Avengers of the New World

LAURENT DUBOIS

Avengers of the New World

THE STORY OF THE
HAITIAN REVOLUTION

THE BELKNAP PRESS OF
HARVARD UNIVERSITY PRESS
Cambridge, Massachusetts
London, England

First Harvard University Press paperback edition, 2005

Library of Congress Cataloging-in-Publication Data

Dubois, Laurent, 1971–

Avengers of the New World : the story of the Haitian Revolution / Laurent Dubois.

p.   cm.

Includes bibliographical references and index.

ISBN 0-674-01304-2 (cloth)

ISBN 0-674-01826-5 (pbk.)

1. Haiti—History—Revolution, 1791–1804.   I. Title.

F1923.D83 2004

972.94′03—dc22   2003063010

For Haiti

ACKNOWLEDGMENTS

My greatest debt is to the many historians whose research and writing made this book possible. Some are ancestors, like Beaubrun Ardouin, Gabriel Debien, and C. L. R. James, the others part of a small and scattered group who often work in isolation. John Garrigus was encouraging about the project throughout, and our conversations were crucial in determining the final shape of the book. David Geggus, whose writings have transformed the study of the Haitian Revolution, has been a supportive and insightful interlocutor over the years. Malick Ghachem has taught me a great deal through his work and our conversations. Stewart King played a crucial role in my early research on the Caribbean. Michel Rolph Trouillot and Carolyn Fick have profoundly influenced the way I think about the revolution. Laennec Hurbon and Michel DeGraff shaped my ideas on Haiti's cultural history. Richard Turits read some early chapters of the book and gave me encouragement and good advice. And Julius Scott has been a constant inspiration because of his passion for reconstructing the lives of the often-elusive figures who built the Haitian Revolution.

I must also thank Julius, and Ada Ferrer, for having—over a greasy breakfast in Ann Arbor years ago—first planted in my mind the idea of writing this book. I owe a debt to three early mentors who guided my first research on Haiti: Barbara Browning, Joan Dayan, and Peter Johnson. I am grateful to Robert Bonner, who read many of the chapters of this book, as well as Christine Daniels and the students in our Atlantic history seminar for their comments. I thank Monique Dubois-Dalcq and Donald Brophy for having read and commented on the manuscript. The members of the "Club Littéraire du Gentilsart," André and Marie-Claude Dubois, were avid readers and insightful critics throughout.

A grant from the Intramural Research Grant Program at Michigan State University funded research in the United States, France, and Haiti, as well as the work of my extremely able research assistant, Marco Meniketti. The

Comparative Black History Program helped me to cover the cost of illustrations. Marcel Chatillon kindly gave me permission to reprint some of the images from his collection *Images de la Révolution aux Antilles,* and Peter Berg helped me to track down and reproduce several engravings. Parts of the manuscript were presented at Yale and Vanderbilt universities, and some material from Chapters 4 and 5 was included in "Our Three Colors: The King, the Republic and the Political Culture of Slave Revolution in Saint-Domingue," in *Historical Reflections,* 29:1 (Spring 2003): 83–102.

I wrote much of this book while I was a visiting scholar at the Clark Center for Seventeenth and Eighteenth Century Studies at the University of California, Los Angeles. I thank Lynn Hunt and Peter Riell for having given me this home in Los Angeles. And I am grateful to Christine Lazaridi for our lunches spent discussing the different stories we were tracking down and weaving together.

In Haiti, Chantalle Verna was a generous host and made much of my research possible. I thank the Fouchard family for their generosity in giving me access to their library. Patrick Tardieu, of the Bibliothèque Haïtienne des Pères du Saint-Esprit, enthusiastically showed me some of the treasures of this collection. And I cannot thank Erol Josué enough for the amazing journey we took to visit Le Cap, and for showing me Gallifet, Sans-Souci, and the Citadel.

Two anonymous reviewers for Harvard University Press gave me encouragement and helpful advice. Ann Hawthorne's expert copyediting was much appreciated. And through her enthusiasm for the project and her guidance, Joyce Seltzer was crucial to making this work what it is.

It was Katharine Brophy Dubois who showed me how to write this book. I thank her, and I thank our son, Anton, who arrived just as I was finishing the manuscript, and who has made everything, once again, into an adventure.

CONTENTS

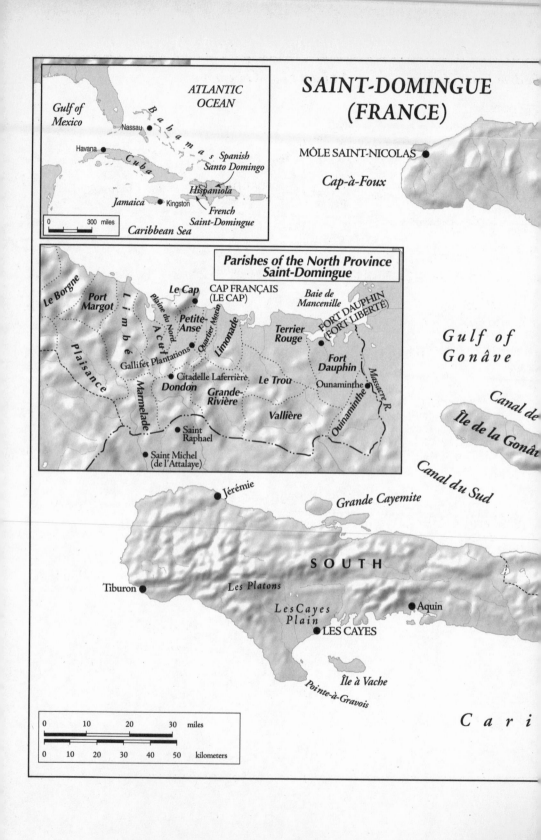

SAINT-DOMINGUE
(FRANCE)

MÔLE SAINT-NICOLAS

Cap-à-Foux

ATLANTIC OCEAN

Gulf of Mexico

Nassau

Havana

Bahamas

Cuba

Spanish Santo Domingo

Hispaniola

Jamaica · Kingston

French Saint-Domingue

Caribbean Sea

0   300 miles

Parishes of the North Province Saint-Domingue

Le Borgne

Port Margot

Limbé

Le Cap

Plaine du Nord

Acul

Petite-Anse

Quartier Matin

CAP FRANÇAIS (LE CAP)

Baie de Mancenille

Limonade

Terrier Rouge

FORT DAUPHIN (FORT LIBERTÉ)

Plaisance

Gallifet Plantations

Marmelade

Dondon

Citadelle Laferrière

Grande-Rivière

Le Trou

Fort Dauphin

Ounaminthe

Vallière

Ouinaminthe

Massacre R.

Saint Raphael

Saint Michel (de l'Attalaye)

Gulf of Gonâve

Canal de

Île de la Gonâve

Canal du Sud

Jérémie

Grande Cayemite

SOUTH

Tiburon

Les Platons

Les Cayes Plain

Aquin

LES CAYES

Île à Vache

Pointe-à-Gravois

Cari

0   10   20   30 miles

0   10   20   30   40   50 kilometers

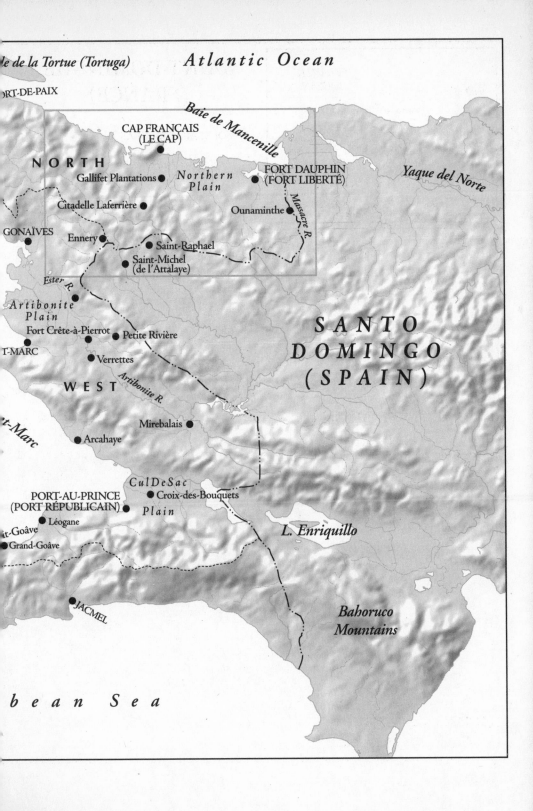

Île de la Tortue (Tortuga)

Atlantic Ocean

PORT-DE-PAIX

Baie de Mancenille

CAP FRANÇAIS
(LE CAP)

NORTH

Gallifet Plantations

Northern
Plain

FORT DAUPHIN
(FORT LIBERTÉ)

Yaque del Norte

Citadelle Laferrière

Ounaminthe

Massacre R.

GONAÏVES

Ennery

Saint-Raphael

Saint-Michel
(de l'Attalaye)

Ester R.

Artibonite
Plain

SANTO
DOMINGO
(SPAIN)

Fort Crête-à-Pierrot

Petite Rivière

T-MARC

Verrettes

WEST

Artibonite R.

Mirebalais

Arcahaye

CulDeSac

Croix-des-Bouquets

PORT-AU-PRINCE
(PORT RÉPUBLICAIN)

Plain

L. Enriquillo

t-Goâve

Léogane

Grand-Goâve

t-Marc

JACMEL

Bahoruco
Mountains

bean Sea

I saw on a magnificent pedestal a negro, his head bare, his arm outstretched, with pride in his eyes and a noble and imposing demeanor . . . At his feet were the words: To the Avenger of the New World!

—Louis Sebastien Mercier,
L'An deux mille cent quarante: Rêve s'il en fût jamais (1771)

I have avenged America.

—Jean-Jacques Dessalines (1804)

Prologue

ON NEW YEAR'S DAY 1804, a group of generals gathered in Saint-Domingue to create a new nation. Their leader, Jean-Jacques Dessalines, had once been a slave. So, too, had several of the men who joined him in signing their declaration of independence. Some had been born in Africa and survived the middle passage; others, including Dessalines, had been born into slavery in the French colony. They signed their names next to those of men who had once been slave owners, including one apparently nicknamed "the good white." Many were men of mixed European and African descent who had been free long before the Revolution began, several of whom had fought against Dessalines in a brutal civil war a few years earlier. Now, however, they stood behind him to declare that they had forever renounced France, and would fight to the death to preserve their independence and freedom. Haiti was founded on the ashes of what had been, fifteen years before, the most profitable slave colony in the world, its birth premised on the self-evident truth that no one should be a slave.[1]

It was a dramatic challenge to the world as it then was. Slavery was at the heart of the thriving system of merchant capitalism that was profiting Europe, devastating Africa, and propelling the rapid expansion of the Americas. The most powerful European empires were deeply involved and invested in slavery's continuing existence, as was much of the nation to the north that had preceded Haiti to independence, the United States. For decades Saint-Domingue had been the leading example of the massive profits that could be made through the brutal institution. Then, in 1791, the colony's slaves began a massive uprising. It became the largest slave revolt in the history of the world, and the only one that succeeded. Within a few years these Caribbean revolutionaries gained liberty for all the slaves in the French empire. The man who came to lead Saint-Domingue in the wake of emancipation, Toussaint Louverture, had once warned the French that any attempt to bring slavery back to the colony was destined to fail. Although he did not live to see it, he was proven right. When freedom was threatened by Napoleon Bonaparte's regime, the people of Saint-Domingue fought successfully to preserve it. Through years of struggle, brutal violence, and imperial war, slaves became citizens in the empire that had enslaved them, and then founders of a new nation. This book tells the story of their dramatic struggle for freedom.

For many who fought slavery—especially slaves elsewhere in the Americas—the Haitian Revolution became an example of what could be accomplished and a source of hope. For those who defended slavery, it became an illustration of the disastrous consequences of freedom. During the nineteenth century an economically and politically isolated Haiti became the object of scorn and openly racist polemic. Most historians in Europe and North America ignored the Haitian Revolution, but in Haiti itself two scholars wrote detailed histories, basing their accounts on archives and on interviews with surviving witnesses and participants, creating a rich nationalist historiography that was little known outside the country.[2]

On the eve of World War II the Caribbean intellectual and activist C. L. R. James wrote *The Black Jacobins,* which remains the classic account of the revolution. James, looking toward the struggles for independence that he saw emerging in Africa, saw the story as an example of both the possibilities and dangers of such struggles. He understood—as the title of the book makes clear—the potent cross-fertilization between the revolutionary transformations that took place in France and the Caribbean. He also eloquently described the dilemmas faced by Louverture as he sought to defend freedom in a world dominated by slaveholding empires. James insisted that the story he had to tell was deeply relevant for the world in which he lived. The Martinican poet and activist Aimé Césaire similarly noted, a few decades later, that Haiti was where the "colonial problem," which the twentieth century was "trying to resolve," was first posed in all its complexity—where the knot of colonialism was first tied, and where it was first untied.[3]

More recently historians in Haiti, France, and the United States have provided new perspectives on colonial Saint-Domingue and the process that destroyed it through detailed studies of slave life and the communities of free people of color, new histories of the revolution, and examinations of the impact of African culture on its development. At the same time, studies on slavery, slave resistance, and the process of emancipation in the Americas have provided new tools for understanding the Haitian Revolution. All these works make it possible to see with more clarity what the events of the period meant for those who lived through them. And they highlight their crucial importance in the broader struggles over the meaning of freedom and citizenship that shaped the Atlantic world during the eighteenth and nineteenth centuries.[4]

The revolution began as a challenge to French imperial authority by colonial whites, but it soon became a battle over racial inequality, and then over the existence of slavery itself. The slaves who revolted in 1791 organized themselves into a daunting military and political force, one ultimately embraced by French Republican officials. Facing enemies inside and outside the colony, these Republicans allied themselves with the insurgent slaves in 1793. They offered freedom in return for military support, which quickly led to the abolition of slavery in the colony. The decision made in Saint-Domingue was ratified in Paris in 1794: the slaves of all the French colonies became citizens of the French Republic.

These events represented the most radical political transformation of the "Age of Revolution" that stretched from the 1770s to the 1830s. They were also the most concrete expression of the idea that the rights proclaimed in France's 1789 Declaration of the Rights of Man and Citizen were indeed universal. They could not be quarantined in Europe or prevented from landing in the ports of the colonies, as many had argued they should be. The slave insurrection of Saint-Domingue led to the expansion of citizenship beyond racial barriers despite the massive political and economic investment in the slave system at the time. If we live in a world in which democracy is meant to exclude no one, it is in no small part because of the actions of those slaves in Saint-Domingue who insisted that human rights were theirs too.

The goal of the slave insurgents during this first phase of the Haitian Revolution was not to break away from France. Indeed, at the time it was slave owners, not slaves, who clamored most for autonomy and even for independence. And along the way the slave rebels became the allies of imperial power and helped preserve the colony against France's enemies, gaining freedom and citizenship in the process. What one writer called "the worst catastrophe ever to befall an empire" was in fact a dramatic challenge to what empires had been and, for a brief time, a model for a different kind of imperial relationship. Only in the early nineteenth century did a true war of national liberation begin in Saint-Domingue. Ultimately, while emancipation had been won through an alliance with the French Republic in 1794, it was preserved by the defeat of the French army in 1804. The people of the new nation of Haiti avoided the tragic fate of those on another French island, Guadeloupe, where most of the population was reenslaved in 1803.[5]

The period between these two moments of dramatic transformation was dominated by the legendary leader Toussaint Louverture. Serving the French Republic as the highest-ranking general in the colony, he defended Saint-Domingue from foreign invasion. By the end of the decade, as the central military and political leader in the colony, he began crafting an autonomous domestic and international policy, laying the foundation for the struggle for independence that followed his capture and death in 1802. During these years he confronted the major dilemmas that would haunt both his successors in independent Haiti and nationalist leaders elsewhere in the Caribbean. (In a 1963 afterword to his book, C. L. R. James compared him to Fidel Castro.) To preserve emancipation, Louverture decided that he must preserve the plantation economy and encourage the return of white planters who had fled. Locked in conflict with ex-slaves who had a very different vision of what freedom should mean, he maintained and perfected a coercive system that sought to keep them working on plantations.

Historians of "postemancipation" societies have explored how the end of slavery led to new conflicts, and new forms of oppression, in plantation societies such as Jamaica, Cuba, and the United States. Revolutionary Saint-Domingue was the first such society in the Americas, and what happened there became a touchstone in subsequent debates about how best to move from slavery to freedom. Abolition in Saint-Domingue took place abruptly, with no period of transition of the kind that was then under way in the northern United States, and which most abolitionists advocated. Faced with a dramatically new situation, administrators in Saint-Domingue had to invent a regime for containing and channeling the impact of emancipation. Within a few years, those who were overseeing the new regimes of labor that replaced slavery were black, and often ex-slaves. Still, the struggle that developed between managers and plantation workers over the terms of freedom was similar in many ways to the struggle that would shape later processes of emancipation. Placing the Haitian Revolution in this context helps us make sense of the complex social conflicts that defined it.[6]

The Haitian Revolution was a uniquely transcultural movement. The population of Saint-Domingue in the eighteenth century was not just majority slave; it was also majority African. These slaves had come from many different regions and political, social, and religious contexts, and they shaped the revolution with what they brought with them. James recognized decades ago that the Haitian Revolution was a precursor to the struggles for African decolonization. Now we are increasingly coming to understand that it was itself in many ways an African revolution. But as David Geggus has recently noted, the question of how to avoid "the twin perils of exoticizing or occidentalizing the slaves" in order to "imagine the attitudes and beliefs of those Africans and children of Africans of two centuries ago" remains "the most intractable question facing historians of the Haitian Revolution."[7]

Since the moment slaves rose up in Saint-Domingue in 1791, accounts of the revolution have focused a great deal on its violence. The fact that some of the atrocities in the Haitian Revolution were committed by insurgent slaves, and later by black officers and troops, has made them the object of fascination and intensive debate. Many writers have felt the need to answer for the violence of one or another party. Did one side commit horrors first, and others only in retaliation? Were the atrocities of the slave insurgents merely responses to those of the slave owners? Political violence was a major feature of the Haitian Revolution, as it was of all other revolutions before and since. The Haitian Revolution deserves a reading that places the violence in context, acknowledges its complexity, and does not use it as a way to avoid confronting the ideological and political significance of the ideals and ideas it generated.

Understanding the Haitian Revolution also requires avoiding using racial designations—white, mulatto, black—as categories that can generate explanations rather than as social artifacts that demand them. Interpretations of individual and collective action during the revolution that are based primarily on racial or class categories often fail to provide a complete or coherent picture of how and why people acted as they did. The communities of African descent who were not enslaved, for instance, were enormously diverse, both socially and politically. While many within them were of mixed European and African ancestry, not all were, and the common use of the term "mulatto" to describe them is misleading. (For this reason I have avoided using the term, which racializes and simplifies a complex reality, in favor of the term *gens de couleur,* which I translate as "free people of color" or "free-coloreds." This term was favored by many politically active members of this group in the late eighteenth century.) Clearly, racial identification was a crucial part of the revolution and, along with economic, social, and cultural factors, influenced how individuals and groups acted and responded to one another. At the same time, complicated ideological and political forces often divided groups that we might be tempted to see as unified by "race." The most useful approach is to focus on the political projects that emerged at the different stages of the revolution, and on the ways they were shaped by and in turn shaped the individuals and groups that articulated them. Though I do of necessity use racial terminology throughout this work, my intent is to avoid essentializing differences and instead to highlight their mutability and shifting political and social meaning.[8]

Many of the central protagonists of the Haitian Revolution, unlike those of the other Atlantic revolutions of the period, left behind few written traces of their political thought. (The major exception is Toussaint Louverture.) Most of what we know about their actions and ideals comes from the writings of (often quite hostile) witnesses, whose views about slavery and slaves profoundly influenced what they wrote. Those who provided details about the words and actions of rebelling slaves, for instance, generally did so with the purpose of convincing their readers that one group or another was responsible for the insurrection. Many later historians have read such sources "against the grain" to tell eloquent stories of the silenced and the marginalized. Their work is an inspiration for my own attempt here to grasp a fleeting moment that is in many ways beyond us, to spur the imagination as well as to invite response and revision. This is a story that deserves—and indeed demands—to be told and retold.[9]

The impact of the Haitian Revolution was enormous. As a unique example of successful black revolution, it became a crucial part of the political, philosophical, and cultural currents of the eighteenth and nineteenth centuries. By creating a society in which all people, of all colors, were granted freedom and citizenship, the Haitian Revolution forever transformed the world. It was a central part of the destruction of slavery in the Americas, and therefore a crucial moment in the history of democracy, one that laid the foundation for the continuing struggles for human rights everywhere. In this sense we are all descendants of the Haitian Revolution, and responsible to these ancestors.

CHAPTER ONE

Specters of Saint-Domingue

IN THE MID-1790s, Philadelphia, capital of a nation recently born of revolution, was teeming with exiles driven from their homes by a cycle of revolution sweeping the Atlantic world. Some came from France, victims of one or another political purge. But many more had come from the Caribbean, particularly Saint-Domingue, fleeing slave revolution. There were white masters and merchants, previously rich and now reduced to dependence on former trading partners or charity. There were free people of color whose presence in Philadelphia became the subject of some controversy. And there were many slaves, brought as property from colonies where slavery no longer existed, treated as property in a city where the institution was only slowly being extinguished.

Among these exiles was a man named Médéric-Louis-Elie Moreau de St. Méry, a lawyer, writer, and onetime resident of Saint-Domingue. Like many exiles, he had arrived carrying almost nothing. He was in fact lucky to be alive: a warrant for his arrest had been issued in Paris just as he escaped the port of Le Havre in 1793. In his haste he had left behind an irreplaceable possession: a set of boxes filled with notes and documents he had collected over a decade of research for books he was writing on French Saint-Domingue and Spanish Santo Domingo. Friends promised to send the essential notes after him. But in the midst of war and revolution there was little certainty. Would the boxes find him? Had they been burned as fuel on a ship or thrown overboard for want of room? Had they sunk to the bottom of the sea during a storm or an attack? By great good fortune, the boxes reached Moreau in Philadelphia. "It is one of the joys in life I savored the most," he wrote. He at once resumed working on a book that had been

An engraving of Moreau de St. Méry done in Paris, 1789. *Courtesy of the Bibliothèque Nationale de France.*

near completion when, as he put it, the revolution "made me powerless to accomplish my project."[1]

Moreau was a citizen of the Atlantic. Born of an important creole family in Martinique in 1750, he left for Paris at nineteen to study law. He received his degree two years later and took up a prestigious position at the Paris Parlement, the most important court in the nation. In 1774 he suddenly resigned and left for the Caribbean, where he settled in Saint-Domingue. He established himself as a lawyer, married into a well-connected family in 1781, and gradually became an important figure. Moreau was also a freemason, and in one of the lodges of Le Cap, of which he later became president, he rubbed elbows with many of the leading men of the colony.

Through his work as a lawyer in Saint-Domingue, Moreau became irritated about something he would harp on for most of the rest of his life: no one, especially the administrators on both sides of the Atlantic who governed the Caribbean colonies, knew anything about them. He decided to try to solve the problem, and, working with other members of a local scientific society called the Cercle des Philadelphes, he began to gather information on Saint-Domingue's law, history, environment, and economy. It was a classic Enlightenment project, based on the idea that knowledge would promote better governance. Because many of the archives he needed to consult were in Paris, he returned there in 1783. The Colonial Ministry provided him with an allowance and access to its archives. In 1784 he published the first part of what became a six-volume history of colonial legislation. He returned to Saint-Domingue, where he continued his research and his struggles with the royal administration. In 1788 he again left the colony for Paris. He was poised to produce his *Description* of the Spanish and French colonies when the French Revolution began. Moreau quickly became active in politics. He was chosen as the president of the electors of the city of Paris and participated in the raging debates about colonial policy. Meanwhile his project languished. There was little time to write history as he tried to survive it. Like many political moderates, he ended on the wrong side during the Jacobin Terror and had to flee for his life.[2]

He ended up in Philadelphia and returned to his writing. He published a *Description* of Spanish Santo Domingo in 1796, but faced a peculiar problem with regard to the French colony: in the years he had been away from it, much of what he had known there had been destroyed or irrevocably transformed by revolution. Moreau worried that the story of Saint-Domingue, the "most brilliant" of the colonies of the Antilles, might be forgotten if he "did not hurry to offer a truthful portrait of its past splendor." At the same time, he imagined "a crowd of people" accusing him of doing "useless work or hoping to excite regrets for which there was no longer any remedy."[3]

But it was worth telling the story of Saint-Domingue, Moreau insisted. If there was to be a reconstruction of the colony, as he firmly hoped, it would have to be based on knowledge of what the ruined plantations and towns had once been, and an understanding of how the colony had functioned, and why things had ultimately gone so wrong. It was possible, Moreau believed, to make the colony once again "a source of riches and power for France. In these fields still smoking with blood and carnage, we must bring back abundance."[4]

In its "short existence," Moreau wrote, Saint-Domingue was "a colony whose nature, splendor, and destruction" were unique in "the annals of the world," and a part of the "History of Nations," like the great civilizations of Greece and Italy. His book, Moreau hoped, might encourage people to "meditate on Saint-Domingue," and to draw as much from this act of contemplation as they would from looking at the "debris of Herculaneum." A century and a half later, another Martinican, Aimé Césaire, would similarly insist that "to study Saint-Domingue is to study one of the origins, one of the sources, of contemporary Western civilization." Both writers insisted that rather than being seen as a place on the margins of Europe and its development, Saint-Domingue must be seen as central to this history.[5]

Curiously, Moreau shied away from one aspect of Saint-Domingue's history. "Has the time come to write on the colonial revolution? . . . I think not." That was why his book, as he announced, represented Saint-Domingue as it was "on the first day the revolution appeared there."[6] And it was why "1789" was repeated throughout the text, often simply as "this year." Like many exiles, Moreau sought to return home by writing about it. That home had been completely transformed by slave revolution, and his work was a walking tour of a vanished world. But, harboring hope that the colonial world might be rebuilt, the exile was also calling up specters of the past in an effort to exorcise the present. In the process he left a remarkable snapshot of the brilliant and brutal colony of Saint-Domingue.

"One good white is dead. The bad ones are still here." This, Moreau wrote, was what the blacks of Le Cap heard in the melody of the funeral bells of the church. It was, perhaps, a subtle way of saying that the only good white was a dead one. Each time the bells rang, another corpse joined the generations of the dead haunting Saint-Domingue. The colony was a graveyard for its original inhabitants, decimated by Spanish colonizers; for its European settlers and soldiers, who succumbed in large numbers to fevers; and of course for the many slaves who died there from execution, overwork, sorrow, or (though rarely) the weight of years.[7]

The dead were divided as the living were. Some whites—individuals of importance in the colony, or those rich enough to pay the 3,000-livre charge for this honor—were still buried near the church, in a single tomb built for the purpose. (In France they would have been placed under the church itself, but this practice had been given up in the heat of the tropics to spare worshipers from the stench of rotting corpses under their feet.) In the tomb were the bodies of two governors of the colony, as well as the bones of the Jesuits who had died there during the first half of the eighteenth century. When Moreau visited in 1777, he noticed some bones sticking out of the ground in the tomb, but doubted what some said about them—that they were the remains of those Jesuits, miraculously preserved.[8]

The church graveyard was small, however, and most whites were buried in a cemetery at La Fossette, on the outskirts of Le Cap. La Fossette had first been used as an overflow cemetery during an epidemic in 1736, receiving the bodies of two ill-respected groups: blacks and sailors. A few decades later, with the cemetery surrounding the Le Cap church too full, it became the official town cemetery. La Fossette—originally called L'Afrique by the Company of the Indies when it occupied the area as part of its slave-trading operations—also had a cemetery for non-Christians. Unbaptized African slaves—called *bossales*—who had died soon after their arrival were buried around the "Croix bossale." (The 1685 Code Noir, which governed the treatment of slaves in the French colonies, stipulated that unbaptized slaves be buried "at night in a field near the place where they died.") It was perhaps these graves that brought slaves to the area for "dances" on Sundays and holidays. Outside the second-largest town in the colony, Port-au-Prince, African slaves were buried in a swampy site also called "Croix bossale." Animals, however, often disinterred the corpses. Local officials, worried about the "exhalations" through which the "dead seemed to menace the living and punish them for their disregard for humanity and morality," established a better-placed cemetery for slaves.[9]

Throughout Saint-Domingue the enslaved often created their own cemeteries by taking over those no longer used by whites. In one town in the Northern Province an abandoned cemetery was still "recognized by the superstitious veneration of the negroes." In the parish of Aquin, in the south, slaves buried their dead near the ruins of the chapel on the site of an early settlement. Attempts to force them to use the official cemetery failed; the slaves just waited until night to bury their dead. So the bodies of those once enslaved were buried alongside the bodies of those once free. Elsewhere the dead of both groups were united for other reasons. Moreau noted with disgust that in one small town "white and *homme de couleur*, and free and slave" were all buried together because there was no tradition of registering the burials. In another, little-populated part of the colony a small cemetery, marked by a cross, indiscriminately welcomed the bodies of "the whites and negroes." Natural forces sometimes also brought the dead together. In 1787 a ravine overflowed during a powerful tropical storm, drowning two slaves, sweeping away carriages and furniture, exhuming the corpses from a small cemetery, and carrying them into the ocean—itself a giant cemetery for those Africans who had not survived the middle passage.[10]

The dead were inescapable in Saint-Domingue, as Moreau lamented in describing the entrance to one town where the sight of a pleasant fountain was offset by the cemetery beside it. It was as if a vow had been taken always to strike travelers with the "lugubrious" presence of the departed. At the same time, Saint-Domingue was a powerful life-source for the booming Atlantic economy, generating fortunes for individuals on both sides of the ocean. Its plains were covered with sugarcane cultivated on well-ordered and technologically sophisticated plantations, supported by efficient irrigation works. The mountains were full of burgeoning coffee plantations, and the towns bustled with arriving and departing ships, passengers, and goods of all kinds. Within a century it had grown from a marginal Caribbean frontier into the most valuable colony in the world. In the process it had welcomed a bewildering mix of people—Gascons, Bretons, Provençals from France; Ibo, Wolof, Bambara, and Kongolese from Africa. On the verge of a revolution, it was a land of striking contrasts.[11]

Christopher Columbus landed on the island during his first voyage, in 1492. The indigenous Taino seem to have called it Ayiti, but Columbus gave it a new name: La Española. On the northwest coast of the island, Columbus left behind a small group of sailors in the care of a local Taino chief. He returned the following year to find the settlement abandoned and destroyed, with most of those he had left behind buried nearby. The chief he had entrusted with his men claimed that a group of Caribs from another island had attacked and he had been powerless to defend the Spaniards. It is more likely that (not for the last time) the initial peace between Europeans and the indigenous peoples had devolved into violence.[12]

This first European settlement in the Americas had failed, but more followed, and quickly. Española—or Hispaniola, as it came to be known in the Anglophone world—was the ground zero of European colonialism in the Americas. The brutal massacre and bewildering decimation of indigenous people that took place there would be repeated again and again in the following centuries, though rarely with the same startling speed. Under the *encomienda* system, settlers were granted the right to the labor of indigenous people in order to mine for precious metals. It was not technically slavery—workers were not owned by the settlers—but in practice it was little different. Overworked, attacked by diseases against which they had no immunity, executed as punishment for revolt, and often committing suicide to escape their brutal conditions, the indigenous population declined precipitously within the first few decades of Spanish colonization. By 1514, of a population estimated to have been between 500,000 and 750,000 in 1492, only 29,000 were left. By the mid-sixteenth century the indigenous population of the island had all but vanished.[13]

The "devastation of the Indies" was chronicled by Bartolomé de Las Casas, who arrived in Hispaniola as a young settler in 1502, and was transformed by what he saw. Within a decade he became the first priest ordained in the Americas, and a harsh critic of the brutal treatment of the Taino by the Spaniards. He decried those who justified Spanish brutality as a necessary response to the barbarism and violence of the natives: "our work was to exasperate, ravage, kill, mangle and destroy; small wonder, then, if they tried to kill one of us now and then." He documented horrifying acts of violence meant to terrorize the population. "It was a general rule among the Spaniards to be cruel; not just cruel, but extraordinarily cruel so that harsh and bitter treatment would prevent Indians from daring to think of themselves as human beings or having a minute to think at all."[14]

In Moreau's Saint-Domingue there were many reminders of this history. Workers building a canal on a plantation in Limonade discovered, along with several Spanish coins, the bodies of twenty-five Spaniards who had been buried in a traditional Taino manner. They were, Moreau believed, the corpses of those left behind by Columbus in 1492. And the anchor found buried in the dirt on a plantation near the ocean was, he wrote, that of Columbus' *Santa Maria*, which had sunk off the coast of the island in 1492. Elsewhere there was forensic proof of Spanish cruelties. In a cave in the north of the colony were found five skulls with their foreheads flattened—a common practice among the indigenous peoples of the Caribbean—which identified them as "Indian." No other bones were found, however, and Moreau concluded that this was because the "Spanish had dogs to whom they gave over the corpses of their unfortunate victims." He knew his history well: in 1493 Columbus had indeed brought attack dogs—mastiffs and greyhounds—to terrorize the Taino population.[15]

The colony was in fact full of haunting reminders of its vanished inhabitants. In Limonade one encountered "with each step, debris of the utensils of the indigenous people who lived here," and in Quartier-Morin, "everywhere you find their bones, their simple but ingenious utensils, their hideous but sometimes very artistically made fetishes." On one sugar plantation, each hole dug for the cane turned up "some new vestiges of the existence of this race now erased from the list of humans." In the church of the town of Jérémie, in the Southern Province, a stone carved with the figures of four seated women, the work of the "natural" inhabitants of the island, had been turned into a *bénitier*—a holy-water font. Near the town of Les Cayes was a peninsula where it was easy to find "fetishes" left behind by its former inhabitants, as well as small caves they had carved into the rock, and small figurines made of conch shells. "The regret of the philosopher is awakened," wrote Moreau, "when he thinks about the fact that from a people so numerous, there is not one left to enlighten us about its history."[16]

The first site of European conquest in the Americas, Hispaniola became a pioneer in another way during the sixteenth century. Las Casas had, ironically, advocated the importation of African slaves to save the brutalized indigenous population. Soon imported slaves replaced the rapidly dying indigenous ones, serving as laborers in a new industry that supplemented that of mining. Sugarcane had been brought to the colony by Columbus in 1493, and by the early 1500s the Spanish began establishing the first sugar plantations in the New World. By the 1530s there were more than thirty sugar mills in the colony, and by the mid-sixteenth century the annual production of sugar reached several thousand tons.[17]

The capital of Hispaniola, Santo Domingo, flourished, eventually boasting the first Catholic cathedral and the first European university built in the Americas. From there the conquest of neighboring Cuba was launched. Soon the Spaniards continued on to the mainland and the conquest of Mexico. Hispaniola was soon overshadowed by the treasures unveiled, and the opportunities opened up, with the fall of the Aztec and Inca empires. Having been for a few decades at the center of the new Spanish empire, Hispaniola was soon consigned to its margins. The sugar economy in the eastern portion of the island declined by the end of the sixteenth century. Ginger and cacao cultivation briefly took its place, but by the latter half of the seventeenth century cattle ranches were "the only real commercial endeavor on the island." Many slaves gained their freedom, and new slave imports to the colony were limited. By the end of the eighteenth century only 15 percent of the population remained enslaved. Meanwhile the western part of Hispaniola remained for the most part unsettled. The name of the island's capital, Santo Domingo, was increasingly used to refer to the entire island, and the French who eventually settled there in the early seventeenth century simply translated the name into French, calling their colony Saint-Domingue.[18]

During the seventeenth century the French and British successfully challenged Spanish and Portuguese hegemony in the Americas. Pirates opened the way for this new phase of European colonization. Throughout the sixteenth century, ships heavy with silver and gold dug by indigenous slaves out of the mines of the Americas constantly crossed the Atlantic. These floating treasure chests, often traveling relatively unarmed, were all-too-tempting prey. The Spanish and Portuguese defended their ships against these marauders, at significant cost, while English and French governors saw that it was in their interest to support piracy against their enemies. By weakening the Spanish hold on the seas and establishing unofficial settlements elsewhere in the Caribbean, the pirates opened the way for more permanent, colonial settlement supported by European royal governments.[19]

Spanish explorers had found the Carib inhabitants of the eastern Caribbean quick to resist encroachment, and had left these islands for the most part untouched. It was here that British and French settlements initially took root. The first was a colony on the tiny island of St. Christopher, where English and French lived side by side. From there the English founded Barbados, the most important of the early Caribbean slave colonies. It developed so rapidly that within a few decades settlers left a crowded Barbados and established a colony on the mainland—South Carolina. In 1635, meanwhile, the French founded colonies in Martinique and Guadeloupe. Throughout the seventeenth and early eighteenth centuries the Caribs managed to survive by playing off the French and the British against each other. Gradually, however, they were isolated on certain islands, and by the end of the eighteenth century even those were colonized by the British. Only a few small indigenous communities remained.[20]

As the colonies of the eastern Caribbean grew, a motley crew of pirates and settlers from St. Christopher, both French and English, settled on the island of Tortuga, northwest of Saint-Domingue. The pirates—called *flibustiers* by the French—were joined by another group, called *boucaniers,* who lived on mainland Hispaniola. The Spanish had introduced new species there—not only dogs, many of whom escaped into the wild, but also pigs and cattle—which, without human or animal predators, had thrived in the intervening century. The *boucaniers* hunted the wild cattle, smoked the meat using an indigenous method called the *boucan,* and sold it to sailors on passing ships. Gradually settlers on both Tortuga and the mainland began to grow provisions and tobacco.[21]

The Spanish repeatedly tried to dislodge these interlopers in Tortuga and the northern coast of Saint-Domingue, but the French settlement survived and continued to grow. The French named a royal governor to oversee Tortuga and the coast of Saint-Domingue in 1664, and he personally recruited settlers for the colony from his native region of Anjou. A population of 400 Europeans there when he first arrived grew to 4,000 by 1680. The *flibustiers* and *boucaniers* were joined, and ultimately outnumbered, by colonists who founded small plantations.[22]

In 1697 a French commander arrived in the growing colony of Saint-Domingue. Preparing to attack the Spanish port of Cartagena, he nailed an invitation on the church of the settlement at Petit-Goâve calling on *flibustiers* and inhabitants of the "coast of St. Domingue," including "negroes," to join him. The recruits from Saint-Domingue participated in the siege, capture, and brutal pillage of Cartagena. One of the officers taking part in the raid, Joseph d'Honor de Gallifet, who later served briefly as governor of the colony, invested his portion of the loot in land, establishing plantations that were to become some of the most successful in the colony. The defeat suffered by the Spanish in Cartagena contributed to their decision to cede the western portion of the colony of Hispaniola to the French with the 1697 Treaty of Rhyswick. A century later the siege of Cartagena was still remembered for other blessings it had brought to the French colony. There was a roadside statue of the Virgin Mary looted from the Spanish port town in 1697 in the Southern Province; under it a candle usually burned. The most famous of the stolen relics was a cross revered in the church of Petit-Goâve. Moreau described the powerful devotions of the worshipers who gathered around it each evening, especially on Fridays, and most of all on Good Friday, placing hundreds of burning candles underneath it, so that the floor was covered with wax and the walls stained with smoke. Normally the climate of Petit-Goâve bred masses of mosquitoes, but there were few in the town thanks to the cross from Cartagena.[23]

Having gained official status as a French colony, Saint-Domingue—one of the last colonies founded in the Americas—would soon outshine all others. The earliest plantations in Saint-Domingue were worked by both African slaves and European *engagés,* or indentured laborers. The latter worked alongside the slaves, but for limited terms—in the French case for three years—after which they became free. Along with the remaining *flibustiers* and *boucaniers,* many of these former indentured laborers started farming small plots of land, notably with tobacco, a crop that required little initial investment and could quickly turn a modest profit. But the competition of Virginia tobacco, changing colonial policies, and the emergence of other crops soon ended tobacco cultivation in Saint-Domingue. The second crop to take off in the colony, indigo, involved a more sophisticated processing procedure that turned the harvested grasses into a blue dye, and so required a bit more capital. Nevertheless, small indigo plantations appeared throughout the colony. This crop would remain an important part of the island's economy, but it was soon overshadowed by the crop that came to dominate Saint-Domingue for the rest of its century-long existence: sugar.

Sugar was the economic miracle of the eighteenth century. Originally from the Middle East, sugarcane had been cultivated on Spanish and Portuguese islands of the eastern Atlantic for centuries. The Spanish in Hispaniola and the Portuguese in Brazil pioneered cane cultivation in the Americas, and the French and English drew on their examples and on the knowledge and finances of the Dutch in establishing their plantation societies in the Caribbean. These colonies both depended on and drove the expansion of the emerging capitalist system of the Atlantic world. Starting in the seventeenth century a remarkable spiral of cause and effect transformed sugar from a luxury enjoyed by only the wealthiest Europeans to a necessity that was a central part of many Europeans' diets.[24]

Slavery was deemed essential to the production of sugar. In the Caribbean, plantations often had several hundred slaves carrying out the difficult tasks of planting and harvesting cane, and a smaller group specializing in its transformation into sugar. Once harvested, cane must be processed quickly, and during certain periods work continued all night. The highly diversified and industrialized sugar plantations of Saint-Domingue and its nearby British competitor Jamaica had some of the largest numbers of slaves of any colonies in the Americas. A fifth of the slaves on these plantations worked in occupations other than fieldwork, as specialists who processed the sugarcane, as artisans making barrels to transport it, or as domestics serving masters or managers. The combination of "field" and "factory" made the plantation regions of the Caribbean some of the most industrialized in the eighteenth-century world.[25]

At first many plantations were worked by a combination of African slaves and white indentured laborers. In Saint-Domingue in 1687, whites outnumbered slaves, 4,411 to 3,358. But by eighteenth century, labor in the Caribbean had been deliberately and obsessively racialized. With the exception of a few managers and overseers, plantation workforces were entirely of African descent. In Saint-Domingue by 1700, the population of slaves had grown to 9,082, while the population of whites had decreased by several hundred. As sugar plantations proliferated over the next decades, the numbers of enslaved increased dramatically; by midcentury there were nearly 150,000 slaves and fewer than 14,000 whites, and on the eve of the revolution, 90 percent of the colony's population was enslaved.[26]

The number of plantations in Saint-Domingue increased with startling rapidity as well. From 1700 to 1704 they jumped from 18 to 120. In 1713 there were 138, 77 of them in the Northern Province. All of these produced raw sugar, which contained many impurities. Bigger profits were available to those who could afford technology to purify sugar on-site, removing the molasses and turning it into an edible (though still brown) sugar, which could be sold at a higher price. The number of plantations removing molasses grew; in 1730 there were 5 in the north, but by 1751 there were 182, compared with 124 that did not refine sugar. In 1790 there were 258 of the former and only 30 of the latter.[27]

Sugarcane production required good land, irrigation, a large labor force, and expensive equipment. It promised major profits, but it required an initial investment far greater than tobacco or indigo. Once the sugar boom hit Saint-Domingue, there was a rush to purchase the best land and a vertiginous rise in prices. The governor wrote in 1700 that a plantation that had sold for 70 écus eighteen months earlier could now not be purchased for 2,000, even when nothing was being cultivated there.[28]

As the fertile land in the colony was bought up for sugar plantations, some whites were left behind. Many retreated to the interior, scraping by farming small plots of land. Others turned to crime: throughout the eighteenth century, the colony's mountains were home to armed bands of whites who preoccupied administrators. Along the coasts, other small communities existed outside the world of the plantations. Moreau described a group in the south as "amphibious beings" whose lives as farmers and sailors recalled those of the colony's early settlers. At the estuary of the Artibonite River there was a "kind of Republic" composed of men who worked as saltmakers and had renounced marriage, and whose property could not be inherited by their offspring but must instead be returned to the community. In the late eighteenth century local plantation owners, disgruntled by the presence of a community that "was a source of problems for the discipline of their negroes," managed to expel the saltmakers from their land, to which they had no official title. A governor, however, intervened when the saltmakers threatened to leave the island forever.[29]

Such holdouts were a small minority. Most whites on the island, many of them recent arrivals from Europe, wanted a plantation and the profits that came with it. But even with good land still available, such a goal was hard to achieve. Most plantation owners took out loans from merchant houses in France to get started. If all went well, these loans could be paid off over time and the planter could grow wealthy. But in many cases the planters failed, and the merchant houses acquired the plantations that had been the collateral for their loans. By the end of the eighteenth century, many merchant houses in France's major port towns of Bordeaux, Nantes, and La Rochelle owned plantations in Saint-Domingue. These were managed by salaried administrators and overseers. Many young men came to the colony seeking such positions, but despite the booming economy there were not enough of them, and those who failed swelled the ranks of poor and unemployed whites. In 1776 one observer noted the "great misery" of many whites on the island and opined that those who came to the colony with no useful skills were likely to end up dead on the side of the road. This was the fate of one "unknown white man, aged 14 or 15, without a beard," who was found by police in 1779; a surgeon determined that he had died of misère—poverty—and he was buried anonymously in a local graveyard.[30]

The second half of the eighteenth century saw Saint-Domingue's population and economy expand dramatically. With France's cession of Canada to the British in 1763, the Caribbean became the main destination for Frenchmen seeking their fortune in the Americas. Saint-Domingue, with its reputation for transforming colonists into rich men, was the most attractive in the region. During these decades a new plantation crop boomed:

coffee. Coffee plantations were less expensive to start up and maintain than sugar plantations, and they had another important advantage: they could be established in the mountainous regions of Saint-Domingue, where there was still land available. Mountainous terrain, accounting for 60 percent of the colony, was useless for cultivating sugar. Thus the coffee boom did not compete with the continuing sugar boom. Instead, it added to the already enormous wealth produced in the colony. By the eve of the revolution Saint-Domingue was "the world's leading producer of both sugar and coffee." It exported "as much sugar as Jamaica, Cuba, and Brazil combined" and half of the world's coffee, making it "the centerpiece of the Atlantic slave system."[31]

Three-quarters of sugar and coffee produced in the colonies and sent to France was reexported to other countries in Europe. Because restrictive French trade policies kept the prices planters could demand for their products down, metropolitan merchants in the port towns made extraordinary fortunes from this business. The livelihood of as many as a million of the 25 million inhabitants of France depended directly on the colonial trade. The slave colonies of the Caribbean were an engine for economic and social change in metropolitan France. The historian Jean Jaurès pointed out the "sad irony" that the fortunes created in Nantes and Bordeaux during the eighteenth century were a crucial part of the struggle for "human emancipation" that erupted in the French Revolution. Many among the bourgeoisie who were frustrated with the limits placed on them by the Old Regime system were wealthy thanks to the sugar and coffee produced by slaves in the Caribbean. In 1789, 15 percent of the 1,000 members of the National Assembly owned colonial property, and many others were probably tied to colonial commerce. The slaves of Saint-Domingue who had helped lay the foundation for the French Revolution would ultimately make it their own, and even surpass it, in their own struggle for liberty.[32]

A passenger arriving by ship from France in the late eighteenth century would generally journey along the coast, first of Spanish Santo Domingo, and then of the French colony. If it was night there would be lights shining from the plantation houses and flames dancing in the mills, where, wrote Moreau, "the sugar crystals that are the principal richness of the colony, and which bring us so much enjoyment, are being prepared." Aboard ship, everyone would be changing into clean clothes saved for the landing.

Reaching the port of Le Cap, the ship would anchor, and the passengers would descend into small boats to be carried into the harbor: "What a spectacle! How different from the places left behind! One sees four or five black or darkened faces for every white one. The clothes, the houses . . . have a new character."[33]

For residents of Le Cap, a ship from France meant the arrival of goods and news from across the Atlantic. On Sundays, in the area called the "marché des blancs" (the "white market"), sailors trying to supplement their meager salaries offered for sale treasures they had brought from France: dry goods, pottery, porcelain, jewels, shoes, hats, parrots, monkeys. Efforts by the administration to stop this practice failed, and the market was very popular with townspeople. "It is fashionable," wrote Moreau, "to take a turn in the *marché des blancs*, even if one has nothing to buy there." The trading of the ship's actual cargo occurred along the Rue du Gouvernement, where merchants and naval captains had shops. In front of each store was a board, usually decorated with a drawing of the ship whose cargo it advertised. In a matter of a few steps, one could "journey through the whole of France," hearing Gascon, Normand, and Provençal accents. Slaves constantly brought goods back and forth from the port.[34]

Ships brought something else of great value: news. Residents gathered in houses near the port to speak to new arrivals or to pass along what they had heard to one another. Arriving news found its way into a newspaper called *Affiches Américaines*. Starting in 1788, where the wealthier residents of Le Cap could gather in a *cabinet littéraire*, a club whose members paid annual dues for access to an "elegantly furnished" room with a library containing "all the interesting newspapers" along with a billiard room. The same building was home to the Cercle des Philadelphes, the scientific society that supported Moreau's work on his *Description*. Its members pursued a wide variety of intellectual pursuits, from botanical experiments to the ill-fated attempt by one plantation owner to introduce camels from Africa.[35]

Le Cap was the size of Boston. It had a population of 18,850, though several thousand of these were soldiers and the majority of the rest were slaves. Its fifty-six streets were organized in a grid, marked with signs and street numbers, and in the wealthiest part of town close to the port were partially paved. There were imposing buildings scattered throughout Le Cap: Le Gouvernement—the house of the administration—which had been the home of the Jesuits until their expulsion from the colony in 1763;

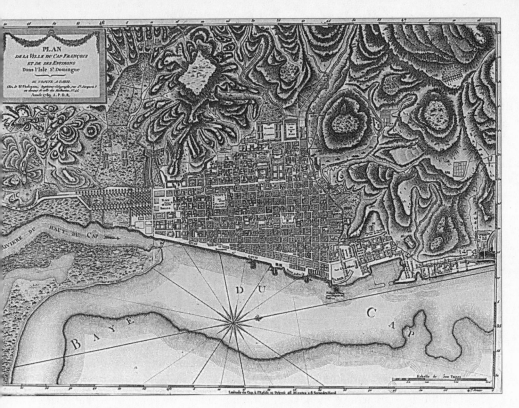

"Plan de la ville du Cap François," 1789. By 1789 Le Cap was a thriving town, its well-ordered pattern of streets a contrast to the surrounding mountains. The map is drawn with North to the right. *Courtesy of the Bibliothèque Nationale de France.*

the military barracks behind it, which could house more than a thousand soldiers; a convent; a large church with an imposing facade; a prison that held (separately) both black prisoners, often runaway slaves, and white criminals and debtors; and several hospitals. There were twenty-five bakeries and, on the outskirts of town, a slaughterhouse. An elaborate municipal water system fed several fountains that provided "fresh and limpid water" from the "neighboring mountains" in public squares. To the south, in a neighborhood called "Petite Guinée," free people of color were concentrated, although others lived elsewhere in the town. In contrast to the other cities of the colony, notably Port-au-Prince, most of Le Cap's 1,400 houses were built of stone. They had "gardens or thick trellises shading them from the sun," and many were inhabited by exotic birds from Senegal, Guiana, and the Mississippi. Those from Senegal had the striking ability to "change in color without changing their feathers."[36]

Le Cap, which one resident called "the Paris of our island," was a lively cultural center, one of the most important in the eighteenth-century Americas. It boasted a theater with a 1,500-person capacity, where Molière's *Le Misanthrope* was performed in the 1760s. In 1784 *Le Mariage de Figaro* opened there soon after its premiere in Paris. A local play, *Monday at the Cap, or Payday,* was also performed. Racial segregation was strictly maintained in the theater, where the ten boxes at the top were reserved for free people of African descent, three for "free blacks" and the rest for "mulattos." As a result, many mothers could not sit with their daughters. Free-coloreds were also banned from participating in the dances at the theater, though they were allowed to watch from their boxes. Le Cap was also full of "cabarets," some legal and many more not, where liquor and gambling were available. There were other forms of public entertainment, such as a traveling wax museum where visitors could see Voltaire and Rousseau, Louis XVI and Marie Antoinette, and, in 1789, George Washington in his uniform. Le Cap's public bathhouses, unlike those in France, did not separate men and women, so that "husband and wife, or those who considered themselves as such, could go to the same bath and the same bathtub"—an arrangement that, Moreau mused, was probably what made them so popular.[37]

Le Cap was built on an extensive and protected bay, and its large and well-constructed port was the most important in Saint-Domingue. It was the first port of call for most ships arriving in the colony, and the easiest from which to join the transatlantic convoys. There were roughly a hundred larger ships in the harbor at any given time, and sometimes as many as six hundred. A visitor in 1791 described workmen "busy with all kinds of labor" at the port, loading "hogsheads of sugar or kegs of indigo." Another later recalled that the harbor was "filled with merchandise being shipped," where "all was bustle, noise, and cheerful labor." The port was fed by the thriving plantation region that surrounded it. The northern plain, traversed by streams from the mountains, was an ideal place for sugar plantations. In 1789 the Northern Province, which included Le Cap, the plain, and the surrounding mountains, contained 288 sugar plantations, most of them producing refined sugar; 443 indigo plantations; and more than 2,000 coffee plantations. The population included 16,000 whites and at least 160,000 slaves. Among the latter were many who would participate in the

"Veue en perspéctive du Cap François," 1717. This watercolor was done by an artist looking west across the water toward Le Cap. The bay was an ideal sanctuary for ships, a fact that propelled the town's rapid development into the colony's leading port. *Courtesy of the Bibliothèque Nationale de France.*

"Vue du Port au Prince," late eighteenth century. The colony's second-largest port developed on this protected bay. *Courtesy of the Bibliothèque Nationale de France.*

uprising of 1791. The province was also home to several free men of African descent who would become important revolutionary leaders. Vincent Ogé, a free man of color, lived in the town of Dondon; a decade before the revolution Toussaint Bréda, once a slave and now a free man, rented a small property near the plantation where he had been born.[38]

Saint-Domingue contained two other provinces—the Western and the Southern. They were separated from the North, and from one another, by high mountain ranges. Only in 1751, when Port-au-Prince—the largest town in the Western Province—became the island's capital, was a passage cut across these mountains. The royal government paid for the road, but slaves built it, carving a 100-foot stairway into the rock. Not until 1787, however, was it possible to travel from Le Cap to Port-au-Prince by carriage. Each region had its mountains, its plains, and its port towns. For most of the colony's history, people and goods moved from region to region by sea.[39]

The Western Province was the second in the colony in population and wealth. Its capital, Port-au-Prince, was the second-largest town in Saint-Domingue. One man who traveled to Saint-Domingue in the 1780s made fun of the grand idea French planters had of Port-au-Prince, which they described as a "throne of luxury and voluptuousness" and considered their "Jerusalem." Having heard their tales, he wrote, he approached the town with "that vague anxiety that precedes admiration and prepares enthusiasm," only to find himself in front of "two rows of cabins" arranged around "dusty air they call a street." Port-au-Prince had the look of a "tartar camp," though the presence of the government, garrisons, and the port made it an active city and the "rendezvous for all conspirators and fortune-seekers" in the colony.[40]

There are two plains in the Western Province: the Cul-de-Sac surrounding Port-au-Prince and, to the north, a plain traversed by the snaking Artibonite River bordered by the port towns of Gonaïves and Saint-Marc. Both plains were dry, the Artibonite plain so much so that one writer described it as "Egypt." During the second half of the eighteenth century, government-sponsored irrigation projects put slaves to work building canals that ultimately irrigated nearly half of the land on the Cul-de-Sac. Consequently, sugar production in the area boomed. In 1789 there were 314 sugar plantations in the Western Province, more than in the north, although many of them were smaller and produced unrefined sugar. Indigo

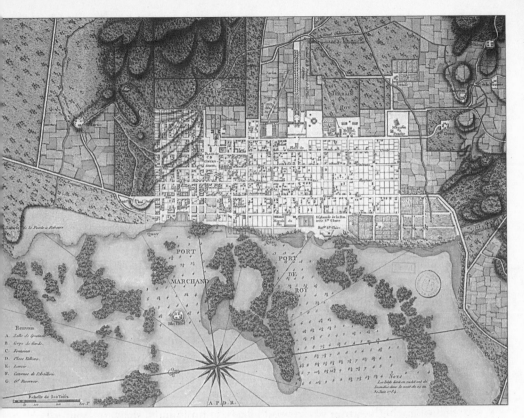

"Plan de la ville des rades et des environs de Port-au-Prince," 1785. Port-au-Prince was less densely constructed than Le Cap. Irrigation works channeled water from the surrounding mountains through a reservoir and into the town. The map is drawn with North to the left. *Courtesy of the Bibliothèque Nationale de France.*

cultivation was much more important in this region than in the north, involving over 1,800 plantations. There were more than 500 cotton plantations and more than 800 coffee plantations. Slaves were again the largest group in the province.[41]

On a long peninsula to the south and west was the Southern Province, whose capital was Les Cayes. It was both cut off from the Western Province and divided internally by the highest mountains in the colony—indeed in the Caribbean. The province included two plains that surrounded Les Cayes, and another smaller plain around the town of Jerémie. It was the least developed of the colony, with only 191 sugar plantations, most of them making unprocessed sugar, and approximately 300 coffee plantations and 900 indigo plantations. It had the smallest population of the three.[42]

Moreau noted that the customs in this region were different from those elsewhere in the colony, as was the creole spoken there. The clothes of the residents had changed little since the first European settlers had arrived. The Southern Province was the last to be fully settled by the French, and remained the most isolated from Atlantic shipping and from the rest of the colony. It was in many ways more connected to the nearby British colony of Jamaica than it was to France, and something of an "English enclave." The inhabitants of the region traded consistently and illegally with the British, as well as with ships from Spanish Cuba, Curaçao, and other areas. Contraband trade was carried on throughout the colony, but it was particularly developed in the south. Huge quantities of indigo were traded to the British, although in official statistics they made up only a tiny portion of the exports of Saint-Domingue. Many free people of color profited from this expanding trade, including a man named Julien Raimond. One day he would carry the demands of this group to Paris.[43]

"Geography," writes one historian, was in Saint-Domingue "the mother of history." Each region had its own landscape, customs, and demography, and these would shape the revolution to come. The geographic location of the colony in the wider world would likewise profoundly shape its political history. Saint-Domingue was at the heart of the Americas, connected in many ways to the empires that surrounded it, and quite far from the nation that governed it. It was part of an evolving Atlantic world, one in which many of the subjects of empires gradually came to dream of one day being citizens of their own nations.[44]

In 1777 a crowd gathered in the main plaza of Le Cap to watch the hanging of a ship captain convicted of stealing. But when the executioner opened the trap below his feet, the rope snapped, and the captain found himself sprawled on the ground. He cried "grace," and several people in the crowd repeated the word. The executioner, unmoved by the miracle, prepared to hang the captain again. The man resisted, wrapping his feet around the ladder and refusing to move, and the crowd erupted and attacked the executioner. Mounted policemen tried to stop the crowd but were showered with rocks and fled. The executioner dragged the captive away down the street, but two big sailors—perhaps from his ship—attacked him and freed the captain. As the executioner returned toward the Place des Armes, he was attacked by a group of blacks, who pummeled him with stones until he was dead. "I saw the corpse of this unfortunate under a pile of stones," Moreau wrote of the murdered executioner; "his head was completely flattened." There was one unlikely survivor from the incident: "a little mouse," which the executioner had adopted, "was in his pocket" and "found living and unharmed."[45]

The port towns of the Atlantic world were notorious for their unruly crowds of sailors, slaves, market-women, small-time crooks, prostitutes, and others who were scraping by on the margins of their colonial societies. They were also, of course, prone to more widespread sedition and revolt on the part of wealthier individuals who, having left their European homes, came to have very different perspectives and interests from those of their European governors. Saint-Domingue was no exception. In its short history it saw two major uprisings before the one that ultimately destroyed it.

In November 1723 a crowd of a hundred women attacked the Maison de l'Afrique, the island seat of the powerful Company of the Indies. Led by a onetime actress named Sagona, owner of a bar in the town, they smashed the windows of the building, broke in, and threw furniture, books, and papers into the street. They tracked some of the company's officials down to a nearby house, where Sagona placed a gun against the throat of one of them and said, "Drink, traitor, it'll be your last." Reportedly he was saved just in time by the intervention of an officer. The next night the rioting continued as a larger crowd again attacked the Maison de l'Afrique and then set fire to a plantation owned by the company at La Fossette. In the crowd were 60 men, armed and dressed like women, and more than 300 women, some covered in flour and others wearing fake moustaches. The uprising, triggered by the granting of trading privileges to the company, lasted several months. Although many of the participants were poor whites, some wealthy men in the colony supported it, with one declaring that if the rebels won there would be open commerce "with all nations," "Republican liberty," and no more taxes. The revolt was so widespread that the governor briefly considered offering freedom to those slaves "who abandoned their masters and gathered under the flag of the king."[46]

Such revolts were a part of a broader refusal by many in Saint-Domingue to accept the plans of the royal administrators for the colony. Wealthy slave owners also consistently flouted and opposed the royal laws and regulations imposed on them. In doing so they took advantage of the division of administrative power in Saint-Domingue between a governor-general, who was in charge of the military aspects of colonial governance, and the intendant, who was in charge of civilian life. However, their powers overlapped considerably, and they were often at odds with each other, a circumstance that suited many planters as it made the application of royal policies difficult. Moreover, laws passed in the metropole had to be registered in the colony by the local *conseils,* or courts, which sometimes refused to do so in protest.[47]

This administrative structure was similar to that of many provinces of France, but there was much that made Saint-Domingue unique. It was, first and foremost, a slave colony, one in which white settlers and other free people were a minority of the population. In 1789, according to official figures, there were roughly 465,000 slaves in the colony, 31,000 whites, and 28,000 free-coloreds. Masters, who were taxed on the basis of the number of slaves they owned, had an interest in underreporting the true numbers, so that it is likely that the slave population was higher, probably near a half-million. (The United States, in contrast, had a total population of 700,000 slaves in 1790.) Furthermore, the towns harbored 26 percent of the colony's whites, who made up only 4 percent of the rural population. A few examples from the northern plain highlight the startling imbalance in the population. In the parish of Limbé there were 300 whites, 200 free-coloreds, and 5,000 slaves, while in the neighboring parish of Acul, where the 1791 insurrection would begin, there were 3,500 slaves and 130 whites.[48]

Masters and colonial administrators agreed that it was vital to contain this slave population. But they often disagreed vehemently about how to do it. The King's 1685 Code Noir laid out detailed regulations regarding the treatment of slaves—their hours of labor, food, housing, clothes, and punishment—as well as related issues such as the process of emancipation. For the next century slave masters brazenly, openly, and consistently broke almost every provision of this code. As one planter activist, Tanguy de la Boissière, wrote in 1793, the Code Noir was always "judged absurd" and its implementation "never attempted." Indeed, over the course of the eighteenth century, local legislation as well as new royal legislation reversed many of its key provisions, particularly those relating to the status of emancipated slaves. Masters in Saint-Domingue, as in North America, responded to any attempt to interfere with their power over slaves with violent hostility and stubborn resistance.[49]

In the mid-1780s reform-minded administrators in the Colonial Ministry in Paris, driven in part by reports of small uprisings on plantations, passed two royal decrees meant to improve the condition of the slaves in the Caribbean. Many of their provisions were aimed at curbing the autonomy of plantation managers—and therefore their power to abuse their slaves—by requiring them to keep careful registers of the work and production on the plantations. The reforms also improved the provisions of the Code Noir by granting slaves not only Sundays but also Saturday afternoons off, limiting the hours of work that could be demanded, and guaranteeing improvements in food and clothing. Slaves were given the right to complain about abuses against them, and severe punishments were provided for masters and managers convicted of murdering slaves.[50]

The masters of Saint-Domingue and some merchants in France publicly attacked the new regulations. One merchant who owned property in Saint-Domingue argued that they would make the work of plantation managers impossible. "How can we contain the negroes if they can accuse whites?" he asked. "To believe the accusations of the slaves is to open the door to revolt and arm them against the whites." He saw in the royal decrees a sinister goal, that of "emancipating the negroes and placing the whites in chains." An officer in the colony who admitted that slavery was "terrible" nevertheless wrote that the decrees were an attack on "the sacred right of property." By placing their work regime and discipline under the control of people "other than their masters," the decrees put a "dagger in the hands of the slaves." The court in Le Cap refused to register the ordinance, setting off a battle between the local administrators and Versailles that led to a 1787 royal edict shutting down the rebellious court and transferring its powers to Port-au-Prince. In the same year, while Martinique and Guadeloupe were granted the right to create colonial assemblies, Saint-Domingue was not. Moreau was in Saint-Domingue at the time, and he and his colleagues in the Cercle des Philadelphes openly attacked these decisions and the "despotic" administration that passed laws without consultation with the colony. In the process they helped lay the foundation for the demands for self-government that would later explode into open rebellion.[51]

Another bone of contention between planters and French officials was the economic policies of the royal government. In the late seventeenth century, under the leadership of the administrator Jean-Baptiste Colbert, the *exclusif*, or monopoly, was put into place. The monopoly meant that only ships from French ports could trade with the colonies. From the perspective of the royal government, the colonies existed to contribute to the economy of the metropole, and it was therefore perfectly logical that the planters should be constrained in this way. France, after all, protected the colonies with its navy, supported their growth with its slave and merchant ships, and supplied settlers and government. It was to be a monogamous relationship of control and support in which colony and mother country would expand in power and wealth together. French ships would buy slaves in French ports in Africa, bring them to French colonies in the Caribbean, and bring back plantation commodities to Europe to be sold by French merchants. The money and the profits would stay within the family.[52]

This was the theory. In practice, of course, things were very different. First of all, French ships consistently failed to deliver sufficient supplies—notably provisions and slaves—to the rapidly expanding colony. The planters contributed to their own problems by focusing obsessively on producing commodities for export, making it necessary to import provisions. French merchants, meanwhile, paid less for colonial commodities than the planters thought they should. It was an illogical system in many ways. Saint-Domingue was next to the thriving British colony of Jamaica, near Spanish Cuba, and quite close to both the North and South American mainlands. There were markets all around. But trade with these prosperous neighbors was prohibited; everything had to travel thousands of miles across the Atlantic.

The *exclusif* was consistently honored in the breach. Pirates, the midwives of the French colonies, had woven links among various Caribbean islands and with the nearby mainlands, and there were always individuals happy to make a profit transporting contraband from one colony to the next. To acquire slaves, planters, especially in the Southern Province close to Jamaica, developed an ingenious system that allowed them to circumvent French merchants in two ways. British traders would bring slaves from Jamaica, and French planters would purchase them with barrels of sugar and coffee. Among the slaves the Jamaicans sold this way were some they especially wished to get rid of because they were rebellious. One slave who probably came from the British West Indies, Boukman, would lead the 1791 slave revolt in the colony.[53]

In addition to nearby British and Spanish colonies, not to mention Dutch traders, the inhabitants of Saint-Domingue found other willing partners in crime among the merchants of New England. The "subproducts" of sugar—particularly rum and molasses—were traded for a wide variety of provisions. (In the early 1790s U.S. ships brought "flour, corn, oats, rice, biscuits, salt beef, salt cod, herring, mackerel, salmon, fish, oils, peas, potatoes, onions, and apples," as well as "live animals including pigs, cows, sheep, and turkeys.") Although many North American merchants came to Saint-Domingue, often the trading took place on small islands such as the Turks and Caicos and the Bahamas, where there was little imperial control. New England merchants in turn traded rum with Native Americans or used it to purchase slaves in Africa. Although their empires were often at war during the eighteenth century, the colonies of North America and the French Caribbean depended on one another as they grew.[54]

Saint-Domingue's economy was sustained by the contraband trade. Small boats plied the shores, buying and selling illegally, and even the leading citizens of the colony participated. It was impossible for the colonial government to repress this trade; harsh legislation against such dealings only highlighted the royal government's impotence. "I am alone against the entire colony" lamented one governor in 1733 when he was criticized for having been too lenient in his punishment of planters convicted of participating in the contraband trade. In the wake of the Seven Years' War, and again after the American Revolution, which opened the way for more intensive trade between North America and Saint-Domingue, administrators made concessions to planters and loosened monopoly regulations, allowing foreign ships to trade certain goods in certain French Caribbean ports. But they excluded some products, and levied heavy import taxes, so the contraband trade continued. The dependence on illegal trading enticed settlers with the possibility that their profits would be greater in a context of lesser imperial control. Many French planters, furthermore, envied the boisterous assemblies of the British colonies. Indeed, as early as the Seven Years' War, some openly supported British attempts to take over the colony, believing their interests would be better served within a different empire.[55]

Saint-Domingue, like all the other colonies of the Atlantic world, was an evolving paradox. While it held out the promise of wealth to its white settlers, it also disappointed many of their hopes. As an extension of the mother country, it was meant to contribute to its power and expansion, and many whites who migrated to Saint-Domingue retained close ties with France and sought to return as soon as they had made their fortunes. But many settlers stayed, as did their children, and in the process they developed new ways of living and seeing the world. Saint-Domingue survived and thrived because its settlers flouted the regulations imposed on them from Paris, trading consistently with their British and Spanish neighbors—especially during times of war. Colonists had different interests from those of the royal governments that controlled them and the metropolitan merchants with whom they traded. They had more in common with British sugar planters in Jamaica than with their cousins in Paris or Bordeaux. The term "creole"—a descriptor that referred to something that was born in the Americas, and could be applied as much to animals and plants as to people, and as well to those of European descent as to those of African descent—captures this difference.

Some writers explained the difference of white Caribbean creoles in racial terms. The English-born planter Bryan Edwards, for instance, identified two physical differences from the "natives of Europe": their "considerably deeper" eye sockets guarded them "from those ill effects which an almost continual strong glare of sunshine might otherwise produce," and their skin felt "considerably colder than that of a European; a proof, I think, that nature has contrived some peculiar means of protecting them from the heat." Others fixated on the corruption fostered in the personalities of creoles by the limitless power they had over their slaves. Moreau described dangers faced by creole men who never left the colony, shaped by their constant ability to turn their "will into law for the slaves," and who ended up abandoning themselves to music and dance and existing "only for the voluptuous pleasures." The naturalist Michel Etienne Descourtilz, who visited Saint-Domingue in the late 1790s, similarly blamed the climate for corrupting the "virtue" of creole women, whose "sedentary life" excited their "voluptuous affections." He claimed that although creoles were born good and virtuous, they were corrupted by the fact that they were destined to command slaves, and developed a "savage, ferocious, egotistical and dominating instinct." He blamed the looseness of their upbringing, in which every "extravagant desire" was entertained by their parents, and so created men who were the "burden of European societies who disdain the ridiculous." Viewing the colonies as distant realms of excess and violence, and their inhabitants as fundamentally different, served to create a distance between slavery and the Europeans who profited from it and consumed what it produced.[56]

Fantasies of depravity and rapid evolutionary adaptation among the creoles were a skewed response to the fact that settlers did create societies distinct and different from those of their fellow nationals across the Atlantic. This circumstance was something the creoles of the Caribbean shared with those of the mainland to the north and south. But their destiny would be quite different. When the thirteen colonies revolted, the wealthiest colonies of the British empire—those of the Caribbean—did not join them, in part because concern about controlling their slaves overshadowed a desire for independence. While slaves played a major role in the American Revolution, primarily by escaping to join the British, who held out the promise of freedom, in the new United States slavery was ultimately consolidated rather than destroyed. In contrast, the victorious struggle for national independence that soon followed in Saint-Domingue became a successful struggle against slavery. And its major protagonists were not slave owners but slaves themselves.[57]

The creoles of Saint-Domingue, after all, were a tiny minority surrounded by a vast population with their own interests and interpretations of the world. The enslaved were "omnipresent and attentive observers" who had an astute sense of the divisions among their oppressors and developed a rich vocabulary to describe it. They referred to the newly arrived whites who often served as their overseers as *moutons France*—French sheep. (The term would be used later to refer to the French troops that arrived, and were decimated, in 1802.) They coined the term *petit blancs*—little whites—to refer to those who did not own land, contrasting them to the *grand blancs* (big whites), also called *Blancs blancs,* or "White whites," whose ownership of property made them true whites. The vocabulary of the slaves was eventually adopted by everyone on the island, and in turn helped to "aggravate the tensions between whites." In this way, slaves' interpretations of the fissures in their masters' society provided categories that deepened them, laying kindling that would help set the colony alight.[58]

CHAPTER TWO

Fermentation

"**Y**OUR MISFORTUNE IS THAT I AM BLACK,**"** wrote the slave Philipeau to his owner, Madame de Mauger, in 1784. "I am black; that is my only fault. If I could whiten myself you would see, with the will of God, an increase in your wealth." Philipeau lived on a plantation located in the rich Artibonite plain of Saint-Domingue. He had been born there, and had served as Madame de Mauger's domestic slave until the 1760s, when she and her husband left to settle permanently in France. By the next decade Philipeau had become the *commandeur*—slave driver— on the plantation. He was its most important slave: he oversaw the daily work in the fields, made sure the other slaves were fed and taken care of, and punished those who failed in their duties. He took his orders not directly from Madame de Mauger, but from the salaried manager she had hired to oversee her properties in the colony. Under pressure to de- liver profits to their distant bosses, and eager to gain a foothold in the colony through the commissions they received on plantation production, such managers were often brutal to the slaves, stinting their food and med- icine, forcing them to work on Sundays, and punishing them with great violence.[1]

This, Philipeau warned Madame de Mauger, was what was happening on her plantation. "Your manager is killing your negroes," he announced. "He is working them too hard." Four had run away, including one old man named Lamour who had always been a faithful worker, and who left be- hind his four children. The manager, furthermore, was making the slaves work on his own crops, for his own profit, taking them away from the work of the plantation. Philipeau pleaded with Mauger to believe him: "I speak to you as if I were explaining myself in front of God." He also pleaded with her to keep his letter a secret. If the manager of the plantation found out that he had written to her, he would be "mistreated." He signed the letter "your very humble and obedient slave." Madame de Mauger did not respond to his entreaties.[2]

Philipeau's letters highlight the paradoxes of life on the plantations of absentee owners. Although such plantations were not the majority—in the north, where they were most numerous, slightly less than half of those producing processed sugar were owned by absentees—they were among the largest and wealthiest. Absentee owners generally had a *procureur* in the colony to whom they had given their power of attorney to oversee their plantations, and who hired the *gérants*, or managers. The *procureurs* rarely visited the plantations, leaving the managers with enormous autonomy, which many exploited. One planter opined that of 100 plantations being run by managers, 95 were in ruins, while their managers had grown rich. Managers could steal plantation commodities, use the slaves for their own profit, and often get away with it. Slaves sometimes protested, as did Philipeau, and one group of slaves on a sugar plantation in the south declared in creole to an official: "We know we have to work for our master on his plantation, but we don't have to work on our manager's plantation." But it took courage to complain, for masters were all too likely to take the word of a manager over that of a slave, and a manager who discovered such complaints had little to restrain him from inflicting brutal punishment. Slaves on larger plantations also had to contend with *économes* (overseers) hired by managers or plantation owners to monitor the slaves in the fields and track their sicknesses, deaths, and infrequent births. These men at the bottom of the hierarchy of white society were paid poorly, hired and fired easily because many were looking for such work, and had fewer possibilities for self-enrichment.[3]

Just below the overseers and at the top of the slave hierarchy were drivers like Philipeau. These slave drivers were, according to one planter, the "soul of the plantation." Masters, managers, and overseers were extremely dependent on them. Drivers were consistently valued very highly on the slave market, and could be worth twice as much as a slave of similar age. Most drivers, like Philipeau, were creoles—they had been born in the colony. They quite literally drove the work of the plantation. A half-hour before sunrise, they woke up the slaves with the crack of a whip or by ringing a bell or blowing a conch shell. They spent the day in the fields with the slaves and reported any misbehavior. They usually inflicted whippings. Their masters rewarded them with better food, clothes, and housing in order both to increase their prestige among the slaves and to secure their loyalty. They were collaborators with the master, playing a central role in the management of the plantations.[4]

At the same time they were community leaders among the slaves. Often chosen because of the respect they already enjoyed on the plantation, as drivers they achieved more power, adding fear to this respect, as well as the ability to help weak or sick slaves and to allow some to leave the plantations at night or on weekends. A manual for prospective plantation masters advised them to be wary of their drivers, who excelled at maintaining an illusion of perfect devotion to the whites but were also close to the most rebellious of the slaves on the plantation, whom they spared from punishment. The author wrote this manual in the wake of the slave revolts of the 1790s, which had probably shaped his perspective on the matter. Indeed to the surprise of many masters, drivers took a leading role in organizing and carrying out the insurrection of 1791.[5]

Revolution was still years away when Philipeau wrote again to Madame de Mauger in 1787. He complained again about the "abominations being committed" by a new manager assigned to the plantation, who took little interest in the work of the slaves and spent his days entertaining in his house. He was selling cotton grown on the plantation, along with lumber cut from the Mauger lands, for his own profit. "Your manager will grow rich at your expense," Philipeau warned. The slaves, meanwhile, were "dying of hunger" even though the warehouses of the plantation were full of food. The manager kept it to feed his personal slaves and his pigs.[6]

This time Mauger wrote back, but her response disappointed Philipeau. We cannot know exactly what she wrote; after reading her letter, the woman who had helped Philipeau write to Mauger burned them, as he had asked Madame de Mauger to do with his. But his response suggests the content: "There is no need to advise me, dear mistress, to make sure the plantation is productive," he wrote. Mauger apparently encouraged him to work harder but ignored his urgent pleas; the plantation manager would not be removed. "You do not want to listen to us. What will we do?" he wrote despairingly. The friend who wrote for him added in a postscript that as he heard her response, the "miserable" Philipeau cried and said that "he would no longer work with the same courage to expand the fortune of a stranger." But the story was not over. In a few years the loyal Philipeau would have his revenge.[7]

For those Africans who survived the horrors of the middle passage, arrival in Saint-Domingue was followed by another torture: branding. Masters marked their ownership by burning their initials into the flesh of their human property. For some, this was a second branding, as slave traders sometimes branded the captives loaded onto their ships. And each time a slave was sold, the process was repeated. According to one seventeenth-century priest, one man "who had been sold and resold several times was in the end as covered with characters as an Egyptian obelisk." Newspaper advertisements for some runaway slaves described the many brands on top of one another. Some Africans, however, had knowledge of herbs that could erase the scars caused by burning—an old art that took on a new value in the context of American slavery. During the revolution, observers noted that many former slaves had managed to render the old brands on their bodies unreadable.[8]

From its founding as an illegal settlement in the 1600s until the abolition of slavery in 1793, hundreds of thousands of slaves were led off slave-trading vessels onto the shores of French Saint-Domingue. According to the most exhaustive inventory of slave-trading journeys, 685,000 slaves were brought into Saint-Domingue during the eighteenth century alone. Over 100,000 slaves were reported to have died during the middle passage, and many more deaths probably went unrecorded. Starting in the late 1730s, between 10,000 and 20,000 African men, women, and children were imported to Saint-Domingue each year. By the middle of the 1780s that number had risen to 30,000 to 40,000. Imports reached their peak in 1790, when nearly 48,000 Africans were disembarked in the colony. This number does not include the slaves imported into the colony before the eighteenth century, nor does it account for the constant influx of slaves brought in via the thriving contraband trade, which naturally left few written traces. We will never know exactly how many slaves were brought to Saint-Domingue. Estimates range from 850,000 to a million. Even though it became a full-fledged plantation society later than other Caribbean colonies and was destroyed decades before the end of the Atlantic slave trade, Saint-Domingue accounted for perhaps 10 percent of the volume of the entire Atlantic slave trade of between 8 and 11 million.[9]

The fact that in 1789 the slave population numbered 500,000 highlights the brutality of slave life. "They are always dying," complained one woman in 1782. On average, half of the slaves who arrived from Africa died within a few years. Children also died at incredible rates, reaching nearly 50 percent on some plantations. Each year 5 to 6 percent of the slaves died, and the situation was worse during the frequent epidemics in the colony. Birthrates, meanwhile, hovered around 3 percent. Focused on short-term gain and for the most part unburdened by humanitarian concerns, many masters and managers in Saint-Domingue coldly calculated that working slaves as hard as possible while cutting expenses on food, clothing, and medical care was more profitable than managing them in such a way that their population would grow. They worked their slaves to death, and replaced them by purchasing new ones.[10]

As a result, by the late eighteenth century the majority of the slaves in Saint-Domingue were African-born. They came from homelands throughout the continent. Early on, many slaves came to Saint-Domingue from Senegambia, home to fledgling French slave ports. During the first quarter of the eighteenth century, the major source of arrivals shifted to the Bight of Benin. Some of these slaves were captured in wars initiated by the Yoruba Kingdom of Oyo, others in raids carried out by the kingdom of Dahomey. A third source was a series of ports along the lagoons of West Africa. The most important was the port of Allada, which came to control a cluster of nearby ports. In Saint-Domingue the complexities of African identifications were often simplified and distorted, and most of the slaves from this region were called "Arada," a version of Allada, or Ardra as it was called by the French. Those from Yoruba kingdoms, meanwhile, were sometimes called "Nago."[11]

As the Atlantic slave trade expanded over the eighteenth century, west-central Africa became the largest source of slaves deported to the Americas. These slaves were supplied through Portuguese raids into the interior from the port of Luanda, from civil wars in the kingdom of the Kongo, and from kingdoms that captured slaves or received them as tribute from regions in the interior. In Saint-Domingue, these slaves were categorized under the generic term "Kongo" (which at the time was usually spelled "Congo"). They made up the majority of the slaves imported into the colony, accounting for 40 percent of the imports during the eighteenth century.[12]

Planters placed great importance on the origins, or "nations," of slaves and used an "elaborate lexicon" that was "the product of both African and

European observation" to categorize them. Although many planters, especially those without access to the larger ports, had little choice in purchasing slaves, those who could expressed preferences for certain "nations" of slaves. Many sugar planters preferred the Arada, whom they saw as good agriculturalists. Some noted that Kongo women had traditionally been given the task of working in the fields, and so were more desirable for fieldwork than the men. The small number of slaves from the cattle-herding Fulbe of West Africa were disproportionately assigned to herding livestock. Moreau de St. Méry wrote extensively about the characteristics of different nations of Africans. The "Sénégalais," he wrote, were "very sober, very clean," and, "most of all, quiet." The Bambara had long marks from temple to neck, and in the islands they were often called "turkey-stealers" or "sheep-stealers" because of the way they satisfied their taste for meat. The Ibo were good fieldworkers but also believed in "the doctrine of the transmigration of souls"; they often killed themselves so that their souls would return to Africa. To dissuade others, planters sometimes cut off or mutilated the head of an Ibo who had committed suicide, reasoning that the Ibo would not want to appear in their homeland disfigured.[13]

By the late eighteenth century many plantations in Saint-Domingue had significant concentrations of slaves from particular African regions. The slave population of one indigo plantation in the Western Province reflected the broader history of the slave trade: among its 92 slaves were 10 older Arada and 29 recently purchased Kongos. On one sugar plantation in the Southern Province there was a bewildering array of African groups: out of the 348 slaves, 58 were Kongos, 28 Ibos, 55 Nagos, 13 Bambara, 25 Arada, 23 Mines, 13 Morriquis, and 16 Sosos; there were smaller groups of Thiabas, Bobo, Mondongues, Senegals, Mocos, Hausa, Tacouas, and Yolofs (Wolofs). On another sugar plantation owned by the same man, of 439 slaves 112 were Kongos, 64 Aradas, 40 Nago, 9 Bambara, and smaller numbers of several other groups. Within each of these groups there was cultural and linguistic diversity, but African languages and customs were undoubtedly kept alive. Some planters placed new arrivals under the tutelage of a slave on the plantation who came from the same homeland to facilitate their integration into plantation life. In the process they also facilitated the maintenance of African communities in their midst. The enslaved recalled, and sometimes called upon, their homelands. In one Vodou song recorded in the 1950s, probably a relic from the days of slavery, a singer calls on the King of the Kongo to "look at what they are doing to me."[14]

The Kongos were especially dominant in the mountains, where many coffee plantations had been founded in the second half of the eighteenth century. In the decade before the revolution they made up at least half the slave population on coffee plantations in the Northern and Western Provinces. In some mountain regions of Saint-Domingue, languages of the Kongo region were probably spoken as commonly as creole and French. In the Northern Province they also accounted for 40 percent of slaves on sugar plantations in the years before the revolution. Among these Kongo slaves were men like Macaya and Sans-Souci, who would become leaders of insurgent bands, and eventually of revolutionary armies, in the Northern Province.[15]

On the eve of the revolution, according to Moreau, two-thirds of Saint-Domingue's slaves—and therefore more than half of the colony's population—had been born in Africa. The relationship between these African-born slaves and the creoles was complex. Creoles had many advantages in facing the daily struggles of slavery. They had grown up speaking creole and had networks of kin in the colony. They generally held more of the specialized and privileged positions on plantations and had a better chance of emancipation. Meanwhile, slaves who had been raised in Africa had their own cultural, political, and military experiences, their own languages and religion. However, sharp distinctions between the groups are misleading: many creoles were only a generation away from Africa, and the African-born who had spent much of their life in the colony became creolized in many ways. Nevertheless, the particular life histories of members of these two groups would shape their participation in the revolution.[16]

The culture of Saint-Domingue—that which shaped all its inhabitants, whether African-born or creole, white or black—was deeply influenced by the constant infusion of African slaves. On plantations and in towns, this culture was inevitably present in musical traditions, language, daily habits, fashions, beliefs, and dreams. Moreau wrote of the use by African slaves in Saint-Domingue of "little figurines made out of wood representing men or animals," which they called *garde-corps*—bodyguards. In the Southern Province, African slaves brought their "comrades to the cemetery" in large crowds, with the women leading the procession, clapping, singing, and drumming. Another observer, visiting in the late 1790s, noted that the Kongos wore feathers in their hair, and that many had filed and sharpened teeth.[17]

Moreau claimed that "all the Africans are polygamous in Saint-Domingue."

African women married to the same man, he noted, called one another *matelots*—"sailors." They were imitating the pirates who had settled the island the century before and formed "societies" whose members called one another by this name. "Among these women, as among all others, there is a kind of conspiracy against men," Moreau opined, especially when it came to tricking their lovers. The use of the term *matelot* among wives in a polygamous marriage is one small example of the rich process of adaptation and transformation that took place in Saint-Domingue.[18]

Moreau wrote of the "African become colonial" who took on "a way of life that can neither resemble that which they had in their place of origin or differ from it absolutely." One of the enduring cultural legacies of the process of encounter and transformation that took place in the cauldron of the colony is Haitian Creole. In parallel with the different creoles that developed in other colonial societies, this language emerged through the mingling of dialects of French with African languages. It was forged over several generations by many speakers: early French settlers and their slaves, free people of color, domestic and urban slaves, adult Africans brought to plantations during the height of the sugar boom, and especially children born into slavery in Saint-Domingue.[19]

African religions also put down roots in the soil of plantations, changing in the process. They entered into dialogue with the practices of Catholicism, whose saints were imbued with a new meaning by worshipers in both Africa and the Americas. In Saint-Domingue the Arada slaves from the Bight of Benin, who were the majority during the first decades of the eighteenth century, brought the traditions of the Fon and Yoruba peoples, which were joined by those brought by the Kongo slaves who eventually became the island's majority. In a world organized to the production of plantation commodities, where slaves were meant to be laborers and nothing more, religious ceremonies provided ritual solace, dance and music, but most importantly a community that extended beyond the plantation. They also provided an occasion for certain individuals to provide advice and guidance. Out of the highly industrialized and regimented plantations, then, emerged a powerful set of religious practices that celebrated and reflected the human struggles of those who participated in them. Religion was, in some sense, a space of freedom in the midst of a world of bondage, and helped lay the foundation for the revolt that ultimately brought complete freedom to the slaves.[20]

Administrators and slave owners had long recognized the subversive po-

Engraving of a sugar plantation from the *Encyclopédie,* 1751. The idealized image identifies (1) the master's house, (2) the slave quarters, (3) the pasture, (5) the fields of sugarcane, (6) the water mill, (7) the building where the cane juice is boiled, (10) the building where the cane stalks are crushed to make the juice, (12) the building where the *pains* ("breads") of sugar are dried, and (13) the heights where manioc, bananas, and other provisions are grown. *Courtesy of the Michigan State University Library.*

tential of the religious ceremonies of slaves. They criminalized and sought to suppress them, though they were never entirely successful. Moreau described in detail a "danse vaudoux" that involved the worship of a snake that had "the knowledge of the past, the science of the present, and the prescience of the future." It involved dialogue between worshipers, who wore red handkerchiefs, and two religious leaders to whom they referred by "the pompous name of King and Queen, or the despotic master and mistress, or the touching father and mother." The worshipers asked these two for favors; "the majority," wrote Moreau, "ask for the ability to direct the spirit of their masters." At one point during the ceremony, the Queen was "penetrated by the god," and "her entire body convulsed," and "the oracle spoke through her mouth." All this was followed by the singing of "an

African song" and dancing. The spiritual power itself was such that some whites, caught spying on the ceremonies and touched by one of the worshipers, themselves began to dance uncontrollably, and had to pay the Queen "to end this punishment." "Nothing is more dangerous than this cult of Vaudoux," asserted Moreau. He lamented the power of the religious leaders and the dependence of worshipers on them. Such relations of power, presumably, were acceptable only between master and slave.[21]

For plantation owners and managers, the slaves were laboring machines, cogs in a system meant to produce as much sugar or coffee as possible. "It is in the time and strength of the negroes that the fortune of the planter resides," wrote one contemporary commentator. The majority of slaves spent their entire lives doing harsh and difficult labor in the fields. On sugar plantations they were organized into several *ateliers,* or work-gangs, each under the command of a driver. The strongest slaves were assigned the hardest agricultural tasks: digging canals, tilling the soil, planting cane, and harvesting it. A second group of children and older slaves, as well as new arrivals from Africa who were often weak from the middle passage and more prone to disease, took on more varied tasks, such as growing provisions, fertilizing planted cane, or trimming cane plants. Field laborers started work at five, stopped for a few hours at midday, then returned to their labor until sundown. The grueling work of harvesting, worsened by the danger of cutting oneself with a machete or on the sharp stalks of the cane, usually lasted from December through July.[22]

Harvested stalks of cane were fed twice through a mill—usually driven by mules, and sometimes by water—that crushed them to release their juice. This task, usually assigned to women, was particularly dangerous. If the slave was tired or distracted, and allowed even a finger to be pinched in the grinders as she guided a stalk into the mill, "the finger goes in, then the hand, then the arm and the whole body except the head." Since during the harvest season the grinding of cane was often done all night in successive shifts of slaves, exhaustion was common. Many lost their arms, and some died of tetanus.[23]

The juice from the cane was boiled in a series of vats heated with fires made with the *bagasse*—the dejuiced sugarcane stalks—which had been gathered in the mills by children or old women. A white *maître sucrier* (master sugarmaker) oversaw this boiling process, assisted by trained slaves who were among the most valued and well-treated on the planta-

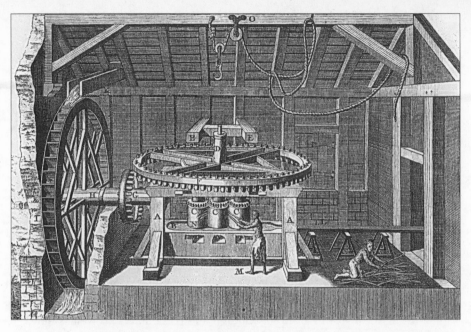

Engraving of sugar processing from the *Encyclopédie,* 1751. This image shows a very advanced machine for crushing the harvested cane stalks and collecting the juice, driven by a water mill. A woman is performing the dangerous job of feeding the stalks into the machine. *Courtesy of the Michigan State University Library.*

tions. Their work required a great deal of care and precision. So did the work of other "elite" slaves—the artisans who made the barrels to transport the sugar, and those who drove the wagons that transported the cane from the fields to the mills and also took care of the horses and mules. Another group of relatively privileged slaves were the domestics who worked in the master's house. Among them were laundresses who washed clothes in nearby streams or rivers, cooks, valets, and coachmen. They were clothed and fed better than the field slaves and could take advantage of their position. Some cooks collaborated with field slaves, using leftovers from the kitchen to raise livestock. Laundresses sometimes sold the soap given to them and washed the clothes with plants or fruit instead. Daily proximity to the master could be an advantage. Along with drivers and artisans, domestic slaves were the most likely to be emancipated. But they were also isolated from the other slaves and more subject to sexual exploitation by their masters.[24]

Coffee harvesting and processing was also difficult work, and involved some periods of night work. But on coffee plantations the labor was more varied and in some ways less difficult and dangerous than that on sugar plantations. Even large coffee plantations were generally smaller than sugar plantations, so there was more contact between masters and slaves. These plantations were also much less often in the hands of absentee owners. Coffee planters often assigned their slaves piecework, in which they had to harvest a certain amount of coffee and would get a small monetary reward if they picked more. A prisoner of the insurgents in late 1791 claimed to have noticed a contrast between those who had been slaves on the sugar plantations of the plain, who were "enraged," and those who had been slaves in the mountains, who were less ferocious.[25]

Enslaved women confronted particular challenges on the plantations: they were responsible for both production and reproduction. Excluded from the most prestigious occupations—drivers, sugarboilers, and artisans—most of them worked in the fields. Those who worked as domestics were in particular danger of rape and other forms of abuse by their masters. And those who were mothers faced particularly wrenching and difficult struggles and choices. During the second half of the eighteenth century, some planters became concerned about the low birthrates among the slaves and instituted incentive programs to encourage women to have children. The manager of the thriving Gallifet sugar plantations in the Northern Province gave monetary rewards to mothers—one for giving birth, and another, probably larger, for weaning the child two years later. Programs of encouragement were often accompanied by new and cruel forms of punishment for those accused of having had abortions. In the Southern Province some women suspected of having them were forced to wear a human-shaped figurine symbolizing the lost baby around their necks. Women who had had abortions were considered to have deprived their masters of a piece of human property. In the late 1790s legends circulated about a midwife named Samedi who during the time of slavery took advantage of her profession to kill the children she delivered. She wore a belt with seventy knots, each a reminder of one of her victims, for whom, she proclaimed, she had been a "liberator."[26]

Enslaved women were prey to sexual exploitation and assault by masters, managers, and overseers. Although some resisted, they had little power to refuse predatory men who legally owned their bodies. Sometimes long-term relationships developed between enslaved women and masters or managers. The slaves involved in such relationships were rewarded with better clothes and food, and sometimes gained liberty for themselves and their children. In seeking to understand these relationships it is difficult—perhaps impossible—to disentangle emotion from interest, sex and sentiment from power and coercion. The little insight we have into them, as with so much of slave life, comes from the sparse and distorted writings of whites.[27]

Despite the deeply unequal relationship between masters and slaves, life and labor on the plantations was the product of constant negotiation and adjustment. The enslaved resisted in small ways as they worked in the fields, and they developed, and defended, customary rights. The most important of these was access to garden plots of land on the plantations. The Code Noir required masters to feed their slaves with a set number of provisions each week. Relatively quickly, however, many masters began using a practice borrowed from Dutch colonies, in which slaves were given a small plot of land to cultivate rather than being given weekly provisions. They were also given all or part of Saturday, in addition to the free Sunday they already had, to cultivate these plots. This arrangement was a way for planters a way to save money, although it could backfire if slaves were unable to grow enough food to feed themselves, as was the case especially in times of drought.[28]

On most plantations the enslaved were fed through a combination of common provisions, cultivated by groups of slaves taken from other tasks under the command of a driver, and food they grew on their own small plots. From the common grounds came potatoes, manioc, and other staples, while from individual plots came squash, spinach, cucumbers, peppers, and sometimes tobacco. Slaves also chewed bits of sugarcane taken from the fields, and drank *tafia*—rum—which masters and managers sometimes handed out when the work was particularly hard. Some supplemented their diets in other ways, gathering oysters or land crabs. The crabs, however, often ate the poisonous leaves of the mancenillier tree, and the poison was transferred to those who dined on them. For this reason, slaves sometimes burned down the mancenillier trees around their plantations. Hungry slaves living around one lake took even greater risks, knocking out crocodiles with stones so that they could take their eggs.[29]

What slaves caught or harvested, and what they grew on their own plots of land, they also often sold, supporting an important internal economy. In one section of the large market of Le Cap a "multitude of vendors" from plantations offered oranges, pineapples, guavas, papayas, apricots, and avocados. Other vendors sold decorative crafts such as calabashes that had been carved on the outside in an "ingenious or bizarre" way. The inhabitants of the towns, whether white or black, depended on such markets; the residents of one southern town, Moreau noted, suffered during periods of heavy rain or the coffee harvest, when plantation slaves did not come to the market.[30]

To sell what they produced in their garden plots, slaves had to be given permission to go to the towns on Sundays. Such journeys also provided valuable opportunities for worship and socializing. Many slaves shed the threadbare clothes they wore in the field—which were given them by the master—for a clean, fancier set they had bought for themselves. In Le Cap there was a special "messe des nègres" after the regular mass, during which slaves and free people of African descent gathered to pray and sing, led by elderly members of their community. The fact that slaves were leading Catholic ceremonies bothered some authorities, and indeed the accusation that Jesuits had encouraged such independent worship helped propel the expulsion of the order from Saint-Domingue in the 1760s.[31]

In the afternoon, after the market was closed, there was music and dancing. Accompanied by drums, calabashes filled with seeds, hand-clapping, improvised singing, and sometimes the music of a four-stringed instrument called the Banza, pairs of dancers would enter a circle formed by the others to dance what Moreau called a "Calenda." Another dance he described was the "Chica"—called the "Congo" in the French colony of Cayenne—a "lascivious" dance in which women moved their hips while keeping the rest of their bodies still. Slaves also gathered in "cabarets," which offered liquor and gambling. In Port-au-Prince there was a curfew: the church bell rang at 9:30 to call slaves back to their homes. There were also places to gather in the countryside. Near Petite-Anse in the north were two *guildiveries* (where alcohol was made), which provided a "meeting-place for a considerable number of negroes," especially on Sundays and holidays.[32]

The Code Noir of 1685 had outlawed "slaves of different masters" to gather "under the pretext of weddings or otherwise," especially along roads or in isolated areas. The stipulated punishment was whipping and branding with an iron shaped as a fleur-de-lis, the symbol of the French crown; recidivists could be executed. Masters who permitted such assemblies on their property could be fined. These regulations were never consistently enforced, although the *maréchaussée,* the colony's police force, sometimes broke up slave gatherings. It was impossible for authorities to prevent slaves from socializing in either towns or countryside, and many masters gave tacit approval to such gatherings, seeing them as harmless diversions.[33]

Although they were able to carve out some spaces of autonomy, the enslaved remained subject to the control of their masters. This control was maintained, as was the entire system of slavery, through violence. In 1802 the British abolitionist James Stephen would note that what had "secured in great measure the tranquility" of the French colonies "before their revolutions" was "the nameless and undefined idea of terror, connected in the mind of a negro slave, with the notion of resistance to a white man and a master." Physical punishment was both a constant threat and a frequent reality in the lives of the slaves. The most common punishment was whipping, which according to the Code Noir was the only punishment allowed on plantations. Masters or drivers tied the hands and legs of the enslaved to posts stuck in the ground, or else tied them to a ladder or hung them by their hands from a post. Whippings were used as torture and as spectacle. "Slow punishments make a greater impression than quick or violent ones," wrote one wealthy plantation owner to his managers. Rather than fifty lashes "administered in five minutes," he recommended "twenty-five lashes of the whip administered in a quarter of an hour, interrupted at intervals to hear the cause which the unfortunates always plead in their defense, and resumed again, continuing in this fashion for two or three times," as being "far more likely to make an impression." The message was aimed as much at the other slaves, who were forced to watch, as at the victim.[34]

Hot peppers, salt, lemon, or ashes were sometimes rubbed into open wounds, which might also be burnt with an open flame to increase the pain. Cases of even more extreme torture appear in the documents. One man wrote in the 1730s about the practice of placing gunpowder in the anus of slaves and lighting it. Another wrote of the castration of male slaves. A master brought to court in the 1750s had tied a slave, suspended, above a fire. Moreau documented cases in which slaves were splashed with burning wax and women's "shameful parts" were burnt with hot coals, and one in which a master attacked some of his slaves and bit off pieces of their flesh. Another late eighteenth-century writer described slaves being doused with boiling cane juice and others being buried alive after having been forced to dig their own graves.[35]

Some slaves collaborated in the master's violence, driven by the fear of becoming its target or by the hope of channeling it elsewhere. Many other slaves simply avoided it and survived as best they could, following orders and trying desperately to work tiny plots of land to feed themselves and their families, crafting small spaces of comfort and community. Some, however, responded by sowing terror among their masters.

In January 1758 a fugitive slave named Makandal was made to kneel in a plaza in Le Cap, wearing a sign that read "Seducer, Profaner, Poisoner." He was then tied to a post in the center of the plaza, and a fire was lit underneath him. As the flames reached his body, he struggled to break free, and the post to which he was attached gave way. The blacks in the watching crowd shouted, "Makandal saved!" and panic broke out. Soldiers quickly cleared the plaza, and Makandal was tied to a board and thrown back into the fire. Makandal had often boasted that he was able to change form, and before his execution he declared that he would transform himself into a fly to escape the flames. Few had seen him die, and many believed he had indeed escaped and was once again in the hills, plotting a new rebellion.[36]

Makandal, who became legendary among both blacks and whites in Saint-Domingue, had been born in Africa. Though his occasional evocation of Allah suggests that he was a Muslim (and thus probably from West Africa), his name may have been derived from the Kongo word for amulet, *mak(w)onda*. Moreau claimed that after his death slaves used the term "Makandal" to refer to ritual talismans as well as to the priests who made them. But in fact the term seems to have been used in this way before he came along—he perhaps chose it, or was given it, for this reason—though his life and death imbued it with a new significance. Makandal was convicted of "mingling holy things in the composition and usage of allegedly magical packets." One of those he made included a crucifix, and Makandal invoked Allah, Jesus Christ, and God when he created them.[37]

Like these packets, Makandal's life and the legends that emerged from it were the result of a potent encounter between African traditions and the world of plantation slavery. Makandal was a slave on a plantation in the parish of Limbé in the Northern Province, where he lost one of his arms while working in a sugar mill. Subsequently relegated to guarding the animals on his plantation, he eventually ran away into the hills. Later legends claimed that he gathered together a large band of fugitive slaves who attacked plantations, but in fact he sowed terror primarily by using poison.

He knew how to make it from harvested plants, and coordinated its use against livestock, slaves who were deemed enemies, and masters. In order to carry out his attacks, Makandal developed an extensive network among the slaves of the Northern Province, including those who worked as merchants traveling from plantation to plantation. Makandal was not the first or the only slave rebel who used poison in Saint-Domingue. But the extent of his activities and the publicity they gained helped set in motion a cycle of paranoia and violence that continued in Saint-Domingue for decades.[38]

The practice of *marronage*—running away from the plantations—was as old as slavery itself. In Saint-Domingue it took many forms. Africans brought into the colony by slavers, refusing their condition as property, often ran away soon after their arrival. They were prone to recapture because they lacked knowledge of the geography of the island and connections who could help them hide, although some residents did help them, sometimes by telling them the way to Spanish Santo Domingo. Plantation slaves sometimes left the direct supervision of the managers but remained nearby. The organization of plantations, with cultivated land, fields for grazing, provision grounds, and slave quarters scattered in different locations, facilitated this evasion. Some maroons stayed on the margins of their plantations for years, eating cane from the fields or food brought to them by friends and kin. Sometimes they also stole from provision grounds or garden plots, impelling slaves to build or grow fences around them. Other slaves ran away to the towns, where they could often blend into the population of urban slaves and free-coloreds, especially if they were trained in a craft. The towns were a preferred destination for women, who were a minority among maroons.[39]

Administrators did what they could to prevent such illegal mobility. Those who left the plantations, even to go to markets on Sundays, were required to carry a pass from their masters permitting them to do so. Any white person could stop a slave and ask him to show these documents. But, as one commentator lamented in 1778, it was easy to counterfeit them. Escaped slaves took advantage of "friends who know how to write" to create false passports, and moved about "with impunity," coming into town to sell and buy provisions before returning to the woods. There was also a traffic in real passes, whose dates could be forged.[40]

Shorter-term absences were often tolerated by planters, who referred to this form of escape as *petit marronage.* Individual returns might be negotiated by whites, sometimes an older woman in the planter's family or a neighbor, with slaves promising to return if they were spared punishment. On absentee-owned plantations, mass *marronage* was sometimes used as a form of protest against a manager. On a plantation in the Cul-de-Sac plain in 1744, for instance, sixty-six slaves left the plantation during the day but came back to sleep in their quarters at night, demanding the removal of the overseer. One day the overseer killed one of the protesting slaves, a pregnant woman, with a knife. Two months later the slaves surprised him, carried him away, and executed him. They were condemned to death, but the governor intervened on their behalf, recognizing that their actions were justified by the particular brutality of their overseer. Such strikes occurred with some regularity and often led to the negotiated return of the slaves. Masters had a great deal of capital invested in their human property, and it was often cheaper to negotiate a return and to replace a white manager than to risk the loss of many slaves and the disruption of plantation labor.[41]

Maroons who were repeatedly absent for several weeks or more were, however, usually punished harshly. The Code Noir stipulated that a slave who had been away from the plantation for more than a month was to have one of his ears cut off and a fleur-de-lis branded on his shoulder. A slave who ran away again for a month was to receive a second brand and have a hamstring cut. The punishment for the third offense was death. Rather than follow these prescriptions for mutilation, however, most masters and managers devised other punishments that caused suffering but did not damage their property. Maroons were usually whipped, and sometimes their garden plots were confiscated. They might be locked up in the plantation hospitals, which often doubled as prisons and were outfitted with bars or posts used to immobilize punished slaves at night, or else in the *cachots*, small stone prisons that proliferated on plantations during the late eighteenth century. Chains might be attached to the slave's legs, sometimes with a ball added to make running difficult, and iron collars with spikes placed permanently around the neck. Only a blacksmith could remove them. Even such devices did not always keep slaves from running away again; some maroons were caught wearing them.[42]

Some individuals broke permanently with the world of the plantations by escaping to the mountains and forming or joining maroon bands. Such bands were a presence in the colony throughout the eighteenth century, and they left their traces on the landscape. As Moreau reported of the eastern parts of the Northern Province, hills with names like Flambeaux (torches) or Congo "recalled the era when fugitives lived in nearly inaccessible locations." Many remembered "Polydor and his band, his murders, his banditry, and most of all the difficulty we had in capturing him." Polydor was killed in 1734, but another maroon leader named Canga emerged in the same region in the 1770s, and after his execution there came another named Yaya.[43]

These bands, who conducted raids against plantations, were a major concern for colonial administrators. The administration maintained the *maréchaussée* to police the slaves and hunt maroon bands. In one case they opted for negotiation. In 1785 the colonial administrations of both the Spanish and French colonies signed a treaty with a group of more than 100 maroons living in frontier region of Bahoruco. The treaty granted them amnesty and liberty in return for their promise to pursue any new runaways in the area and hand them over to the authorities. Many whites decried such agreements, believing that the only way to deal with rebel slave communities was to destroy them. But in pursuing this policy Saint-Domingue's administrators were simply following the lead of those in Jamaica and Suriname who had signed such treaties with maroon groups in the 1730s as a way of ending long wars and creating a buffer against continuing escapes.[44]

During the eighteenth century the maroon communities of Saint-Domingue maintained open, armed conflict with the plantation society that surrounded them, claiming and defending their liberty. As a result some consider them the precursors—and the ancestors—of those who rose up in the slave revolt of 1791. (During the reign of François Duvalier, a statue to the "Unknown Maroon" was erected across from the National Palace in Port-au-Prince to celebrate these nameless rebels as the founders of the nation.) Others express skepticism about the relationship between *marronage* and revolution in Saint-Domingue. The maroon communities of the colony were much smaller than those in Jamaica and Suriname, in part because many of the mountainous regions where maroons might have sought refuge had been invaded by coffee plantations. Indeed it may have been the limits on the expansion of maroon communities that propelled slave revolution, since those who wished to escape slavery had to develop a direct and systemic attack against the world of the plantations rather than seeking a refuge outside it.[45]

The presence of maroon communities in Saint-Domingue contributed to the fissures in colonial society. In order to fight maroons the administration ultimately turned to free people of color. In so doing they laid the foundation for demands for inclusion that ignited the colony during the revolution. Maroons, by successfully flouting slavery, were also an inspiration and example for the enslaved, as well as for antislavery writers. The 1791 revolt, however, emerged from the heart of the thriving sugar plantations of the northern plain, and the existing maroon communities were not involved in its planning. More important for the revolt were the practices of *marronage* on the edges of plantations, or in the towns, which had helped sustain a culture of autonomy and the networks that connected various plantations. Like religious ceremonies and Sunday gatherings, the practice of running away laid the groundwork for an uprising that united slaves across plantations and in so doing enabled them to smash the system from within. Once they had risen up in 1791, however, slave insurgents did use tactics pioneered by maroons in defending their mountain camps against French attacks.[46]

Makandal was a part of the long tradition of *marronage* in the colony. In developing his cross-plantation network of resistance, meanwhile, he also drew on another long-standing practice: the use of poison by slaves. Starting in the seventeenth century, colonial legislation outlawed the use of poison, in the process repressing forms of traditional healing practiced within the slave community that whites often used as well. The reasons for this proscription were clear enough. Poison granted power. Slaves who used poison against whites aimed "to dominate their masters" and humiliate them by making them feel "a power that was hidden, but very close." Poison could be placed in food by the domestics who surrounded whites, and there was often no way to detect it or to identify who had placed it there. Commentators pointed out that since many planters put stipulations in their wills granting freedom to certain slaves, there was a strong incentive for those named slaves to accelerate their access to freedom by killing their masters. Poison could also be used against the master's property, killing animals in ways that were often difficult to distinguish from death by disease. Often it was used by slaves against other slaves. Those who knew how to use poison could gain power and respect within the slave community.[47]

It is difficult to know how extensive the use of poison by slaves actually was. Evidence of its use comes primarily from trials conducted in a context of rampant paranoia. Masters often imagined that poison was being used when in fact their animals were dying of disease, and their slaves of overwork and misery. Surrounded by slaves, knowing that some might know how to concoct poisons, and that many had plenty of motivation to use it, many masters responded by burning suspected slaves alive without the formality of a trial. In 1775, according to one doctor, every plantation had its stake. "To intimidate the other negroes," he wrote, the masters forced "each of them to carry a bundle of wood for the stake, and to watch the execution."[48]

It was illegal for masters to torture and kill their slaves in this way. A few masters were in fact deported from Saint-Domingue after committing atrocities against their slaves. For the most part, however, they acted with impunity. In 1788 a planter name Nicholas Le Jeune tortured two female slaves whom he suspected of having used poison against other slaves. He burned their legs, locked them up in a cell, and threatened to kill any slave who attempted to denounce him. Nevertheless, a group of fourteen slaves brought a complaint to the local court. White judges who went to the plantation to investigate found the two women chained, their burned legs decomposing, and one being strangled by the metal collar around her neck. Both died soon afterward. The judges also found that a small box that Le Jeune claimed contained poison in fact contained "nothing more than common smoking tobacco interspersed with five bits of rat stool." Le Jeune was put on trial on the basis of the slaves' denunciations. He defended himself by arguing that if slaves saw planters punished on the basis of their testimony, there would be a breakdown of authority and, ultimately, a slave revolution. Others agreed, and one man even suggested that each of the slaves who had denounced Le Jeune should receive fifty lashes. The investigating officials who took over the case, on the other hand, argued that punishing brutal planters was the only way to prevent an outbreak of revolution: if the violence of planters was not kept in check, and if slaves found no recourse from the administration, they would have no option but violent vengeance. Ultimately, however, the officials bowed to pressure from the planters, and Le Jeune was never punished.[49]

For fearful masters, Makandal came to symbolize the danger of a mass uprising that would destroy the whites in the colony. One famous account of his life described a speech he made to slaves, during which he placed three scarves in a vase full of water—one yellow, one white, and one black. The first symbolized the original inhabitants of the island, the second the "present inhabitants." Pulling out the third, he declared: "Here, finally, are those who will remain masters of the island: it is the black scarf." A 1779 memoir presented Makandal as a "Mohammed at the head of a thousand exiled refugees" who, imagining "the conquest of the Universe," had planned to massacre all the whites in the colony. All that was lacking to bring about a "general massacre" and "a revolution similar to that of Suriname or Jamaica" was a leader, "one of those men, rare in truth, but who can emerge at any moment," like Makandal, "whose name itself" made the inhabitants of the Northern Province "tremble." In 1801, in a "grand new spectacle" presented in London, the romantic hero was a rebellious slave named Makandal who declared himself "one unawed by fear."[50]

Writers in France also prophesied the imminent emergence of a black revolutionary leader. In his 1771 fable of time travel, Louis Sebastien Mercier imagined waking up after a 672-year nap and finding himself in a changed and perfected world. In one plaza he saw on a pedestal "a negro his head bare, his arm outstretched, with pride in his eyes and a noble and imposing demeanor." Under the statue were the words "To the Avenger of the New World!" Mercier learned that "this surprising and immortal man" had delivered the world "from the most atrocious, longest, and most insulting tyranny of all." He had "broken the chains of his compatriots" and transformed those "oppressed by the most odious slavery" into heroes. In an "instant" they had "spilled the blood of their tyrants." "French, Spanish, English, Dutch, Portuguese all fell prey to iron, poison, and flame. The soil of America avidly drank the blood that it had been awaiting for so long, and the bones of their ancestors, murdered by cowards, seemed to stand up and shake with joy." The "Avenger" became a god in the New World and was celebrated in the Old. "He came like a storm spreading across a city of criminals that is about to be destroyed by lightning." He was an "exterminating angel," granted power by justice and by God.[51]

The Abbé Raynal's famous history of European colonialism, which went through many printings in the 1770s and 1780s, contained a passage that drew on Mercier's vision. After critiquing the institution of slavery, the work warned readers that the slaves did not need their masters' "generosity or advice" to break the "sacrilegious yoke of their oppression." Already, it noted, "two colonies of fugitive negroes have been established" in Jamaica and Suriname and had won recognition of their freedom. These signs were the lightning that announced the storm. "All that the negroes lack is a leader courageous enough to carry them to vengeance and carnage," the work warned. "Where is he, this great man, that nature owes to its vexed, oppressed, tormented children? Where is he? He will appear, do not doubt it. He will show himself and will raise the sacred banner of liberty. This venerable leader will gather around him his comrades in misfortune. More impetuous than torrents, they will leave everywhere ineffaceable traces of their just anger." The "American fields," the text continued, riffing off Mercier, would get drunk on the blood that they had been awaiting "for so long," while the bones buried over the course of three centuries would "shake with joy." Monuments to this "hero who reestablished the rights of the human species" would be erected in the New World and the Old. But the Europeans might reap what they had sown: "the *Code Noir* will disappear, and the *Code Blanc* will be terrible, if the victors consult only the law of revenge!"[52]

The passages in Raynal and Mercier were intended as both indictment and warning. Mercier appended a note to his powerful portrait of the "Avenger," spoken from the eighteenth-century present: "This hero will probably spare the generous Quakers who have just granted liberty to their negroes in a memorable and touching era that made me cry tears of joy, and will make me detest those Christians who do not imitate them." There, was, then, a way to avoid carnage and revenge. Slavery must be abolished by the Europeans, before the slaves abolished it—and their masters—themselves.[53]

Such warnings developed out of a complex network of colonial administrators and Enlightenment intellectuals who came during the last decades of the eighteenth century to believe that slavery had to be reformed and ultimately eliminated. Such thinkers saw clearly that the daily resistance of slaves through poison, suicide, abortion, as well as *marronage* and revolt, and the violent response of the planters formed a cycle that had to be stopped before it spun out of control. They were not particularly antiracist, and certainly not anticolonial—Mercier's ideal world was one in which the wastefulness of slavery in the Americas had been replaced by an empire in which Africans grew sugarcane next to their own huts—but they believed that slavery should be gradually replaced by other forms of labor. Enlightenment critiques of slavery attacked the institution as a violation of the natural rights that all human beings shared, and the warnings of Mercier and Raynal suggested that, like all other oppressed peoples, the slaves had the right to resist their oppressors violently.[54]

By the time the French Revolution began, both defenders and enemies of slavery were evoking the specter of a large-scale uprising. As abolitionist activity accelerated in Paris, planters complained that antislavery writings would encourage slaves to revolt by making them think they had allies. Abolitionists retorted that in their cruelty and ignorance the planters were leaving their slaves no choice but to revolt. The masters of the Caribbean, wrote the comte de Mirabeau, were "sleeping at the foot of Vesuvius." In 1789 the Abbé Grégoire echoed Raynal, declaring that "the cry of liberty" was resounding in both the Old and New Worlds; all that was needed was "an Othello, a Padrejean"—the latter a seventeenth-century slave rebel—to awaken the enslaved to an understanding of their "inalienable rights" and push them to violent revolt. But he backed up his claims about the danger of slave revolt by quoting the words of a planter, an opponent of the rights of free-coloreds, who wrote that 400,000 slaves in Saint-Domingue were awaiting their opportunity to rise up. In the political theater, all sides constantly referred to the potential for revolution among the slaves. Yet despite all the talk of revolution, it was a shock when the slaves actually launched one.[55]

CHAPTER THREE

Inheritance

W HAT EARTHLY POWER CAN GIVE ITSELF the right to create unjust laws, when the Eternal itself has abstained from doing so?" So asked Julien Raimond in a 1791 pamphlet tracing the "origin and progress" of prejudice against free people of color in Saint-Domingue. In unveiling this history, Raimond hoped to end it. Free people of color, many of them wealthy planters, others serving in colonial military or police units, had proven their value and loyalty to the French regime, he argued. And yet they were being prevented by whites from participating in the political assemblies of the colony. This act of racial prejudice went against everything the French Revolution stood for. Even Louis XIV's 1685 Code Noir had recognized that once they were no longer slaves, free people of color had the "the right to citizenship." "Will the National Assembly be less just than a despot?"[1]

Raimond was educated, wealthy, and passionate in his struggle against racial discrimination. Starting in the 1780s, he mounted a political struggle on behalf of the free-coloreds of Saint-Domingue by petitioning the head of the Colonial Ministry in Paris. He remained a major political figure through the turbulent years of the Revolution. He was also, in his own way, a despot. Like many of those whose rights he was defending, he owned slaves. His struggle for rights and the stubborn rejection of his proposals by the white planters of Saint-Domingue show both the absurdity and the power of racial prejudice in the colony. Raimond and many other planters had some African ancestry. Economically, culturally, and socially, they and the white planters were in many ways natural allies. Yet white colonists, convinced that slavery could be maintained only through discrimination against free people of color, rejected their requests for political equality.

Julien Raimond's father, Pierre, was born in the Languedoc region of France and emigrated to Saint-Domingue in the early eighteenth century. He settled in the south and married Marie Bagasse, the daughter of a local planter. Bagasse was of mixed European and African descent, but when the couple was married in 1726 she was not distinguished from Pierre in terms of race. Throughout the early eighteenth century, many individuals of African descent in the Southern Province were counted as white in censuses, and when they drew up legal documents they were rarely described with racial terms. This state of affairs changed in the 1760s. Bagasse began to be identified consistently as a *mulâtresse* (mulatto) in notarial documents, while the young Julien Raimond was described as a "quadroon"—a person of one-quarter African ancestry. In the parish of Aquin, where the Raimond family lived, there was a remarkable surge in the free-colored population not because of a baby boom or migration, but because administrators began applying racial terms where they had not done so before. Individuals and families were in effect transformed from white to mulatto or quadroon.[2]

The emergence of racial terminology in the legal sphere was part of the broader progress of racial discrimination during the decades before the Haitian Revolution. The 1685 Code Noir declared that emancipation was the legal equivalent to "birth in our islands," and therefore granted the *affranchi*—the freed individual—the same rights as those born in the kingdom, even if they had been born in "foreign lands." Still, certain stipulations differentiated the *affranchis* from other free individuals. They were enjoined to show respect to their former masters, and they could be re-enslaved as punishment for certain crimes. These provisions, however, applied only to the individual who had been freed, not to his or her children; they were linked to the person's legal trajectory from slavery to freedom, and not to their ancestry. There was, in principle, no discrimination solely on the basis of African descent or skin color. Although they probably experienced racial discrimination in their day-to-day lives, free people of African descent could buy land and slaves, live in any neighborhood in the towns, educate themselves in any school, and practice any profession they wished.[3]

The Code Noir's stipulations about emancipation, however, like those regarding the treatment of slaves, were steadily undermined during the eighteenth century. Attempting to counter the increasing size and power of communities of free people of color, colonial administrators required masters who freed their slaves to pay "liberty taxes," and they gradually made African ancestry a legal liability. In the wake of the Seven Years' War, scattered discriminatory legislation against free people of color was systematized and expanded. A 1764 royal decree forbade people of African descent to practice medicine, surgery, or pharmacy. The next year another decree excluded them from working in legal professions or in the offices of notaries. A 1773 law made it illegal for them to take the names of their masters or white relatives, on the ground that such a practice destroyed the "insurmountable barrier" which "public opinion" had placed between the two communities and which government had "wisely preserved." Unmarried women of color had to choose for their children names "drawn from the African idiom, their profession, or color." (The family of Julien Raimond complied grudgingly by switching from the "Raymond" of their French father to "Raimond.") A 1779 regulation made it illegal for free people of color to "affect the dress, hairstyles, style, or bearing of whites," and some local ordinances forbade them to ride in carriages or to own certain home furnishings. By the time of the Revolution free-coloreds were subjected to a variety of laws that discriminated against them solely on the basis of race.[4]

What had driven the transformation of Saint-Domingue from a relatively open society into one saturated with racial discrimination? For Raimond, the response was simple: sex. Early in the colony's history, he argued, the European men who came to the colonies "burning with the desire to make a fortune" but "weakened by the heat of the climate, often sick, and deprived of the aid wives of their own color could have given them," turned to "African women." These slave women cared for them assiduously, hoping to gain "the greatest recompense, their liberty." "These first whites," Raimond explained, "lived with these women as if they were married" and had children with them. Some freed the women and married them, as the Code Noir stipulated whites who had children with slaves should do. Many whites left land and slaves to their partners and children. Indeed it was generally expected that they would do so, and Saint-Domingue whites resisted royal attempts to institute laws outlawing such bequests. As a result, a class of property-owning free people of color emerged in the colony.[5]

From then on, wrote Raimond, the members of this group married one another, "and the daughters married whites who arrived from France." Young white men who came to the colony to make their fortune "preferred marrying women of color, who had land and slaves as their dowry." Julien Raimond knew about this pattern from the experience of his parents. To their marriage Pierre Raymond had brought little but his white skin; Marie Bagasse brought three times more wealth than he did, as well as her extensive family connections. Unlike her French husband, she was educated enough to sign her name in the wedding contract. It was Bagasse's economic and social power that enabled the new couple to acquire plantations and begin building the fortune that Raimond and his siblings inherited.[6]

There were those who were wary of such marriages and other unions between white men and women of African descent. In 1723 the intendant of Saint-Domingue wrote to request that French orphan girls be sent to provide wives for young men who used the "lack of white women" as a pretext to "stay in their libertinage with the *négresses*," becoming seditious vagabonds instead of productive settlers. But despite the increasing presence of European women in the colony over the next decades, there remained powerful economic motivations for European men to connect themselves with the free-colored community. "There was no dishonor in seeing them, frequenting them, living with them, marrying their daughters," wrote Raimond, especially the daughters "whose parents had become rich." But for the increasing number of French women who came to the colony in the second half of the eighteenth century and were jilted by white men in favor of women of color, jealousy quickly turned to racial hatred. This animus, he argued, drove the expansion of racist laws.[7]

There were, according to Raimond, other sources of jealousy. Wealthy free-coloreds sent their children to be educated in France (the Raimond family sent several of theirs, including Julien), and when they returned their refinement represented a sharp counterpoint to the "vices and ignorance of the whites of the island." Educated free-coloreds "were looked down upon because of their origin, because they could not be looked down on for anything else." Although "honest whites" continued to marry free women of color, during the 1750s and 1760s several of those who did were divested of positions as administrators or militia officers. Laws discouraging interracial marriages were not uniformly applied, but they discouraged many whites from marrying women of color, though not from continuing to live and have children with them.[8]

Raimond's brief history of racial prejudice, with its jealous white villains and unceasingly virtuous free people of color, simplified and sexualized a complex reality. But it did accurately highlight how economic tensions between whites and free-coloreds had helped propel the creation of racist law in the colony. Especially after the Seven Years' War, when they came in increasing numbers, white migrants to the colony found themselves competing with the population of free-coloreds. Seeking to take advantage of the expanding coffee economy, they often found "that the free-coloreds were there before them": many had settled in mountainous areas before the coffee boom and established plantations on land they already owned. Free-coloreds were familiar with Saint-Domingue and less prone to the diseases that wiped out many European colonists within their first year. When they needed help on their plantations, they drew on extensive families rather than turning to paid employees. They invested for the long term, slowly building up their land holdings, while fortune-seeking whites often spent their money quickly only to find themselves in bankruptcy. From generation to generation, many free-colored families secured plantations and grew into wealthy owners of land and slaves, especially in the south, where the Raimond family lived, and in the west. In Port-au-Prince free-colored families made fortunes by purchasing seafront lots early on in the area that became the town's center. They were among the many successful free-colored urban entrepreneurs in the colony.[9]

Whites and free-coloreds were not always at odds. In both the countryside and the towns, social and economic relationships continued across the color line throughout the eighteenth century. As policies of racial discrimination were put into place, some whites objected strenuously, foreseeing (correctly, as it turned out) that these policies would weaken rather than strengthen the colony. But as the eighteenth century progressed, racist sentiments were increasingly buttressed by colonial administrators who, driven by a desire to secure the loyalties of white residents of the colony, encouraged racial division and hierarchy through the complex of discriminatory laws that Raimond railed against. There was, such officials argued, inevitable solidarity between free people of color and the enslaved, and only by highlighting the difference between whites and people of African descent, whatever their legal status, could the hierarchies necessary for the survival of slavery be maintained.[10]

At the same time colonial officials, confronting the refusal of white residents to serve in the standing militias, recruited free-coloreds to serve in both military and police units. Ultimately men of African descent became the majority in the armed forces of the colony, standing as a bulwark against both external enemies and those within: the slave majority. The two policies at first sustained each other: excluded from many avenues of economic and social advancement, free men of African descent readily took advantage of the possibilities opened up by service in the military and police forces. Ultimately, however, they would collide. For as they served as defenders of the colony and of slavery, free men of color also challenged and undermined white supremacy. This contradiction, and the ultimate inability of whites to effectively negotiate it, would ignite the first fires of the Haitian Revolution.

In 1780 a 120-year-old man, Captain Vincent Ollivier, died in Saint-Domingue. His life, an obituary proclaimed, would "serve as proof for those who need it that a truly great soul, no matter what shell it inhabits, is visible to all men and can silence even those prejudices that seem necessary." Ollivier was probably Saint-Domingue's oldest black veteran. He had lived through most of the colony's history, and had gone from being a slave to being a free man, an officer, and a respected community leader. In 1697 his master had volunteered to join the French expedition against Cartagena, and had brought his slave Ollivier with him. Like other slaves who participated in the mission, Ollivier obtained something more precious than loot: freedom. His journey home was a long one; taken prisoner by the Spaniards, he was eventually ransomed to France, where he met Louis XIV and fought in Germany. After returning to Saint-Domingue, he was appointed captain-general of the colored militia of Le Cap by the governor, and for the rest of his life he was called "Captain Ollivier," appearing with his sword and wearing a feather in his hat. He was a frequent guest among the high-ranking whites of Saint-Domingue. Moreau de St. Méry celebrated Ollivier's achievements, along with those of another ex-slave veteran of the Cartagena expedition, Etienne Auba, who had been made a captain of a unit of free blacks in 1723, and in 1779 was granted a military pension. Like Ollivier, Auba always wore his uniform and sword in public. He died the year after Ollivier, 100 years old.[11]

In 1779, a few years before Auba and Ollivier died, a French officer came looking for recruits in Saint-Domingue. He was a former governor of the colony, Charles d'Estaing, and was leading a French expedition to help the rebels of the thirteen colonies on the North American mainland in their struggle against Britain. The majority of those who ultimately joined up were men of African descent. Among them were two of Vincent Ollivier's sons, and Ollivier enthusiastically supported d'Estaing's mission by "recalling his past glories" to the volunteers. The expedition sailed north and attacked the British at Savannah. Although d'Estaing had ordered that soldiers of African descent "be treated at all times like the whites," they were put to work digging trenches for the siege. Nevertheless, the free-colored unit distinguished itself during the campaign, which ended in French defeat, holding a line against the advancing British troops and defending the retreat of d'Estaing's force.[12]

The free-coloreds who supported the American Revolution were part of a long military tradition. Like many other provinces of France, Saint-Domingue had militia units through which inhabitants could be mobilized for defense, but many whites—"status conscious and notoriously single-minded in their pursuit of wealth"—resented and resisted militia service. In the early eighteenth century, segregated free-colored militia units were formed, and over time administrators came increasingly to depend on them to assure the defense of the colony. The first free-colored army units were formed during the Seven Years' War, and although the several hundred men who joined spent the war quietly along the border with Santo Domingo, observers noted their value. Whereas many of the fresh French troops who arrived in the colony during the war succumbed to tropical diseases, the local free-colored troops remained healthy. When d'Estaing arrived as governor a few years after the war, he introduced a plan to make free-coloreds "the backbone of colonial defense." All men of African descent would be required to serve in the militia, without the right to purchase exemptions as whites could. At the same time, d'Estaing declared it would no longer be possible for free-coloreds to serve as officers in their units—as Ollivier, Auba, and others had done for decades. To soften the racial discrimination of the plan, he proposed that anyone who had less than one-eighth African ancestry be decreed officially white. This aspect of the proposal enraged many colonial whites, and d'Estaing was unable to institute his reforms, although a ban on free-colored officers was instituted. When the governors who succeeded him tried to strengthen the militia units in the colony, they triggered an uprising in which white and free-colored planters in some parts of the colony joined forces in violent protest. Administrators suppressed the revolt, but they were never able to overcome white resistance to militia service, and during the decades after the 1760s, men of African descent formed the majority serving in the militias. A colonial administration that sanctioned racist laws depended on the free-colored population as allies and protectors.[13]

A few white planters openly admired the military prowess of the free-coloreds and argued against their legal exclusion. Laurent François Lenoir, the marquis de Rouvray, who was a veteran of the Seven Years' War and an officer in d'Estaing's 1779 mission, encouraged potential free-colored recruits to say to themselves: "I must make the whites blush for the scorn they have heaped on me . . . and for the injustices and tyrannies they have continually exercised over me with impunity. I must prove to them that as a soldier I am capable of at least as much honor and courage and of even more loyalty." A few decades later revolutionary activists such as Julien Raimond and Abbé Grégoire would similarly evoke their service in the militias and their bravery at Savannah in arguing that free men of color were capable and deserving of Republican citizenship. Though it is not certain, some historians have suggested that several of the free-colored leaders who emerged in the revolution—notably André Rigaud—were veterans of the Battle of Savannah.[14]

In addition to assuring colonial defense, free men of color played a central role in defending Saint-Domingue against its dangerous internal enemies: the slaves. The colony had a special police force, the *maréchaussée,* whose task was to monitor slaves on plantations and in towns and to pursue runaways and attack maroon communities. By the 1730s the *maréchaussée* regulations stipulated that the rank-and-file troops were to be free people of color, while the officers were to be whites, though a reform in 1767 allowed free men of color to be noncommissioned officers. Those who served in these units—often drawn from local militias—received relatively low pay but were given rewards for capturing runaway slaves. Masters who wanted to free a male slave were granted an exemption from "liberty taxes" if they enlisted them in the *maréchaussée,* and as a result many in the force were themselves still enslaved, serving for their liberty.[15]

The service of free people of color in such units obviously cultivated tension and distrust between them and the slaves. It also strengthened the case that the only way to prevent a slave insurrection would be to assure the loyalty of the free people of color by granting them rights. In 1785 the marquis de Rouvray noted that these men were vital allies in a slave colony that was like a "besieged city," whose inhabitants were walking on "barrels of powder" that might explode at any time. Other prominent figures in Saint-Domingue concurred. This argument was later advanced by advocates for free-colored rights. The Abbé Grégoire wrote in 1789 that the group's "bravery is well known" from their success in capturing maroons.

Bringing together whites and free people of color, "cementing the mutual interests of these two classes," would create a stronger "mass of force" for containing the slaves. In another pamphlet he asked how France could replace the free people of color as a security force in a colony that devoured "effeminate Europeans and overworked negroes."[16]

Despite various countercurrents on both sides of the Atlantic, however, a majority of planters and officials believed that maintaining racial distinctions toward free-coloreds was vital to preserving slavery in Saint-Domingue. A 1767 ministerial directive declared that, for those whose ancestors had come from Africa, the "first stain" of slavery extended to "all their descendants" and could not be "erased by the gift of freedom." In 1771 administrators in Saint-Domingue argued that in order to maintain a feeling of inferiority in the "heart of slaves" it was necessary to maintain racial distinctions "even after liberty is granted," so that they would understand that their "color is condemned to servitude," and that nothing could make them "equal" to their masters. One of the justifications for policies aimed at limiting the number of free-coloreds was that runaway slaves could easily blend into such communities, and indeed might find sympathizers within them.[17]

At the heart of such arguments, and of the discrimination they justified, was a profound contradiction. Even as racist laws meant to limit the power and numbers of free people of color proliferated, whites continued to have sexual relationships with women of African descent, both slave and free, and to give their partners and children property and slaves. On the eve of his wedding to a white woman in 1781, Moreau gave slaves and money as gifts to a free woman of color, Marie-Louis Laplaine, who had been his housekeeper for several years, and to her daughter, Amenaide. Laplaine was described as a "mulâtresse," and her daughter was described as a "quarteronne" (three-quarters white); she was probably Moreau's daughter. Whites were connected to free people of color by a complex web of familial and social ties; men of European and African descent were, often literally, "sons of the same father." And yet the law created a difference between them, defining them as members of two separate social classes, with their destinies shaped by their ancestry. Saint-Domingue was a schizophrenic society in which the law attacked relationships between those of European and African descent even as the whites who supported such laws continuously flouted them.[18]

A clever solution to this hypocrisy was to portray women of African descent, and particularly free women of color, as seducers of hapless white men. One officer wrote that women of color in Saint-Domingue were "idols" at the feet of which European men deposited their fortunes. Such women made themselves the "absolute masters of their conquests." It was as if, he continued, nature had responded to the "state of slavery in which the men of color live" by granting such women "the power of their charms over the whites." The baron de Wimpffen described them as "the most fervent priestesses of the American Venus," who made "sensual pleasure a kind of mechanical skill which they have brought to its ultimate perfection." Moreau, who theorized that the mix of African and European ancestry caused heightened sexual appetites, was similarly obsessed with the dangerous sexuality of these "priestesses of Venus" whose "entire being" was "given over to sensual pleasure." "Her sole vocation is to bewitch the senses, deliver them to the most delicious ecstasies, enrapture them with the most seductive temptations; nature, pleasure's accomplice, has given her charms, endowments, inclinations, and, what is indeed more dangerous, the ability to enjoy such sensations even more keenly than her partners, including some unknown to Sappho." They were, he added "both the danger and delight of men."[19]

Michel Etienne Descourtilz, a naturalist who lived in Saint-Domingue in the late 1790s, proposed a more sinister theory for why creole men were drawn to slave women—whom he called "animated machines"—and threw themselves into relationships driven by base instinct rather than reason. As soon as creole boys were born, he suggested, their irresponsible mothers gave them to slave wet-nurses. These "libertine" slaves, tricking their masters, continued their illicit sexual affairs even as they gave their milk to their master's children. Black women fed "corrupted milk" to the white boys, and this "pernicious drink" communicated the "germ" of "impudent desires." Creole mothers were to blame for instilling in their boys a lust for slave women by handing them over to them at a young age rather than breast-feeding them themselves as they should have.[20]

Such febrile talk was a way to finesse the contradictions produced by white patriarchy, of abstracting these relationships from the complicated and contorted relations of power that defined them. Sex was enmeshed with racism and slavery, and racist laws shaped the relationships they sought to outlaw. Moreau admitted that many free women of color were "condemned" to "the state of being a courtesan," but claimed that this result was unavoidable and even had the laudable effect of keeping masters from forcing themselves on their slaves. But, as Julien Raimond pointed out, it was racist laws that forced free women of color "to prostitute themselves to whites" rather than marry them. Some free women of color found a new way to formalize the relationships they had with white men by taking on the title of *ménagère,* combining the roles of "professional manager and personal companion." Many white migrants depended on *ménagères* to establish social and business contacts in the colony and to manage their affairs. Women involved in such relationships, whose terms were often laid out in a legal contract, could sometimes make enough money to become independent entrepreneurs in towns like Le Cap. Indeed free women of color were a major economic, social, and cultural force.[21]

Over the eighteenth century, law, economy, and discourse worked together to produce a set of racist practices that, once in place, appeared to many as both natural and permanent. Yet this system of racial hierarchy, which most whites saw as necessary for the survival of the colony, was saturated with contradictions and dangerous fissures. Many free people of color, particularly those who were slave owners, looked down not only on slaves but also on poorer whites. Some free people of color referred to white soldiers derisively as "white negroes," thus insulting both groups at once. Skin color played a role in determining status as well, and many free people of color, like whites, differentiated between those with different degrees of European ancestry. Such distinctions were eventually institutionalized in the colony; the census of 1782 divided free people of color into two categories: "gens de couleur, mulâtres, etc.," who had European ancestry; and "free blacks," who did not. The latter were likely to have been freed in their lifetimes rather than born of free parents. Some writers then and since have drawn sharp distinctions between these two groups, but in reality the differences were blurred: there were many slaves of mixed ancestry who had been freed, and second-generation free people who had no European ancestry.[22]

Moreau sought to order this world by producing a phantasmagoric racial cosmology: a "scientific" formula based on the division of individuals into 128 parts, all either European or African, with different combinations creating different racial identities. He wrote that even after several generations in families that appeared white, there might appear "indiscreet apparitions of an African character" that belied the family's origin, and that even if certain "quadroons" were whiter than a Spaniard or Italian "no one would confuse them." But his certainty in racial identification was misplaced. Families like that of Raimond had long "passed" as white before the latter half of the eighteenth century, and there was often no way to distinguish those with African ancestry from those without. One British officer serving in the colony in the mid-1790s would write that he had "seen many *Mulattresses* as white, if not whiter, than the generality of European women." In 1792, when two rebel envoys presented themselves in front of the Colonial Assembly of Le Cap, they were asked, "Are you white?" While "the face" of one "provided his answer," the other responded simply that he was the son of an unknown father. The question was unanswerable.[23]

Some revolutionaries would ask the same question of planters who defended racial hierarchy. In a 1789 pamphlet the Abbé Grégoire demanded of white planters who their fathers and mothers were, suggesting that many of them were probably descended from men of African descent who had declared themselves "Caribs." It would be impossible for the planter delegates to prove that they were not of African descent, since sometimes "by the second generation, the color is entirely washed away." In a 1791 pamphlet Moreau described Julien Raimond as "mulatto," and Raimond retorted that he was the "legitimate son and the grandson of European fathers and landowners in Saint-Domingue." "Can Moreau de St. Méry . . . count back to his ancestors," he asked, "without covering himself with the ignominy befitting a man who scorns and betrays the class from which he springs?" Raimond was suggesting that the man who had created an elaborate racial system meant to identify the nuances of descent, and who had become one of the most eloquent defenders of white privilege in Saint-Domingue, was a fugitive from his own African ancestors.[24]

Had they looked in on him in the 1780s, Moreau's ancestors would have found him living in the center of Paris as he carried out his research on the law and history of Saint-Domingue, an active participant in the world of Enlightenment science and culture. His masonic connections gained him an appointment as the secretary of a new museum (later the Musée de Paris, and eventually the Musée de l'Homme) intended to showcase and encourage debate and discussion of new discoveries in the natural sciences, geography, history, and art. In a speech at the museum, Moreau celebrated a dream that many Enlightenment intellectuals shared, that through reason the wrongs men had created by "deifying" themselves could be resolved. He did not mention what some intellectuals at the time considered to be one of humankind's greatest injustices: slavery. But

Moreau regularly came in contact with one man who was very concerned with ending the barbaric institution: the marquis de Condorcet, who in 1781 had published an antislavery essay. Moreau shared a friendship with Condorcet, and fact they had much in common. Moreau was concerned with improving the condition of slaves, and Condorcet believed that slavery could be outlawed only through a gradual process that would start by lessening the hardships of slaves' lives. Genteel discussions of slavery between intellectuals, however, would soon become difficult. With the onset of the Revolution, the stage for such debate expanded dramatically, and the two men soon found themselves on opposite sides in a vicious political battle.[25]

Condorcet was part of a broad Enlightenment current of antislavery thought that found its expression in the works of *philosophes* from Montesquieu to Voltaire and Rousseau, in numerous novels and plays whose heroes were rebelling slaves, and in the prophesies of rebellion issued by Mercier and Raynal. Paris had also seen attacks against slavery in the legal realm, where, during the 1760s and 1770s, several hundred slaves successfully sued for their freedom. These advances did not go unpunished; in the 1780s royal administrators passed draconian legislation against people of African descent living in Paris, forcing them to carry an early form of passport under threat of deportation and criminalizing interracial relationships. Indeed, Enlightenment antislavery had many contradictions. Those who accepted the immorality of slavery also often accepted racist ideas about Africans, and many writers accepted that slavery was wrong in principle but was a necessary evil whose benefits ultimately outweighed its disadvantages, both for Europeans and Africans "saved" from "barbarism." Still, by the end of the eighteenth century, a number of the intellectuals and professionals who would become the new Revolution's elite were sincerely committed to attacking slavery.[26]

In 1788 the journalist Jacques-Pierre Brissot de Warville, who had come into contact with the antislavery movement in England and the United States, founded the abolitionist Société des Amis des Noirs in Paris. Like its British counterparts, the society advocated abolition of the slave trade followed by the gradual elimination of slavery in the Americas. Although abolitionism in France never developed into a popular movement as it did in Britain and the United States, the society came to boast a number of influential members: Condorcet, the marquis de Lafayette, the comte de

Mirabeau, and eventually the Abbé Grégoire. In the Revolution they would find an ideal setting for promulgating their views on slavery.[27]

Late in 1788 Louis XVI called for the election of representatives to the Estates General, an ancient consultative body, to help him resolve the urgent budget crisis the kingdom was facing in part because of the support it had lent to the American Revolution. There were three "estates" in the body—the aristocracy, the clergy, and the "Third Estate," meant to represent the remaining majority of the population. Like most professionals and intellectuals, Moreau was taken up in the elections, and was chosen as the president of Paris' electoral assembly. For those like him tied to the slave colonies of the Caribbean, the onset of Revolution was ripe with possibility but also with danger. In the Revolution the colonies might find redress against the despotic policies imposed on them. But there was also a chance that they would find the very foundation of their livelihood challenged, even destroyed.[28]

The Société des Amis des Noirs jumped at the opportunity presented by the calling of the Estates General to further its antislavery cause. An essay by Condorcet was sent to each of the hundreds of districts electing deputies. It expressed hope that the French nation would turn its attention to the slave trade and work to end its "crimes of violence," to improve the lives of slaves condemned "to work without end and without hope, exposed to the arbitrary punishments of their masters, deprived of all social and natural rights, and reduced to the condition of domestic animals." The actions of the society had some effect. Forty-nine of the *cahiers de doléances*—lists of grievances that the king had invited the people to submit—included attacks of one kind or another on the slave trade or slavery. Brissot and the Société des Amis des Noirs also encouraged Jacques Necker, the liberal minister of the king who (though his family's wealth was tied to the Caribbean colonies) was critical of the slave trade, to eliminate subsidies provided by the French state to slave traders. In the speech that opened the Estates General in June 1789, Necker asked the body to look with compassion on the plight of African slaves, "men like us in their thoughts and above all in their capacity to suffer," who were piled up in the hulls of ships and sent across the Atlantic.[29]

It was a promising beginning for the abolitionists. But the society met its match in a powerful group committed to defending colonial slavery. In July 1788 a group of French planters gathered in Paris. Invoking grievances dating from the conflict with royal government during the mid-1780s, they decided to lobby for reforms and demanded the formation of a colonial assembly for Saint-Domingue. Some suggested that the colonies should also request representation in the Estates General. A few perceptive participants pointed out the dangerous implications of such a request: if deputies from the colonies were invited to participate in the creation of national policies, they would put the colonies under the control of the Estates General, where antislavery forces would likely find voice. Nevertheless, the group decided to press for national representation. The demand was rebuffed by administrators in Paris and in Saint-Domingue, but in the colony groups of planters organized in secret and elected deputies. In almost all cases free men of color, even those who were wealthy property owners, were barred from participating. And the *cahiers de doléances* produced by the Saint-Domingue delegates explicitly opposed the integration of property-owning free people of color into the political life of the colony.[30]

When the Estates General finally gathered at Versailles in June 1789, seventeen delegates from Saint-Domingue showed up uninvited. Brissot argued they had been illegitimately elected and should not be allowed in the assembly. The delegation demanded admittance, warning that otherwise France would have to resolve the problem of "colonial representation" with "arms in its hands" as England had a few decades before. Granted "provisional" admittance, but denied the right to vote, the planter delegates took advantage of a crisis. The Estates General had traditionally voted by order, which meant that on any issue the aristocracy and the clergy could outvote the Third Estate, even though the latter had twice as many delegates. The members of the Third Estate therefore argued that the voting should take place by head rather than by order. In the face of the royal government's intransigence, on June 20 most of the members of the Third Estate, along with a few aristocrats and clergy, declared that they were the true representatives of the people of France, naming themselves a National Assembly. It was the beginning of the French Revolution, and nine of the Saint-Domingue delegates—including the marquis de Rouvray—were there. They asked for the right to be united "provisionally" to this new assembly, and took the same oath as the other delegates. Their presence at this event gained them the sympathy of many of their comrades.[31]

Although many supported the full admittance of the Saint-Domingue delegates, a controversy exploded over exactly how many should be allowed to sit in the assembly. The colonial delegates requested a number of seats based on the total population of the colony. Several metropolitan delegates pointed out the irony of this request, most forcefully Mirabeau. "The free blacks are proprietors and taxpayers, and yet they have not been allowed to vote," he noted. "And as for the slaves, either they are men or they are not; if the colonists consider them men, let them free them and make them eligible for seats; if the contrary is the case, have we, in apportioning deputies according to the population of France, taken into consideration the number of our horses and mules?"[32]

It was a powerful statement about the limits of democracy in the colonies, and the hypocrisy of the white delegates who purported to represent a population they held in subjugation. But the colonial delegates and many others in the National Assembly had little desire to open up a discussion on the morality of slavery. A compromise granting six seats to Saint-Domingue (two for each province) was quickly reached and the broader issues shunted aside. It was the beginning of a pattern that would dominate debates over colonial policy for nearly two years. During the night of August 4, as representatives from the aristocracy and the clergy stepped forward to give up the privileges that separated them from other citizens, one delegate brought up the question of the ultimate form of privilege—the owning of slaves—but his intervention garnered little enthusiasm. The planters were busy outside the assembly, too, showing up in force at the Comédie Française to heckle a performance of a play by Olympe de Gouges, a leading activist for the rights of women, which attacked slavery and celebrated the possibility of solidarity between French whites and colonial slaves. The play closed after three nights.[33]

Many representatives in the National Assembly were tacitly committed to maintaining slavery, and abolitionist voices were isolated. Representatives from port towns like Nantes and Bordeaux, which profited from the monopoly regulations governing colonial trade, had important differences with planter representatives. But when faced with a common threat, they banded together. The planter-merchant alliance was crafted and maintained by the Club Massiac, which gathered a broad range of plantation owners from Saint-Domingue, some proprietors of coffee and indigo plantations, others wealthy absentee owners of sugar plantations. The marquis de Gallifet, owner of some of the most prosperous sugar plantations in the Northern Province, was its first president, though he soon resigned the post, apparently because of a stuttering problem. Like the Société des Amis des Noirs, the Club Massiac funded the publication of pamphlets—including one written by the marquis de Rouvray called *L'Etat des nègres*—and also managed to get its views expressed in certain revolutionary newspapers. The planter club developed close connections with parallel merchant political clubs in the port towns. Although in principle the Club Massiac was for colonial landowners only, one of its key members was Moreau. With his "folders of laws, his boxes of colonial history, he was the living law code, the historian, almost the legislator of the colony," and his connections helped the group enjoy considerable power.[34]

The initial face-off between planters organized in the Club Massiac— and their port-town allies—and the Société des Amis des Noirs resulted in a clear defeat for the latter. Discussion of slavery and the slave trade was effectively tabled in the assembly, and the society was saddled with a powerful accusation: that its activities might set in motion another, much more dangerous, revolution in the colonies.

"People here are drunk with liberty," wrote the Saint-Domingue deputies in Paris to their constituents in August 1789. "The peril is great; it is near." If they even said the word "slavery," they complained, the abolitionists might seize the opportunity to demand emancipation. The population in the colony must be extremely vigilant, seizing "writings in which the word 'Liberty' appears," increasing their guard in plantations and towns, and watching for free-coloreds arriving "from Europe." Julien Raimond intercepted this letter and gave it to Mirabeau, whose used it to expose the planters as enemies of the Revolution, men afraid of the word "liberty" itself. In response, the Saint-Domingue delegates published their own annotated version of the letter in 1790, pointing out that it advocated wariness only of writings dealing with the "liberty of the slaves." They included a "post-scriptum" to the letter, which they claimed was written and intercepted at the same time, but never published, in which they advocated a rapprochement between free-coloreds and whites in the colony as the surest way to maintain peace. This suggestion was probably shaped by one of the delegates who signed the letter, the marquis de Rouvray. The delegate's warnings and the abolitionist's response were the opening skirmishes in a war whose battlefields would stretch from Paris and Bordeaux to the plains of Saint-Domingue. It was a war over the meaning of the Revolution itself, over whether the laws of a regenerated France would be applicable in the colonies as well as the mother country, over the very question of whether rights were universal.[35]

What was so dangerous about what might be brought from Europe to Saint-Domingue? A few weeks after the letter was written, the National Assembly wrote and adopted the Declaration of the Rights of Man, whose first article declared that "men are born and remain equal in rights." One newspaper proclaimed that its principles would be applicable in the colonies as well as in metropolitan France. This was precisely what the planters who had eschewed representation in the Estates General had feared: that revolutionary principles accepted in Paris would be applied to the slave societies in the Caribbean. Despite provisions accepting "social distinctions" and declaring property a "sacred and inviolable right," many planters saw the universalist Declaration as a clear threat to slavery, reacting as if it were a disease to be quarantined. Already in July 1789, several slave women who had arrived in a French port from Saint-Domingue had been detained and sent back to the colonies by port authorities concerned about what they might learn in continental France and communicate back to the colony. In August one member of the Club Massiac proposed that all "blacks or mulattoes" arriving from Europe be banned from entering Saint-Domingue, and in September the club wrote to merchants in the port towns asking them to prevent individuals of African descent from embarking for the colonies. Several ship captains sent assurances that they would do so. Attempts to control the flow of information would continue: in April 1790 local officials directed Le Cap's postal director "to stop all arriving or departing letters that are addressed to mulattoes or slaves and to deliver these letters to the municipality." They were to keep this procedure a secret, presumably so that officials could use this surveillance to uncover evidence of sedition or conspiracy.[36]

Of course there was no way to control the circulation of information and the many hopes and fears it raised. Even as attempts were being made to prevent information and people from moving across the Atlantic, many whites responded with excitement to the revolutionary changes. They "spoke loudly of liberty in front of slaves," according to the surgeon Antoine Dalmas, and "bitterly attacked privileges, prejudice and despotism." The poor landless whites of Saint-Domingue—overseers and managers, small-time merchants, unemployed wanderers—saw the Revolution as an opportunity to express grievances against wealthy whites. When news of the fall of the Bastille arrived in the colony, some celebrated by pillaging and setting fires in the towns; many created and joined political clubs.[37]

Property-owning whites, too, jumped at the opportunity to gain local control over economic policy, and lost no time grabbing political power. The committees that had elected representatives for the Estates General created provincial assemblies in the north, west, and south that declared war against the "ministerial despotism" of the colonial governor and the Colonial Ministry in Paris. The assembly of the Northern Province granted itself full legislative and executive power and in early 1790 reopened the Conseil Supérieur of Le Cap, whose closing by the royal government in 1787 had enraged many planters. Fearing for his life, the colony's unpopular intendant fled. With the old administrative structures of Saint-Domingue severely weakened, a new network of provincial assemblies and municipal governments under popular control now governed the colony. In January orders from the colonial minister arrived calling for the formation of a short-term, consultative assembly in the colony; whites in Saint-Domingue instead held elections for a permanent assembly. Elections took place in February 1790, with the vote granted to all whites who had lived in the colony for at least a year. This policy was more liberal than the one currently in place in France (which had economic requirements for suffrage), and helped assure a tenuous unity between white property owners and poorer whites. It was a democratization based on racism: property-owning free people of color were again excluded from political participation. Indeed poor whites in the colony quickly came to exert much of their political energy and violence against wealthy free-coloreds.[38]

When the assembly met in the port town of Saint-Marc in April 1790, the motto hanging in the meeting hall declared, "Notre union fait notre force." (This motto, "Our unity is our strength," would one day be adopted by the Haitian Republic.) The group chose the title General Assembly, pointedly refusing the term "Colonial." Many of those who sat in the Saint-Marc assembly were planters involved in coffee or indigo production who depended on contraband trade and were particularly eager to see an end to the constraints of the monopoly regulations. The majority of the planters who had been serving in the provincial assemblies in the west and south were elected to Saint-Marc, and these local assemblies essentially stopped meeting after the elections. Things were different in the north. There the Provincial Assembly included a significant proportion of merchants and wealthy planters who were connected through family and business to France and were close to the colonial administration. While many of the more radical representatives from the north left for Saint-Marc, the Provincial Assembly remained in the hands of these more conservative men. From then on, the two assemblies were on a collision course.[39]

While the whites of Saint-Domingue were busy carrying out their revolution, they reacted violently to the possibility of another, more radical, revolution that could turn their world upside down. Already in May 1788, the arrival of copies of a French paper that included articles attacking the slave trade and discussing abolitionist movements in England had created a "great sensation" in Saint-Domingue. In the next year news of the activities of the French Société des Amis des Noirs reached the island. Fearing the power of the abolitionists, planters inflated it. Indeed, they gave the society an unlikely ally: Moreau de St. Méry. In June 1789 a man named Louis Charton had published a pamphlet in Paris alleging that Moreau had demanded the abolition of slavery in the colonies. Although Moreau confronted Charton and forced him to admit his accusations were false, he was unable to stop the rumor that he had "adopted the maxims of the Amis des Noirs" from spreading to Saint-Domingue. In October 1789 Moreau's brother-in-law "narrowly escaped lynching," while "calls rang out" for the hanging of the "great creole judge himself." This and other events drove constant talk about the looming possibility of abolition. In late October, in the midst of widespread reports about "movements among the slaves," several whites were imprisoned for harboring abolitionist sentiments. It was said that four emissaries of the Société des Amis des Noirs were about to arrive in the colony, and commissioners were named in Le Cap to question arriving passengers and search their luggage.[40]

By late October fears of slave insurrection had mushroomed. It was announced one day that 3,000 rebel slaves were gathered above Le Cap waiting to attack the town. A detachment of soldiers sent to disperse the gathering found nothing, although they accidentally shot one member of their own party. They were guided by a slave named Jeannot who, two years later, would be one of the earliest and most brutal leaders of the slave insurrection; perhaps his own rebellion began with the wild goose chase outside Le Cap. The whites who imagined masses of slaves gathering outside the town were not completely deluded—simply premature. In fact a few months before, in August 1789, slaves had risen up in Martinique, having been told by their leaders that the king of France and his "distinguished" friends had abolished slavery but that the local government and planters were conspiring to squelch the decree. Masters and slaves shared news about the power of the abolitionists, and while masters sought to imprison and repress those who advocated an end to slavery, many slaves spoke about an imminent freedom. Both groups overestimated the power of the Société des Amis des Noirs, but what they feared and hoped drove them to action.[41]

Whites were also quick to respond to the threat posed by free people of color, who saw in the Revolution an opportunity to ratchet up their protests against their oppression. During 1789 delegations of free men of color had repeatedly demanded inclusion in local political assemblies. Except in rare cases, whites overwhelmingly rebuffed them, and soon began responding with violence. In November 1789, in the town of Petit-Goâve in the Southern Province, an elderly white man named Fernand de Baudière was accused of being the author of a petition written by the free-coloreds in the town. He was arrested and put into prison, but a crowd overpowered the local magistrates and lynched him. Elsewhere in the south, a group of whites broke into the house of a wealthy free man of color, beat him, tied him to a horse, and dragged him down the road. Some friends intervened and saved his life, but one of his sons was killed. In Le Cap a man named Dubois "not only declared himself an advocate of the mulattoes, but with a degree of imprudence which indicated insanity, sought occasions to declaim publicly against the slavery of the negroes." He was arrested and put in prison, and would probably have been lynched had the governor not intervened and expelled him from the island. Soon free men of color were responding by arming themselves. The first skirmishes in the war were under way.[42]

In Paris the battle over the rights of free people of color was raging as well. In October 1789 a delegation of free men of color, including Julien Raimond and Vincent Ogé, appeared in the National Assembly. They presented a petition opining that "there still exists in one province of this Empire a race of men debased and degraded; a class of citizens consigned to contempt, to all the humiliations of slavery." These men, though "born citizens and free," lived as "foreigners" in their own land; they were "slaves in the land of liberty." They demanded an end to racist laws and the right for free men of color to vote in local assemblies in Saint-Domingue and have representatives in the National Assembly. The assembly agreed to consider their request, and the president declared that "no citizen will demand his rights . . . in vain."[43]

Both Raimond and Ogé had begun this crusade for rights by presenting their demands to the planters of the Club Massiac. Raimond had spoken of a plan, which he had put forth to the Colonial Ministry in the 1780s, by which rights would be granted only to "quadroons" who were born of legitimate parents and could claim at least two generations of freedom behind them. In a separate meeting Ogé presented a bolder plan both for the granting of rights to free-coloreds and for the gradual abolition of slavery, declaring that it was the only way to prevent a revolt among the slaves. Having received nothing concrete from the Club Massiac, Raimond and Ogé joined a group of free-colored activists called the Société des Colons Américains. The name was significant, emphasizing that the free people of color were American colonists, just as the whites were. They eventually allied themselves with the abolitionists of the Société des Amis des Noirs. Within a few months Brissot and Grégoire had joined this new battle over the meaning and universality of citizenship. The alliance gave new energy to the abolitionists and helped to radicalize the demands of the free-coloreds. The *cahier des doléances* presented to the National Assembly by the Société des Colons Américains demanded "equality for all non-whites and freedom for mulatto slaves."[44]

The planter-merchant lobby, united on the question of slavery, was less so when it came to the rights of free people of color. A minority of planters, such as the marquis de Rouvray, believed that they should be granted political rights; in fact he had earlier proposed that they be admitted to assemblies in Saint-Domingue through white proxies. Another planter noted that the demand of the free people of color was clearly based on reason and humanity and should not be refused. "Let us avoid the arrogance and rigidity that destroyed the French aristocracy," he warned, which had "refused to give up its coat" and consequently lost everything. Many among the merchants, "who cared above all about the color of sugar," were sympathetic to the demands emanating from a group of plantation owners who contributed to the commerce that enriched French ports. Free-coloreds in Bordeaux organized demonstrations in September 1789 in favor of the demand for political rights, and were received well by many in the town. A club of merchants and planters formed in La Rochelle, which had tight links with the Club Massiac, wrote in November 1789 that it seemed wise to accept the "natural right" of free-coloreds to political representation.[45]

Such support, and the positive response to the free people of color in the National Assembly, gave Raimond and Ogé hope. Many in Paris were receptive to their demands, which were a clear application of the universalism that had found expression in the Declaration of the Rights of Man. Although there were many limits placed on citizenship during the early years of the Revolution (women, servants, and many poorer men could not vote), the justification for such exclusions—that only those who were financially independent could be politically independent as voters and representatives—could not be applied to the educated and wealthy free men of color petitioning in Paris. The only justification for excluding them was race. For many thinkers influenced by Enlightenment universalism and revolutionary egalitarianism, the "aristocracy of the skin" that the planters were defending was a clear violation of everything the Revolution stood for.

But here, as in the earlier antislavery campaign, initial advances were followed by defeat. The Club Massiac, most of whose members were committed to refusing any concessions to the free people of color, counterattacked and managed to isolate the reformers in the National Assembly. Although Grégoire forced a request for free-colored representation through the credentials committee, which he chaired, opponents shouted down attempts to put their recommendation to a vote. Planters and their allies published pamphlets that argued against the granting of rights to free-coloreds, and for strict limits on metropolitan intervention in the colonies. Drawing on the arguments developed during the previous decades by legal thinkers such as Moreau, they went on the offensive with an argument that would remain the foundation for the political activism of the next decade: the colonies, they insisted, needed "particular laws." The great boons of the Revolution had to be adapted to colonies whose societies, climates, and economies differed from one another and from that of the mother country. Colonial policy should be shaped not by Paris but by those familiar with the Caribbean, who understood slavery and slaves from experience. At the center of the argument was a stubborn defense of slavery. As the planter Tanguy de la Boissière argued in a 1789 pamphlet published in the colony, the "pivot" of the "constitution, legislation, and regime of Saint-Domingue" must be "everything for the planter." "There can be in

Saint-Domingue only slaves and masters," he declared, the former serving only as "instruments of cultivation." Such views gained official recognition in an October 1789 memo by the Colonial Ministry and were strongly supported by colonial representatives, notably Moreau, who by then was sitting in the National Assembly as a representative for Martinique.[46]

As Raimond, Grégoire, and others understood all too well, abandoning colonial policy to the planters meant condemning free-coloreds to political exclusion and unchecked discrimination. How, they demanded, could the National Assembly allow one group of France's citizens to so flagrantly oppress another group in this way? How could the planters who had so long oppressed the free people of color be allowed to decide whether they could exercise their natural rights? The response from Moreau was that masters had in fact shown great benevolence and humanity to the free people of color. It was, after all, the generosity of white masters that created the class in the first place, and the free-coloreds demanding rights were little more than ingrates supported by uncomprehending zealots. Segregation, Moreau argued, was inevitable and beneficial. The "color" of individuals of African descent would separate them from whites, and free people of color had gathered in their own segregated neighborhoods because they accepted this difference. Integration was impossible, and free-coloreds should put their faith in the benevolence of those who had given freedom to them or to their ancestors.[47]

Raimond and Grégoire insisted that free people of color were the only ones capable of containing the slaves, and argued that granting them rights was in fact the best way to preserve slavery. But planters doubted their sincerity. Grégoire gave them reason to be suspicious. He demanded that slave owners look to the Declaration of the Rights of Man, and taunted them to "get themselves out of it if they could"; he caused an uproar in the National Assembly when he attacked planters for their cruelty both to free-coloreds and to their slaves; and he regularly invoked the possibility of slave revolt, reminding readers that all people had the right to insurrection against their oppressors. Planters took advantage of such statements—and of fragmentary and exaggerated reports about slave unrest in the colonies, particularly the 1789 revolt in Martinique—to paint Grégoire and his allies as advocates, and even instigators, of slave revolt. One newspaper article proclaimed that Brissot would not stop "intriguing" until there were "five or six children of the Congo sitting in the French National Assembly."[48]

Drawing on an established tradition, the prominent planters in Paris argued that the only way to preserve slavery was to maintain a racial hierarchy among the free. One writer worried that even if slavery were preserved, granting rights to free people of African descent would make them the "kings of the colonies," as they would transform themselves into a majority by emancipating their own slaves and liberating those owned by whites. Moreau insisted that any intervention by the National Assembly into the status of free-coloreds would undermine the power of masters over their slaves. "If our slaves suspect that there is a power that can influence their condition, independently of the will of their masters," wrote Moreau, they would see that they were no longer in a state of "absolute dependence" on the whites. Once this had happened, it would be impossible for "France to preserve its colonies." The representatives in the National Assembly had only one choice: to leave the power of masters intact by allowing them complete legal autonomy. If they did otherwise, they would not only have the blood of colonial whites on their hands; they would also be sounding the death knell of a system that millions of French people depended on for their livelihood.[49]

These scare tactics worked. In March 1790 the National Assembly approved the formation of a specialized Colonial Committee. There were no abolitionists on the committee, and among the twelve were four planters and two merchants who owned property in Saint-Domingue. It was headed by Antoine Barnave, who had ties to the port towns and was sympathetic to their interests. Within a few days the committee proposed a law on colonial governance that reassured colonial representatives. The constitution of France would not be applied to the colonies. Instead, each colony would elect its own assembly, which would propose a constitution regarding the "internal" regimes of the colonies—notably the administration of slavery and the laws regarding free-coloreds—which would be reviewed and ratified in Paris. The colonies would be governed by particular laws developed by their populations, laws unconstrained by the constitution of France or, presumably, the Declaration of the Rights of Man. These provisions granted planters the freedom they had long demanded to govern their colonies internally. But the decree also protected the interests of French merchants. There were to be "no innovations" in "any of the branches of commerce between France and the colonies," the law promised. Final decisions on trade policies would, as before, be made in Paris. Slavery and the slave trade were safe, and so were the regulations that forced the colonies to export their products to the mother country. After the law was presented the comte de Mirabeau rose to speak, but was shouted down from all sides as he denounced those who surrounded him as cowards. The law was rushed to a vote with no discussion, and it passed. The colonies were safe from the dangers of universalism. Indeed, the decree took aim at the abolitionists by declaring that "all those who worked to incite uprisings against the planters will be declared guilty of crimes against the nation."[50]

Although the law seemed to grant the whites of Saint-Domingue complete control over their domestic policies, it contained an ambiguous phrase that provided an opening for the free-coloreds. The law declared that the colonial assemblies would be elected by "citizens," but failed to specify who would be granted this status. During the next weeks, as Barnave drafted a report that was to accompany the March 8 decree to the colonies, the National Assembly received several entreaties from free-coloreds asking to be given the right to vote. Negotiations in the Colonial Committee led to a revision declaring that "all people" who were property owners over twenty-five would be able to participate in the elections. In the assembly, Grégoire complained that the phraseology was still too vague, and requested that free-coloreds be explicitly included; but ultimately no alterations were made to the instructions.[51]

The Colonial Committee had avoided a fight in the National Assembly by not providing clear instructions on the matter of the free-coloreds. It hoped that the planters would "take advantage of the imprecision" of the instructions to refuse the demands of the free people of color, demands that they "did not dare refuse themselves." It was a cynical and cowardly political compromise, and in it were embedded the seeds of a brutal conflict. The National Assembly had abandoned the free people of color, leaving them "facing their enemies" in the colonies. "It was in Saint-Domingue that everything would be decided."[52]

Across the Atlantic the Saint-Marc assembly had been busily reshaping the colony on its own terms, bypassing the governor's authority, passing decrees and applying them without consultation. When the Provincial Assembly of the north attacked this disregard for France's representative in the colony, the Saint-Marc assembly drew up a document called the "Bases constitutionelles"—"Constitutional Principles." It was a bold charter for political and economic autonomy, granting the assembly sweeping powers to control not only the internal laws of the colony but also the "external regime" of commerce. Even Bryan Edwards, a British writer sympathetic to the planters, admitted that "some of the articles are irreconcilable to every just principle of colonial subordination," and that the provision granting the assembly control of trade policies was "an extravagant assumption of imperial authority, in a subordinate part of the French empire, as I believe is without precedent." It was also much too radical for the more established planters and administrators of the Provincial Assembly of the north.[53]

When it received the National Assembly's March 8 decree the Saint-Marc assembly decided to obey the new law only to the extent that it did not contradict its "Constitutional Principles." They invited voters to reconfirm the sitting representatives in an election carried out according to its old suffrage regulations, and declared flatly they would never share political power with a "bastard and degenerate race"—the free-coloreds. The campaign led to the "confirmation" of the delegates at Saint-Marc, who, riding high, opened all the ports of Saint-Domingue to foreign trade. A clear violation of the new laws passed by the National Assembly, this was too much for both the governor and the more conservative Provincial Assembly of the north. In Port-au-Prince an officer mobilized white troops and invited veterans of the free-colored militia to join him in crushing the seditious assembly. Troops were also sent from Le Cap, and the two armies converged on Saint-Marc. Many of the more cautious representatives at Saint-Marc, disagreeing with the radical course the group had taken, had already resigned. Others slipped back to their homes in the face of the attack. But eighty-five representatives took advantage of a sailors' revolt on a ship anchored at Saint-Marc, the *Léopard*, and leapt on board, heading for Paris to present their case and argue that they had been victimized by a tyrannical colonial government.[54]

The *Léopardins*, as the refugee representatives were called, presented a challenge to the compromise between planter and merchant interests embodied in the March 8 decree. Merchants, as well as the conservative planters of the Club Massiac, greeted the *Léopardins* coolly, and on October 12 Barnave and the Colonial Committee condemned the actions of the Saint-Marc assembly as a violation of constitutional law and "public tranquility." But the presence of the *Léopardins* in France publicized the political chaos in Saint-Domingue and gave the Paris planters a new opportunity to attack Grégoire and his allies. Even the Provincial Assembly of the Northern Province, despite its metropolitan leanings, blamed the disorders in Saint-Domingue on the worries of planters about the presence of the members of the Société des Amis des Noirs, notably Grégoire, in the National Assembly. It was crucial, the Provincial Assembly argued, for the government in Paris to put an end to sedition in the colonies by reassuring them that these dangerous abolitionists would not have their way. And it was necessary that the free people of color know that it was only from the planter-dominated colonial assemblies that they could "expect benefits, and that they are to obtain these benefits only by wise behavior and respectful bearing." Barnave decided to clarify his earlier instructions, and in the same law that attacked the Saint-Marc assembly he included a stipulation promising that "no law upon the status of persons shall ever be made for the colonies except upon the precise and formal demand of the colonial assemblies." Protests by Grégoire and Mirabeau were again shouted down, and the National Assembly passed the law. Grégoire warned that the decree, in addition to being an insult to justice and humanity, was impolitic. Who could assure, he asked, that this "degraded caste" would not use force in the pursuit of justice, and join with the slaves or with groups of rebellious whites in the colony?[55]

In July the free-colored leader Vincent Ogé had managed to leave France despite attempts by the Club Massiac to prevent him from doing so. He was, according to one contemporary chronicler, "tired of the uselessness" of the entreaties they had made in Paris. He "resolved to return to his colony, arms in hand, to demand the political rights of his caste." He first stopped in London, where he met with the famed abolitionist Thomas Clarkson. Having purchased arms (perhaps in Le Havre before leaving, or perhaps during a stop in the United States), he arrived in Saint-Domingue undetected in October 1790, and traveled to his hometown of Dondon, south of Le Cap. It was time, Ogé had decided, to back up free-colored demands with something less easy to sidestep than petitions: guns. As he told Clarkson in London, the free-coloreds were ready to take up arms to make themselves "independent and respectable."[56]

Ogé found enthusiastic support in Dondon, where he quickly mobilized an army of several hundred supporters. He marched on nearby Grande-Rivière and occupied the town, then sent letters to the Provincial Assembly in Le Cap demanding that it apply the March 1790 decree granting all free citizens, "without distinction," political rights. If the members of the assembly refused, they would become prey to his "vengeance." In a letter to one administrator, Ogé compared the demands of the free people of color to those of the Third Estate in France. The planters might be "insulted" by having to serve with free men of color, he noted. But were the "nobles and the clergy" consulted in "redressing the thousand and one abuses that existed in France"? He also warned that his troops were ready to "respond to force with force." Soon after some initial victories, however, Ogé's uprising was crushed by troops sent from Le Cap. Groups of free men of color who had gathered in other parts of the colony also dispersed, sometimes after negotiating with white officers. Ogé fled to Spanish Santo Domingo, but the Spanish extradited him to Le Cap. He asked for clemency, but received torture and execution. He and his fellow conspirator Jean-Baptiste Chavannes were condemned to be executed, broken on the wheel, and their heads displayed on pikes to dissuade others. Nineteen other participants were hung.[57]

The execution of Ogé transformed him into a "martyr for liberty" among the free-coloreds and heightened the conflict between them and the whites. Although "nature united them" through family, and they shared interests as property owners, "hate and vengeance" had now "forever shattered these connections." In the next months, free men of color took up arms throughout the colony to demand rights and to defend themselves against continuing attacks by whites. Ogé had assiduously avoided mobilizing slaves to join him and had insisted in his letters that he was not against slavery. But others who fought with him, notably Chavannes, seem to have been more tempted to turn to the slaves as allies. Before he was executed, the desperate Ogé had apparently confessed that throughout the colony there were men of color who were hoping to mobilize the slaves in support of their revolution.[58]

Ogé also became a martyr for many in Paris, where news of his brutal execution helped stir an ever-growing hostility against the "aristocrats of the skin," notably among the increasingly powerful Jacobins. Planters, meanwhile, continued to use the specter of slave revolt to parry the attacks of the abolitionists. In May 1791 Moreau proposed a decree assuring that "no law on the state of slaves in the colonies of the Americas" would be passed except in response to the "formal and spontaneous demand of the colonial assemblies." This move drew the wrath of the formidable Maximilien Robespierre, who retorted famously: "Perish the colonies rather than a principle!" Although planters (as well as later fans of Robespierre) would tirelessly use these words as proof of the radical Jacobins' commitment to the destruction of the colonies, the principle in question was in fact primarily a rhetorical one: Robespierre worried about the "domestic impact" of passing a decree that in accepting slavery in the colonies could help justify tyranny in continental France. Once the term "slave" was replaced with the euphemism "unfree person" the decree was passed. After two years, all attempts to end the slave trade and slavery in the National Assembly had failed. Had it not been for the revolt that soon erupted in Saint-Domingue, the French Revolution would probably have run its course, like the American Revolution, without destroying the massive violation of human rights at the heart of the nation's existence.[59]

Still, the planters were already beginning to lose their complete grip on colonial policy. Although they had successfully convinced many in Paris that any intervention into the question of free-coloreds would undermine slavery in the colonies, they also found themselves increasingly struggling against the current of radical republicanism that was coming to dominate the Revolution. Julien Raimond and Grégoire had convinced many that it would be a travesty for the Revolution to allow the oppression of free people of color by colonial whites. The two sides wrangled behind the scenes in the National Assembly, and eventually a compromise was brought to the people's representatives: political rights would be given to free people of color who had been born to two free parents. The free people of color Raimond had always put forward as the representatives of his class—those, like him, who owned property and slaves—were to be enfranchised. But those who had been recently freed, and who were assumed to have dangerous solidarities with those who were still enslaved, would be excluded from political power. It was a timid granting of rights, and furthermore did not revoke the discriminatory laws in place in Saint-Domingue. Nevertheless, a significant step had been taken: the color line had been crossed.[60]

How many free people of color were given rights by this decree? The question is difficult to answer. Many historians have asserted that only a few hundred met the stipulations of the decree. But Julien Raimond, invested as he was in presenting the free-coloreds as primarily a landowning class, asserted at the time that the vast majority of people of African descent in the colony had in fact been born free of free parents. Such details, though, were ultimately irrelevant, for the Saint-Domingue whites reacted with an enraged refusal to comply with the decree. In Paris the colonial delegates had walked out in protest when the vote was passed, and when news of the decision reached Saint-Domingue later that summer, planters vociferously criticized the National Assembly, and the governor wrote that he could not enforce the decree. Many whites openly proposed that the solution was to "cut the throats" of the free-coloreds, "desert" France, and "call in the English."[61]

The wife of the marquis de Rouvray wrote with disgust about what she called the "Messieurs de France," the "stupid" and "inept" individuals who, having given the colonies the right to make their own laws, had then turned around and taken this right away. Like many planters, she saw the decision as proof that the National Assembly was committed to destroying their lives as masters, and believed that secession from France might be necessary. Saint-Domingue, she argued, should send deputies "to all the powers that have slave colonies" in order to "ask for help in case the Assembly ends up pronouncing the abolition of slavery, which it certainly will do." The slave owners of the Americas, she hoped, would band together to stop the "contagion of liberty." Her husband, having taken part in the formation of the National Assembly a few years before, was now back in the colony, and he was sure that Saint-Domingue would soon be under the power of the British. Although he supported the demands of the free people of color, he saw an irreversible danger in the direction the National Assembly was taking. In the midst of all these troubles, Madame de Rouvray took solace in "high hopes" for the crops of cane and coffee that were growing around her, still worked by obedient slaves. "The cane is magnificent," she wrote in July 1791, and the weather was perfect. The storms had been coming in almost every day.[62]

CHAPTER FOUR

Fire in the Cane

ON APRIL 10, 1784, a balloon rose over the thriving sugarcane fields south of Le Cap. A crowd—which included the colony's governor—watched as it rose to 1,800 feet and then descended slowly to the ground. The men responsible for this spectacle were emulating scientific pioneers across the Atlantic who, the year before, had sent the first balloon in history into the sky. As they read about this triumph in the newspapers of Saint-Domingue, many in the colony were taken with the same excitement for the new machines that was gripping France. A colonial government clerk named Beccard had made a few attempts to send up small balloons, achieving his first success in late March 1784. Meanwhile he had begun building a larger balloon with several other men, among them a man named Odeluc, the *procureur,* or administrator, of three plantations owned by the marquis de Gallifet. Gallifet was far away, living off the profits from his plantations in Paris. In his absence, Odeluc offered one of the plantations he managed as a site for the balloon experiment. So it was that the first large balloon to fly in the Americas went up over a thriving sugar plantation. As they watched the balloon ascend, noted Moreau de St. Méry, the "black spectators" could not stop talking about "the insatiable passion" men had to "exert power over nature." They were perhaps thinking of their own condition. Odeluc may have been a scientific man, but he was also a slave driver.[1]

The balloon "revolved slowly as it ascended," allowing the crowd to see the decorations painted on it. The coats of arms of the governor, the intendant, Beccard, and Gallifet were prominently displayed. Alongside them were allegorical figures representing chemistry, physics, air, and fire—figures whose form we can only imagine, since no image of them was left behind—presumably meant to celebrate the triumph of science over nature: the laws that governed the movement of physical objects; the properties of the elements that could be combined, sometimes explosively, by humans; the versatility of the air, which when heated to the right temperature could produce a movement that had always been thought impossible. On that day, as they watched the spinning, rising balloon, the spectators probably could not imagine that the final element, fire, would within a few years transform everything around them.

"Your houses, Monsieur le Marquis, are nothing but ashes, your belongings have disappeared, your administrator is no more. The insurrection has spread its devastation and carnage onto your properties." With these words the marquis de Gallifet learned of the destruction wrought on his plantations by the August 1791 slave insurrection. The writer of the letter, Millot, owned a neighboring plantation that had suffered a similar fate. Writing from Le Cap, he described an "immeasurable" devastation and lamented that the colony, "once flourishing," now was nothing more than "ashes and rivers of blood." A few weeks later Gallifet received more details from one of his surviving managers, Pierre Mossut, who had carried a telescope to a hill outside Le Cap to survey the damage. The plain around the plantations, wrote Mossut, contained nothing more than "slaves, ruins, and the most complete devastation." Gallifet's plantation, once a centerpiece of the thriving sugar economy of Saint-Domingue, had become a camp for an army of slave insurgents.[2]

Founded in the early eighteenth century by a colonial governor, the Gallifet plantations were so famous by the second half of the century that to describe something sweet, people in Saint-Domingue said "as sweet as Gallifet sugar." And to describe utmost happiness, they said "as happy as a Gallifet negro" (although the question remains: "Who said this, the planters or the slaves?"). One visitor to Gallifet's three main plantations in 1779 described hygienic slave quarters built with masonry and tile roofs (in contrast to the typical mud and thatch huts). Aqueducts brought water not only to the sugar mills but also to the hospitals, gardens, and slave quarters. He described Odeluc as "knowledgeable, wise, and thoughtful" as well as humane.[3]

But Odeluc's job meant that he had one priority: producing as much sugar as possible. "How can we make a lot of sugar when we work only sixteen hours [per day]?" he wondered in a 1785 letter. The only way, he con-

"Révolte des Nègres à St. Domingue." Engraving of the 1791 uprising. The original caption asserted that the "contradictory decrees" of the National Assembly regarding the colonies led to "all the horrors of a civil war." *Courtesy of the Bibliothèque Nationale de France.*

cluded, "was by consuming men and animals." Of the 808 slaves on the Gallifet plantations in January 1791, there were almost none older than sixty, and a small percentage were over forty. "It seems that the happy slaves of Gallifet did not tend to live very long." Of a group of 57 African slaves brought to the plantation in February 1789, 12 were dead within a year. Birthrates were low, and one-third of the children born on the plantations soon died. In 1786 there was an "extreme dryness," and winds blew so hot they cracked furniture and shattered glasses. In 1788 there was drought again, and it was worse in 1790. Sugarcane production suffered, and with it Gallifet's profits, but most of all the slaves. Their numbers decreased over the decade, but the amount of land cultivated did not. They were simply worked harder. The slaves on the smallest of the three plantations, La Gossette, were the worst off. In 1789 20 of them escaped into the woods for two months, demanding the replacement of their manager.[4]

In August 1791 a series of nighttime meetings of slaves took place in the northern plain. Some of the Gallifet slaves attended, and decided to join in the mass insurrection that was being planned. On the night of August 21 the manager of La Gossette, Pierre Mossut, was awakened by a group of slaves who announced that they were "coming to talk to him" and who then attacked him. Mossut was wounded in the arm but fought back and managed to escape. He sent word to the main Gallifet plantation, and soon Odeluc and several other whites arrived at La Gossette. The next morning, accompanied by a judge from Le Cap, they interrogated slaves and extracted a worrisome confession: there was a plan afoot to start "a war to the death against the whites." The slave overseer of the plantation, Blaise, was identified as one of the ringleaders. Blaise, however, was nowhere to be found.[5]

That night, slaves rose up on several plantations in the nearby parish of Acul. A band led by a slave named Boukman "spread like a torrent" through the parish. On one plantation, "twelve or fourteen of the ringleaders, about the middle of the night, proceeded to the refinery," where they seized "the refiner's apprentice, dragged him to the front of the dwelling-house, and there hewed him into pieces with their cutlasses: his screams brought out the overseer, whom they instantly shot. The rebels now found their way to the apartment of the refiner, and massacred him in his bed." These slaves were soon joined by a large troop from two neighboring plantations, and together they burned the entire plantation to the ground. The only person they spared was the plantation's surgeon, whom the slaves took with them, "with the idea that they might stand in need of his professional assistance." From there the insurgent band attacked surrounding plantations, and by early the next morning all but two of the plantations in the parish had risen in revolt.[6]

During the morning of August 23 the revolt spread from Acul to the neighboring parish of Limbé. A troop of nearly 2,000 slaves went from plantation to plantation, killing whites, burning houses, and setting cane fields alight. In parishes farther east, meanwhile, slaves rose up on several plantations. Much of the northern plain was soon engulfed by the rebel-

Painting of the northern plain burning during the August 1791 insurrection. The unknown painter was looking from above the town of Le Cap. The ash and smoke from the burning cane fields covered the sky for days. *Private collection.*

lion. "The fire, which they spread to the sugarcane, to all the buildings, to their houses and *ajoupas* [huts], covered the sky with churning clouds of smoke during the day, and at night lit up the horizon with aurora borealis that projected far away the reflection of so many volcanoes, and gave all objects a livid tint of blood."[7]

Many whites fled the region, but at the La Gossette plantation Odeluc, Mossut, and a small detachment of National Guard troops prepared to confront the insurgents. As soon as they arrived, however, the soldiers threw down their weapons and fled through the cane fields toward Le Cap. "We were attacked by a horde of assassins, and could offer only meager resistance," wrote Mossut. "After the first volley, we took refuge in flight." Odeluc, weighed down by his boots and his age, was surrounded by insurgents and killed. Mossut, however, escaped when a domestic slave of the plantation appeared and presented him with a horse.[8]

Some masters and overseers successfully fought back, sometimes aided by loyal slaves. The conspiracy, however, had involved slaves from throughout the region, and the bands of insurgents often found supporters ready and waiting, and welcomed eager new recruits. The majority of slaves on the Robillard plantation, for instance, joined the group of insurgents who arrived on August 25. The owner had fled, but the driver of the plantation, who refused to take part in the insurrection, was killed. Robillard's house and the lodgings of several slave artisans and the driver were set alight. The slaves preserved their own quarters, however, as well as "two large tables to take their meals." They also smashed to pieces all the sugar-manufacturing equipment on the plantation. Indeed, throughout the region insurgents destroyed "not only the cane fields, but also the manufacturing installations, sugar mills, tools and other farm equipment, storage bins, and slave quarters; in short, every material manifestation of their existence under slavery and its means of exploitation."[9]

On the morning of August 23 a man rode into Le Cap on a barebacked horse, shoeless, hatless, a sword in his hand. "To arms, citizens, our brothers are being slaughtered and our properties are being burned; all the slaves of the plain are advancing with fire and iron in hand!" "At first everyone thought he was crazy," but they gathered around him, asking questions, and soon came to believe him. Refugees from the northern plain were soon pouring into Le Cap. The town's officials issued an order preventing all ships in the harbor from leaving—to keep the sailors around for the defense of the town, and to ensure that there was somewhere for the inhabitants to go if it failed. They fortified the roads and passes and placed troops and cannon around the edges of the city. They also began punishing slaves they suspected of complicity in the revolt. "Above 100 negro prisoners" were "shot in the burying place" during two days in late August. Soon "six gallows" were erected in one square, flanked by a wheel "to put the poor devils to torture, as they are brought in." One man proposed that all the masters in the town hand over their male domestic slaves, who would be placed in preventive custody on ships in the harbor. "The streets were deserted" in Le Cap, though "at times one saw brigands pass by in chains on their way to execution, and wounded soldiers who were being taken to the hospital, or fearful people carrying aboard the vessels their most prized possessions." In the distance there could be heard "the rumbling of burning fires and the explosions and whistling of cannon," but the war was everywhere: "One feared being slaughtered by one's servants."[10]

Several rebel attacks on the town were turned back from the fortified positions. But from their camps outside the city, insurgents taunted the soldiers. They were camped "one league" away, but they frequently approached "in numbers to bid defiance. Many of them are killed by our cannon. They, notwithstanding, come up unarmed." Estimated as 2,000 strong on August 23, by August 27 the insurgents were "reckoned 10,000 strong, divided into 3 armies, of whom 700 or 800 are on horseback, and tolerably well armed," though the rest were "almost without arms." An army was gathering on the plain, and there seemed no way to stop it.[11]

"There is a motor that powers them and that keeps powering them and that we cannot come to know," Pierre Mossut wrote to Gallifet of the insurgents. "All experienced colonists know that this class of men have neither the energy nor the combination of ideas necessary for the execution of this project, whose realization they nevertheless are marching toward with perseverance." Although many had been captured and questioned, "all observed obstinate silence when questioned about who armed them and incited this odious plot." What was happening was impossible, and yet it was happening before his very eyes. Other masters were also bewildered by the success of the insurrection. "How could we ever have known that there reigned among these men, so numerous and formerly so passive, such a concerted accord that everything was carried out exactly as was declared?" one asked. A revolution was under way, but no one—not its victims, not those who were marching across the northern plain of Saint-Domingue seeking freedom and vengeance—knew how far it would go or where it would take them.[12]

Just over a week before the insurrection began, on Sunday, August 14, 200 slaves gathered on the Lenormand de Mézy plantation in a parish called Morne-Rouge. They were delegates from plantations throughout the central region of the northern plain, including the parishes of Limbé, Petite-Anse (where the Gallifet plantations were), Port Margot, Limonade, Plaine du Nord, and Quartier Morin. There had been meetings like this before, and in fact they were common enough that several planters had given their slaves permission to attend what they described as a "dinner." But this meeting was special: final plans were made for a mass uprising.[13]

Most of the delegates at the meeting were privileged slaves, and many of them were the drivers on their plantations. These men, of necessity trusted by their masters, had a relative freedom of movement and were leaders on the plantations. Because of their position, they generally carried swords that, meant to threaten the slaves, could also be used for other purposes. Still, they were in a curious position, since while field slaves respected (and also feared) them, they also might well have felt ambivalent about having them as representatives. Acting as driver in the service of a master was not the same thing as leading slaves against him, even if both roles required similar qualities. Yet if anyone was capable of leading slaves in a coordinated and widespread revolt, it was these elite slaves, who came as representatives of thousands and thousands of others back on their plantations.[14]

All we know of the meeting comes to us from fragments of testimony. One participant described how, during the meeting, a man—a "mulatto or quartaroon"—read a statement announcing that the king and the National Assembly in Paris had passed a decree abolishing use of the whip by masters and provided slaves three free days a week instead of two. Local masters and authorities, the statement added, were refusing to apply the new decree, but luckily troops were on their way to the colony to force them to do it. Like the rumor that had circulated in Martinique in 1789, this one served to inspire and perhaps reassure potential insurgents. It also highlighted the possibility that, given the open conflict between local assemblies in Saint-Domingue and the National Assembly, the latter might be an ally in the battle against local slave masters. The rumor was an effective call to arms, and it was productive in its own way. The powers in Paris had in fact done nothing to improve the lot of the slaves, and were not about to, but that would change once the slaves took action on their own.[15]

Several delegates at the meeting argued that they should wait for the arrival of French troops before taking any action themselves. But others argued that they should rise up immediately. The revolt almost started that night, but cooler heads prevailed and a more careful plan was finalized. It required careful coordination among large numbers of slaves, who were to rise up and start the burning and killing in unison. The date set for the event was, as best we can tell, the night of Wednesday August 24. It was a surprising choice; with remarkable consistency, slave conspirators in the Americas during the eighteenth century planned their uprisings for Sundays or holidays, days when it was easier for slaves to circulate without inciting suspicion, and when they would not have to fight after a long day of work in the fields. But on August 25 a meeting of the entire Colonial Assembly was scheduled in Le Cap. It would have been, as one historian notes, "not only a day when the population of Le Cap would have been distracted by the big event, but also a unique opportunity to eliminate the entire political elite of Saint-Domingue." The choice was a measure of their ambition.[16]

In the week after the meeting of August 14 some slaves, unable to contain themselves, carried out premature acts of rebellion. On the sixteenth, for instance, slaves were caught setting fire to a building on a plantation in the Limbé parish, and under interrogation one told the plantation owner that "all the drivers, coachmen, domestics, and confidential negroes" had "formed a plot to set fire to the plantations and to murder all the whites." He named several slaves on the nearby plantation as fellow conspirators. All the slaves on this plantation were gathered and asked if there was such a plot. The slaves answered "with one voice" that this accusation was a "detestable calumny" and swore "inviolable attachment" to their manager. He believed them, and, as one account lamented when it was too late, "his credulity has been our ruin." Still, whites were aware that something was afoot, even if they had no idea how extensive the conspiracy really was. For the conspirators, weeks of planning, not to mention many lives, were on the verge of being lost. So, starting with the attack against Mossut at La Gossette, and then the uprisings in Acul, the revolt was set in motion early. The insurrection was more fragmented and haphazard than the plan of the fourteenth had envisioned. The early launching of the insurrection may have short-circuited a plan for the slaves in Le Cap to rise up on August 25 as insurgents attacked from outside the town. The 1791 insurrection, for all it ultimately achieved, might have been an even greater success.[17]

How was it that these slaves, at this time, were able to do what no other group of slaves had ever done before or would again? What made their insurrection so powerful? The success of the insurrection lay in the capacity of the conspirators to organize across plantations, bringing together slaves separated by significant distances and working under the watchful eyes of overseers and masters. The conspiracy required leadership and, just as importantly, trust, for its discovery could have led to the capture and execution of the participants.

The most visible leader during the first days of the insurrection was Boukman, who had worked first as a driver and then as a coachman. Boukman was, it is believed, a religious leader, a role that would have earned him respect among many slaves. Before the revolt, in the woods at a place called Bois-Caïman, Boukman led conspirators in a religious ceremony. (Various accounts describe him officiating alongside an old African woman "with strange eyes and bristling hair" or else a green-eyed woman of African and Corsican descent named Cécile Fatiman.) Although the service is usually described as having taken place after the meeting on August 14, it probably took place on the following Sunday, August 21, at a plantation halfway between those of Gallifet and Le Cap. It was a convenient gathering place for slaves on their way back from the town's markets. At the ceremony Boukman apparently proclaimed: "The god of the white man calls him to commit crimes; our god asks only good works of us. But this god who is so good orders revenge! He will direct our hands; he will aid us. Throw away the image of the god of the whites who thirsts for our tears and listen to the voice of liberty that speaks in the hearts of all of us." Those assembled took an oath of secrecy and revenge, sealed by drinking the blood of a black pig sacrificed before them. It was a form of pact probably derived from the traditions of West Africa.[18]

Antoine Dalmas, the only person who wrote about Bois-Caïman at the time, portrayed it as the ultimate expression of African barbarism. Dalmas had served as a surgeon at the Gallifet plantation and survived the insurrection on the northern plain before fleeing into exile to the United States. There, in 1793 and 1794, he wrote a memoir in which he described how "before executing" the plan they had made at the August 14 meeting, the conspirators had a "kind of celebration or sacrifice" in which "a black pig, surrounded by fetishes, covered with offerings each one stranger than the next, was the holocaust offered to the genius of the black race." "The religious ceremonies that the blacks practiced in slitting the pig's throat," he continued, "the eagerness with which they drank its blood, the value they placed on possessing some of its hairs—a kind of talisman that, according to them, would make them invulnerable—serves to characterize the African." He concluded that "it was natural for such an ignorant and stupid class to take part in the superstitious rituals of an absurd and bloody religion before taking part in the most horrible of assassinations." Dalmas's work—which, when it was finally published in 1814 was followed by an essay arguing that the Haitian Revolution was illegitimate and that the French should take back their former colony—is the only surviving account of the event written soon after it took place.[19]

Dalmas's account was taken up by another writer, the French abolitionist Civique de Gastine, who added the (now canonical) detail that it was a dark and stormy night. In 1824 a Haitian writer named Hérard Dumesle penned a poetic description of the ceremony, drawing on oral accounts he heard during a journey in the region of Le Cap. Dumesle was a great lover of classical Greek and Roman culture, and many of the details he ascribed to the religious practices of the slaves—such as a divination based on the entrails of the sacrificed pig, performed by a "young virgin"—would have been more familiar in ancient Rome than in revolutionary Saint-Domingue. But Dumesle's text provided the earliest written version of the speech given at the ceremony, although it did not attribute the speech to Boukman, as later writers did. Over a decade later, another account of the ceremony appeared through an interview with a man who recalled his participation in it. Incorporated into a famous history of Haiti written by Beaubroin Ardouin, this account mentioned an "oath" taken during the ceremony.[20]

The story of the Bois-Caïman ceremony symbolizes the place religious practice had in the slave insurrection. The insurrection of 1791 required community and leaders, and there is little doubt that, in one way or another, religious practices facilitated the process of its organization. Once the insurrection began, religion helped inspire insurgents, and solidified the power of certain leaders. One French soldier reported how insurgent troops advanced to the tune of African music, or amidst a silence broken only by the "incantations of their sorcerers." Another contemporary described how, as insurgents prepared to fight, religious leaders prepared *ouanga* (fetishes) and so "exalted the imagination of the women and children, who sang and danced like demons." One young slave, Hyacinthe, who became a leader in the Western Province, was a religious leader, and carried a talisman made of horsehair into battle. And when insurgent leaders were killed, ceremonies were held in their honor. One insurgent leader was buried by the troops who had defeated him, but later "the negroes took him up and buried him again with great pomp." The invocation of the mysterious ceremony at Bois-Caïman serves as shorthand for the complex and varied presence of religion in the planning and execution of the insurrection.[21]

Though religious practices facilitated and spurred on insurrection, it was only their combination with careful political organization that made the 1791 uprising successful. The plantations and towns of the colony had been the site of a productive and complex encounter between African traditions and Catholicism throughout the eighteenth century. But the dramatic social transformations brought about by the Revolution—the movement away from plantations and into insurgent camps, the encounters between groups of slaves from different regions in a context of cultural liberty—helped propel a new set of religious developments in the colony. Slave insurgents who had drawn on their religious traditions in seeking solace and strength became part of new communities in which religious practices were reconfigured and strengthened.

Before the insurrection of 1791 there may in fact have been two ceremonies: one in which a cow was sacrificed, perhaps to serve the deity Ogou, who is still served in this way; and the other, at Bois-Caïman, in which a pig was sacrificed. These were perhaps early versions of two traditions of worship that were later brought together in Haitian Vodou—the "Rada" and "Petro." The Rada rites have their roots in West Africa, while the Petro seem to have evolved from Kongolese traditions. The Petro *lwa*—Vodou gods—are more unpredictable, temperamental, and at times violent than the Rada, and carry the marks of both slavery and resistance. One 1950s ethnographer described Petro ceremonies dominated by the "crack of the slave-whip sounding constantly, a never-to-be-forgotten ghost" that recalled the "raging revolt of the slaves against the Napoleonic forces" and "the delirium of triumph" of the Haitian Revolution. The history of the revolution, then, became part of the religion, some of whose practitioners see the Boïs-Caïman ceremony as the founding moment of their religion, a charter both for the gathering of different African nations and for the unification of African-born and creole slaves in pursuit of liberation. Thus Bois-Caïman remains a symbol of the achievement of the slave insurgents of Saint-Domingue, a symbol not of a specific event whose details we can pin down, but rather of the creative spiritual and political epic that both prompted and emerged from the 1791 insurrection.[22]

A few weeks after the insurrection began, an insurgent was captured by a troop of white soldiers. He tried to escape by pleading his innocence, but, according to one soldier, when he "saw that his fate was sealed," he began to "laugh, sing, and joke" and "jeered at us in mockery." Finally, they executed him. "He gave the signal himself and met death without fear or complaint." When they searched his body, they found "in one of his pockets pamphlets printed in France, filled with commonplaces about the Rights of Man and the Sacred Revolution; in his vest pocket was a large packet of tinder and phosphate and lime. On his chest he had a little sack full of hair, herbs, and bits of bone, which they call a fetish." The law of liberty, ingredients for firing a gun, and a powerful amulet to call on the help of the gods: clearly, a potent combination.[23]

Many planters believed the ideals of the French Revolution, spread by uncomprehending and overenthusiastic whites, were responsible for bringing fire and carnage to the colonies. In early September the colony's assembly passed a "provisional decree, prohibiting the sale, impression, or distribution of any pieces relative to the politics and revolution of France." Pierre Mossut, writing to Gallifet in Paris, blamed the insurrection on "the various writings published in your capital in favor of the Negroes," which had circulated in the colonies and were known to the slaves. The planter Madame de Rouvray wrote that the insurrection was the direct result of the actions taken in metropolitan France by abolitionists. "The *scelerats* [villains] swore they would have us slaughtered by our slaves!" she exclaimed, perhaps thinking of the famous passage prophesying insurrection in the Abbé Raynal's *Histoire philosophique*. Madame de Rouvray found further proof of her assertion in reports claiming that there were whites leading the slave insurgents in battle. Along with the 150 slave insurgents her husband had killed just the day before, she wrote in September, was one white man who was *carbonisé*—covered in carbon as a kind of blackface. Another account claimed, similarly, that there were whites leading the insurgents "with blackened faces," and who "were discovered by their hair." One priest captured among the rebels confessed, probably prodded by the fear that he would be executed (as he indeed soon was), that he had been "sent over with four more from France" in order to "teach negroes to revolt." An even more extreme version of this paranoia was expressed in a September letter claiming that "fifty *new* emissaries were coming" to the colony "to raise insurrections among the slaves." It accused Julien Raimond of "making numerous levies of rogues and ragamuffins in the streets of Paris," and attacked Robespierre and Condorcet, "members of the National Assembly," as "dangerous enemies to the colonies." The letter was taken quite seriously. A decree was passed in response, ordering that "every emigrant from France should be sent back to the mother country, at the expense of the colony," unless they possessed property on the island or were related to someone who did.[24]

There was a long-lived chorus of writers who blamed the revolt on the spread of egalitarian ideals within Saint-Domingue, as if these ideals all by themselves had the power to set the colony on fire. The front page of the inaugural issue of the *Moniteur Général* of Saint-Domingue, a vehicle for the colony's planter-dominated assembly, was a poem titled "Philanthropy." It identified a "ferocious and blood mania" called "philosophy" as the "invisible and perfidious arm" that was driving "one hundred thousand rebel slaves." Antoine Dalmas, our source on the Bois-Caïman ceremony, provided a list of the accused that included the entire Enlightenment. It began with the Société des Amis des Noirs, "who had as their avowed goal the loss of the colonies," but continued with "those numerous sects" who called themselves "economists, Encyclopedists, etc.," and who formed "a kind of Republic" that, to their great misfortune, had influenced the rulers of France. Those like Dalmas who made such claims implicitly viewed the slaves as capable of interpreting and transforming Enlightenment ideals, and of applying them to their own ends.[25]

Dalmas, meanwhile, scoffed at those who offered a mirror image of this theory, claiming that the king and the aristocrats were behind the revolt. But some took this allegation quite seriously. A lawyer named Gros, who was a prisoner of the insurgents, claimed that they all believed that the king had been imprisoned, and that they had been given orders "to arm themselves and give him back his liberty." He concluded that "the revolt of the slaves is a counterrevolution." The marquis de Rouvray found credence in both theories. In December 1791 he wrote to his daughter that "the Amis des Noirs were probably the initial cause of our misfortunes," having sent emissaries to the colony, two of which had been hung for "having preached their dogma among our slaves." But he added that it was also "very certain" that "the partisans of counterrevolution" had played a major role in inciting the slave revolt in the hope that the loss of Saint-Domingue would help stir up the coastal provinces of France and turn their inhabitants against the revolution. The idea that white counterrevolutionary planters were behind the revolt would have a long life. In 1793 the Republican commissioners in the colony would arrest some planters, accusing them of having "advised, encouraged, excited, or protected" slave revolt, as well as of having supplied insurgents with ammunition and provisions. In a proclamation on slavery issued in May of that year, they announced that it was not "among the slaves" that the "causes of their insurrections" would be found. It was neither "for themselves" nor "from themselves" that they had revolted, but rather the result of external "impulsions" by men who had no "African blood."[26]

But of course the insurgents had their own ideologies, their own histories, and their own hopes for the future. While the actions of royalist and Republican whites helped set the stage for the insurrection and contributed to its development, the slave insurgents were the true force behind it. As Jean-Philippe Garran-Coulon, author of a long official report on the "troubles" of the colonies published in the late 1790s, argued, the slaves of Saint-Domingue (like those who followed Spartacus in Rome) had been moved to action not by the actions of instigators but rather by the "genius of liberty," which had incited them to "break their chains." If they had been encouraged by the talk of liberty in the colony, and by the "unthinking" statements of some whites, the slaves had no "instigator" other than "the love of liberty and hatred for their oppressors." "Slaves are in a permanent state of war with their masters and the government that maintains slavery. They have the right to demand liberty by any means, even violence," he wrote. Taken up in a violent and no doubt at times exhilarating process of revolution, they drew on a variety of ideals as they struggled to find their place in a rapidly changing world. Their voices, for the most part screened out of the voluminous accounts of the insurrection of 1791, nevertheless bleed through in ways that can help us understand the complicated process of political invention that took shape during the Haitian Revolution.[27]

Early in the insurrection, one group presented a clear set of demands. They approached a French officer and told him that they would surrender if "all the slaves should be made free." But they were "determined to die, arms in hand, rather than to submit without a promise of liberty." The whites and free-coloreds who were sent with the official French response—which rejected emancipation but offered an amnesty to all insurgents who would return to the plantation and denounce their leaders—were attacked, and six of the nine were killed by the disgusted insurgents.[28]

In a few cases, slave insurgents explicitly phrased their demands in the language of Republican rights. When a group of slaves were questioned about the meetings they had attended just before the insurrection began, they declared that "they wanted to enjoy the liberty they are entitled to by the Rights of Man." The next day several "leaders of those mobs" were "taken and interrogated," and their answer "was like the first received." Another account of the 1791 insurrection described how "an innumerable troop of negroes presented themselves almost underneath the batteries of Le Cap, asking for the rights of man." The pamphlet of the "Rights of Man" found on one executed insurgent also suggests the important role of this document in inspiring certain slaves.[29]

But insurgent leaders more commonly called on the authority of the king of France himself. This was the case of a remarkable free-colored man who took on the name Romaine la Rivière (also known as Romaine-la-prophetesse), who emerged as a leader in the Southern Province of Saint-Domingue in late 1791. Having established himself in an abandoned church, he conducted mass before an upside-down cross and claimed to be "inspired by the Holy Spirit and in direct communication with the Virgin Mary, his godmother, who answered his solicitations in writing." He repeatedly told slaves that the king had already freed them, but that their masters were refusing the decision, using this assertion to encourage them to join his armed band. Romaine la Rivière was remarkable for the strength of the claims he made on both the earthly and heavenly powers, but he was not unique. When Boukman was killed in mid-November, insurgents lamented that he had been "killed for the most just of causes, the defense of his king." The insurgent leader Jean-François, "the supreme chief of the African army," wore a gray and yellow uniform decorated with a "cross of Saint-Louis," an aristocratic military order. His guards' uniforms were decorated with the royal fleur-de-lis. He and the leaders he fought with called themselves generals and officers of the "army of the king." Some insurgents spared some white sailors they had captured because "they were in the king's service." Garran-Coulon concluded: "It is certain that the *nègres* armed themselves in the name of the king; that they had a flag soiled by the fleur-de-lis, and by the motto 'Long live Louis XVI'; that they constantly invoked his authority, and called themselves *gens du roi*."[30]

The insurgents had complex motivations for evoking the king of France, whom many saw as a potential ally and liberator because of the rumors that had circulated about his actions in their favor. Many probably recalled the royal decrees of the 1780s which were meant to improve the lot of the slaves, and which had incited such hostility among their masters. When in December 1791 the insurgent leaders Jean-François and Georges Biassou were negotiating with colonial officials, they explained that their followers were prey to "false principles," notably the idea that "the king has given three days per week to the slaves," and that they would feel betrayed if they were not granted them. In the same letter they noted their "obstinacy" in expecting the favors they had been told they would receive from the king. Three days of freedom a week was not complete liberty, but as a change that carried the seeds of a more autonomous existence it would have been an inspiration for many slaves. In some parts of the colony, meanwhile, insurgents passed on the news that the king had abolished slavery completely. Not unlike the peasant rebels in France during the Great Terror of 1789, the slave insurgents of Saint-Domingue invoked a powerful and distant figure—who they rightly understood might have the power to counteract the assemblies of the colony—against their all-too-local enemies. As Garran-Coulon noted in his report, the evocation of the king was a logical political strategy. Even if the royal government protected them very little against their masters, it was the only protection they could "invoke against the tyranny of their masters." "Is it surprising that in such circumstances, the negroes tried to take advantage of the division of the whites, and even to increase it as much as they could in order to diminish the strength of their enemies, and gain the support of those they considered their [the whites'] enemies?" The insurgents of Saint-Domingue evoked the king in pursuit of concrete political goals that were, in the local context, quite revolutionary.[31]

Evocations of the king did not imply a rejection of the language of Republicanism. By mid-1791, despite the increasing radicalization of events in France, the country was still nominally a constitutional monarchy, not a republic, and many did not see the Rights of Man and the authority of the king as mutually exclusive. The rumored decree discussed at the meeting of August 14, after all, was said to have been passed by the king *and* the National Assembly. Later in 1791, Biassou wrote of his readiness to "serve his king, the nation, and its representatives." Such ideological syncretism continued in Saint-Domingue even after the break between the Republic and the royalty was accomplished in France. In early 1793 one insurgent leader named Joseph flew a tricolor flag decorated with three fleur-de-lis, freely mixing Republican and royalist symbols. Later that year the Republican commissioner Léger Félicité Sonthonax recalled that some insurgents who had been recruited to the Republican side had proposed to make him "king in the name of the Republic" as a way of ending the war against their enemies. But when the conflict between republicanism and royalty finally became a clear conflict between slavery and freedom, many—though not all—former slaves threw in their lot with the Republic.[32]

Insurgents had a powerful incentive to take a "royalist" tone: the collaboration, and ultimately alliance, they developed with the Spanish across the border in Santo Domingo. The Spanish had "an open market with the brigands," who arrived with money, but also with dishes, jewels, furniture, and animals taken from plantations to buy supplies, as well as weapons and ammunition to supplement those they took on plantations or during battles. This trade, as well as some direct military aid given by the Spanish, provided crucial support for the insurgent army, and indeed was probably one reason it succeeded as well as it did. Insurgent leaders traveled to the border, and Spanish officers visited their camps. The insurgents cultivated such contacts, adopting an "extravagantly royalist rhetoric" and "posing as defenders of church and king" at least in part to encourage the Spanish to support them.[33]

Insurgents also often described their own leaders as kings. In the Southern Province in early 1792, a group of insurgents ultimately created the "kingdom of the Platons" and chose a king to be their leader. Romaine la Rivière had, according to one observer, the ambition to become the "king of Saint-Domingue." In the north, too, certain leaders were elected as kings. On a Sunday two weeks after the revolt began, insurgents who had taken over Acul celebrated two weddings in the town's church with an imprisoned Capuchin priest officiating. "On the occasion, they assumed titles, and the titled blacks were treated with great respect." "Their colours were consecrated, and a King was elected"—a free black named Jean-Baptiste Cap. A few weeks later, after a clash between insurgents and French troops, "a negro superbly dressed and decorated, with a crown on his head, was found upon the field of battle."[34]

For the majority of the population of the island who were African-born, the form and content of kingship were probably defined by the traditions of their homelands. Garran-Coulon attributed the royalism of the insurgents in part to their "ignorance," since "in Africa as well as in Saint-Domingue, they knew only royal government." The Republican commissioner Léger Félicité Sonthonax similarly wrote in late 1793 that "the most stupid of Africans" could understand the "simple" idea of a king, while "even the most sophisticated of them" could not "conceive of the idea of a republic." Such interpretations and oppositions were of course misleading. Kingship meant something quite different in Africa—for instance, in the Kongo, whence many slaves had come in the decades before the revolution—than it did in Europe. In Kongolese political culture, there was a long-standing conflict over the nature of kingship, between traditions that emphasized a more authoritarian form of rule and others that limited the power of kings and provided for more democratic forms of rule. Such traditions drove conflicts in which many of those enslaved in Saint-Domingue would have participated. Indeed, the Kongo might even "be seen as a fount of revolutionary ideas as much as France was." As with so much of the insurrection of 1791, the only evidence we have of the transcultural development of insurgent political ideologies is extremely fragmented, but the naming of "kings" among the insurgents likely involved a transcultural dialogue between European and African visions of leadership and government.[35]

African slaves from the Kongo arrived with another kind of experience that they made useful in Saint-Domingue. Many of them had been soldiers fighting in the civil wars that ripped apart the kingdom of Kongo before they had been captured and sold into slavery. They were "African veterans," who had knowledge and experience of warfare and knew how to use firearms. The warfare practiced in the Kongo was quite different from that of European armies, involving organization in small, relatively autonomous groups, repeated attacks and retreats aimed at confusing the enemy, and firing from a prone position and, when possible, from behind shelter. Soldiers in Saint-Domingue consistently described similar tactics among the insurgents. One contemporary wrote that instead of exposing themselves as a group like "fanatics," they fought "spread out and dispersed," and positioned themselves in places that made them seem ready "to envelop and crush their enemies by their numbers." They were careful in their observations of the enemy. "If they encounter resistance, they don't waste their energy; but if they see hesitation in the defense, they become extremely audacious." A report from 1793 described how a group of insurgents, surprised by an attack, took refuge behind rocks and, "following their cowardly custom, *hidden,* fired on us." As the French troops charged the insurgents, they retreated "from ambush to ambush until they had reached some inaccessible rocks." These tactics were successful; the "inaccessible" rocks were clearly accessible to the insurgents, who escaped the attack, though they left behind their dead and paths of blood. The insurgent leaders Jean-François and Biassou made the importance of African military tactics clear in a letter they wrote late in 1791, in which they asserted that most of their followers were "a multitude of *nègres* from the coast"—that is, from Africa—"most of whom can barely say two words of French but who in their country were accustomed to fighting wars."[36]

African veterans were not the only ones who brought military experience to the insurgents. Although they were a minority, there were also free people of African descent in the insurgent camps, some of whom had experience of serving in the French colonial militia or the *maréchaussée*. Many of them brought more than just experience. In late September a group of "mulattoes and free negroes" who had been serving against the insurgents deserted "with arms, baggage, and military stores" and "joined the rebels." The towns of Fort-Dauphin and Ouanaminthe, near the Spanish border, were taken over by the insurgents thanks to the desertion of Jean-Baptiste Marc and Cézar, two "free blacks" who had fought for several months against the "brigands" before joining them, bringing ammunition and cannon. Slaves who had been employed hunting for their masters had experience with firearms. One visitor to the colony in the late 1790s described some hunters, who seem to have developed their skills as slaves before emancipation, who each week were given enough powder for seven shots. With this they were to provide enough food for a week. They hunted birds by crawling through the lagoons with their rifles over their heads, until they found several birds "living in society," killing several with a single shot. Such skills could be put to use in other kinds of ambushes as well.[37]

When they lacked weapons, as they often did, the insurgents used startling "ruse and ingenuity." "They camouflaged traps, fabricated poisoned arrows, feigned cease-fires to lure the enemy into ambush, disguised tree-trunks as cannons, and threw obstructions of one kind or another into the roads to hamper advancing troops." Some insurgents advancing on Le Cap stood firmly up to three volleys of shot, each of them "wearing a kind of light mattress stuffed with cotton as a vest to prevent the bullets from penetrating." Some demonstrated a suicidal courage when they "suffocated the cannon of the enemy with their arms and bodies, and so routed them." Although at first many insurgents did not know how to use the cannon they captured, loading them improperly, they soon learned. One group took control of a battery along the coast, and when a French ship fired on the battery to dislodge them, they braved a barrage of 250 cannon shots. They then used the cannon balls that had landed around them to fire back at the ship, which was seriously damaged before its crew managed to sail it away.[38]

Violence, in the form of military engagements with French troops and the massacre of white planters and their families, was a central part of the insurrection. Many of the accounts of the event that were soon produced and disseminated throughout the Americas and Europe presented tales of savage and unthinkable atrocities committed by the slaves. One well-known account—presented to the National Assembly in France in

November 1791 and quickly published in English translation in 1792—included a description of the attack on the Gallifet plantations that claimed that the insurgents carried as their "standard the body of a white child impaled upon a stake." This detail was not mentioned in the descriptions of the attack on Gallifet by Pierre Mossut or Antoine Dalmas, neither of whom would have been likely to suppress so memorable an image had they been aware of it. But it was accepted as true by many readers, and often repeated as a symbol, and condemnation, of the insurrection. In Paris the famed revolutionary Camille Desmoulins used the potent image when he declared that his political enemy, the abolitionist Brissot, was to blame "if so many plantations have been reduced to ashes, if pregnant women have been eviscerated, if a child carried on the end of a pike served as standard of the blacks."[39]

The same account described many other horrors—a carpenter named Robert tied between two boards and sawed in half, husbands and fathers killed and their wives and daughters taken by the insurgents and "reserved for their pleasures," one woman raped on the body of her dead husband. Drawing on this text, and on what he heard during his stay in Saint-Domingue in 1791, Bryan Edwards embellished some of these horrors (the carpenter Robert was sawed in half because his assassins declared that "he should die in the way of his occupation") and provided descriptions of others (a policeman was nailed to the gate of his plantation and his limbs chopped off "one by one with an ax") when he wrote what would become a standard reference for later histories of the revolution. The insurrection, he wrote, had produced "horrors of which imagination cannot adequately conceive nor pen describe" and a "picture of human misery" that "no other country, no former age, has exhibited": "Upwards of one hundred thousand savage people, habituated to the barbarities of Africa, avail themselves of the silence and obscurity of the night, and fall on the peaceful and unsuspicious planters, like so many famished tygers thirsting for human blood." Death awaited "alike the old and the young, the matron, the virgin, and the helpless infant," and within "a few dismal hours the most fertile and beautiful plains in the world are converted into one vast field of carnage;—a wilderness of desolation!"[40]

But Edwards also described an "unexpected and affecting" act by a slave who saved his owners, Mr. and Mrs. Baillon, and members of their family. This slave, "who was in the conspiracy," hid them in the woods and brought them provisions from a nearby insurgent camp during the first days of the uprising. After they failed to make it to nearby Port Margot in a canoe he had found for them, the slave "appeared like a guardian angel" and escorted them to sanctuary in the town. In contrast to the stories of black atrocity, which Edwards presented without indicating from whom they came, this story of black heroism required a footnote: he explained that he had learned the story secondhand, from a friend who had heard it from Madame Baillon herself. This perhaps explains why his version differed from that presented in another account of the same event, which identified the insurgent in question as "one of the negro generals," a man named Paul Blin. (Blin, an overseer on a plantation in Limbé, did play an important role in the planning and execution of the insurrection.) In this version, Blin helped the family only at the insistence of his wife (who was the Baillons' nurse), and led them to a rickety boat only so that they would die in a manner less horrible than that "prepared for the unhappy family" by the insurgents. Whatever the truth was, Blin ultimately paid the price for having gained a reputation for mercy. The notorious insurgent leader Jeannot had Blin brutally killed under the pretext of treason because he had heard the story of the assistance he had given to white planters.[41]

Stories about insurgent slaves saving white masters powerfully highlighted the drama of a world turned upside down, and raised the question of how the contorted human relationships developed in slavery would be transformed in a new context. Having long justified slavery as a relatively benign system, and taken comfort in the relations of kindness and charity they imagined they had with certain privileged slaves, many planters were shocked by the sudden transformation of these men and women into dangerous enemies. What made the "horrors" of the insurrection even worse was the betrayal of especially trusted slaves such as drivers and domestics. One account lamented that it was the slaves "which had been most kindly treated by their masters" that were "the soul of the Insurrection." "It was they who betrayed and delivered their human masters to the assassins' sword: it was they who seduced and stirred up to revolt the gangs disposed to fidelity." It was a "heart-breaking discovery" to the planters, who would see nothing but despair in the future were it not for certain acts of "invincible fidelity" by certain slaves. Such loyal slaves had received their liberty in thanks, but—and this was crucial—this liberty was "the gift of their masters." Seeking to hold onto a world that was burning all around them, white masters sought relief in stories of fidelity that provided the consoling mirage that their world could once again be as it had been.[42]

The insurgents of 1791 were enormously diverse—women and men, African-born and creole, overseer and fieldworker, slaves on mountain coffee plantations and sugar plantations—and carried with them many different motivations, hopes, and histories. Using violence against a violent system, they shattered the economy of one of the richest regions of the world. During the first eight days of the insurrection they destroyed 184 plantations; by late September over 200 had been attacked, and "all of the plantations within fifty miles of either side of le Cap had been reduced to ashes and smoke." In addition, almost 1,200 coffee plantations in the mountains surrounding the plain had been sacked. According to one observer, "one can count as many rebel camps as there were plantations." Estimates of the numbers of insurgents varied widely, but by the end of September there were at least 20,000, and by some estimates up to 80,000, in the insurgent camps.[43]

"They are spurred on by the desire of plunder, carnage, and conflagration, and not by the spirit of liberty, as some folks pretend," one white merchant wrote of the insurgents. But plundering masters' homes, destroying the infrastructure of the plantations on which they were enslaved, and killing those who had enslaved them were powerful ways to pursue liberty. Indeed, they were the only ways available to most of the slaves. We can only imagine the exuberance and exhilaration the rebels must have felt as they took vengeance, turned the tables on their masters, and saw, perhaps for the first time, the extent of their power. We can only imagine, too, the wrenching pull of divided loyalties that many must have experienced, between staying with families on plantations and leaving with insurgent groups, between participating in a revolt that might very well lead to their brutal execution and trying to stay neutral in the midst of a war, between serving masters and hoping for rewards and fighting for an uncertain liberty. For what lay ahead was profoundly uncertain. The insurgents knew they would have to continue to fight French forces in order to hold on to what they had gained. But what might victory look like? What would it take to turn Saint-Domingue into a place where they could live with hope and possibility?[44]

For one slave of the Gallifet plantation, the insurrection had ironic consequences. In February 1791 Marie-Rose Masson had given Odeluc 3,342 livres. It was what a slave trader would ask for the purchase of two babies, and it was the price of Masson's freedom and that of her mother. Masson's father was the man who had preceded Odeluc as the manager of the plantations, and who had died soon after she was born. Odeluc had raised her, and agreed in 1787 to let her buy her liberty, but it took her four years to amass the required money. When she paid him in February, he gave her a receipt but put off signing the emancipation papers. Then, in August, he was killed at La Gossette. Masson, perhaps because she was so close to gaining her liberty, did not join the insurrection, and remained in the service of Odeluc's replacement, Mossut. He, however, refused to acknowledge the agreement she had made, and kept Masson and her mother as slaves. The insurrection, in killing Odeluc, had taken away the purchased freedom of these two slaves, even as all around her other slaves powerfully demonstrated the freedoms they had seized from their masters. It is unlikely that Mossut, Masson, or the insurgents who surrounded them could imagine that within two years there would no longer be any slaves in Saint-Domingue.[45]

CHAPTER FIVE

New World

I N EARLY SEPTEMBER 1791 Madame de Rouvray wrote to her daughter from a very different world. She was comparatively lucky. Her slaves had not rebelled, and no insurgents had reached her plantation. Her husband, the marquis de Rouvray, was leading troops that had kept the insurgents out of the region. Still, Madame de Rouvray announced resolutely that they would have to leave Saint-Domingue, "for how can one stay in a country where slaves have raised their hands against their masters?" They might go to Havana, where they could find land and rebuild a plantation with their slaves—"if we are lucky enough to preserve them from the contagion." If it became impossible to live as slave masters in Saint-Domingue, Cuba would have to do—even if its customs were "quite opposed to our own."[1]

While the marquis de Rouvray was fighting insurgents in the eastern part of the northern plain of Saint-Domingue, an officer named Anne-Louis de Tousard, a veteran of the American Revolution, was leading troops south of Le Cap. Tousard had led a first attack on two plantations in Acul on August 24 and 25, though he made little headway against the 3,000 to 4,000 insurgents concentrated there. By late September, however, he had achieved several victories. On the twenty-third he surprised a group on one plantation and quickly routed them with "a great slaughter." A counterattack by the insurgents, among them "cavalry commanded by king Jeannot," was pushed back by "well-directed fire." Two days later the insurgents were again defeated after they charged three times but were driven back "with great loss."[2]

Since the beginning of the insurrection, the main Gallifet plantation had grown into a fortified base from which frequent raids were launched. In late September about 900 troops under Tousard's command attacked before dawn and soon overran the camp. Most of those who had been living there had fled a few days before, carrying "an immense quantity of valuable effects." Most of the 2,000 who had stayed behind were old, sick, or simply wished "for an opportunity to escape; being reduced to an allowance of two bananas a day" in the insurgent camp. The attackers, however, "had orders to give no quarter to men, women or children," and once they took the camp a "horrid carnage ensued." As the soldiers ransacked and burnt the buildings, the "many sick, and old negroes" they encountered "were all either destroyed in the fire or by the sword." The troops freed several white prisoners and found proof that the insurgents were receiving aid from the Spanish: a cannon with a Spanish inscription and a letter from a commander named Don Alonzo.[3]

Despite such successful attacks, the insurgents survived. They were "repulsed but not dispersed," and as they held on to their weapons they "learned better each day how to use them." An October report described how the insurgents, who "in the beginning made their attacks with much irregularity and confusion," armed for the most part only with "instruments of labor," "now come in regular bodies, and a considerable part of them are well armed with the muskets, swords, &c. which they have taken and purchased." They marched "by the music peculiar to the negroes" and began fighting "with a considerable degree of order and firmness, crying out Victory!" Before them they flew a "bloody banner" with the motto "death to all whites!" "We were crushed by this war," recalled one soldier.[4]

It had become an "exterminating war." Because of the indiscriminate killing of slaves by French troops, many who might have opted for the relative safety of their plantations fled to the insurgent camps. There was little room for neutrality. "The country is filled with dead bodies, which lie unburied. The negroes have left the whites, with stakes, &c. driven through them into the ground; and the white troops, who now take no prisoners, but kill everything black or yellow, leave the negroes dead upon the field." The two sides were at a gory stalemate. "The heads of white prisoners, placed on stakes, surrounded the camps of the blacks, and the corpses of black prisoners were hung from the trees and bushes along the roads that led to the positions of the whites." And the insurgents were still holding out after several months. As Madame de Rouvray wrote: "We kill many of them, and they seem to reproduce themselves out of their ashes."[5]

Le Cap had been preserved from the insurgents, but much of the property in the northern plain had been destroyed. Sugar production, the lifeblood of the region, was at a standstill. And for many planters the government of France, prey to a powerful revolutionary movement, was almost as dangerous and unpredictable as the slave insurgents themselves. For some, exile was the only choice. One man announced his departure for New England with a poem that began "Adieu France." A woman "recently arrived from France" had soon seen enough, and offered her services as a chambermaid to anyone headed back across the Atlantic.[6]

Others stayed, hoping to resolve the situation, or at least to survive it. Administrators sought aid from nearby Jamaica, whose governor sent several ships with provisions and ammunition, though no troops. The planter Bryan Edwards, who joined the convoy, described how as the ships arrived in Le Cap townspeople "assembled on the beach" and "with uplifted hands and streaming eyes, gave welcome to their deliverers (for such they considered us)." The white population, he claimed, was unanimous in its "outcry against the National Assembly, to whose proceedings were imputed all their disasters." Indeed many were ready to "renounce their allegiance to the mother country," and "without scruple or restraint" declared that they wished the British would "conquer the island, or rather receive its voluntary surrender from the inhabitants." One prominent planter sent a letter to British prime minister William Pitt requesting an English occupation of the colony, which he saw as the only way to preserve the institution of slavery.[7]

But in the end the aid provided by the British was, as one embittered colonist wrote, "limited to sterile wishes and useless demonstrations." Pitt apparently responded to the news of the insurrection by commenting dryly: "It seems the French will be drinking their coffee with caramel." Whatever sympathies the white slave owners of the Caribbean might have for one another, the competition between empires was ultimately more important to the British, and when they finally did come to Saint-Domingue, it would be as invaders seeking internal allies in a war of conquest rather than as friends providing aid.[8]

Without troops from the British, and with months to wait before any troops could arrive from France, the governors of Saint-Domingue faced a serious problem. How could the fight against the insurgents be sustained? The available soldiers had been sent into the field, along with many civilians recruited into this desperate war. But by early November the two most important officers leading the campaign were convinced that this would not be enough. The only way to assure a victory, they argued, was to enlist the support of the free-coloreds. "What is the white population compared to the multitude of rebel slaves?" asked Rouvray in a speech to the assembly in Le Cap. "Isn't this enemy enough, without continuing to provoke the free-coloreds?" Invoking the "authority of history"—and drawing on his experience as a commander of free-colored troops during the American Revolution—he reminded his audience that these troops were superior to soldiers arriving from Europe, who were always decimated by disease. Tousard seconded Rouvray, pointing out that the only way to win the war against the insurgents was to harass and pursue them continually. Where were the soldiers—men "used to the climate"—who could carry out such a war? "Do you have any other than the mulattoes? No." Why, then, did the assembly persist in refusing their help, pushing them into the camp of the enemy rather than welcoming them as allies?[9]

Since many of them had served in the militia and in the pursuit of maroons in the *maréchaussée*, the free-coloreds indeed seemed the ideal soldiers for fighting the insurgents. Although there were some among the insurgent camps, many free-coloreds had already shown their willingness to combat the insurrection. In the first days of the uprising a group of free-coloreds in Le Cap had formed a troop to fight the rebels. During the attack on the Gallifet plantation, the first to enter the camp were "the free mulattoes and negroes, chiefly mounted." Nevertheless, the assembly rejected the interventions of the veteran officers, deferring any discussion of the status of the free-coloreds until after the insurrection was defeated. Having successfully held the free-coloreds at bay through violence in Saint-Domingue and lobbying in Paris, they were unwilling to relent, even in the dramatic situation that surrounded them. "One day," Rouvray warned them, "the pitying laughs with which you greet the important truths I share with you will turn to tears of blood."[10]

Not all whites in the colony were as intransigent. Some saw that the threat of sharing political power with a small group of free-coloreds was nothing in comparison to the threat of losing everything. During September and October several local administrators signed a remarkable series of treaties with groups of free-coloreds. This happened not in the Northern Province, but rather in the west (and subsequently in the south), where free-coloreds were armed and well organized, and where the slaves were relatively contained even after August 1791. While the slave insurrection was the major force shaping events in the Northern Province, then, the vexed relationship between free-coloreds and whites took center stage in other regions of the colony.

Early in August 1791 free-coloreds organized a mass political assembly in the town of Mirabalais. A well-respected, French-educated man named Pierre Pinchinat was elected president, and forty delegates were chosen to address demands for political rights to the National Assembly, as well as to local assemblies and the colony's governor. Just as the revolt began in the Northern Province, however, the governor responded by ordering them to dissolve their "illegal" assembly. The angry free-colored assembly soon decided to take up arms. Among their leaders was André Rigaud, a goldsmith who had been educated in Bordeaux and had a long military career that, according to many accounts, stretched back to the siege at Savannah during the American Revolution. He was at the beginning of an illustrious political career that would ultimately lead him into a brutal conflict with Toussaint Louverture. But all that was still far in the future.[11]

The free-coloreds of the Western Province, expecting open warfare with their white enemies, were eager for military allies. They found them in a several groups of rebellious slaves who were active in the region. The free-coloreds promised these slaves—who became known as the Swiss (a reference to the Swiss mercenaries who served the French king)—that they would receive freedom in return for their service. The "Confederates," as the alliance of the free-coloreds and the Swiss called themselves, quickly proved to be a daunting military force. In early September a troop of whites from Port-au-Prince attacked them near Croix-des-Bouquets. The Confederates pushed many of their white opponents into the nearby cane fields. It was not a good place to take refuge; as they should have known by then, sugarcane burns all too easily. The Confederates set fire to the cane fields, and the whites trapped in them were burned to death.[12]

In the wake of this victory, a wealthy planter from the town named Hanus de Jumecourt stepped forward with an audacious plan. At odds with the radical whites of Port-au-Prince, many of whom came from the class of "petits blancs," and intent on preventing slave rebellion from breaking out in the region, he decided to make peace with the free-coloreds. He led the administrators of Croix-des-Bouquets and Mirabalais in signing an agreement with the Confederates, promising to abide by the decrees of the French National Assembly, including that of May 15, 1791, which had given political rights to some free-coloreds. This first agreement became the template for another signed soon afterward between representatives from Port-au-Prince and the "citizens of color," as the Confederates pointedly named themselves. It began with a history lesson. The "citizens of color" declared that the provisions "passed in their favor" in the 1685 Code Noir had been "violated by the progress of a ridiculous form of prejudice," which had continued when the assemblies in the colony denied them the vote, and they had therefore been compelled to take up arms to defend their "violated and misunderstood rights." Having set the record straight on their own actions, they noted (undoubtedly with considerable satisfaction) that it was good to see the "return of the white citizens to the true principles of reason, justice, humanity, and healthy policies."[13]

The "citizens of color" presented themselves as defenders of the National Assembly, and the whites as rebels against its authority. They demanded the "literal execution of all the points and articles of the decrees and instructions of the National Assembly," insisting, as Ogé had the year before, that these had granted them political rights. Since they had been illegally excluded from voting, furthermore, they declared that all the assemblies then in existence were illegitimate and must be replaced through new, racially integrated elections. Whites in the region had been furiously resisting any grant of political rights to free-coloreds for years, but with slave revolt looming to the north, times had changed. The Port-au-Prince delegates accepted all the free-coloreds' demands. Another "Concordat" signed in October 1791 added more provisions, ordering the integration of local militia units and abolishing the use of racial distinctions in public discourse. All free men would simply be "citizens."[14]

A procession and a mass were organized in Port-au-Prince to celebrate the agreement. Alongside the victorious free-coloreds were the Swiss—several hundred rebel slaves turned victorious soldiers—whose presence thrilled slaves in the town and galled many whites. They walked, wrote one observer, "with the assurance of free men," and reportedly told urban slaves: "If you had done like us, the country would be ours!" There had been no mention of the Swiss in the numerous agreements signed during the previous month, but there had been a debate among the free-coloreds about what to do with them. Many free-coloreds supported a proposal by which the Swiss would be freed but forced to serve eight years in the *maréchaussée*. But the white patriots in Port-au-Prince were against any such action, convinced that rewarding rebellious slaves with freedom was a bad precedent. Although a number of free-coloreds, including André Rigaud, spoke out in defense of the Swiss, the free-colored leadership, led by their more conservative leaders such as Pierre Pinchinat, acquiesced in the decision of the administrators of Port-au-Prince: the Swiss were to be deported. "I knew all along that the blacks would get screwed," one disgusted slave in Port-au-Prince exclaimed. He was right: the Swiss were to be sent to the Mosquito Coast of Central America, a place where, as one planter wrote, "even the devil couldn't survive." In fact, though, they suffered a worse fate. The captain who was supposed to bring them to the Mosquito Coast tried, and failed, to sell them in Belize, then dumped them along the shore of Jamaica. The British, alarmed at the prospect of having such slaves in their colony, shipped them back to Saint-Domingue. There, imprisoned in a boat in a remote harbor under the watch of French soldiers, sixty were executed, and most of the rest died of sickness and starvation. It was a tragic betrayal that would not be forgotten, and a taste of the internal conflicts among different groups of African descent in the colony that were to come.[15]

Meanwhile the brief period of cooperation and peace between the free-coloreds and whites ended in a new outbreak of violence. On the day the municipality was scheduled to ratify the Concordat, a black Confederate soldier named Scapin was insulted in the street by a white soldier. They began to fight, and when the police arrived they arrested Scapin. News of the incident spread, and an angry white crowd pushed the police aside and lynched him. Enraged free-coloreds responded by shooting down a white "patriot." A battle broke out in the streets of Port-au-Prince. The outnumbered free-colored soldiers retreated from the town, but whites killed free-colored civilians in the streets and murdered them in their homes. As the killing progressed, a devastating fire broke out in the city. Eight hundred houses were burnt to their foundations, and the city reduced to a "mound of ashes."[16]

"Only a perfect union between the white citizens and the citizens of color," officials from the nearby town of Saint-Marc wrote to the governor, "can preserve the colony from dangers that may bring about its complete ruin." But the possibility of an alliance had gone up in smoke with Port-au-Prince. The brutality of the clashes there left the free-coloreds enraged, and several issued open declarations of war against the whites. One called on his brethren to besiege Port-au-Prince and to plunge their "bloody arms" into the bodies of these "monsters from Europe." It was time to uproot "this tree of prejudice" and "avenge God, nature, the law, and humanity, outraged for so long in these terrible climates." André Rigaud issued a similar call to his followers in the Southern Province: the free-coloreds must respond to the brutality of the whites by killing, pillaging, and burning in turn, seeking vengeance against the "barbarians" who wished to slaughter them and reduce them to slavery. By late November the Western and the Southern Provinces were, like the north, in a state of war. The slaves had not started the war there, but they were a part of it. In the next months both sides in the conflict increasingly recruited slaves to fight for them. They assumed that once the conflicts were over, slavery could be rebuilt. In this expectation they were sorely mistaken. For a time the slaves would serve the white and free-colored armies, learning how to fight, biding their time. But in the end many would choose to leave these masters, and all masters, behind.[17]

In late October 1791 elderly slaves gathered at the gates of their plantations on the northern plain to enjoy a novel sight. Down the road marched a group of white prisoners, flanked by insurgent soldiers who were hitting them with sticks. The "old negroes and negresses humiliated us with their words," recalled one of the prisoners, a local official named Gros, "and celebrated the exploits of their warriors." For nearly a century, escaped slaves had been similarly captured and marched off to prison. Now the roles were reversed.[18]

Gros and the other prisoners had been guarding a post outside their town when they were attacked and captured by a group of insurgents. As they were marched away they saw their houses and fields go up in flames. They were first brought to a camp under the command of Sans-Souci ("a very bad subject"), where they were insulted and given only "a few drops" of *tafia*—rum—to drink. A white priest in the camp frightened them by announcing that "one must know how to die." For the next part of their journey the prisoners were carried in carts, in which they were so thoroughly jolted about that they would have preferred to walk. They were brought to a camp under the command of a slave named Michaud, who, according to Gros, had "a great deal of sensitivity," and who helped the prisoners as best he could.[19]

Michaud, however, was outranked by a leader notorious for his brutality: Jeannot. He kept the white prisoners chained, giving them only a glass of water and three bananas per day, supplemented only rarely by a piece of "beef's ear." The residents of the camp surrounded them, and although a few "seemed pained" by their situation, most jeered and "rejoiced." At night, remembered Gros, "our terror worsened because of the speeches that we heard; and their sad songs, accompanied by instruments, seemed to be a prelude to new tortures." Then Jeannot announced to the prisoners that two of them would be killed every twenty-four hours, "to prolong his enjoyment." One white prisoner received "over 400" strikes of a whip, and gunpowder was rubbed into his bleeding wounds. Other prisoners, escorted out of their prison to the sound of a drum, were chopped to pieces or strung up and bled to death. One was executed by his own domestic slave. The whippings and executions described by Gros were a terrifying mirror image of the tortures long inflicted by white masters upon slaves. But Jeannot was not brutal only to whites; he also imprisoned slaves "who were still loyal to the whites." A group of free-coloreds operating in the area lamented that "his only joy was spilling blood" of whites and blacks. "If on earth there are two principles," they wrote, "Jeannot was animated only by that of evil."[20]

One day, as Gros and the remainder of the prisoners awaited their promised execution (they were, apparently, to be roasted alive), they heard shots in the distance, and mounted troops led by Jean-François, who was Jeannot's superior, arrived in the camp. He arrested Jeannot and, after a quick military trial, had him tied to a tree and shot. Jean-François promised the white prisoners that their tortures were over and that they would be treated humanely from then on. The prisoners were "walking ghosts": "pale and disfigured, attacked by vermin who were spread over all parts of our bodies, covered with blood and dust." But they were treated more kindly from then on. As they marched some insurgents dismounted from their horses and let the exhausted prisoners ride. At the next camp, where the insurgents' *salle du gouvernement*—the central seat of the insurgent government—was located, they were greeted by a man named Jean-Louis, a domestic slave who had lived for several years in France and for this reason was nicknamed "the Parisian." He fed them and provided them with "an excellent mattress," and they rested well.[21]

From then on the prisoners were allowed to circulate freely in the camps, and Gros was recruited to be Jean-François's secretary. Many of the "mulattoes" in the camp, he reported, felt ambivalent about being a part of the revolt. A small number of them, who had been partisans of Ogé in 1790, were active participants, even instigators, of the insurrection, while others saw in it an opportunity to fight for their own rights once it began. But many, he claimed, were kept in the camps under duress, constantly watched to prevent them from leaving. Even Jean-François—who may have been a slave, and a maroon, before the Revolution—presented himself to Gros as a kind of hostage to the mass of the insurgents. He told Gros that he had been made "general of the negroes" by the masses of the insurgents, but that unlike them he was not fighting for "general liberty," which he believed was an impossible goal and would have been dangerous for the "uncivilized hordes" that surrounded him. He had lesser ambitions: he railed against plantation managers and wanted them banned from Saint-Domingue. Most of the insurgents, however, were committed to the "complete destruction of the whites." Among them, Gros wrote, the women were much "more insolent, harsher," and less disposed to return to their plantations than the men. The insurgent leader Georges Biassou concurred, singling out the "negresses of the plantations" as a particularly rebellious and recalcitrant group.[22]

By late November Jean-François and Biassou were the most important insurgent leaders in the northern plain. They had survived as other leaders had fallen. Jean-Baptiste Cap, who was elected king of Limbé and Port-Margot in late August, had been captured trying to recruit slaves on a plantation and broken on the wheel. And in mid-November Boukman was surrounded by a troop of cavalry and gunned down during a battle. He was decapitated, his body burned by the French troops in view of the insurgent camps, and his head displayed on a stake in the main plaza of Le Cap. The man who killed him was awarded the large bounty promised to anyone who brought in the "heads of the different chiefs of the rebels." The death of the man who had set the uprising in motion made a deep impression in the rebel camps, where insurgents launched into a three-day *calenda*—dance—during which they taunted white prisoners (whom some wanted to put to death in revenge for their leader's death) and told stories of their exploits in the war.[23]

Several months of war had taken their toll. Many thousands of insurgents had died in the fighting. Those who had survived were often hungry and sick. How long could the insurrection hold out if troops arrived from France? What, ultimately, was to be gained? Jean-François and Biassou decided it was time to sue for peace. Other officers, including one who went by the name Toussaint, agreed. It would be a test of their leadership and of the extent of their power, for many in the insurgents' camps were determined never to return to the old world.

In late November three civil commissioners sent by the National Assembly arrived in Saint-Domingue. When they had left France, no one there had yet learned of the 1791 slave insurrection, so they were not armed with an official response to the event. Instead they brought a decree that deepened the impasse in the colony. On September 24 the National Assembly had proclaimed that whereas it and the king would have control over the "exterior regime" of the colonies, notably trade policies, the "laws concerning the state of unfree persons and the political status of men of color and free blacks" would be established by the local assembly. The law of May 15, which had incited such protest among the whites of Saint-Domingue, had been overturned by the very authority that had decreed it a few months before. The news overjoyed many whites, but it was a bitter disappointed for the free-coloreds. After several years of struggle, the death of Ogé and Chavannes, months of killing in Port-au-Prince, they were in the same place they had started: with no political rights and no recourse against the local assemblies.[24]

The commissioners also brought other news. France had a new constitution, which had, as the commissioners put it, destroyed "stone by stone" the "edifice of the Old Regime" and created a constitutional monarchy. The king had accepted the constitution and proclaimed hopefully that the Revolution was over and that it was time to bring peace to the nation. In this spirit the National Assembly had decreed a general amnesty for "acts of revolution," and this decree had been extended to the colonies. Those who "returned to order" would be forgiven for any acts of war or violence they had committed.[25]

"We must be included in the general amnesty pronounced for all indiscriminately," argued Jean-François and Biassou in a letter to the commissioners. But others disagreed. A deputy from Le Cap serving in the assembly argued that the amnesty did not apply to those in rebellion in the colony. It was for those who had committed "acts of revolution," and "certainly the crimes committed in Saint-Domingue must be considered differently." Granting amnesty to the "free-coloreds and free blacks" would establish "a perfect equality between them and the whites." Extending it to the slaves would have an even more disastrous effect: it would free them from their dependence on their masters and make it impossible to guarantee their future subordination. To accept the insurrection as an "act of revolution" was, this deputy recognized, to legitimize it. It meant defining their struggle as politics rather than as "crime," and recognizing them as revolutionaries rather than as "brigands." If amnesty was granted, slavery would never be secure again.[26]

In fact the insurgents had already profoundly undermined slavery, freeing tens of thousands of slaves from their (often dead) masters through violence. They had won the right to be treated as a political force. As the commissioners realized, there was little choice but to offer them amnesty in the hope of ending a conflict that could not be won by military means. Jean-François and Biassou took advantage of the opportunity presented them and put forth a plan to end the insurrection. The assembly would grant several hundred "liberties" to the insurgent leaders, who would distribute them among their officers. The mass of the insurgents who were not granted freedom would be granted an amnesty from punishment. In return, the leaders would end the war and bring them back to their plantations. Jean-François and Biassou presented themselves as leaders eager to contain their more radical followers, and recommended that a proclamation be issued to the slaves assuring them that the assembly would "take care of their situation." But they also threatened that if their proposals were refused, "a horrible carnage" might ensue, including the death of "the white prisoners, and white women."[27]

The planter-dominated assembly, however, refused to deal with "rebel negroes." Speaking as if they were still powerful masters, they told the insurgents that if they returned to their plantations and showed themselves to be repentant, they might be forgiven. Tousard, who had been approached individually by the insurgents, responded in a similar vein: "Do not believe that the whites, and especially the members of an assembly of representatives from the colony, would lower themselves so far as to receive conditions dictated and demanded of them by their rebel slaves." He demanded, before any negotiation could take place, a complete end to hostilities, the release of all prisoners, the return of all plantation slaves to their plantations, the disarmament of all "negroes," and the surrender of all their weapons. As one of the commissioners noted months later, a major opportunity to end the slave insurrection was lost. The assembly was clearly incapable of confronting the actual situation on the island. Having summarily rejected the entreaties of the "brigands," and with Saint-Domingue smoking around them, they engaged in an interminable debate about whether to call themselves a "General Assembly," as they had before, or a "Colonial Assembly," as they eventually did.[28]

The commissioners, more receptive to the proposals of the insurgent leaders, tried to salvage the negotiations. But Jean-François and Biassou's letters began to take a harsher tone. They warned the commissioners that neither "searching for the authors" of the revolt nor "deploying the forces that the nation has put under your command" would lead to peace in the colony. Those who had demanded that the rebels return to the plantations clearly did not understand "the nature of the revolution": "One hundred thousand men are in arms," they declared. "Eighty percent of the population" of the north had risen up. Jean-François and Biassou explained that they were "entirely dependent on the general will" of this mass of insurgents. This will was defined by the "multitude" of African slaves. Only the insurgent leaders and officers selected for either "their influence over the negroes" or "the fear they inspire in them" would be able to bring these men back to the plantations. And only they, backed by the presence of royal troops, could successfully pursue those who refused. If the commissioners agreed to the conditions they had set, however, the fortunes of the colony could be "reborn out of their ashes." The commissioners met with Jean-François to discuss the terms of an agreement. The encounter started off poorly when a planter accompanying the commissioners stepped forward and struck the resplendent leader as if he were a misbehaving slave. Jean-François stepped back among his troops, but one of the commissioners walked into the group of "irritated blacks" and secured an arrangement by which white prisoners would be released and brought to Le Cap. Jean-François asked that his wife, who was imprisoned in the town, be released in return.[29]

The original offers made by the insurgent leaders made only vague reference to a reform in slavery, emphasizing the amnesty and the limited "liberties" to be granted. But Jean-François and Biassou were clearly under pressure from those in the camps to wrest more significant concessions from the governors of the colony. In one letter to the commissioners, they passed on some "representations made to us by the negro slaves," who emphasized that they would not return to the plantations without being promised significant reforms. They complained of "the bad treatment they receive from their masters, most of whom make themselves the executioners of their slaves, mistreating them with all kinds of torments, taking away their two hours [of free time], their holidays and Sundays, leaving them naked, with no care when they are sick, letting them die of misery." Jean-François and Biassou agreed that there were many "barbarous masters" who took pleasure in "exercising cruelties on their miserable slaves," and administrators and managers who, in order to stay in the good graces of the plantation owners, committed "a thousand cruelties against the slaves." They asked the commissioners to take steps to assure that the slaves would no longer be treated so poorly, and to abolish the "horrible *cachots*" in which slaves were imprisoned on the plantations. "Try to improve the situation of this group of men who are so necessary to the colony, and we dare assure you that they will go back to work, and return without resistance to their duty." Propelled by the "general will" in the camps, Jean-François and Biassou asked for minor reforms, similar to those put forth by the royal government in the 1780s that had been vehemently opposed by planters. The situation, of course, was different, and they perhaps hoped that, when faced with a mass uprising, slave masters would be willing to make some concessions. Although there was already talk of a "general liberty," Jean-François and Biassou, like most European abolitionists of the time, pursued the goal of reforming slavery rather than dismantling it.[30]

They were, however, being carried along by a revolution. As negotiations progressed, many among the "multitude" in the camps became suspicious of their leaders. Some openly menaced the prisoner Gros, knowing that as Jean-François's secretary he was facilitating communication with the whites, while others threatened the "mulattoes" they believed were behind the negotiations. They made clear that they would resist, forcefully if necessary, any negotiation aimed at making them return to the plantations. When a delegation of leaders, including Toussaint, marched to Le Cap to bring the white prisoners to the commissioners, they were stopped on the way by a crowd of "negroes," who, as Gros described it, "swords in hand, threatened to send only our heads to Le Cap, swearing against peace and against their generals." Only the firmness of the escorts saved the whites.[31]

In the end, although the prisoners were exchanged as planned, the negotiations broke down soon afterward. The September 24 decree made it difficult for the commissioners who brought it to override the decisions of the assembly, which technically controlled "internal" affairs in the colony. No deal materialized. If it had, it might in any case have provoked open hostilities between the "multitude" of insurgents and their leaders.

By mid-January the insurgents under the command of Jean-François and Biassou were attacking again. They captured the district of Ouanaminthe, on the border with Spanish Santo Domingo, and attacked the outskirts of Le Cap. Biassou attacked the hospital outside the town of Le Cap to free his mother, who was a slave there. The sick who were left behind were killed by the attackers. For the time being, there seemed no end in sight to the "exterminating war."[32]

By November news of the slave insurrection was arriving steadily in France through official correspondence as well as personal letters. Planter representatives demanded a massive shipment of troops to suppress the revolt, and assailed the Société des Amis des Noirs with accusations that it had incited the slaves to revolt. The society's correspondent in England, Thomas Clarkson, wrote a pamphlet refuting this idea; slave revolts, he noted, had existed in every slave society going back to Greece and Rome, long before there were abolitionists. The "real cause" of the insurrection, he insisted, was the "Slave Trade." As long as it continued, revolts were inevitable, and far from being a reason to stop abolitionist efforts, they were a reason to "redouble" them. In Paris the revolutionary firebrand Jean-Paul Marat presented a different kind of defense for the revolt. If the white residents of Saint-Domingue had the right to reject "laws emanating from a legislator who was two thousand leagues away" and to proclaim independence, as he believed they did, the other groups in the colony also had, like all human beings, the right to resist oppression. The whites had made themselves "despotic masters of the mulattoes and tyrannical masters of the blacks," and if the latter wished to "overthrow the cruel and shameful yoke under which they suffer, they are authorized to use any means available," even "massacring their oppressors to the last."[33]

But the violence of the revolt also repelled some in Paris. Olympe de Gouges, whose 1789 play had celebrated slave resistance and white-black friendship, was shocked by the violence of the uprising and admonished the slaves. When in their "blind rage" they failed to "distinguish between innocent victims and your persecutors," they justified their tyrants by imitating them. "Men were not born in irons," she lamented, "and now you prove them necessary." French abolitionists were clearly in a bind: the group's careful plans for reform, too much for many whites, were also clearly too little for the slaves. Superseded by the events in the colonies, and with many of its members finding themselves in increasing political trouble in the midst of the unfolding revolutionary events in Paris, the Société des Amis des Noirs soon ceased its regular meetings, though its founder, Brissot, remained active in colonial politics.[34]

"What will stop the revolt of the slaves in Saint-Domingue?" asked a deputy in the National Assembly in March 1792. Brissot and other abolitionists had long insisted they had the answer: the free people of color. With the news of the uprising arriving in Paris, the arguments in favor of racial equality at last carried the day. Brissot and some of his allies gained control of the Colonial Ministry. They blamed the planters for the revolt and, publicizing the overtures some of them had made to the British, painted them as dangerous counterrevolutionaries. The only way to save the colony, they argued successfully, was to give political rights to the free-coloreds. Their victory was facilitated by the increasingly radical tone of the Revolution in France, and by the looming possibility of war with Great Britain, but it was driven by the events in Saint-Domingue, and based on the principle of the "Concordats" signed between whites and free-coloreds there. The argument about free-coloreds' political rights, as Robin Blackburn notes, "had been transformed by the sight of the smoke rising from burnt-out plantation buildings and cane fields."[35]

On April 4, 1792, the National Assembly declared: "the *hommes de couleur* and the *nègres libres* must enjoy, along with the white *colons,* equality of political rights." They would be allowed to vote in local elections and be eligible for all positions if they had met the financial criteria for "active" citizenship. The decree was presented as a way of responding to the "the uprising of the slaves"; it noted that the "unity" of citizens was "the only thing that can preserve their property from pillage and fire." The "odious conspiracy" of counterrevolutionary planters was, the law declared, "linked to the projects of conspiracy against the Nation of France, which are about to explode simultaneously in the two hemispheres." But the Republic would triumph against its enemies by granting equality to those who had been excluded, and by integrating these "new citizens" into the nation. From that day forward, there would be only two categories of people in the colonies, free and enslaved; and there would be no racial distinctions among the free. It was a dramatic step. In the heart of the slave societies of the Americas, legal distinctions on the basis of race were outlawed. With free-coloreds so numerous in Saint-Domingue, the decree assured that people of African descent would have significant political power. The slave insurgents of Saint-Domingue had expanded the political horizon in a paradoxical way, making it necessary to grant racial equality in order to save slavery.[36]

A new set of commissioners was sent to Saint-Domingue to apply this decree, and given the power to dissolve the existing assemblies and oversee the formation of new, racially integrated ones. Like the commissioners sent in 1791, they faced the daunting task of bringing order to a colony at war with itself. Unlike those who preceded them, however, they would use their power against that of the white planters of Saint-Domingue and ally themselves with the newly enfranchised free-coloreds. But in the end the commissioners would carry out a mission very different from that which they had been handed. Accompanied by a law and by a convoy of troops meant to put an end to the slave insurrection, they would instead end up embracing it and its demand for liberty.

CHAPTER SIX

Defiance

I N LATE 1792 the slave Philipeau wrote again to his owner, Madame de Mauger, in France. "I am black, but, my dear mistress, I am true and loyal," he declared. He was raising his children to love and fear God, he announced, and to faithfully respect their masters. Philipeau did not complain about the plantation manager, as he had years before. Instead, he wrote to Mauger of the profits "I made this year." He was now—as he had long argued he should be—the manager of her indigo plantation. It was not, however, Mauger's generosity or farsightedness that had brought this about. Indeed, although he must have assumed she knew what had happened, Philipeau was reticent about announcing the change too openly. His new power had come from revolt: sometime during the previous months, he and other slaves had risen up and forced their hated manager off the plantation.[1]

In a world overshadowed by the smoke of the slave revolt in the north, slaves throughout the colony were emboldened to speak and strike out against the hierarchies of slavery. Indeed Mauger had, within a few months, completely lost control of both of her plantations. Early in 1792 the slaves on her sugar plantation had risen up against their manager. "Your blacks have forced me out of your plantation, having pillaged and stolen everything and threatened to kill me," the deposed manager wrote in May. "Right now they are doing as they please." Even before this had happened things were difficult on the plantation; it had been impossible to build a needed mill because the carpenter had been killed fighting the insurgents. "The colony is depopulated of whites," the manager lamented. He had seen enough. Fearing for his safety, he left for France.[2]

Mauger's slaves presented their demands with a confidence that shocked those who confronted them. When a group of whites from Saint-Marc, acting on Mauger's behalf, went to her sugar plantation two months later to replace the expelled manager, the slaves responded unequivocally. "Our surprise was extreme," wrote the visitors, "to hear them all shout that they didn't want any more whites." It turned out that a free man of color named Enard had "taken over the management of the plantation without anyone asking him to." When Mauger's representatives came to the plantation, the slaves announced they were quite happy with Enard's services and wanted "no others." The visitors explained that Enard was less qualified than the white manager they had chosen. They had every legal right to choose who would manage the plantation, and the slaves had, in principle, no right to refuse. But when Mauger's representatives insisted, the assembled slaves made "murmurs and threats" and showered them with jokes and insults, and the whites retreated.[3]

Faced with such united resistance, whites found they had little power to respond. Mauger's representatives asked local administrators to punish the rebellious slaves. But with so few troops at their disposal in front of widening slave resistance, there was little they could do. A month later Mauger's administrators named another man, a sugar refiner, to take control of the plantation, but the slaves expelled him too. In the end, Mauger's representatives accepted Enard's presence, and even paid him and sent food to the plantation. "Men are vindictive, and we are in a century in which it seems everything is permitted," they wrote apologetically to Mauger. Only the defeat of the slave insurgents of the north could bring the slaves of the Western Province back under control. Although on many plantations slaves remained "tranquil," they were not "working too hard." "We are forced to close our eyes and reward them anyway. It is quite cruel, but the hope of a different future gives us patience."[4]

These events paralleled those on Mauger's indigo plantation, where Philipeau had taken charge. In his letter to Mauger, Philipeau at first distanced himself from what had happened: he wrote that the slaves had "taken advantage of the revolution to fire your manager." But then he made clear that he had both approved and participated: "You know that if I had been master, he would have been kicked out of here six years ago for his bad behavior." He assured Mauger: "We did nothing bad to him. We did not hurt him." And then he gave her an order of his own. Rather than being angry with her slaves, he told Mauger to "bless God that this man is no longer on your property." She could depend on him to keep things running on the plantation, he insisted. The slaves had not left, and they had not killed or hurt anyone. Indeed, "since the revolution" there had been three "little creoles" born. Her property was increasing under his care.[5]

In his letters Philipeau presented himself as his mistress' humble servant. He declared he would be happy to accept a new manager, whether "white" or "mulatto." In a letter they wrote several months later to Mauger, a group of other slaves from the plantation declared they were repentant about what they had done. "All the subjects in Saint-Domingue have felt the loss of reason," they noted. But at the same time they justified their behavior, describing how the old manager had "tyrannized" them, and pointing, as Philipeau had years before, to the financial losses she suffered as proof of this. "We are slaves and your subjects, and we give ourselves over to work as we should, but humanity must interest itself in our fate." They had a right to be treated according to certain rules, they asserted, and to take action when they were wronged by those in power. Philipeau had taken a bold step years before in writing to his mistress to ask her to intervene on behalf of her slaves. In the new context created by the insurrection of 1791, he and the other Mauger slaves had gone further, using their numbers and their determination to take over the plantation themselves. They understood that those in charge had little power to resist and would ultimately be forced to negotiate with them over the terms of their labor. Like slaves elsewhere in the Artibonite region, and throughout the Western Province, they did not destroy or abandon the plantations, but they began to make them their own.[6]

At the beginning of 1792, while much of the Northern Province had been overtaken by slave revolt, the west and the south were still relatively untouched by open insurrection. During the year, however, the compass of slave action expanded dramatically in these regions. Some slaves attacked their masters and took control of their plantations, and by the end of the year independent bands of insurgent slaves had established themselves in parts of the south. Slave revolution, initially limited to the Northern Province, now engulfed much of the colony. It was groups of whites and free-coloreds—many of them plantation owners—who laid the foundation for this expansion of slave revolution by arming slaves to fight alongside them in their violent battles against one another.

Free-colored leaders had initially shied away from using this tactic. In his 1790 revolt Vincent Ogé refused to mobilize slaves, as some suggested he should. And in the south in January 1791 free-coloreds turned down an offer of support from a group of several hundred conspiring plantation slaves. These insurgents, like those who would set in motion the revolt in the north several months later, were inspired by the rumor of the king of France's grant to plantation slaves of three free days per week; they were determined to force the local administration to enforce the decree. The free-coloreds, though they promised to issue such a demand, were not willing actually to join forces with the slave conspirators. Although the latter decided to go ahead with their revolt anyway, their plans were discovered and their leaders arrested and imprisoned before they could act. The slaves of the south would have to wait for the slaves of the north to open the way.[7]

A year later most of the slaves of the south were still on their plantations. But male slaves increasingly found opportunities for individual freedom. As their battles with local whites continued, some free-coloreds concluded that they could not win without slave recruits. Bands operating in the countryside held out the promise of liberty to men from the plantations who would join them in fighting the whites. Slaves had reason to be wary of such promises. Many probably knew of what happened to the Swiss—the slave insurgents who had joined with the free-coloreds in the early 1790s—most of whom had found death instead of liberty. Nevertheless many slaves responded. Sometimes they were given little choice. Troops of free-coloreds occupied plantations, seeking to win over the drivers on plantations abandoned by their owners. If the driver resisted, they sometimes cut up his whip—a symbol of his power—or, worse, shot him. In some cases these bands also pillaged and burned the houses of the slaves. Once the free-coloreds were drawing recruits from among the slaves, whites had little choice but to respond in kind or be overwhelmed. By the end of 1791 whites in several parts of the south had freed their own slaves and made them soldiers. Les Cayes passed a decree ordering that one-tenth of the local slaves be recruited to fight the free-coloreds.[8]

Most free people of color (many of whom, like the Raimond family, owned plantations in the area) shared with whites a desire to see slavery maintained in the area, and assumed—reasonably enough, given the long history of slave recruitment in Saint-Domingue and elsewhere in the Americas—that the granting of freedom to some slaves in return for their service would not fundamentally undermine their own power or wealth. But, called on to be auxiliaries in a war that was not their own, slaves gained military experience and new political perspectives. Once they were serving "as equals in arms" they took "as an accomplished fact the freedom they were promised." As one planter wrote, the slaves who had left plantations for military camps had "lost the habit of working" and in the process became "accustomed to thinking." Once the war between the whites and free-coloreds came to an end, many of them began fighting their own war.[9]

In the west, where conflicts between whites and free-coloreds had been raging since the disintegration of the various "Concordats" signed in 1791, slaves were also increasingly recruited as auxiliaries. Port-au-Prince, still the stronghold of the white radicals, was under siege by the troops of free-coloreds. But the latter had enemies outside the town as well. In the Artibonite region a planter named Claude Isaac Borel—who was a representative in the Colonial Assembly—turned his plantation into an armed camp and, fighting under a red flag, launched attacks against free-coloreds in the area. He transformed the community of white saltmakers who lived in the region into an armed band to fight with him. In the face of Borel's successes, free-coloreds in the region began recruiting slaves from local plantations. As in the south, when the slave drivers on certain plantations refused to cooperate, the free-coloreds sometimes killed them. The civil war profoundly undermined the authority of masters in the Artibonite plain and created new fissures in the system that held slaves in check.[10]

The white radicals of Port-au-Prince, too, began recruiting slaves to fight for them. Jean-Baptiste de Caradeux, a planter who had previously armed his own plantation slaves, created the "Company of Africans," recruiting among urban slaves. They carried out raids on the Cul-de-Sac plain and in March 1792 joined with troops of white patriots in attacking the free-colored stronghold at Croix-des-Bouquets. As these troops marched across the plain, they raided plantations, taking the pigs and chickens of many slaves, and forced some to join their ranks. The fortuitous arrival of a solar eclipse as they marched added to the terror they inspired in their opponents. Although slaves on one plantation fought back, for the most part the Port-au-Prince troops encountered little resistance from them or the outnumbered free-coloreds, who retreated from Croix-des-Bouquets. Soon, however, the tide turned. An army of slaves, angered by the depredations against them and encouraged by emissaries from the free-coloreds, rose up on the plantations of the plain and converged on Croix-des-Bouquets. Ten to fifteen thousand strong, armed with sticks and machetes, they marched into battle behind Hyacinthe, who waved a horse-hair talisman meant to protect them from enemy fire. "Don't be afraid; it's only water coming out of the cannon," he called as they charged. Although many fell, others braved the murderous artillery to meet the Port-au-Prince troops in hand-to-hand combat and retook Croix-des-Bouquets. In the process they faced off against the Company of Africans: during the battle thousands of slaves fought one another in a war that was not their own.[11]

The mass mobilization of slaves severely disrupted slavery and encouraged new uprisings throughout the region, but the leadership of Hyacinthe shaped and limited slave action. He established himself on a plantation, promising to bring his followers back to the plantations. Hyacinthe invited the planter Hanus de Jumecourt—the architect of the first Concordat between whites and free-coloreds, signed in 1791—to return to Croix-des-Bouquets and head the police force there. Using his considerable influence and the threat of violence, Hyacinthe oversaw the partial reestablishment of sugar production on the plain and helped preserve the plantations of the west from the destruction that had occurred in the north.[12]

The slaves who had risen up in Cul-de-Sac had saved the free-coloreds—something their leader Pierre Pinchinat would recall when he wrote that the blacks had served as a "rampart" against the whites—and in doing so they opened the way for the final defeat of the white radicals of Port-au-Prince. After the free-colored victory at Croix-des-Bouquets, the Republican commissioners in Le Cap decided to seek peace in the west. Under the leadership of Pinchinat, the free-coloreds demanded the arrest of the leaders in Port-au-Prince and dissolution of the local assembly, and the commissioners agreed. With the administration and many whites in the west turned against them, the radicals fell into disarray. Caradeux left the colony, carrying fifty of his slaves to the United States; Borel was arrested and soon left Saint-Domingue. In early July the army of free-coloreds, led by André Rigaud and Louis-Jacques Bauvais, entered Port-au-Prince. The remaining radical leaders were arrested; one of the most hated was executed in secret. Rigaud and Bauvais, having proved themselves as the military leaders of the free-colored insurgents, became French Republican officers.[13]

Meanwhile, by May 1792 news had arrived from France about the April 4 decree granting full political rights to free-coloreds. The looming danger of slave revolt and the turnabout in Paris combined to weaken the political will of those whites who still resisted the demands of the free-coloreds. The first stage of the Haitian Revolution was coming to a close. The free

people of color had taken advantage of the opening provided by slave revolt and, through effective lobbying in Paris and armed struggle in Saint-
Domingue, unraveled the racial hierarchy that had oppressed them for
decades. In the process they had become essential allies for the Republican administrators from France in Saint-Domingue. Many of them would
embrace this role in the coming year, and in so doing would break with
those among their white planter allies who turned against the Republic.
General Bauvais would explain that the free-coloreds had never been the
"dupes" of the wealthy planters, having joined with them only because they
needed "auxiliaries" as they struggled for their rights. "If the devil had presented himself, we would have recruited him," he declared. The free-
coloreds, in any case, no longer needed their local white allies, for they had
gained an even more powerful ally: the metropolitan government, which
increasingly came to depend on them as its base of power in the colony.[14]

There was, of course, one problem: what to do with the slaves who had
been central in securing victory? Most free-coloreds, as well as their white
allies, wanted the slaves who had risen up to return to their plantations.
Having at last realized that times had changed, however, they made an important concession to the slave insurgents, granting freedom to several
hundred of their leaders. This promise came with one condition: that the
leaders allow themselves to be organized into a police unit to keep order
on the plantations from which many of their followers had come. Among
those included was Hyacinthe, whose success in keeping order in Cul-de-
Sac highlighted the effectiveness of employing formerly enslaved leaders
to contain slave resistance. The Republican commissioner Philippe Rose
Roume de Saint-Laurent noted with satisfaction that these slaves-turned-
police spread out among the plantations like "preachers," and that their
success in restoring order amply justified the decision to grant them freedom. Men who had led slaves into war now helped lead them back to work.
Still, a precedent had been set, one that in the words of one contemporary
provided a "dangerous example for all thinking blacks": insurrection and
war against whites could lead to an officially sanctioned freedom.[15]

In the Southern Province many slaves who had fought for the free-
coloreds resisted attempts to bring them back to work. In mid-July 1792
the local commander invited two leaders of bands of armed slaves, Armand
and Martial, to a conference with their masters to work out a return to the
plantations. Martial wore a uniform with epaulets and carried a sword and

a gun to the meeting. Armand, dressed less impressively, sat across the table from his own master, who had owned him for twenty-five years, and who just as the revolution began had promised him his freedom. The two men refused the whites' entreaties to surrender and bring their followers back to the plantations. They left the meeting as they had arrived, as political leaders who no longer felt any allegiance to the men who still technically owned them. A few days later they riposted with their own demands: three free days a week for all slaves, liberty for several hundred leaders, and the abolition of whipping. White authorities refused to negotiate, and Armand and Martial retreated to a mountainous region called the Platons, where they were joined by other bands and new recruits from plantations. Elsewhere in the south, in Port-Salut, one of the leaders of the January 1791 conspiracy, who had managed to escape from prison, led a new slave revolt. The Southern Province, like the north, was gradually being taken over by strong bands of rebel slaves.[16]

The governor, Philibert François Rouxel de Blanchelande, arrived in late July and offered Armand and Martial an amnesty for all their followers who returned to their plantations. Unimpressed, the slaves responded by attacking the plantations around Les Cayes. In the midst of a storm Armand led troops onto his master's plantation and burned it to the ground. The revolt in the north was his model; he told one slave that at Le Cap "the slaves did not leave a single structure standing" and that "the same must happen here."[17]

Blanchelande sent white troops and a regiment of free-coloreds commanded by Rigaud against the insurgents. As the columns marched up into the mountains, they were "assailed from all sides by blacks they could not see," who shot at them and rolled rocks down from above. Two hundred white soldiers were killed and several captured. Blanchelande watched in horror as the head of one of his officers—recognizable from a distance because of his white hair—was lifted on a pike above the insurgent camp. The victorious rebels shouted "Long live the king!" and "Long live Blanchelande!" in order to make the whites think there were "traitors among them." The expedition was an embarrassing and costly failure. "The blacks remained the absolute masters of the Platons."[18]

In the wake of this victory the rebel band sent a new set of demands to Les Cayes: freedom for the all insurgent slaves in the group, and three free days per week for all slaves in the region. In another missive they went further, asking for territorial rights over the Platons. As had been the case in the north, there were tensions within the band itself about the negotiations, and some criticized Armand for trusting Rigaud, who was acting as an intermediary between them and the officials at Les Cayes. The whites balked at any concessions, but when Armand threatened to attack Les Cayes and burn the city down, the Provincial Assembly offered to grant freedom to several hundred slaves.[19]

The freedom papers were signed by Rigaud and the Provincial Assembly, and some slaves were suspicious of their validity because they had not been signed by their masters. Furthermore, freedom was granted only to those who had been armed by free-coloreds, and not to those who had been armed by whites or who had risen up independently. Only a little more than half of the eligible 700 accepted the offer. The others stayed at Platons, trusting their weapons rather than the papers offered to guarantee the freedom they had claimed for themselves. New recruits streamed up toward Platons. Although they lacked weapons, and were forced to fabricate poison arrows and to use pots filled with stones to add to the noise of their attacks, they defended themselves successfully. They were building a new life in the mountains. They had several camps protected by entrenchments built on the edges of cliffs, each with 800 to 900 cabins, as well as hospitals for the sick. The residents called their home the "kingdom of the Platons," and chose a king to govern them. They descended to raid plantations, stealing mules and horses and attacking army camps. In the plain, meanwhile, most slaves "simply stopped working altogether." By late 1792 one-third of the plantations in the south had been burnt, and all of the nearly 100 sugar plantations on the once-thriving Plaine des Cayes had been destroyed or damaged.[20]

To fight the rebels, the government deployed troops recently arrived from France, many of them poor rural men unprepared for the difficulty of the fighting. As one soldier wrote, it was "brigandage" rather than war, for the soldiers "killed without seeing the enemy," who approached them in the bushes "without being seen" until they were in pistol range. The French had some successes against the insurgents, and took brutal revenge when they could. In one engagement in the south near the end of 1792, 100 insurgents were gunned down in a cane field, where the white troops found the dead and the wounded "lying like dogs." "We cut off their heads and ears to bring them back to our camp," announced once soldier. "It was a real joy for us." Another bragged to his girlfriend about the "pleasure" he took in carrying the head of a slave back to his camp. But such victories came at a steep cost. Prone to tropical disease, exhausted during difficult missions against the mountain strongholds, lacking meat and other provisions even when they were in their garrisons because of the destruction on the plain, many died within months. "This is the graveyard of the French," wrote one soldier. "We die here like flies."[21]

In the north the tone of the insurgents was changing. Jean-François and Biassou, who in late 1791 had negotiated for a small number of emancipations and limited reforms in slavery, joined with a young leader named Charles Belair and issued a letter to the Colonial Assembly and the commissioners. The French, they pointed out, had "formally sworn" to follow the Declaration of the Rights of Man. This declaration, they continued, pronounced that "men are born free and equal in rights" and that their "natural rights were liberty, property, security, and resistance to oppression." In resisting slavery, then, the insurgents were clearly "within their rights" as stipulated in the Declaration. Nevertheless, there were French officials who had "crossed the oceans" to combat them. In place of such hypocritical behavior, the insurgents suggested an alternative. They would lay down their arms if two major demands were met: "general liberty for all men retained in slavery" and a "general amnesty for the past." The leaders would then oversee the return of the insurgents to the plantations, where they would go back to work not as slaves but as laborers receiving a yearly salary. With a keen awareness of the political forces that might shape the future of the colony, the insurgent leaders requested that the plan be presented to both the king and the National Assembly and be guaranteed by the Spanish government. Nothing came of this proposal at the time. But it stands as a testament to the expanding goals and ambitions of the insurgents. A year later, in August 1793, another insurgent leader named Jean Guyambois approach Biassou and Jean-François with a more radical plan by which the slaves would be freed and given land ceded by the Spanish.[22]

Over a year after the uprising had started in the northern plain, much of Saint-Domingue was beset by powerful groups of insurgents with no intention of laying down their weapons, and some of their most powerful leaders were calling for freedom for all slaves. The enemy, lamented one planter, was "too numerous" and "their means of defense too great" for them to be defeated. There was, in any case, no victory to be had. "Whichever way things turn out, our ruin is total. If we do not defeat and destroy the rebel slaves, we will all end up being slaughtered by these monsters, and by destroying them we destroy our fortunes. For it is in these slaves that our fortunes exist." Some whites sympathized with the rebels. In early 1793 one resident of the south who had fought the insurgents there wrote to his mother wondering: "Why is the desire to be free seen as a crime? . . . While all of Europe resounds with the cries of liberty and equality, Saint-Domingue rings with the voices of innumerable victims whom one slaughters without pity and who more than anyone have the right to revolt against the hand that crushes them. What a century! What a philosophy!" Others saw hope only in exile. Many, however, were determined to fight, such as the planter who announced to "vile slaves" and "rebels" who had killed many of his friends: "I will follow them coldbloodedly into the grave, and I swear that you will see all my blood flow before I consent to your freedom, because your slavery, my fortune, and my happiness are inseparable." In November 1792 another stated clearly an opinion that would be reiterated by other planters in the next months: "We did not fetch half a million savage slaves off the coast of Africa to bring them to the colony as French citizens." He was wrong. Within the year the "savage slaves" he saw as nothing but property would be just that: citizens.[23]

On September 17, 1792, the ship *America* arrived in the port of Le Cap. On board were the three commissioners sent by the National Assembly to govern Saint-Domingue: Léger Félicité Sonthonax, Etienne Polverel, and Jean Antoine Ailhaud. Sonthonax and Polverel (having been abandoned by Ailhaud soon after their arrival) would oversee a dramatic transformation in the colony. Both had spoken out against slavery in previous years and were bearers of a radical republicanism that was increasingly taking hold in France. Their actions in Saint-Domingue would show a remarkable courage and commitment to those radical ideals. But the transformation they oversaw in the colony was determined less by what they brought from Europe than by their encounter with the power and political vision of the slave insurgents who had begun their war for freedom in 1791.[24]

It was the first time that either man had set foot in Saint-Domingue. Sonthonax came from a provincial family, wealthy though not aristocratic, and in the 1780s had studied law at the University of Dijon. He then moved to Paris, where he worked—as Moreau de St. Méry had a few years before him—as a lawyer at the Paris Parlement. Polverel also came from the provinces, from an aristocratic family, and was also trained in law. He was a freemason, and in the decades before the Revolution was a member of a Bordeaux lodge whose members included several free-coloreds from

Saint-Domingue. Although neither joined the Société des Amis des Noirs, they were familiar with the antislavery thought of the Enlightenment. After 1789 both wrote for some of the new newspapers that sprang up to chronicle and propel the French Revolution. In 1789 Polverel wrote that "nature has made men for liberty, for equality, and for society. No man was given by nature the right to command other men or to sell them." The next year Sonthonax penned a remarkable prophesy in the newspaper *Révolutions de Paris:* "Yes, we dare to predict with confidence that the day will come—and the day is not too far off—when you will see a curly-haired African, relying only on his virtue and good sense, coming to participate in the legislative process in the midst of our national assemblies."[25]

It was their encounter with the prominent abolitionist Jacques Brissot de Warville that set them on their road to Saint-Domingue. Brissot acted as a patron to both Sonthonax and Polverel in the Paris Jacobin Club, where the two men gained experience dealing with colonial matters. In 1791 Polverel led a move to expel several members of the Club Massiac from the Jacobin Club, asserting through his actions that there was no place for proslavery views in his revolution. The next year Sonthonax sat on a committee that issued a letter on behalf of the Jacobin Club supporting the May 15, 1791, decree granting political rights to some free-colored men.[26]

When, in March and April 1792, Brissot and his allies gained control over colonial policy and pushed through the April 4 decree granting political rights to all free-coloreds, they turned to Sonthonax and Polverel. The task of applying this decree in the colonies, as Brissot well knew, would be a difficult one, and would require more firmness and ruthlessness than the previous metropolitan representatives in Saint-Domingue had mustered. Confident in their principles, Brissot supported the candidacy of Sonthonax and Polverel to the position of commissioners for Saint-Domingue. (He also supported the candidacy of Julien Raimond, but the planters in the National Assembly successfully blocked this nomination.) So it was that two provincial lawyers turned revolutionary journalists, neither of whom had any experience in the Caribbean, were handed the fate of what had until recently been the most profitable colony in the world.[27]

Sonthonax and Polverel left the French port of Rochefort in late July 1792. According to their orders from the government, the commissioners had the power to suspend or dissolve the existing colonial assemblies and to take "all measures necessary" to apply the April 4 decree. They were accompanied by 6,000 troops and a printing press. Also on board was the new governor-general of Saint-Domingue, Desparbès, who was supposed to take control of military matters in the colony. As had often been the case in the Old Regime, the division of power created problems. The commissioners and governor clashed as they crossed the Atlantic, and within a few months of their arrival in Saint-Domingue Sonthonax and Polverel deposed Desparbès.[28]

Predictably, the appointment of Sonthonax and Polverel was contested by the planters in Paris. Unable to stop the departure of the new commissioners, the planters did what they could to make their landing difficult. One planter wrote in colorfully alarmist terms to the Colonial Assembly about "secret" plans they were carrying from the National Assembly for the "general emancipation" of the slaves. Their convoy, he claimed, was carrying 20,000 rifles with which to arm the slaves, who, once they had been freed, were to be turned against all "the foreign colonies" in order to carry "revolt, and then independence, throughout the New World." The commissioners he added, loved only the blacks and would attack all the whites and free-coloreds "without distinction." He called on the people of Saint-Domingue to reject the "those tigers thirsty for blood" and to suffocate their "barbarous projects."[29]

On their arrival in Saint-Domingue the commissioners did what they could to dispel such fears, announcing clearly that they had come to grant political rights to free-coloreds in order to salvage slavery, not destroy it. Sonthonax declared that the colonial assemblies were the only bodies with "the right to rule on the lot of the slaves" and that slavery was "necessary to the cultivation and prosperity of the colonies." It was neither his nor the National Assembly's intention to attack the rights of the planters in this regard. (Several months later, in a private letter to Brissot, Sonthonax noted his opposition to any sudden emancipation, which would "undoubtedly lead to the massacre of all the whites.") The commissioners also made clear, however, that they would no longer tolerate racial prejudice. "Henceforth," announced Sonthonax, "we recognize only two classes of men in the French part of Saint Domingue: free men without any distinction of color, and slaves." They were ready to use the extensive powers they had been granted to confront any "defiance" by the colony's residents.[30]

There was enough defiance to go around. An increasing number of white planters, wary of the radicalization of the Revolution, were joining the royalist opposition that existed throughout France. They shared with it many general concerns, but they also had a particular worry: many believed that "having proclaimed equality" the French National Convention would soon "proclaim general emancipation." Rejecting republicanism and embracing the white flag of the royalists would not only strike a blow for the king but might also save slavery in the colony. Planters with royalist sympathies could look to the examples of Martinique and Guadeloupe, where in late 1792 white planters had successfully expelled Republican administrators.[31]

Sonthonax and Polverel might have expected to find a supportive counterweight to the royalists among poorer, pro-Republican whites. Some residents did support their regime: "Things are better now that the commissioners are here," one would write in mid-1793. But many who were partisans of revolutionary change tended to support autonomy for Saint-Domingue, and were often as hostile to the threat of a "tyrannical" metropolitan authority as planters were. Furthermore, despite the various official attempts to encourage cooperation between whites and free-coloreds, racial conflict continued to polarize the colony. Just before the commissioners arrived, fighting between whites and free-coloreds in Le Cap had left several dead. And wealthy planters such as de Jumecourt and the marquis de Rouvray, who had led the move for reconciliation with free-coloreds, were already firmly anti-Republican, and indeed would soon turn to enemy powers. As the commissioners quickly came to understand, they were to find little support anywhere among the white population.[32]

In October 1792 startling news arrived in the colony: an August uprising in Paris had led to the suspension of the king by the National Assembly. A new assembly, based on universal manhood suffrage, was to be elected: the National Convention. France had become a republic. Many were violently opposed to this change, both inside and outside France. For the more radical leaders of the Revolution, notably those concentrated in the Jacobin Club, it was vital to defend the fledgling republic by any means necessary. With enemies rallying at the borders—the threat of war with all the kings of Europe was looming on the horizon—internal dissent was branded as treason and repressed with increasing violence. Power was increasingly concentrated in the hands of a few powerful leaders in the National Convention's committees, such as the Committee of Public Safety. Sonthonax and Polverel received expanded powers: they could suspend all administrators and officers who were disloyal enough to oppose them.[33]

Over the next months the two commissioners eliminated most of their enemies and consolidated their political power. Having expelled Desparbès, they replaced him with General Donatien Marie Joseph de Rochambeau, who had been sent to Martinique as the new governor but, because of the royalist takeover there, had been forced to continue on to Saint-Domingue. The commissioners disbanded all existing assemblies in the colony, including the Colonial Assembly, announcing they would be replaced with new ones elected by both whites and free-coloreds. In fact, though, there were not to be new elections in Saint-Domingue—not yet. Instead, Sonthonax and Polverel replaced the assembly with an "Intermediary Commission." Six of its members were chosen by the outgoing Colonial Assembly, who selected six whites. The other six were to be chosen by the commissioners, who selected six free men of color, including Pierre Pinchinat. The racially integrated commission—the first of its kind in the colony—was a powerful symbol of what the commissioners hoped to achieve. But it had little power—or will—to oppose the Republican commissioners who had formed it.[34]

In late October the three commissioners split up, with Polverel and Ailhaud leaving to assume governance in the west and south. Ailhaud took advantage of the move to escape from Saint-Domingue, leaving Polverel in charge of both regions. Sonthonax, more strident and combative than Polverel, was soon embroiled in conflict in Le Cap. When a group of whites broke into a prison and massacred whites and slave insurgents locked up there, he blamed the attack on a political group in Le Cap and disbanded it. When Polverel criticized his actions, Sonthonax retorted: "You accuse me of having violated in this the rights of man and citizen, as if the rights of men could be claimed in a land of slavery."[35]

Sonthonax struck out against the racial segregation in the army. With the support of Rochambeau and another officer, Etienne Laveaux, he placed at least one officer of color in each of the army units stationed in the town. The local Regiment du Cap, however, boldly refused to accept any such officers. Sonthonax commanded that they assemble, along with other units, on the town plaza to take an oath declaring they would obey the April 4 decree. The troops assembled, but, as several hundred free-coloreds led by Pierre Pinchinat watched, they refused to take the oath. Soon afterward Sonthonax announced that he would deport the entire regiment. The city erupted: as rumors spread that the free-coloreds were planning to massacre the whites, the Regiment du Cap took over the arsenal and attacked free-colored troops, who retreated to the edge of the town. But Sonthonax, aided by Rochambeau and Laveaux, rallied the loyal white troops, turned the tables on the rebels, and managed to arrest several of them and take back control of the town. The free-colored troops, led by Pinchinat, marched back triumphantly. A few weeks later Sonthonax created several new regiments of free men of color in Le Cap. He had survived a violent challenge to his authority. It would not be the last such challenge; and the next time, Sonthonax would take more dramatic measures to ensure his survival.[36]

From outside Le Cap, bands of slave insurgents were watching. Although the April 4 decree was passed with the explicit intention of defeating the slave uprising, the commissioners had made little progress in doing so in the months after they arrived. Many of the French troops that accompanied them succumbed to disease; by one account half of them died within two months. In late October and early November 1792 a large and well-armed expedition led by Rochambeau flushed insurgent bands out of the northern plain and captured their stronghold at Ouanaminthe, along the border with Santo Domingo. But most of the insurgents simply retreated into the mountains, and in the end the mission did little but "inflame the pride of the enemy," who had realized that they could survive even when an impressive army was sent against them. The rebels remained "masters of the mountains, from which they could, at will, bring fire and iron to the plains." With the majority of troops back in Le Cap, the insurgents advanced across the plain again, and by December some bands were once more camped close to the town.[37]

After Rochambeau left to take up his post in Martinique, now back in the hands of the Republicans, the task of fighting the insurgents fell to Etienne Laveaux. The tide of the war began to change under his command. In mid-January Laveaux unleashed a well-coordinated attack against the insurgents on the northern plain. His soldiers charged Biassou's troops, gathered in the town of Milot on the southern edge of the plain. They took refuge in a fort in the hills nearby, and Biassou led the defense courageously, marching around on the ramparts in view of the French attackers. But Laveaux's troops took a hill above the fort, and after a unit of free-coloreds scaled the walls, the insurgents retreated into the mountains.[38]

In early February Sonthonax wrote that Laveaux had "performed miracles." A song published in a newspaper promised the women of the colony that their "lovers would defend them" and soon they would no longer hear the drums of war. During February the residents of Le Cap could read many accounts of victories over the insurgents. Several strongholds around Grande-Rivière, in the center of the northern plain, had been destroyed. Attacked at night by "brigands" who came on with an "incredible ferocity," one unit nevertheless pushed the insurgents back and killed five of their "chiefs." Soon afterward the commander of this unit, General Desfourneaux, captured an insurgent camp near Sainte-Suzanne and killed several of the "most feared chiefs." He had burned everything he found to the ground, as he did in another nearby camp, destroying several hundred *ajoupas*—huts—built by the insurgents. Their blood, he wrote, was so thick after the battle that it covered the soles of his boots. He was fighting a war against the land as well, uprooting provisions and cutting down banana trees. Doing so, he declared, would hurt the insurgents "more than our guns." Elsewhere free-colored troops carried out nighttime attacks on camps built by slaves who had left their plantations. They shot those who tried to escape. Many frightened slaves, the newspaper declared, were returning to their masters. And there was reportedly disarray in the insurgent camps, with Jean-François and Biassou no longer coordinating their attacks. Jean-François narrowly escaped capture several times. Sonthonax declared that victory was near: the insurgent slaves, "those miserable valets," appropriate soldiers for "royalism and its agents," would soon suffer the fate of their "wicked protectors."[39]

There were victories in the south as well. In early January Polverel sent a new expedition against the "kingdom of the Platons." The insurgents fought back once again, setting up ambushes against the approaching troops. They were short on ammunition, however, and as the columns approached, Armand and Martial decided to evacuate their camps for higher ground. Several hundred residents in the camp, "mostly women, children, the aged and the sick," stayed behind, as had been the case at Gallifet in late 1791. They were too tired or weak to run, and perhaps ready to go back to the plantations. They weren't given the chance. The attacking troops massacred everyone they found at Platons and destroyed the insurgent town. The attack was celebrated as a "tremendous victory."[40]

The success of the mission against Platons depended on the service of several hundred slaves led by a charismatic leader named Jean Kina, a slave who had made a name for himself serving whites against the free-coloreds starting in early 1792. Kina's ragged, barefoot soldiers—who were later described as attacking to the sound of African music—played a crucial role in shoring up slavery in the Southern Province. Kina himself, ultimately freed for his services, remained loyal to the whites, going on to serve the British when they invaded the colony. The whites in the south also had the support of a Mandingo slave named Coacou. According to one French soldier, Coacou had "given himself the title of general" and wore a French general's uniform. (The unanswered question of where he had got it should probably have suggested the need for some suspicion about where his loyalty ultimately lay.) His hat and his swordbelt were decorated with the red, white, and blue of the Republic. Coacou carried out nighttime attacks against insurgent camps, and sometimes captured, tortured, and killed rebels who were raiding plantations. In the north, too, slaves played a crucial role in attacks against insurgent camps. One group of soldiers noted the crucial role played in a recent victory by slave recruits who "seconded us" in pursuing "the enemies of our species, and not of theirs," suggesting that they deserved to be rewarded.[41]

Even with such allies, the victories against the insurgents were only partial. Attacked in one area of the plains, insurgents spread out as they retreated, "burning and bringing terror" to surviving plantations. Insurgents frequently retreated before they could be captured or massacred, creating new camps higher in the mountains, which became the "boulevards of liberty." Although French officers continually declared they had killed several "important chiefs," there always seemed to be others to take the place of the dead. In fact, despite the campaigns against them, the insurgents operated with impunity in many parts of the colony. One frustrated writer in the town of Limonade saw several hundred members of an insurgent camp under the command of the leader Sans-Souci unworriedly gathering salt along the coast near the town. It was vital, he insisted, to deprive them of this "necessity," and also to prevent them from communicating and trading with the canoes that met them along the coast. The insurgents had developed networks of communication that stretched across the colony and beyond. The general Joseph, forced to retreat from his camp in February 1793, left behind letters sent to him by an insurgent chief in another part of Saint-Domingue, as well as one sent to him from a correspondent in Philadelphia. Indeed the currents of communication among slave communities in the Americas buzzed with news of the uprising in Saint-Domingue.[42]

Free-colored recruits to the French side played an important role in the campaigns against the insurgents. But there were still never enough of such troops to assure a final victory. General Desfourneaux criticized local whites who were shirking their duty to fight the insurgents. Many residents were, understandably, doing their best to stay away from fields of battle. The Intermediary Commission proclaimed in early March that many inhabitants of the northern plain had retreated to Le Cap, where they were "vegetating with an insouciance that was as revolting as it was unacceptable, safe from the fatigues and dangers of the war," and ordered that they all report to military duty in their rural parishes. But many whites flouted such orders, leaving many areas depopulated and essentially in the hands of the insurgents.[43]

Some whites sold their belongings and left the colony, harboring little hope for the return of peace and prosperity. A newspaper advertisement offered a coffee plantation several miles from Le Cap for sale, seeking to make the best of a relatively unattractive proposition: all the buildings had been destroyed, although a few walls were still standing; of the forty-eight "heads of negroes" that were to be included in the sale, thirty were off fighting the insurgents; the remaining slaves, including seven that were "lost with the brigands," would be included on the off chance they ever returned. Some planters, having lost their workforce, sought to rent gangs of slaves for the time it took to complete the harvests on their plantations. One wanted ten to twelve slaves to bring to a region "that had not been burnt," while another was seeking twenty to twenty-five slaves to harvest coffee for a few months. One desperate planter who had "armed the few negro males who had not joined the brigands" to defend his property, only to have most of these recruited for missions against the insurgents, offered money to any men who were willing to go back to his plantation with him.[44]

In the meantime, in Le Cap there were still simple pleasures to be had, such as a crate of 1788 Médoc, as well as some Bordeaux, recently arrived from France. One merchant offered a locally made chocolate made of pure cocoa that he claimed was superior to chocolate that arrived from France, which was "falsified" with nuts and therefore prone to infestation by worms. There were unexpected dangers, too. One writer wrote indignantly that each Sunday, citizens of Le Cap were beaten up by drunken North American soldiers from the merchant boats that were regularly anchoring in the harbor. For those who were not tired of hearing about—and fearing—the slave insurrection, there was literature to be purchased:

Gros's account of his time as a prisoner among the insurgents in 1791 went into its second printing.[45]

In the midst of war and revolution, society was being transformed. The historian Thomas Madiou noted that by 1792 in the Southern Province, "everything was changed: habits, customs, many new words in the language." Relationships between slaves and masters were being reshaped. One "free black" slave owner had read the Declaration of the Rights of Man to his slaves—a crime for which he was imprisoned in Le Cap until the commissioners Sonthonax and Polverel released him. There were new ways of speaking about race and community. A man named Laurent Jolicoeur presented a petition to the administration in Saint-Marc, introducing himself as "formerly described as a *citoyen de couleur*," but emphasizing the inappropriateness of the term by noting that he was in fact "as black as the white is white." He was seeking freedom for one of his slaves, Zaïre, a woman of the Ibo nation, asking the administrators for "your benevolence, or rather your justice," in taking her "out of captivity." "Zaïre is no common subject," Jolicoeur wrote, "and if she were not in servitude, she could rival any *citoyenne* with the elevation of her sentiments." Because of this, however, her state made her deeply miserable, and, "especially since the Revolution," she was inconsolable. She was the mother of three children "of her color," a fact that proved not only her "wisdom" but also her "virtue." "What *citoyenne* can claim to have, as she has, accepted only the caresses of those similar to her?" Jolicoeur powerfully reversed the common hierarchy of racial terms by calling himself "black" and dismissing the term *citoyen de couleur*. And he based the claim that Zaïre was qualified for freedom by highlighting her refusal to participate in interracial sex, which he presented as ubiquitous in the old world of the colony. Her loyalty to her race became proof of her "wisdom" and "virtue."[46]

Meanwhile, in March 1793 a boat called *La Nouvelle-Société* came to anchor in the harbor of Le Cap. Outfitted in Nantes, it had just made the crossing from the Zaire River, on the "Angola coast," and had a "beautiful" cargo of 331 slaves for sale. Slave imports into Saint-Domingue had dropped dramatically since their peak of nearly 50,000 in 1790; fewer than 10,000 were brought in by French slavers during the course of 1792. Yet even with many of its cane fields turned to ash, there were still African men and women being brought to the colony in chains.[47]

CHAPTER SEVEN

Liberty's Land

I
N EARLY 1793 a new war came to Saint-Domingue: an imperial war.
In January Louis XVI was executed in Paris, and the next month the
monarchies of Spain and Britain declared war against France, joining
Austria, which had done so the year before. All the Republic's borders
were now battlefields. It was a new kind of war, for the outnumbered
French government responded with a mass mobilization of soldiers. It was
also an Atlantic war, for soon the Caribbean was swept up in the battle over
the fate of the Republic.

Though wounded by slave insurrection and internal warfare, Saint-
Domingue remained an extremely valuable colony. But given the difficulties of colonial warfare and the susceptibility to disease of European
troops, both Spanish and English military leaders understood that the
best way—perhaps the only way—to conquer Saint-Domingue was to
take advantage of the internal dissension there and to rally part of the population to their side. They hoped to "gain an enormous prize at relatively
little cost." In another island, or at another time, this objective would have
involved inviting the white planters into alliance. But in Saint-Domingue
in 1793, power was fragmented, and the slave insurgents, as well as the
armed free-coloreds, were just as important as potential allies as the divided white population. Indeed, "as soon as war was declared, all parties
immediately looked to the slaves for assistance."[1]

For the Spanish, the war presented an opportunity to regain the colony
they had lost a century before. Since 1791, Spanish residents and officers
along the border had been in consistent if informal contact with the slave
insurgents under the command of Jean-François and Biassou. After war

was declared in 1793, officials in Madrid ordered the governors of Spanish Santo Domingo to recruit slave insurgents as "auxiliary troops," offering them freedom and land in return for military service. Although there was a long tradition of arming slaves in the Spanish Americas, this decision was a "daring experiment." Rather than inviting the enslaved to serve for liberty, the Spanish were calling on "people who had effectively already freed themselves." These were experienced and independent bands of fighters, and they would prove difficult to control and dominate once they had been recruited. Still, the policy was initially a success. By May and June 1793 Jean-François and Biassou had brought upward of 10,000 soldiers to the Spanish side. The Spanish were able to keep their own troops in reserve, stationing them for the most part along the border, while their "auxiliaries" did the fighting for them. Meanwhile Spanish aid breathed new life into the insurgent army, helping it to recover from the losses suffered during the previous months.[2]

The British cultivated other allies. Since 1791, white planters had made several overtures to the British government, and some had aired the possibility of handing the colony to an imperial power whose commitment to maintaining slavery seemed much stronger than that of the French Republic. The outbreak of war provided an opportunity to concretize these plans. In late February 1793 a group of French planters in London drew up a detailed proposal offering to transfer their allegiance to the British government in return for protection and a suspension of debts. In the Caribbean, meanwhile, exiled French planters in Jamaica, as well as those chafing under the commissioners' rule in Saint-Domingue, talked of calling in the British. Many planters were shocked by the execution of the king, and in early 1793 a group of refugees in Jamaica publicly burned tricolor symbols and effigies of Republican leaders. It seemed to many that the French Republic, besieged by the great powers of Europe, was doomed, and that therefore British control would be temporary, with the colony returned to France once the monarchy was restored there. But what truly tipped the balance in favor of British intervention for many planters was the fear of slave liberation. Having experienced, often firsthand, the violence of slave revolt and the disintegration of slave discipline in general, frustrated by the commissioners' autocratic ways and their close ties to free people of color, and most of all deeply suspicious of them and worried that slave emancipation would soon be decreed, many white planters saw British occupation as the only hope to preserve a world they once had mastered. Once the war had begun, the British decided to take advantage of the invitation issued to them by many French planters.[3]

Turning to the enemy was a reasonable and a pragmatic choice for the planters. In the end, however, instead of saving slavery, it created the conditions for its final destruction. In making themselves traitors to the Republic, they opened the way for slaves to become citizens and defenders of France. The planters pushed the beleaguered Republican commissioners to find new allies. Like the Spanish, the French turned to the rebel slaves. In February 1793 the colonial minister suggested to Sonthonax that he offer freedom to those insurgents who would fight for France. The commissioners did so, organizing slaves who had been mobilized by whites in the Western and Southern Provinces into "Legions of Equality," but at first they had little success recruiting allies from among the insurgents in the north. Eventually, however, the Republic outdid its enemies, destroying the foundations of the old Saint-Domingue in order to save the colony for France.[4]

The "slaves of the New World," Sonthonax wrote in a private letter in February 1793, were "fighting for the same cause as the French armies." If only the National Convention would "do something for the slaves," they would stop fighting for the king and join the Republic. France would gain new and valuable allies if its leaders were courageous enough to admit that they and the insurgent slaves were fighting a common struggle against tyranny. In an official letter to the Convention, Sonthonax made the same point, though more cautiously, arguing that it was "essential" that it "hasten to fix the lot of the slaves" without waiting for the colonial assemblies in Saint-Domingue. The colony, he insisted, might be lost to France if the Convention did not act quickly. Preoccupied with war and sedition in France, however, the Convention provided no response, and no new instructions or reforms. Even if it had, they probably would not have arrived for some time: the war brought communication across the Atlantic to a near standstill. The commissioners were, as Sonthonax wrote, "the lost sentinels of the Republic." And they were leading it toward its most radical act.[5]

In early May Sonthonax and Polverel issued a proclamation regarding the treatment of slaves. It was essentially a reiteration of the royal edict of 1784, which had never been applied in the colony because of planter opposition. It protected the slaves from being forced to work on Sundays and provided for shorter working hours for pregnant and nursing women. Perhaps most importantly—and most infuriatingly to the planters—it invited slaves to bring complaints against their masters and managers to the attention of local officials. Especially when those local officials were part of Sonthonax's regime, planters could expect that—as had never really been the case before—slave complaints might be taken seriously and lead to punishments for violent planters. Indeed, a petition presented several months later on behalf of the slaves of Saint-Domingue complimented Sonthonax for having, with this decree, "much diminished the rights our former masters pretended to have over us." The regulations still clearly were meant to enforce slavery. Up to fifty lashes of the whip were allowed to punish slaves; maroons were still to be punished by being branded (though no longer, presumably, with a fleur-de-lis) and having their ears sliced off. But they also included some articles aimed at encouraging insurgents to return to their plantations, promising amnesty to those who left their camps. To make sure slaves understood their new rights and responsibilities, the proclamation was to be translated into Creole, displayed in a central spot on each plantation, and read aloud to the assembled slaves.[6]

About the time that these new regulations were issued, a new governor, François-Thomas Galbaud du Fort, arrived in Saint-Domingue. Born in Port-au-Prince, he owned property in Saint-Domingue. When Galbaud arrived in Le Cap, Sonthonax was in Port-au-Prince with Polverel. Galbaud installed himself as governor and named his brother, Cézar—who had been living in Saint-Domingue and was quite hostile to the commissioners—to second him. There was a great deal of discontent against the commissioners in Le Cap, and Galbaud got an earful. One planter named Tanguy de la Boissière, who had advocated autonomy in 1789 and been active as a journalist and publisher in the colony since then—and had recently been sniping at the commissioners in Le Cap's papers—sought to convince Galbaud to strike out against Sonthonax. He attacked the recent decree on the management of the plantations, reiterating the old argument that it was "absolutely against the spirit of slavery for an intermediary authority to place itself between master and slave." The new proclamation proved either the "delirium" of the commissioners or their firm commitment to complete the "disorganization of Saint-Domingue." Resistance was necessary, as it had been in the 1780s. Now the situation was more dangerous and called for more dramatic action. The commissioners were on the verge of making "all the rebel negroes" into "free soldiers" to fight the "miserable whites." Galbaud was the only one who could prevent all the whites from being massacred.[7]

In Port-au-Prince Sonthonax and Polverel heard the news of Galbaud's arrival. They also heard that he had openly claimed that they had been acting "like dictators," and that he was hostile to free people of color, whom he called "mulattoes." They were certainly disturbed by the simple fact that Galbaud had established himself as a competing power, and saw clearly that he would become a rallying point for their enemies. The conflict between the governor and the commissioners was a replay of the competition between governors and intendants that had long been a feature of the administration of Saint-Domingue. But now, in the midst of war and revolution, with the commissioners involved in a reform of slavery, the stakes of the conflict were higher than ever.[8]

Polverel and Sonthonax returned to Le Cap "in a very bad mood." There they received a joyous greeting from many free-coloreds but an "icy" response from many whites. The relationship between the commissioners and Galbaud immediately degenerated into open hostility. According to one account, when Galbaud complained to Sonthonax about his actions against whites in the town, the commissioner responded, "Understand, citizen, that the only thing white about me is my skin." Galbaud retorted that he had heard that Sonthonax had a "black soul" but was surprised that he admitted it so readily. The perhaps apocryphal story of the exchange played on the two meanings of "black," suggesting Sonthonax as both evil and a friend of the slaves and enemy of the whites. Another account described how the commissioners turned down Galbaud's invitation to a banquet, prompting the jilted governor to entertain the guests who did show up by attacking Sonthonax and Polverel. His wife declared that they should "flee this land of blood" for Paris, where they would gather forces to return to the colony to punish the commissioners and "avenge the whites for the atrocities committed against them." Convinced that Galbaud was spreading sedition, Sonthonax and Polverel arrested and imprisoned the governor.[9]

Imprisoned on a ship in the harbor of Le Cap, Galbaud found himself surrounded by friends. In addition to prisoners locked up by the commissioners (among them de la Boissière), many of the sailors on the ships were hostile to the Republican commissioners. Galbaud, with the help of "a few eloquent men," launched an audacious plan: seconded by the sailors, he would lead an attack on Le Cap and depose the commissioners. Several thousand strong, Galbaud's supporters stormed the town on the afternoon of June 20. Sonthonax and Polverel escaped capture thanks to the protection of a troop led by the African-born officer Jean-Baptiste Belley, and many soldiers fought back against Galbaud. After several hours the town's assailants were forced to retreat to their ships. But the next morning they came on again with more success. They captured the arsenal of Le Cap after the white commander of the detachment guarding it ordered his troops (most of them free-coloreds) not to fire against his "brothers." The outnumbered commissioners fled to the outskirts of the city to a camp on the Bréda plantation that had been set up to defend Le Cap against slave insurgents.[10]

As Galbaud's followers spread out through Le Cap there was chaos in the city. The prisons were opened, releasing hundreds of slaves "captured in the battles against the insurgents." Many of these freed prisoners, along with other slaves in Le Cap, managed to obtain rifles and other weapons—according to one account, free-coloreds distributed weapons to domestics from stashes in their houses, while many later accused the commissioners of having ordered the distribution of guns to the urban slaves—and some began fighting Galbaud's troops. Random killing, looting, and fires soon followed. The question of who started the fires would animate colonial polemics for years to come. Republicans blamed the unruly sailors who made up Galbaud's troops, while accounts written by whites who fled Le Cap described rampant pillaging and arson by slaves. Some claimed that the destruction was part of a sinister plot carried out under the direct orders of Sonthonax and Polverel.[11]

As they watched the town burn, Sonthonax and Polverel made a bold declaration aimed at recapturing it. It was "the will of the French Republic and of its delegates," they announced, to grant freedom to all "black warriors" who would "fight for the Republic." Any slave who took up arms in their defense would become "equal to all free men" and receive "all the rights belonging to French citizens." They sent officers out to invite any slaves who wanted freedom to join them. Enemies of the commissioners would later declare that beneath the offer of freedom and citizenship was a more sinister invitation: the new recruits were won over with an offer of booty from the town. Whether responding to the promise of liberty or loot

"Incendie du Cap Français." This engraving depicts the burning of the town in late June 1793 during the battle between Galbaud and the commissioners Sonthonax and Polverel. *Courtesy of the Bibliothèque Nationale de France.*

or both, a band of insurgents several thousand strong under the command of Pierrot, who had been camped in the hills above Le Cap close to the Bréda plantation, stormed into the burning town.[12]

One merchant noted with disgust that the commissioners had rewarded "men who for two years had been fighting for their Papa King" while threatening the lives of those whites who had been defending the "interests of the mother country." But the commissioners' invitation won new and daunting allies for the Republic. In their official account of the event to the National Convention, they described how groups of insurgents—some of whom had already abandoned their "royal symbols" for those of the Republic—had presented themselves and asked to serve "the nation against kings." "We promised them liberty in the name of the Republic, and declared that all those who took up arms for her would become the equals of their former masters." Some still carried Spanish flags or the white banners of the French royalists, but when the commissioners explained that it was kings who "made people slaves," they threw them down and took up the flag of the Republic. Mixed together with free men of color and white troops who had remained loyal, they formed a remarkably integrated army unit: former slaves, free-coloreds, and whites, united in the service of the Republic.[13]

The descent of these new recruits into the town turned the tide of the battle. Outnumbered, Galbaud's followers retreated to their ships. As the Republic's new allies spread through the city, looting and burning continued. Some whites were stopped in the streets and detained by bands of free-coloreds and armed slaves. Many fearful residents scrambled aboard ships, carrying whatever they could. When the ships weighed anchor and sailed away, heading for the United States, they were carrying thousands of white refugees, along with many of their slaves. They would settle in towns like Philadelphia and Charleston, and many would never return to Saint-Domingue.[14]

Within a few days Sonthonax and Polverel returned to the smoldering city. Together with their old allies—including the free-colored officer Jean-Louis Villatte, who played a crucial role in restoring order to Le Cap—they had a new army of black Republicans behind them. They named Pierrot a general. Born in Africa, a survivor of Saint-Domingue's slavery, the elderly Pierrot had since 1791 become the trusted and respected leader of a band of insurgents camped near Le Cap. Now he was no longer fighting the French for freedom. He and his followers were free men and citizens, and he was an officer in the army of the Republic.[15]

"It is the kings who want slaves," announced Polverel and Sonthonax. "It is the kings of Guinea who sell them to the white kings." "The French nation," in contrast, "was committed to shattering "all chains." Calling on all the slave insurgents to follow the example of Pierrot and come to the Republican side, the commissioners criticized the "unworthy chiefs" who were still fighting for the Spanish. These leaders, they claimed, were themselves slave traders, capturing children in Saint-Domingue and selling them to the Spanish. (Contemporary reports do indeed suggest that Biassou, as well as Jean-François, sold women, children, and some men described as "troublemakers" as slaves for their own profit.) The choice was clear: the Republic was for freedom, its enemies devoted to tyranny and slavery.[16]

The commissioners sent a letter to Biassou promising him and his band freedom—as well as improvements for plantation slaves—if he would change sides. Along with the letter they sent an envoy, one of Pierrot's lieutenants, the Kongolese-born Macaya, to convince Biassou and Jean-François to join the French. The rebel leaders responded with a proud statement of their loyalty to the king of Spain and to all kings. Kings had ruled since the "beginning of the world," and if the king of France had been "lost," the king of Spain remained, and had given them his protection. The authority of the Republican commissioners would mean nothing until there was again a king on the throne behind them. Jean-François and Biassou not only rejected the entreaty but also recruited Macaya back to their side. The next month he himself issued a powerful rejection of the commissioners' entreaties: "I am the subject of three kings: of the king of Congo, master of all the blacks; of the King of France, who represents my father; of the king of Spain, who represents my mother," he announced. Invoking the biblical magi, he wrote: "These three kings are the descendants of those who, led by a star, came to adore God made man." If he "went over to the Republic," he concluded, he might be "forced to make war against my brothers, the subjects of these three kings to whom I have promised loyalty."[17]

Jean-François and Biassou launched a new round of attacks and, aided by other defections among the troops fighting the Republic, made significant advances across the northern plain. While Polverel left for Port-au-Prince to oversee the defense against the Spanish in the Western Province, Sonthonax stayed in Le Cap and tried to gain more supporters for the Republic. It was, he declared in early July, "with the natives of this country, that is, the Africans, that we will save Saint-Domingue for France." But the liberty Sonthonax was offering the "Africans" in return for military service was nothing more than what the Spanish had been offering for several months, and there were few new converts. On July 11 Sonthonax sought to make service in the Republic more enticing by declaring that, in addition to those who joined the Republic, their current—and future—families would be freed.[18]

Polverel extended the commissioners' offer of freedom to the west and south. Working with André Rigaud, he sent envoys into the mountains of Les Cayes, where the survivors of the "kingdom of the Platons" were gathered, to invite them to join the Republican army. Those who agreed would, along with their families, be granted freedom. They would have the responsibility of overseeing the return of other slaves to their plantations. This time, most of them accepted the terms. The main insurgent leaders, notably Armand and Martial, became captains of companies in the newly formed Republican legions.[19]

Many rebels remained aloof, however. The commissioners, desperate to gain the allegiance of the mass of the insurgents, understood that they had to offer more. As early as July they had warned a free-colored commander in the north that if the members of his class resisted their gradual preparation of "an emancipation that is now inevitable," it would happen "all at once" through "insurrection and conquest." They challenged the free-coloreds to embrace a "pure republicanism," reminding them that equality was not "the only principle," and that liberty preceded it. This letter, according to one contemporary, proved that the commissioners already saw "the torrent that would carry everything away." In fact, though, it suggests the opposite. They imagined, as did abolitionists in France, that it would be possible to oversee a gradual emancipation that would not "hurt cultivation." Soon, however, they would be decreeing a very different kind of emancipation, seeking to channel and contain a torrent they could not control.[20]

At the end of August Polverel issued a proclamation acknowledging the crucial role that "warriors"—slaves turned Republican soldiers—were playing in defending the colony. "Those who own nothing," however, should not have to "sacrifice their lives for the defense of the property of others." The "warriors" deserved more than freedom. They deserved land. Following the policies of the French revolutionary government, Polverel had already decreed that the property of those who had "abandoned or betrayed" Saint-Domingue would be confiscated by the state. In his August proclamation Polverel announced that he would distribute this state-owned land "among the good and loyal Republicans"—whether "insurgent Africans" or Spanish defectors—who fought "for the defense of the colony." He hoped his call would encourage all to rally around France and go on the offensive against Santo Domingo, so that the Republic on the island "would have no limits but the ocean."[21]

Polverel explained that loyal "cultivators"—that is, the plantation slaves—also deserved rewards. While those whose masters were still in the colony would remain slaves, those whose masters had fled, but who nevertheless had continued to work on their plantations, were declared free. Since those who worked the land were "first to whom nature had destined its fruits," they would also be granted the "right of property" and receive a portion of their master's plantation. The offer of land was extended to other groups: those who had fled their plantations because of the "cruelty of their masters" or through the encouragement of the "chiefs of the revolt," but were tired of "their life of vagrancy"; those who were "already enjoying independence" in the mountains under Spanish control, but wished to return and "cultivate a happy and fertile land and live under the laws of equality." In addition to land and freedom, "all Africans and descendants of Africans" who fell within these categories would enjoy all the rights of "French citizens."[22]

Polverel's proclamation provided no details about how and when land would be distributed. The plantations belonged "in common" to the "universality" of the "warriors" and eligible "cultivators," but as long as the war continued they would remain "undivided." They would be broken up only once victory was assured. In the meantime, everything produced on the Republic's plantations—where the now-free cultivators were ordered to remain and "fertilize the soil with their labor"—would be divided up among the workers and the "warriors." They would receive different amounts according to their age, gender—women received half as much as men—and rank in the hierarchies of the army and the plantation. The freeing and payment of former slaves were themselves radical steps, and the deferred promise made by Polverel had dramatic implications: when the war was over, fields of cane and coffee were to become homesteads, and slaves independent farmers.[23]

Since the beginning of the revolution, rumors of imminent emancipation had circulated continually in the colony. In June 1793 one such rumor had reached the insurgent camps: the leader Pierrot, who a few weeks later would join the Republic, heard that the French (as well as the Spanish and English) were advocating a general emancipation of the slaves. By August 1793, with the power of the planters all but smashed, the slave insurgents fighting for Spain steadily advancing across the colony, and the plantation economy at a standstill, the possibility of emancipation was closer than ever. Many in Le Cap—including many whites—were openly clamoring for it. A white official drew up a petition on behalf of the colony's slaves demanding "the Rights of Man" and "general liberty." Although a symbolic "tree of liberty" had been planted recently during the ceremonies of July 14 in Le Cap, it complained, there was still slavery in the land. "Are we not men?" the petition asked. "Say one word," it asked Sonthonax, "and Saint-Domingue will be happy and free." A few days later the municipal government of Le Cap declared that, in a colony haunted by the "ashes" and "piles of dead" created by slavery, it was time to grant the "cultivators of Saint-Domingue" the "Rights of Man." Their rights could not be denied them by any power, whether "human" or "divine." Those "expatriated" from Africa by Europeans and brought to this new country wanted it to become their own. They wished to be "recognized and free and French!" Granting their wish would save the colony: France would "acquire thousands of soldiers, and the land an infinity of cultivators"; the nation would still receive "rich products" that were "even more valuable" because they came from "free hands."[24]

On August 24, at an open meeting in Le Cap, 15,000 "souls" voted in favor of the emancipation of the slaves of the north. Finally, on August 29, when Sonthonax issued a decree that began "Men are born and live free and equal in rights," all who were "currently enslaved" in the Northern Province were declared free. They would "enjoy all the rights attached to the quality of French citizenship." Slavery had been abolished in the richest region of Saint-Domingue, on the plains out of which the revolt of 1791 had emerged, in the mountains that had served as "boulevards of liberty" to the insurgents. The specter of liberty that had loomed over Saint-Domingue for years, haunting and taunting masters and slaves, had become a reality.[25]

"General Liberty has just been proclaimed in the island," an elated insurgent allied to the Republic, Bramante Lazzary, announced to his "brothers in revolt" in the north. They must all swear loyalty to France and "march under its flag," the Republican tricolor, whose red, white, and blue symbolized the "reunion of the three colors." "Our flag makes clear that our liberty depends on three colors: black, mulatto, and white; we are fighting for these three colors." All the races of Saint-Domingue were to form "one family" and fight those who "are against our liberty." Against the "aristocrats and the Spanish" who flew the white flag of royalism, who wanted "only the white," and who hoped for a return to the "old order," all should rally and proclaim: "No, we are French," and "we want to live free or die."[26]

In the next months Polverel followed suit, though more gradually, in the west and south. Having already freed many of the slaves in the regions under his control with his August proclamation, in early September Polverel announced to those who were still enslaved that that they should wait patiently for the imminent "day when you will finally be permitted to enjoy the Rights of Man." A few weeks later he freed state-owned slaves and—in an effort to maintain some peace between former masters and former slaves in the new order—invited whites "penetrated with the principles of liberty and equality that form the foundation of the French Republic" to emancipate their own slaves. His proclamation made that clear there was ultimately little choice in the matter: "the slavery of a single individual is incompatible with the principles of the Republic." Finally, on October 31, Polverel decreed that all "Affricains & Affricaines" (African men and African women), as well as all descendants of Africans—and all those who were to arrive in the colony or to be "born there in the future"—were "free" and "equal to all men." They would enjoy "all the rights of French citizens and all the other rights pronounced" in the Declaration of the Rights of Man. The Declaration itself was translated into Creole and posted and distributed so it would be accessible to all. All men over eighteen were to present themselves to the local administration, where after taking an oath they would receive a printed declaration of their French citizenship.[27]

"You will no longer be the property of another; you will be your own masters, and you will live happily," declared Sonthonax. But, as Polverel had, he demanded that they show themselves worthy of this gift of freedom by "forever rejecting indolence and banditry." They were required to remain on their plantations, where they would be paid for their work. Domestics would be paid yearly salaries, while plantation workers as a group were granted one-third of the goods produced on the plantation each year. This portion was divided up unequally, with drivers receiving the largest shares, followed by male cultivators, then women (who received two-thirds of what men received), and finally children. Though required to stay on their plantations for at least a year, the ex-slaves could be moved for reasons of "incompatibility of character"—a judgment presumably to made by the manager or property owner—or at the request of the other workers on the plantation. After a year they could request a transfer to another plantation. But except for service in the army—an option open only to men— there was no provision for those who wanted to leave the plantations, to go into the mountains to settle their own land, or to depart for the cities. Any men who were not either soldiers or property owners and any women found "errant" would be imprisoned.[28]

Sonthonax did not offer any land to the ex-slaves. And the redistribution of property promised by Polverel, at first deferred, eventually vanished completely from the rules he put in place. In the end, the commissioners did not even make a small concession that certainly would have been ap-preciated by former slaves—granting them official ownership of the gar-den plots they had farmed as slaves. Polverel, however, did go further than Sonthonax in assuring plantation laborers some control over their labor. He gave them the right to participate in the selection of managers and to elect their drivers in plantation assemblies. Women—banned from voting in po-litical assemblies of Saint-Domingue, as they were France—were given the right to vote in these elections. Polverel also gave the cultivators six months to move to a new plantation if they wished. Polverel's regulations promised a dramatic transformation meant to turn plantations once oper-ated through a brutal hierarchy into farms worked by salaried workers and run with their active participation.[29]

During the coming years, ex-slaves in Republican-controlled areas would struggle to expand the limited freedom they had been given. The British would soon occupy much of the colony and would reestablish slavery as they went. Nevertheless, everything had changed for Saint-Domingue, for France, and in some sense for slaves and masters everywhere. A step for-ward had been taken, one that shaped the debates and struggles over slav-ery that engulfed the Atlantic world during the next decades.

There was no precedent for what had happened. The small-scale, grad-ual elimination of slavery launched earlier in several U.S. states had opened the way for what Sonthonax and Polverel did in 1793. But the scope of emancipation in Saint-Domingue was massive in comparison. The colony had until recently boasted the most profitable plantation regions in the world, and the slaves freed in 1793 made up the vast majority of the population. And although they did place conditions on the liberty they de-creed, Sonthonax and Polverel did not provide for any period of transition between slavery and freedom. In this omission they disregarded the argu-ments of the great abolitionists of the day, such as Condorcet, who be-lieved strongly that slavery could be extinguished only through a gradual process. In decreeing a universal and immediate emancipation, they cre-ated an example that would be both celebrated and vilified, held up by some as a model of uncompromising and principled action, and denounced by others as an example of the dangers of giving liberty to slaves who were not ready to be free.

Perhaps the most radical part of their proclamations was the granting not just of liberty but also of citizenship to the slaves. The new order was, in principle, to be based on uncompromising equality. Race was to have no place within it. This, too, was a dramatic challenge, not only to the pathologically stratified society of Saint-Domingue, but to the forms of democracy that reigned in the Americas and in Europe. The promise of 1793—a transracial citizenship in which ex-slaves and ex-masters would live together as political equals—was a great step forward, indeed in many ways out of its time. Undermined and attacked almost immediately, it produced in later years eloquent defenders of the principle that all people, of all races, were equal in rights. Distorted and eventually destroyed during the next decade, it nevertheless lingered as a fleeting possibility, one that would not find its home again in the Americas for many years.

The abolition of slavery gained new recruits for the commissioners, but it also helped solidify the opposition of many whites—and many free people of color—to the Republican regime. And the most important insurgent leaders—Jean-François, Biassou, and the as-yet-elusive figure named Toussaint—remained steadfastly loyal to the Spanish, choosing the autonomy they had carved out for themselves over an alliance with a Republic whose fate seemed uncertain. Throughout September and October they advanced steadily across the north and west under the banner of the Spanish king.

And then another conquest began—that of the British. In late September 600 redcoats disembarked at Jérémie, on the edge of the Southern Province, and were greeted by residents crying "Long live the English!" In the Northern Province the French officers in control of the naval fort at Môle Saint-Nicolas, "the Gibraltar of the Antilles," handed it over without a shot—a victory "announced to the British public by the cannon of the Tower of London." The British then turned their attention to a greater prize: the control of the productive plantation regions of the colony, notably those of the west. There, too, they were hoping that their advance would be facilitated by defections.[30]

In much of the west, notably in Saint-Marc, free people of color dominated political life. Like white planters, most free-colored property owners were infuriated by the emancipation decree and sought a solution that would allow them to remain masters. At the same time, however, they did not want to give up the right to racial equality they had gained through the April 4 decree. When, in February, Saint-Domingue planters in London had offered to hand over Saint-Domingue to the British, they proposed that propertied free people of color retain "the same rights as the whites."

This initial proposition for equality was "whittled down," however, and the articles of capitulation agreed upon in September by Saint-Domingue planter representatives and the British stipulated that free-coloreds would be given "all the rights given to this class in the English colonies." This was a major step backward from the full equality they currently enjoyed.[31]

Some free-colored leaders insisted that they should accept emancipation and remain loyal to the Republic. Others, unwilling to accept emancipation, favored siding with the Spanish, who retained slavery but had relatively liberal traditions regarding free people of African descent. In Saint-Marc the leading free-coloreds crafted a compromise. At a town meeting the majority voted to accept British occupation on the "condition that racial equality be maintained." By late December the Union Jack was flying over the port that had once been the home of the colony's seditious assembly. Next came the town of Arcahaye, farther south toward Port-au-Prince. There the free-colored mayor declared that France would not blame those residents of Saint-Domingue who turned to the British seeking to preserve the "unfortunate remains of the men and the property of this colony." "If ever there is a case in which it is excusable to abandon one's flag," it was this one. Arcahaye was soon placed in British hands. "You forget that you have African blood in you," the free-colored Pierre Pinchinat declared in disgust to those who had defected. Even if the "voice of humanity" found no place in their "hardened hearts," they should save the blacks from slavery out of gratitude for the services they had rendered them against the white planters. For with British occupation came the return of the slavery that had been abolished just a few months before.[32]

One great prize remained: Port-au-Prince. But there the Republicans—who had renamed the city Port-Républicain—managed to hold on. Sonthonax had come to join Polverel to direct the defense of the town, and the commissioners strengthened their forces as they had in Le Cap by recruiting soldiers from among the bands of insurgents in the surrounding plain. In his bid to secure the loyalty of such ex-slaves, Sonthonax announced in late February that the National Convention had abolished slavery in all the French colonies. He was, of course, guessing—there was no way that he could have known of the decree passed several weeks before in Paris—although, as it turned out, he was right. He also crafted personal connections with certain leaders. He invited the leader Alaou, who had been born in West Africa, to enter the town with several thousand of his followers, and treated him to a "magnificent meal." "It would be hard to portray the joy, the pride, the enthusiasm of these bands of Congos, Ibos, Dahomeys, Senegalese," wrote one nineteenth-century historian, "as they watched their supreme chief, nearly naked, covered in fetishes, hold a white cock at his side, sitting next to the representative of France, covered in tricolor ribbons."[33]

The commissioners had left the north in the hands of Etienne Laveaux. He put free-colored officer Jean-Louis Villatte in charge of Le Cap and moved his headquarters to Port-de-Paix, on the front lines facing the British. "Even if the entire colony hands itself over to the English," he commanded, "let us hold fast, and conserve for the Republic a place where the forces it will send can disembark and find an immediate welcome." If they could not defend Port-de-Paix, they would destroy it and retreat from "hill to hill," fighting until reinforcements arrived. The desperation of the French created a kind of equality: most of the white troops were serving "with bare feet, like the Africans." Laveaux himself, the child of the French aristocracy, had nothing he could claim as his own. When the British noted that if he surrendered he could keep all his possessions, he shot back that "the only loot I have is my uniform, which is that of a soldier." Villatte, too, responded defiantly to calls to surrender, answering one Spanish summons to put down his weapons by sending, in place of a written letter, a packet of cartridges and bullets. Le Cap and Port-de-Paix became the "boulevards of liberty" in the north. And they would hold fast, though the saviors they were awaiting would not come from across the ocean, but from among the slave insurgents of Saint-Domingue.[34]

Slavery had been abolished in Saint-Domingue. But would it be defeated in Paris? How would the independent, unsanctioned, and boldly creative decisions taken by Sonthonax and Polverel be greeted by the Republic they represented? The mission of carrying the news of emancipation across the Atlantic, and of convincing the National Convention of the action's wisdom, fell to three men: one white, one of mixed European and African descent, and one born in Africa and raised in slavery, the officer Jean-Baptiste Belley. They had been elected in Saint-Domingue in September 1793 and had left the colony for Paris, with two others, soon afterward.[35]

It was not a comfortable journey. Crossing the Atlantic in the midst of a war against the greatest naval power on earth, Great Britain, was difficult enough for a French delegation. But the British were not their only enemies. The delegates left Saint-Domingue on a ship packed with whites fleeing into exile, who were openly hostile to the delegates and to the regime they represented. The ship took them to Philadelphia, a city thronged with the refugees from Saint-Domingue who had left with Galbaud's convoy. As soon as they anchored there, they were accosted by French sailors who shouted that the delegates should be hung or shot. One of the white delegates, Louis Dufay, entered the town and was immediately surrounded by a murderous crowd, surviving thanks to the protection of a woman who led him through the side streets of the city. Another crowd boarded the ship and attacked the other delegates. They were particularly brutal to Belley. They took his sword, his watch, his money, and his papers, and attacked him for "daring" to serve as an officer and "commanding whites." Belley responded that if he knew how to "save whites and defend them" there was no reason he could not command them. The crowd demanded that he remove his tricolor cockade, shouting that a black man should not be allowed to wear one. When he refused, they tore it off. The crowd then pillaged the quarters of the absent Dufay, declaring that "whites who sided with blacks were the guiltiest of all." One of the five delegates was spirited off the ship by the crowd and taken hostage, though he managed to escape and rejoin the delegation later in New York. To make sure that some of them made it to Paris, the delegates split into two groups. Three of them—Belley, Dufay, and Jean-Baptiste Mills—finally made it to Bordeaux and, after being briefly imprisoned by local authorities, arrived in Paris in mid-February.[36]

When the men entered the Convention, a deputy rose and announced that it was a great day. While the "aristocracy" of both nobility and church had been destroyed by the Revolution, the "aristocracy of the skin" had remained strong. All that, however, had just changed. "Equality is consecrated; a black, a yellow [i.e., mulatto], and a white have taken their seat among us, in the name of the free citizens of Saint-Domingue." The Convention erupted with applause, and another deputy asked that particular recognition be given to the two free men of color—Belley and Mills—whose class had been oppressed "for so many years." The next day Dufay stood before the Convention and delivered a powerful speech describing the events that had transformed Saint-Domingue. He recounted how the slaves in Le Cap and on surrounding plantations had come to the rescue of the Republican commissioners when they were attacked by the counter-revolutionary Galbaud. "'We are negroes, and French,' they said . . . 'we will fight for France, but in return we want our freedom.' They even added: our *Droits de l'Homme.*" Dufay argued that the commissioners had taken the only reasonable course of action in creating "new citizens for the Republic in order to oppose our enemies." Immediately after his speech, a deputy rose and asked that the National Convention declare that slavery was abolished throughout the Republic. There was no opposition, and the law was quickly written and voted: "The National Convention declares that slavery is abolished throughout the territory of the Republic; in consequence, all men, without distinction of color, will enjoy the rights of French citizens."[37]

Belley shouted: "I was a slave during my childhood. Thirty-six years have passed since I became free through my own labor, and purchased myself. Since then, in the course of my life, I have felt worthy of being French." "It is the tricolor flag that has called us to our liberty," he continued, and vowed "on behalf of my brothers" that it would fly upon the shores and mountains of Saint-Domingue "as long as there is a drop of blood in our veins." "This is the death of the English!" the famed revolutionary leader Danton proclaimed. The colony would have a powerful army born out of emancipation and ready to die to defend it.[38]

The dramatic decision made by Sonthonax and Polverel in Saint-Domingue had become the law of the French Republic. Throughout this empire, whose prosperity rested on a foundation of slavery, there would be no more masters and no more slaves, only citizens. It was a truly radical change, the most dramatic of the many inaugurated by the French Revolution. It took individuals who had been stripped of all human rights and made them members of a democratic republic. French colonial slavery had, at the onset of the Revolution, been at its height, and within five years it had been destroyed. The emancipation decreed in 1794 was major step in the long, contorted journey that would ultimately lead to the elimination of slavery in the Americas. But for the people of Saint-Domingue, it was only the end of the beginning of a long struggle for freedom.

CHAPTER EIGHT

The Opening

TOUSSAINT LOUVERTURE was waiting. Part of the torrent of revolution that had swept away slavery in Saint-Domingue since 1791, serving under the command of Jean-François and Biassou, he was by 1793 a powerful and independent leader in the insurgent camps allied with the Spanish. By the beginning of 1794 he was still leading his troops against the Republic in Saint-Domingue. That situation, however, was about to change.

When he joined in the insurrection in 1791, Toussaint was already a free man. He had been born in slavery just outside Le Cap on a plantation owned by the Bréda family. He worked as a coachman and took care of livestock on the plantation. Sometime in the 1770s the plantation manager, Bayon de Libertat, emancipated Toussaint. Within a few years Toussaint had acquired his own slave, an African-born man named Jean-Baptiste, whom he freed in 1777. Toussaint tried his hand at agriculture, renting a small coffee plantation near the town. After two years, when he ended his lease, he owed the owner the cost of two slaves, one woman and one child, who had died during his tenure.[1]

In the mid-nineteenth century one of his sons, Isaac Louverture, wrote a brief account of his father's early life. Toussaint's father, he wrote, was an African prince, the second son of an Arada king, who had been captured and sent to Saint-Domingue as a slave. In the colony the exiled prince sometimes met other Aradas, the former subjects of his father. They "recognized him as their prince" and saluted him according to the "customs of their homeland." The sorrows of exile, wrote Isaac, were softened by the kindness of his master, who gave Toussaint's father a plot of land and "five blacks" to cultivate it. The African prince converted to Catholicism, married a woman of his "nation," and had several sons. The oldest of them was Toussaint. He learned the African language of his Arada parents and, after their death, was also educated by his godfather Pierre Baptiste, a free black living in Le Cap, who had been educated by missionaries. He studied geometry, French, and some Latin under his tutelage. Drawing on Isaac Louverture's description of his father Toussaint's education, another nineteenth-century biographer claimed that the future revolutionary leader had read the writings of the Abbé Raynal. This assertion inspired C. L. R. James to pen a passage describing the slave Toussaint reading about the prophesied "black Spartacus" and seeing in himself the answer to the question "Where is he?"[2]

As with the Bois-Caïman ceremony, it is difficult—probably impossible—to separate reality from legend in the story of Toussaint, including how he took on the name Louverture—"the opening." Isaac Louverture attributed the name to a comment by Etienne Polverel. After Louverture conquered Dondon and Marmelade for the Spanish in late 1793, Isaac wrote, the commissioner admiringly noted that his enemy could make "an opening anywhere." As another early biographer who repeated this story put it, the "public" had given him his nickname to celebrate his successes, and "history had left it to him." Perhaps, though, rather than tracing its origin to the comment of a white administrator, it is safer to assume that the man who ultimately made it famous chose it for himself and that, with "its cryptic connotations of a new beginning," it had a particular, still hidden, meaning for him.[3]

"Judged according to the interests of the moment, through the prism of passions," wrote the French general Pamphile de Lacroix, "Toussaint Louverture has been represented in turn as a ferocious brute, or as the most surprising and the best of men, as often as an execrable monster as a saintly martyr: he was none of these." Louverture was a brilliant political and military leader who, over the course of his career, gathered around him individuals from all walks of life, from white planters and officers to creole and African-born slaves. He "greatly impressed most who met him," and although whites sometimes privately made fun of him, "in his presence no one laughed." He had this effect even on some of the most powerful personalities of the revolution; one contemporary wrote that Jean-Jacques Dessalines "didn't dare to look him straight in the face." He was "a leader of acute intelligence" who was "totally adept at confusing his opponents." He was "both ruthless and humane, capable of making barbarous threats but of sparing even those who had double-crossed him." Throughout his career he would regularly invoke the possibility of brutal punishment, both human and divine, but also show a remarkable tendency to forgive, evoking the teachings of Catholicism as his inspiration. He was a consummate politician who cultivated personal loyalty and effectively used secrecy and trickery as he sought and found openings in his rise to power. He was also a great political thinker, not only the "first and greatest of West Indians," as C. L. R. James put it, but also one of the towering figures in the political history of the Atlantic world.[4]

Louverture's extensive correspondence allows us to explore his actions and ideals. These letters were not written by his hand. Indeed, Lacroix recalled that he "spoke French poorly" and often turned to creole in communicating his ideas. "Nevertheless a divine instinct enlightened him about the value of words" in French. He kept his secretaries working constantly, with several of them writing different versions of a letter until they had found "the turn of phrase that was the appropriate expression of his thought." He never stopped thinking: "Journeying across the colony on horseback at lightning speed, seeing everything for himself, he prepared his actions. He meditated as he galloped; he meditated as well when he pretended piously to pray." He had much to think about, for the challenge he faced was enormous: channeling the only successful slave revolt in history, overseeing the first great transition from slavery to freedom in the Americas, and redefining the political terms of empire.[5]

From the time he joined the French Republic in 1794, Louverture took on the task of protecting, and defining, the liberty the slaves of Saint-Domingue had won. As he managed the daily details of military and civil administration, he struggled to lay the foundation for a kind of order that had never been seen or even really imagined. His problems were those faced by subsequent generations of administrators overseeing the transition from slavery to freedom in the British Caribbean, the United States, and Cuba. Though he differed from most of these later administrators in one crucial way—he had himself experienced slavery—his post-emancipation policies were similar to those of the administrators who followed him. Intent on maintaining and rebuilding the production of sugar and coffee, he sought to limit the liberty of the ex-slaves, responding to their attempts to move freely, acquire land, and escape plantation labor by constructing a coercive legal order. His administration marked the beginning of a longer story of how emancipation ultimately failed to bring true

"Toussaint Louverture." There are numerous, and startlingly diverse, images of Louverture from the period. This well-known engraving was first published in Marcus Rainsford, *A Historical Account of the Black Empire of Hayti* (1805). *Courtesy of the Bibliothèque Nationale de France.*

equality and independence to former slaves. Though his ultimate inability to construct a multiracial, egalitarian, and democratic society in Saint-Domingue might strike us as particularly tragic, given his origins, this was a failure he shared with the leaders of every other postemancipation society in the Atlantic world.

The situation Louverture faced was particularly challenging. He came to power in a colony devastated by insurrection and war, inhabited by a fragmented and diverse population, and for much of his time in power

Portrait of Toussaint Louverture on horseback, circa 1800. *Private collection.*

received little support, either material or political, from metropolitan France. As a black officer committed to the participation of men of African descent at the highest levels of administration, he confronted a lingering—and eventually resurgent—racism within the French government. And as he sought to assure the preservation of liberty in Saint-Domingue, he had to navigate a complicated set of imperial conflicts and relationships that placed constraints on his social and economic policies.

Toussaint Louverture was, as one novelist has suggested eloquently, the "master of the crossroads" of the Haitian Revolution. Descendant of West African royalty, but also raised Catholic and educated in European arts and sciences, he emerged from the crossing of these two traditions, though as a leader he would emphasize the virtues of Catholicism and repress the African traditions of his colony. But as he faced the political challenges of the postemancipation colony, the other part of his education was perhaps more important. He had been in his life both a master and a slave. He would draw on both experiences in governing the evolving colony of Saint-Domingue.[6]

"I am Toussaint Louverture. My name is perhaps known to you. I have undertaken vengeance. I want Liberty and Equality to reign in Saint-Domingue. I work to bring them into existence. Unite yourselves to us, brothers, and fight with us for the same cause." With these words, Louverture announced his emergence as an independent political force in Saint-Domingue. He issued the proclamation on August 29, 1793, the very day Léger Félicité Sonthonax abolished slavery throughout the Northern Province. Although he was calling for liberty, he was not announcing his alliance with the Republic. Instead, he was positioning himself against Sonthonax as the true defender of liberty in Saint-Domingue. In a letter written at the same time, he declared that he had been "the first to stand up for" the cause of emancipation and had "always supported" it. Having started the battle for it, he promised, he would finish it.[7]

The insurgent leader Bramante Lazzary, having just issued a call for the "three colors" of Saint-Domingue to unite behind the Republic, wondered why Louverture was still fighting for the wrong side. "Father Sonthonax," the "representative of the will of all of French," had issued a decree of general liberty, which Lazzary had sent to Louverture. If Louverture supported freedom, why was he still fighting for the king of Spain, embracing the "old regime" instead of joining the Republic? Lazzary addressed his letter to "Citizen Toussaint Louverture," but added sarcastically "supposed General of the Armies of his Most Catholic Majesty today, yesterday supposed General of the King . . . perturber of the order and the tranquility of our brothers." He hoped, however, that they would soon be fighting side by side for their "three colors." In this, he was to be disappointed.[8]

Louverture's actions and motives during this period and the months that followed remain shrouded in mystery. Since his moderating participation in the negotiations between the insurgents and administrators in late 1791, he had become an increasingly important figure within the insurgent army. During these negotiations—and again in 1792—he participated in and supported plans meant to end the insurrection by bringing the majority of the insurgents, minus some leaders who would receive freedom, back to the plantations. He did not sign the July 1792 letter in which Biassou and Jean-François proposed an end to slavery in the colony. In June of 1793, a few weeks after Jean-François and Biassou joined the Spanish, Louverture followed them to serve as an "auxiliary." He therefore agreed to the terms initially presented by the Spanish: liberty, along with land and other rewards, for those men who fought against the French.[9]

Sometime in May or June 1793 Louverture made contact with the Republican officer Etienne Laveaux in Le Cap. Unfortunately, there is only one enigmatic trace of the communication that took place between the two men. A year later Louverture reminded Laveaux that "before the disaster at Le Cap"—that is, before its destruction in June 1793—he had proposed "avenues of reconciliation" that had been "rejected." The surviving letter does not say what these were. One of Louverture's early biographers thought he knew, and when he reprinted Louverture's 1794 letter, after the words "avenues of reconciliation" he inserted the phrase "the recognition of the liberty of the blacks and a full amnesty." Historians from Victor Schoelcher to C. L. R. James have taken these words as Louverture's own. In fact, however, there simply is no concrete trace of what he put forth in 1793. All we know is that there was, in 1793, no reconciliation. It would be another year before Laveaux and Louverture would become allies instead of enemies.[10]

Once Louverture issued his proclamation in favor of "liberty and equality" in August 1793, why did he keep fighting for Spain? Louverture had good reasons to be suspicious of the solidity of the Republic and its policy of emancipation. Sonthonax's hold on the Northern Province was tenuous, and, like many others in mid-1793, Louverture probably thought that the French Republic was heading toward defeat in Europe as well. There was no reason to join the losing side. Sonthonax's abolition, furthermore, was a local decision, and Louverture understood that it would not be secure until it had been ratified by the government in Paris. Louverture, meanwhile, enjoyed a great deal of autonomy, commanding—with little Spanish supervision—territory stretching from Santo Domingo all the way to the west coast of the colony. In October, when the British sought to enter the port town of Gonaïves, they found "a Negroe, who they called the Spanish general, commanding the place." His name was "Tusan."[11]

In early 1794 increasing numbers of white émigrés, many returning from exile in the United States, were rallying to the Spanish side. They hoped to return to a Saint-Domingue in which slavery, or at least plantation agriculture, was safe. Tensions between the black auxiliaries and these white émigrés contributed to growing problems between the auxiliaries and the Spanish. Meanwhile, their hold on certain parts of Saint-Domingue was loosening. When the Spanish attempted to reinstitute the use of the whip on plantations, slaves in some parts of the northern peninsula rose up in revolt. Free-colored auxiliaries of Spain revolted in the same region, declaring that it was vital to follow the "maxims of the Republic" in order to "keep the freedom" they had fought for. There were similar defections in Gonaïves and the mountains of the Artibonite region. The British, too, found some of their erstwhile allies turning against them. In March and early April several free-colored commanders in the northern peninsula joined the French side, leaving the British in control only of the region around the Môle Saint-Nicolas. The Republic's fortunes seemed to be improving.[12]

Louverture began to chart a course increasingly independent both from his Spanish commanders and from his superior in the insurgent army, Biassou, with whom he was in open conflict by late March 1794. In early April a representative of the French émigrés serving with Spain complained that in the region under Louverture's control "rebel negroes" were "assassinating, pillaging, and burning our properties in the name of the execrable Republic." Instead of fighting them, Louverture was "arming all the slaves and removing them from their plantations," promising them "general liberty" and telling them that they would be free if they dared "to kill the whites." These accusations had little influence on the treatment of Louverture by the Spanish, who recognized him as one of their most valuable allies. One commander had written of him earlier that if God "descended to earth," he would find no heart "more pure" than that of Louverture.[13]

On April 29 a "strange circumstance," both "extraordinary" and "mysterious," took place in Gonaïves. Spain's black auxiliaries in the town suddenly attacked their erstwhile Spanish comrades, demanding "in the name of the King of the French" that they surrender. Some Spanish troops were killed; others, along with several hundred of the town's inhabitants, fled into the countryside. On May 5 Louverture wrote to these refugees that he regretted the "unfortunate" events, and explained that he had "not participated at all." At the same time a Spanish officer wrote to Louverture complimenting him for not forgetting the oath he took "before God" to "serve His Majesty faithfully and die for him." Louverture rode up into the nearby mountains, promising the refugees that he would soon return and advising them to stay out of Gonaïves until he did.[14]

On the same day Etienne Laveaux dispatched a letter to Louverture, inviting him to join the French side. Louverture accepted. Within a few days he had gone into "open revolt" against the Spanish. He raised the tricolor flag over Gonaïves and put the parishes of Gros-Morne, Ennery, Marmelade, Plaisance, Dondon, Acul, and Limbé, all under his command, in the hands of the Republic. Writing to Laveaux on May 18, Louverture admitted that he had been "led astray by the enemies of the Republic and of the human race." After the "avenues of reconciliation" he proposed had been rejected by the French in mid-1793, "the Spanish offered me their protection and liberty for all those who would fight for the cause of kings; I accepted their offer, seeing myself abandoned by the French, my brothers." After many months, however, he had come to understand that the Spanish aim was to have the blacks "kill one another to decrease our numbers" so that they could force the rest "back into their former slavery." "Let us unite together forever and, forgetting the past, work from now on to crush our enemies and take vengeance against our perfidious neighbors." As an elated Polverel wrote in June, "Toussaint Louverture, one of the three royalist African chiefs who were fighting with the Spanish," had finally understood his "true interests" and those of his "brothers." He understood that kings could never support "liberty and equality," and was now fighting for the Republic. Along with Louverture came more than 4,000 troops and three veteran officers who would leave a profound mark on Saint-Domingue: Henri Christophe, who had been free before the revolution; and the former slaves Moïse and Jean-Jacques Dessalines.[15]

News of the National Convention's February abolition of slavery had been sweeping into the Caribbean along unofficial channels, and it had probably reached Louverture, triggering his defection. In ratifying the emancipation proclaimed by Sonthonax and Polverel, the French government had won his loyalty. Louverture was nevertheless cautious during the following weeks. He kept in contact with the Spanish, and although he defended his positions he did not attack his former allies. In fact, soon after they gained the territory he brought to them, the French lost Port-au-Prince to the British, who had just received long-awaited reinforcements. In early July, however, Louverture received the confirmation he needed: a printed version of the National Convention's abolition decree. It was "consoling news" for all "friends of humanity," he wrote to Laveaux in a letter he signed as "servant of the Republic." He suddenly went on the offensive against the Spanish. "I almost captured Jean-François," he gleefully reported. He had escaped only thanks to the "thickness of the bushes" into which he had fled, leaving all his effects, including his papers, behind. "He saved only his shirt and pants."[16]

The defeated Jean-François took a curious revenge, one that reflected the unraveling of Spanish designs on Saint-Domingue. In the town of Fort-Dauphin, while an "immobile" Spanish garrison looked on, he had his troops slaughter 700 of the French planters who had rallied to the Spanish side. The brutal act made clear that the alliance the Spanish had tried to build between exiled white planters and black auxiliaries drawn from slave insurgents was untenable. On the battlefield, meanwhile, the Spanish suffered new defeats at the hands of Laveaux, who wrote that there was not a "single day" in the "happy month" of July that was not "marked by victories."[17]

The same boat that had carried the official news of the abolition of slavery to Saint-Domingue had also, ironically, brought an order for the commissioners Sonthonax and Polverel to report back to Paris. There they would have to face charges levied by exiled planters who were set on taking revenge against them. For Sonthonax, a "more curious mixture of triumph and humiliation could scarcely be imagined." His actions in Saint-Domingue had been vindicated by the Convention, but he was being called back to stand trial in front of the "aristocrats of the skin" whose power he and Polverel had destroyed by proclaiming emancipation. The commissioners left the colony in the hands of Etienne Laveaux and of his new converts to the cause of the Republic. For the next two years, in the midst of war, the colony received no assistance from France, and no concrete directives on policy. Left on their own, Laveaux and Louverture pushed back the colony's attackers and built a new order on the smoking foundations of slavery.[18]

"They want to disarm you in order to kill you," Laveaux warned the slaves of the British-controlled Saint-Marc region in September 1794. How long, he demanded, would they remain the "passive instruments" of their "former masters"? And how long would the free-coloreds of Saint-Marc, who had been given so much by France, continue in their treason? The "citizens of April 4" should make peace with emancipation. Those who feared that work on the plantations would cease were wrong: "How blind you are! Must one be a slave to work?" The "free man" who had "nothing" felt "the need to work," and did so with "patience and satisfaction," knowing he would take home the "fruits of his labor." The free-coloreds, Laveaux insisted, would be better off under Republican rule. His entreaties were well timed: many free-coloreds in the "occupied zone" were beginning "to feel they were on the wrong side." Having accepted the British takeover on the condition that racial equality be maintained, once the occupation was under way they had seen a "regression to old norms" of discrimination among the French planters. The British, worried about the precedent that might otherwise be set for their own colonies, decided in mid-1793 to apply discriminatory British law in Saint-Domingue. Men of color were divested of positions in the police force and administration, and some were threatened with deportation by British officials suspicious of their loyalties. In case the principles of self-interest were not enough to convince the free-coloreds in Saint-Marc to support the Republic, Laveaux added another inducement: if they did not surrender, he warned, would send Louverture to sack the town, sparing only the "former slaves."[19]

For several months Louverture had been advancing on Saint-Marc from his base in Gonaïves. To take the town, he set in motion a complicated ruse. In mid-August he announced to the British officer Brisbane that he intended to surrender, and had two of his loyal officers go over to the other side with their troops. They were in fact infiltrators whose mission was to "spread disaffection" within the British camp. Having gained the trust of Brisbane, Louverture's agents turned on him and nearly managed to assassinate him. As the mayor of Saint-Marc led an uprising in the town, Louverture's forces attacked.[20]

Despite its intricate preparation, the Republican attack on Saint-Marc failed. Louverture claimed that it all went wrong because he had crushed his hand moving a cannon. "If I had been able to fight as I usually do at the head of my troops the enemy would not have held an hour, or else I would have died, one or the other." He also blamed the "treason" of the many free-coloreds who had stuck with the British. Still, Louverture had further weakened the alliance between the British and the local free-coloreds by sowing distrust between them.[21]

Indeed, the fortunes of the British in Saint-Domingue were reaching their "lowest ebb." They held Port-au-Prince, but the city was besieged by

Republican insurgents who held the mountains around it and were in a position to cut off its water supply. British soldiers at Fort Bizoton, an isolated outpost south of the city, were repeatedly attacked by Republican troops. Sickness decimated the Port-au-Prince garrison; in October 1794 fewer than half of the British troops in the city were fit to fight. In the south the British suffered a series of defeats at the hands of André Rigaud. In early October Rigaud took Léogane, a step on the road to Port-au-Prince. A few months later, on Christmas Eve, he attacked the British-held Tiburon, at the extreme west of the southern peninsula, routing and decimating the British garrison along with black troops under the command of Jean Kina fighting with them.[22]

The Spanish, too, continued to suffer defeats. In October 1794 Louverture captured the inland towns of Saint-Michel and Saint-Raphael, slaughtering many of the Spanish defenders with his cavalry, capturing valuable ammunition and cannon. Lacking troops to set up an adequate defense, he burnt the town to the ground and retreated. In late December Louverture set in motion a well-coordinated campaign using several columns—one led by Dessalines and another by Moïse—that succeeded in surrounding and routing Jean-François's troops and capturing the Grande-Rivière region.[23]

As Louverture and Jean-François traded bullets on the battlefield, the former comrades also traded harsh words. "The liberty the Republicans tell you about is false," Jean-François declared in a letter to his "brothers" serving on the French side. Saint-Domingue was France's most valuable colony, and without it the "arts" and "industries" of the mother country would be destroyed. Once the French secured a peace with their European enemies, he asserted, they would turn on their black allies. "They will arm convoys that will be full of white soldiers, who will reduce you to a state of servitude." The liberty that Jean-François and his followers enjoyed in the Spanish camp, meanwhile, was "very different." It had not been granted to them by a benevolent authority; they had won it for themselves. "Having already become independent men, we were adopted as subjects by the kingdom of Spain."[24]

"You say the liberty the Republicans offer is false," retorted Louverture. But it was not the Republicans who had offered them liberty. "We are Republicans and therefore free by natural laws." Only kings would dare give themselves the right to reduce to slavery men who were naturally free. In fact all those who were "subjects or vassals of kings" were nothing more than "vile slaves." "The only true man is a Republican." Mocking Jean-François's pride in the titles granted to him and his officers by the Spanish, Louverture told him he could keep them: "one day they will be as useful to you as the luxurious titles of our former aristocrats were to them."[25]

In October Jean-François and Biassou attacked troops under Moïse's command. Louverture rushed to support him and, leading troops crying "Long live the Republic!" managed to repel the attack. As he later wrote to Laveaux, however, many of his courageous soldiers were killed, and "even though we destroyed many of our enemy, this does not compensate us for our losses." But Jean-François's days were numbered. In June 1795, across the Atlantic, a defeated Spain signed the Treaty of Bâle with France. One of the articles ceded Spanish Santo Domingo to the French. Although they would not act on this cession—it would be Louverture himself who would finally occupy the Spanish half of the island, and only in 1800—the fighting between the two colonies was to cease. By late 1795 the news of the treaty had arrived in Saint-Domingue. "Praise be to God, Jean-François is going to leave," Louverture announced joyfully to Laveaux in November. Before he left, Jean-François sent a parting shot to Laveaux: when he saw "Mister Laveaux and other French men of his position giving their daughters in marriage to the negroes," then he would be convinced that they truly believed in equality.[26]

The British sought to recruit Spain's abandoned auxiliaries, promising them freedom, and a few accepted and continued to oppose the Republicans under a new banner. Biassou "tried on the red jacket the British sent," and seems to have been tempted to continue fighting Louverture. Under the British, however, he would have had to fight under the command of white officers, and would have had much less autonomy than he had under the Spanish. Ultimately Biassou, Jean-François, and many other officers among the auxiliaries chose instead to leave their homeland under the protection of the Spanish, who resettled them throughout their empire. Biassou, a pioneer of slave revolt, became a pioneer of another kind, securing a retirement in Florida. Others ended up along the coast of Central America, where they established long-standing communities. Jean-François and his entourage lived for many years in Spain.[27]

There was now only one enemy in Saint-Domingue: the British. In August 1795 they invaded the Mirabalais region, extending their control east toward Santo Domingo. Louverture counterattacked and routed a troop of French planters serving with the British. He wrote with satisfaction that the "brave and impertinent" commander of this unit, surrounded, had jumped off his horse and "ran into the bushes with the debris of his army, shouting 'Sauve qui peut!'" There were, Louverture reported, enemy corpses scattered all along the road where the battle had been fought. With the recapture of Mirabalais, new allies were won. A man named Mademoiselle, chief of a maroon band who had long lived in the area and called themselves the Doco, led his followers to met with Louverture, and offered to join the Republic side. There were among the Doco several "Africans of the Arada nation," and Louverture delighted them by speaking to them in their native language. In late September, however, the British attacked the region again. Louverture was forced to retreat, and ordered his troops to burn the plantations and to take the cultivators with them.[28]

Louverture's troops were ragged, poorly paid, and often hungry. He regularly pleaded with Laveaux to send him more guns, more ammunition, more paper for cartridges. In early 1795, having received powder from Laveaux, he wrote that it was as if he had received medicine for a sickness. In late 1795 he noted that his soldiers were "as naked as worms"; three-quarters of them had no pants or shirts. After one battle in the Mirabalais region in September 1795, Louverture's troops found a manual written by the British to help train the troops of French whites fighting with them. He sent it to Laveaux for inspection, but asked that he return it so that he could use it for the "instruction of my troops." Despite the hardships he faced, over time Louverture created a daunting and disciplined fighting force. "It was remarkable to see these Africans, naked, carrying nothing but a cartridge belt, a saber and a rifle, showing exemplary and severe discipline," the French general Lacroix wrote of them. He described how, having occupied the town of Port-de-Paix in 1798 after months of campaigning with barely anything to eat, they did not loot the town's stores or the produce brought to the markets. Such soldiers were the heart of the army that sealed the defeat of the British occupation of the island and one day, when Louverture was no longer its leader, the defeat of the French.[29]

Even as he built his army of ex-slaves, Louverture went to work coaxing those who were not soldiers back to their plantations. Building on the policies of Sonthonax and Polverel, Louverture committed himself to forcing former slaves to keep working on the plantations. The decision put him in conflict with the aspirations of many of the newly freed people of the colony.

Since emancipation in 1793, ex-slaves throughout Saint-Domingue had struggled against the constraints placed on their freedom by administrators. Just as they had contested the power of their masters, they contested the power of their managers. In doing so they took advantage of the new rights they had gained. The daily struggles that took place on the plantations during this period were, for the most part, undocumented. But in February 1794, just a few months after he had emancipated the slaves, Polverel issued a new set of regulations revising his earlier policies on plantation labor. By looking at what Polverel outlawed, we can gain a sense of what the former slaves had been doing in the intervening months. On many plantations abandoned by their former masters, ex-slaves expanded the size of their garden plots and also took over other parts of the plantation to cultivate for their own subsistence and profit. They felled wood and gathered fruit in and around the plantations, and many harvested the produce grown on the provision grounds and sold it in town markets, using plantation horses and mules to transport it, as well as for "personal pleasure." Some migrated and settled on abandoned plantations. One group "cut down and burned" a coffee grove in order to "build houses for themselves in its place." Throughout the colony, the former slaves had taken to heart the idea that they deserved portions of the land. To dispel the confusion that he himself had encouraged the year before, Polverel announced in his decree: "This land does not belong to you. It belongs to those who have bought it or inherited it from those who first acquired it."[30]

Plantation workers had also protested the terms under which they were ordered to work. Both Sonthonax and Polverel had decreed that women—who, as in slavery, had the same work responsibilities as men—were to be paid less. Many women had clearly protested, for in his February decree Polverel suggested to the men on the plantations that they should beware of the "exaggerated pretensions" of their women. He criticized the women for being unwilling to accept that the "inequality of strength that nature has placed between them and the men" as well as the "intervals of rest which their pregnancies, their childbirth, their nursing, oblige them to make" justified the difference in salaries. He was hoping, it seems, to encourage men on the plantations to stifle the resistance of the women. But women continued to protest on many plantations. When the owner of one plantation read Polverel's decree to the assembled workers, a number of them, led by the women, "openly questioned its legitimacy, saying that it sounded like a plot against them orchestrated by 'whites,' rather than a decree form the official government of the Republic." They refused to follow the new regulations until an official came to confirm what the plantation owner had said.[31]

From the beginning of the insurrection, many slave insurgents had issued a demand for three free days a week for the slaves. In the wake of Polverel's late-1793 emancipation decree, which had maintained the six-day work week of slavery, many slaves had demanded they be given at least two days a week, rather than just one, to cultivate their own plots. Polverel sensed that this was an important, and potentially explosive, issue. He gave plantation workers the choice between a six-day and a five-day work week, but provided a substantial incentive for them to choose the former: on plantations where workers chose a six-day work week, they would receive one-third of the plantation's production. If they chose to work five days per week, their portion would be cut in half, to one-sixth. It was a dramatic difference for one day a week less of work. But the laborers on several plantations—again led by women—nevertheless chose more free time and less pay. They had more faith in the revenue they generated themselves from their garden plots than in the salaries they were promised from plantation managers. Plantation workers struggled in other ways to maintain control over some of their own time. Two women laborers refused their manager's request that they work at night, announcing that if anyone worked in the cane fields after dark, it would be he.[32]

Polverel and Sonthonax used the threat of punishment to contain the "pretensions" of the former slaves. Indeed the system instituted by Polverel in February was eerily prophetic of the social formations that would emerge throughout the Americas in the wake of slavery. No longer owned as property, laborers were now imprisoned by law and poverty. When they resisted their plantation managers, they were subject to imprisonment or forced labor on public works. When found guilty of theft—a charge leveled against them not only if they took provisions or commodities produced on the plantations, but even if they took the "spontaneous fruits of the land" that grew on the property—they were fined. But of course few had any money to pay the fines, so they usually ended up in prison. There were some who refused an existence that stank of slavery, and ran away, as maroons had for decades. Others found a kind refuge—or at least a broader set of possibilities, along with new dangers—by joining the military. Women, of course, could not follow this route away from the plantations. Their war was the daily struggle over the terms of freedom that shaped the postemancipation world of Saint-Domingue.[33]

As he gained control of more and more territory in late 1794, Louverture confronted same challenges earlier faced by Sonthonax and Polverel. When he won back British-controlled territory, he brought a second emancipation to the men and women who had been reenslaved. In such areas, however, despite the efforts of the British and the French masters who lived there, many of the plantations had been left in ruins by years of insurrection and war. In the once-thriving Artibonite region, Louverture wrote to Laveaux in July 1794, the plantations had "all been destroyed." "Everything has been broken and shattered." In Plaisance only one plantation had escaped burning, and in the nearby plains only a few were still "intact." Louverture explained that he was unable to follow Laveaux's instructions to pay the cultivators because there was nothing to pay them with. They would first have to produce something. In the meantime Louverture used his authority—and probably the threat of force—to maintain order. He noted with satisfaction that the "workers" from Plaisance, who had fled during the fighting, had all "returned to the plantations" under his orders.[34]

In November 1794, when Laveaux went to visit the lands under Louverture's command, he was delighted to see that reconstruction of the plantation economy was under way. "All the inhabitants," he wrote, "especially the whites," never tired of "honoring the virtues of Toussaint." He helped those of all "colors" and "opinions." Many white planters had returned to their plantations, and many white women talked about the assistance they had received from this "surprising man." In Petite-Rivière, 15,000 cultivators had come home. They were, Laveaux gushed, grateful to the Republic that had made them free, and worked assiduously thanks to Louverture. "Whites, blacks, mulattoes, soldiers, cultivators, property owners, all bless the virtuous chief whose care maintains order and peace among them."[35]

Looking back in the middle of 1795, Louverture remembered how with all the mountains "in rebellion" and the plantations "abandoned," he had been forced to use all his "patience and activity" to bring the cultivators back to work. He had also, however, used threats. The French constitution, declared Louverture in a March 1795 proclamation, assured the "conservation of the property of citizens," and his officers would make sure that property was respected. The propertyless ex-slaves, meanwhile, were ordered to return to their plantations within twenty-four hours. They would be paid a salary for their work, but they did not have the freedom to say no. "Work is necessary, it is a virtue," Louverture announced. "All lazy and errant men will be punished by the law." Writing to Laveaux a few months later, Louverture noted that he was "busy gathering the cultivators, the drivers, and the managers, exhorting them to love work, which is inseparable from liberty."[36]

Louverture was, from the start, generous and forgiving toward white planters in the regions he captured from the British. Although he knew that many of them had actively supported the British occupation and even carried arms against the French, he showed little interest in punishing them for their treason. In this he went against the grain of French policy, which was often quite harsh to those deemed traitors to the Republic; in 1794 in Guadeloupe, for instance, several hundred French planters who had fought for the British were executed and buried in mass graves by order of the Republican commander of the island, Victor Hugues. Louverture's own experience suggested the benefits of forgiving and forgetting; he had, after all, been greeted with open arms by the Republic in 1794 despite the fact that he had been fighting for the Spanish enemy for nearly a year. But he also believed that the colony needed these former masters in order to rebuild the plantation economy.

When in August 1795 Louverture captured the Mirabalais region from the British, he found "magnificent plantations" in the "best possible state" where the ex-slaves were "working well." In the town were several hundred white planters from other parts of Saint-Domingue who had gathered under the protection of the British. Louverture gave them passports to return to their homes and wrote to Laveaux requesting permission to give them back their properties, which had been sequestered by the Republic. Such abandoned properties, as Louverture saw it, were more likely to be rebuilt if they were put in the hands of their former owners, who had the expertise necessary to rebuild them, than if they were kept in the hands of a strained administration. Louverture was confident enough in his own power not to fear that these planters would challenge the order of emancipation from within. Indeed many of the planters who returned, seeing that the likelihood that slavery would be restored was diminishing day by day with Louverture's conquests, were willing to accept the new order, which offered them continuing, if somewhat diminished, possibilities for enrichment. The planters' return home was not always easy. Often, facing bureaucratic hurdles and the resistance of the managers put in charge of their plantations by the local administration, they were unable to reestablish ownership of their lost estates. Nevertheless many returned. Louverture pursued his policy of welcoming returning planters throughout his career in Saint-Domingue, generating both allies and enemies in the process.[37]

Louverture was comfortable working with former masters as a way of maintaining and rebuilding the shattered plantation order. Indeed, in 1795 he became a property owner himself, acquiring a plantation at Ennery, in the mountains above Gonaïves, which provided him with a refuge throughout the next years. By 1799 Louverture owned several plantations; an article published in France in early 1799 described one as being in the "best of condition," with a house where "everything exuded order and decency" surrounded by the "houses of the cultivators" and thriving groves of coffee trees. In the new regime, of course, property owners did not have the unfettered power over their laborers they had enjoyed under slavery. The colonial state was committed to emancipation. But it was also committed to making the former slaves stay on their plantations and forcing them to work at the same tasks they had before they were free. With their choices circumscribed by the policies of Louverture's regime—enforced by "agricultural inspectors" appointed in the areas under his command—ex-slaves did what they had in 1793 under Polverel's regulations, expanding their garden plots as much as they could, negotiating the terms of their labor, and sometimes illegally leaving the plantations to seek something better.[38]

Some plantation workers rose up against Louverture, claiming that his goal was nothing less than the resurrection of slavery. As early as January 1795 one of his officers, Blanc Cazenave, rallied cultivators in the Artibonite to rise up by claiming that Louverture intended to reinstitute the "old regime." In June, in the parish of Marmelade, another man encouraged cultivators to rebel by announcing that Louverture was "making them work" in order to return them to the "slavery of the whites." Several plantation managers whom Louverture had installed were killed. "I went myself to preach" to the rebellious laborers, wrote Louverture, but "in thanks for my pains I received a bullet in the leg, which is still causing me a great deal of pain." Much of the region's harvest had been lost to fire during the insurrection. Louverture used his disciplined troops of ex-slaves to repress these revolts. But rumors that he was preparing a restoration of slavery haunted him continually throughout the next years. Facing such rumors, and the revolts they helped stir up, Louverture defended his policies by insisting that it was necessary to limit liberty in order to sustain it.[39]

In February 1796 plantation workers in the mountains above Port-de-Paix, in the Northern Province, rose up in revolt. Several whites were killed. Louverture rode all night from the west to confront the rebels personally, demanding that they explain why they had risen up. He summarized the conversation he had with the rebels in a letter to Laveaux. Though the exchange was probably more complicated, and tendentious, than Louverture described it, his letter provides insight into the leader's evolving political philosophy. He had, he explained, criticized the rebels for the killings they had committed, and told them that "if they wanted to conserve their liberty they must submit to the laws of the Republic, be docile, and work." "God has said: ask and you shall receive, knock on my door and it shall be opened," he told them. "But he never said to commit crimes to ask for what you need." The rebels told Louverture they knew he was "the father of all the blacks" and had been working hard for their "happiness and liberty." But, the rebels insisted, they had good reasons for taking up arms. Etienne Datty, who "from the beginning of the revolution" had always been their leader, and had "always eaten misery with us so we would win our liberty," had been dismissed by local officials, and they did not understand why. Triggered by Datty's dismissal, the uprising was nourished by a broader set of grievances against the local administration. "They want to make us slaves; equality does not exist here," the rebels explained. Where Louverture was in command, "whites and men of color" were "united with the blacks." All seemed "like brothers, born of the same mother." "That, my general, is what we call equality." In Port-de-Paix, however, things were different. The blacks were disdained and mistreated. Those who worked on the plantations were not given a large enough share of what they produced. And they suffered daily, and potentially devastating, harassment. "They make us give them our chickens and our pigs when we go to sell them in town, and if we try to complain, we are stopped by the police, and they put us in prison and don't feed us and we have to pay to get out." This, the insurgents declared, was "not liberty."[40]

Louverture responded gravely that although all the reasons they had given him seemed justified, they were wrong to have risen up. They had put him in an impossible position. He had just dispatched emissaries to the National Convention to "thank them in the name of all the blacks for the benevolent decree that had given them liberty," and to "assure them that they would work hard" to prove to France, and to all other nations, that they deserved their freedom. He had triumphantly declared that, with the aid of France, the people of the colony would demonstrate to the "entire universe" that a colony "worked by free hands" could flourish. What would the Convention think when it learned what the insurgents of Port-de-Paix had just done? "Tell me," he demanded. He would be "shamed" and proven wrong. The French government would accept the arguments of the enemies of liberty, who had argued that "blacks are not made to be free, that if they become free they will no longer want to work, and will do nothing but steal and kill." They would demand that Louverture make sure the blacks remained obedient from then on.[41]

A few months later Louverture issued a similar proclamation to rebellious cultivators in the nearby parish of Saint-Louis du Nord. What would the French people say, he demanded, when they learned that rather than being thankful for freedom, the ex-slaves had "soaked their hands in the blood" of France's children? How could they dare claim that France wanted to reestablish slavery when the nation had sacrificed its flourishing commerce and its most prosperous factories to bring them liberty? "Be very careful, my brothers; there are more blacks in the colony than there are men of color and whites combined, and if there are disorders it is against us that the Republic will act," he warned. He demanded that all "good citizens" denounce those who "blasphemed against the French Republic."[42]

Louverture sought to placate the rebels, notably by naming Etienne Datty to a local military post. But his interventions ultimately had little effect. In May Datty took arms once again. "All the cultivators of the mountains have risen up," Louverture wrote; they were "destroying provisions" and refusing to deliver what was produced on the plantations. Rumors were circulating that Louverture was planning to "give the country over to the British and return them to slavery," and some claimed that the French government intended to reestablish slavery. He sent Dessalines to the area with 500 soldiers, who restored order in the area, at least for a time.[43]

In the end, if Louverture kept having to send troops to Port-de-Paix it was because he had provided no concrete response to the rebels' eloquent complaints that what they were living was "not liberty." His reply was simply that they had to live according to the rules of the Republic if they wanted to keep liberty at all. They should be grateful to France, and had to demonstrate that they deserved their freedom. Such statements, of course, obscured a great deal. For the liberty of the ex-slaves of Saint-Domingue had not been a magnanimous gift from a benevolent Republic. The National Convention had taken the important step of ratifying and sanctifying the principle of emancipation, and in so doing had courageously put principle before profit. They had done so, however, following the lead of Sonthonax's emancipation decree, which was a response to the powerful bid for liberty by the insurgents of Saint-Domingue. It was these insurgents—those who had "eaten misery" in pursuit of liberty, who were the real authors of abolition. Having suffered years of slavery at the hands of a French colonial regime, they had finally won emancipation through two years of war. Why, then were they indebted to France? Why, now that they were free, did they owe the nation the very same obedience and work that had previously been expected of slaves?

Louverture had been at the heart of the insurrection, and knew well enough that liberty had been won, not given. His concern, however, was how to preserve that liberty. He understood that, however principled France's leaders had been in 1794, ultimately the French nation would stick to the principle of emancipation only if Saint-Domingue continued to send the commodities it had produced for the past century across the Atlantic. Freedom was sweet, but it had a cost. France still needed the sweetness of sugar, and the coffee to go with it. According to one contemporary, Louverture's dictum was: "The liberty of the blacks can be consolidated only through the prosperity of agriculture." There was, perhaps, an alternative to maintaining plantation agriculture. The abolitionist Condorcet had suggested that as slavery was dismantled, small plots of land could be distributed to the former slaves, who would grow cane individually, and then bring it to state-run mills for processing and export. Louverture, however, like other French administrators, never truly considered this alternative, which certainly would have involved both costs and risks that perhaps seemed too much to bear. Instead he decided that it was vital to rebuild the plantation economy, whatever the costs, for the costs of not doing so would be even greater. As Louverture knew, the enemies of liberty were active, in the camps of the British in Saint-Domingue that he confronted each day, as well as in exile in the United States and in Paris. They had long argued that abolition would be a disaster, and would eagerly put to use any information they got that confirmed their suspicions about the incapacity of the slaves to be free. Emancipation was a fragile thing. To save liberty,

Louverture decided, was to accept that it might be something less than what slaves had dreamed it would be.[44]

Some ex-slaves garnered enough money to purchase land outside their plantations, or else headed into the hills and simply claimed it for themselves. But many—probably the majority—toiled away as laborers on the plantations where they had once been slaves. In the 1950s the ethnographer Odette Menesson-Rigaud recorded a Vodou song, a lament that seems to date from the period of the Haitian Revolution, probably from 1800. At the time Saint-Domingue was in the midst of a civil war, and Louverture's general Dessalines was leading troops against André Rigaud in the south. The two enemies had something in common: both were leaders of militarized labor regimes in the areas they controlled. Indeed, Dessalines himself, a former slave, controlled several large plantations. If, in much of Saint-Domingue, the old white masters had gone, the vast majority of ex-slaves still had no claim to the land that they, and often their ancestors, had worked. The Vodou song recorded in the 1950s perhaps provides us with a trace of the irony the ex-slaves registered about the situation, and the sorrow they felt as they came to see that the land they worked was not to be theirs. "Mister Rigaud, Mister Dessalines," the song announced, "this land is not for us. Understand? It's for the whites."[45]

CHAPTER NINE

Power

DO YOU BELIEVE, citizens and colleagues," Jean-Baptiste Belley asked the National Convention in early 1795, "that nature is unjust, that she has, as the planters assert, made some men to be the slaves of others?" Belley had been serving as one of Saint-Domingue's representatives since the year before, when he and his colleagues had precipitated the vote abolishing slavery throughout the French empire. Already, however, some of the men who served alongside him were clamoring against the liberty decree. A representative from the Indian Ocean colony of Ile de France, the planter Marie-Benoît-Louis Gouly, delivered a speech to the Convention portraying the ex-slaves of Saint-Domingue in starkly racist terms.[1]

It was absurd, Gouly insisted, to grant freedom and citizenship to people whose souls were accessible "only through the organ of hearing," animated only by the "loud sounds of a drum or a voice expressed with force," whose eyes had no "vivacity," and whose very "figure" presented "the image of stupidity." "He acts and does not reflect; he seldom speaks and often sings; never does a profound sentiment of pain or pleasure cause tears to stream from his eyes." "He suffers and never complains," Gouly continued. "He has no desires, loves repose, and absolutely hates work; his pleasure is to do nothing, and he finds all his happiness in sleeping." Such individuals had, in short, none of the capacities required for citizenship. Having made this argument, Gouly reiterated the arguments made before emancipation by thinkers like Moreau de St. Méry, asserting that the colonies must be governed by particular laws different from those applied in the metropole.[2]

Gouly's racism was nothing unique; it was part of a proslavery tradition that would haunt the Atlantic world for a long time to come. What was unique was the presence, at the heart of France's government, of a former slave who could counter these assertions through his words and his very presence. "I was born in Africa," Belley announced proudly in response to Gouly's "bizarre portrait" of the ex-slaves. Although the blacks had been brutalized by their masters, he explained, they had remained men. Their insensitivity was not an essential attribute, but the result of the degradation they had experienced at the hands of "cruel masters" like Gouly, "a tiger who for twenty-five years devoted himself to torturing Africans" while making his living "on the sweat and blood" of slaves.[3]

Belley explained how, brought "as a child to a land of tyranny," he had gained his liberty thirty years before through "hard work and sweat." Since that time, he announced, "I have always loved my country." The same was true of the blacks recently made "free and French" in Saint-Domingue, who "bravely" defended "the rights of the Republic." The white slave masters—"born dominators"—had, in contrast, busily handed over as much of the colony as they could to the British. The ex-slaves were clearly quite capable of serving France. It was the disloyal planters who were undeserving of citizenship. Gouly wished to see only "chains, slaves, and tyrants" in the Caribbean, and his "negrocidal" ideas were a threat to France and to the Rights of Man.[4]

"Let it no longer be said that the African cannot be submitted to discipline," demanded another representative in the National Convention a few months later. "The love of liberty makes him capable of anything, and the strikes he has made against the Spanish and the British are incontestable proof of his courage." He was speaking on behalf of the powerful Committee of Public Safety, which had just completed a report about the situation of the colonies. It confirmed many of Belley's claims. The white planters of Saint-Domingue were as "attached to slavery as nobles were to their vassals," "blinded by prejudice," and guilty of choosing to "throw themselves under foreign tyranny rather than give up their slaves." But where slavery had been abolished, all colors—Africans, whites, "yellows" ("mulattoes")— were fighting "with equal devotion for the cause of liberty." The threats of defenders of slavery, who had always claimed that without slavery there would be no work, had been proven wrong. "Let us no longer speak of the necessity of slavery for cultivation," the speaker demanded. Ex-slaves were working on many plantations as they had before, but were paid a salary instead of being forced to work for nothing. Any decrease in the productivity of the colony was a result of the "torrent of the revolution." Soon "new cultivators, assured of their liberty," would return to the plantations and "devote themselves to work." Freedom would give them "an energy that is never found in men burdened with slavery."[5]

These speeches were part of a larger battle over the consequences, and future, of emancipation that raged throughout 1795. While planters reworked their proslavery arguments in the new context, portraying the ex-slaves as lazy and barbarous, defenders of emancipation presented the ex-slaves as ideal Republicans, courageous soldiers, hard-working laborers, and loyal citizens. The two sides faced off in the lengthy trial that pitted Sonthonax and Polverel against a committee dominated by planters, who painstakingly attacked the actions of the commissioners during their stay in Saint-Domingue. As the trial wore on, Polverel fell ill and died. Sonthonax continued on alone, responding to his accusers and accusing them in turn. In the end he vindicated himself and the decree of general liberty. For the time being, the critics of emancipation were kept at bay.[6]

In the middle of 1795 a new constitution was passed in France. It replaced the National Convention with a Corps Législatif (Legislature) composed of two parliamentary bodies—the Conseil des Anciens (Council of the Elders) and the Conseil des Cinq-Cents (Council of the Five Hundred)—overseen by an executive branch called the Directoire (Directory). The constitution institutionalized a retreat from the more radical phase of the French Revolution, but it also confirmed the decree of emancipation, and declared that the colonies were an "integral part" of the French Republic. There were no legal or political distinctions between the departments of France and those of Saint-Domingue. In early 1796 the Directory appointed a new set of commissioners to bring the constitution to Saint-Domingue. Among the five appointed were Philippe Rose Roume de Saint-Laurent, who had served as a commissioner in 1791; the free-colored activist Julien Raimond, returning to the colony after a decade of exile; and Léger Félicité Sonthonax. Even he, who had been absent from Saint-Domingue for the shortest time of the three, would find a colony profoundly different from the one he had known.[7]

Eighteen months of war had produced a new group of military leaders of African descent. The four most important—André Rigaud, Louis-Jacques Bauvais, Jean-Louis Villatte, and Toussaint Louverture—had been rewarded for their service in early 1795 by the National Convention, which had promoted them to the rank of brigadier general. They loyally served the Republic by fighting against the British, but in the regions they commanded they operated autonomously, acting as both military leaders and local administrators, cultivating a political and social power that depended on their ability to mobilize and control the citizens of Saint-Domingue. Among the four there was one who would emerge, at the expense of the other three, as the central political figure in the colony. Having joined the revolution, Toussaint Louverture was busily making it his own. And he would prove himself ready and able to push aside all those who stood in the way.[8]

Unlike Louverture, André Rigaud had never fought against the Republic. Since 1792, when he and Louis-Jacques Bauvais had led the free coloreds of the Western province to victory and been named officers by Sonthonax, he had been fighting in the French army. The next year, when Sonthonax and Polverel fled the colony, they placed Rigaud in command of the Southern province. Alongside Bauvais, who controlled nearby parts of the Western province, he fought steadfastly against the British invasion in the name of the Republic. But, cut off almost entirely from the north, and therefore from Laveaux in Le Cap, he did so independently, forging an autonomous regime.

Rigaud's administration resembled that in place in the north in many ways. It pursued the goal of maintaining the plantation economy, building upon Polverel's regulations. But Rigaud introduced an innovative approach to managing abandoned plantations. Seeking alternatives to direct management by the state, he began to rent them out to private citizens. The policy had two major advantages: the administration gained badly needed revenue, and the work of reconstruction and production on the plantations was placed in the hands of individuals working for their own profit. It also, of course, had a potential political liability: many of those who had the money to take advantage of this policy were members of the wealthy class of people of color who had once been slave masters in the region. Those who had owned nothing in the old order—not even their bodies—found few opportunities to do anything but remain on the plantations, as they were ordered to do, and serve as laborers to these new masters. The placing of abandoned plantations in private hands represented another step away from the thrilling promise, made by Polverel in August 1793, that this land would be distributed to the ex-slaves. Disappointed ex-slaves in the south, as in the north, saw the ghosts of slavery in the new order.[9]

There were also tensions between ex-slaves and ex-masters in the military. Before the commissioners had left, they had ordered Rigaud to "lead and coordinate the insurgent bands of Africans" in the region. But the leaders of these powerful and independent bands—particularly a Kongolese-born man named Dieudonné, who commanded 3,000 soldiers camped in the mountains above Port-au-Prince—cherished their independence and did not wish to submit to the authority of Rigaud and Bauvais. Ex-slave troops and their officers had good reason to be suspicious. In 1792, after all, the Swiss—slaves who fought on the side of the free coloreds—had been sold out by their erstwhile allies, and most paid with their lives. In early 1793 the insurgent leader Alaou, soon after his triumphant meeting with Sonthonax in Port-au-Prince, was assassinated by troops loyal to Bauvais in what they presented as a preemptive strike meant to stop a planned assassination of their leader. Sonthonax himself had contributed to Dieudonné's hostility to the colored leaders: in June 1794 he had placed his commissioner's medallion around Dieudonné's neck, warning him that the free coloreds were a threat to freedom.[10]

In late 1795 the tensions between Dieudonné and Rigaud and Bauvais reached a breaking point. Dieudonné complained of their discrimination against black officers, pointing out that there were none in the towns under their command. Fed up, he opened negotiations with the British in Port-au-Prince. During the previous years his army had besieged the city by damming up the streams that brought water from the mountains to the city. Now, as a goodwill gesture, his troops let the water flow down once again. Dieudonné requested that a market be opened where his followers could sell the harvests from their mountain plots, and in early January his soldiers, "armed and defiant," sold poultry and vegetables to the hungry residents of Port-au-Prince.[11]

It was at this point that Louverture, who commanded stretches of the Western province bordering those held by Dieudonné and was worried that the Republic might soon lose several thousand fighters to the British, intervened. "Although I have not had the pleasure of meeting you," he wrote to Dieudonné in February, "I know that, like me, you are in arms for the defense of our rights, and for general liberty, and that our friends Polverel and Sonthonax had the greatest confidence in you, because you were a true Republican." Why, just as France had granted them "all the rights we are fighting for," was Dieudonné allowing himself to be tricked by the Republic's enemies? "The Spanish had, for a time, dazzled me," Louverture admitted, but he had seen the error of his ways. "I encourage you, my brother, to follow my example." Even if Dieudonné had "little problems" with Rigaud and Bauvais, he could trust General Laveaux, "who is a good father to us all." And he could trust Louverture, who was "black like him." The only path to happiness, Louverture insisted, was in "serving the French Republic." "It is under its flags that we are truly free and equal."[12]

Louverture sent two emissaries to carry this letter to Dieudonné. He also gave them secret instructions: if Dieudonné was unwilling to come over to their side, they should encourage his followers to rise up against him. As Louverture reported with satisfaction to Laveaux days later, his plan worked beautifully. Dieudonné refused Louverture's entreaty, but one of his lieutenants, Laplume, led an uprising that brought the several thousand troops who followed him to the Republican side. Dieudonné was imprisoned and died soon afterward. Laplume's troops, however, did not submit to Bauvais and Rigaud, but instead put themselves under Louverture's protection. Laveaux promoted Laplume to the rank of general. The tensions that had been smoldering between the colored officers and the leaders of the "African bands" were not resolved, just transferred into the beginnings of a conflict between Rigaud and Louverture.[13]

In the Northern province, meanwhile, Louverture was increasingly at odds with another officer of color, Villatte, who controlled the area around Le Cap. As Louverture and Villatte fought alongside each other against the Spanish, there were conflicts over the ill-defined borders between their zones of command. In January 1795, 180 of Louverture's troops defected and placed themselves under Villatte's command. Louverture wrote to Laveaux in April that he was willing to forgive Villatte for encouraging this defection—Catholicism, he wrote, taught men to forgive those who had "offended them"—but complained that the action put him in a difficult position. In June Louverture suffered a greater blow when, in the midst of a revolt in Acul, Louverture's commander in the area, Joseph Flaville, put himself under Villatte's command, bringing a substantial number of troops with him.[14]

Such insubordination, Louverture wrote to Laveaux, was like a river overflowing its banks, "ravaging" all in its path, and stopping the torrents in one place would only give them more force elsewhere. Laveaux intervened and removed Flaville from the area, but Louverture's resentment against Villatte continued. In January 1796 he complained that "men from Le Cap" were circulating among his troops trying to recruit them to join

Villatte's forces. "They say that the troops are well paid and taken care of in Le Cap," while those under Louverture's command lacked pay and food.[15]

Villatte had good reasons to be suspicious of Louverture, a man he had fought against during 1793 and early 1794, before his late rallying to the Republic, and whose power was increasingly in competition with his own. His conflict with Louverture put him also at odds with Governor Laveaux, who was already unpopular with many in Le Cap. Under Villatte's regime, free coloreds had taken up places in the town's administration, but some resented the fact that they were still under the orders of Laveaux. They were disappointed when he named a white officer, rather than Villatte, general of the army of the Northern province. As Laveaux wrote in January 1796, some free coloreds despaired that it was not "one of them" who was governor of Saint-Domingue in his place. "It is my country and not his," they said. "Why send us whites to govern and administer our country?" They also had more immediate grievances. Since the fires and mass exodus of 1793, many people of color had occupied and rebuilt abandoned houses in Le Cap. They saw the ownership of these houses as recompense for the service they had rendered the Republic, as well as a contribution to the restoration of the shattered city. But one of Laveaux's administrators, a local merchant named Henry Perroud, insisted that since these abandoned houses were the property of the Republic, those who occupied them should pay rent to the state.[16]

These grievances eventually boiled over in late March 1796. On the morning of the twentieth a group of "citizens of color" entered Laveaux's house and announced that they were arresting him "in the name of the people." He was dragged to prison and found Perroud already there. The municipal government issued a decree declaring that the governor had "lost the confidence" of the people and had therefore been replaced by Villatte. But some resisted the coup. One of Villatte's officers, Pierre Léveillé, circulated throughout Le Cap speaking out against Laveaux's arrest. The governor, he declared, was the "protector of the blacks," and if he died the free coloreds would turn over the colony to the English, and slavery would be reestablished. Léveillé was stopped by Villatte's followers, but not before he sent a message to the officer Pierre Michel, who commanded outside Le Cap, asking him to help. Michel rallied together his officers—including Pierrot, Sonthonax's first recruit in 1793—and demanded that Laveaux and Perroud be released.[17]

Michel also sent word to Louverture. "He who attacks Governor

Laveaux attacks the mother country and all of us," Louverture wrote back to Michel. He issued a proclamation to the inhabitants of Le Cap, criticizing them for sowing conflicts in the midst of war. "You asked for liberty and equality, and France gave it to you." Why didn't they wish to follow the governor whom France had given them? "What will the mother country say," he asked, when she learned of their treasonous actions? She would treat them all as "barbarians." "Blindly obey the laws," Louverture commanded sternly, "and those nominated to execute them." Meanwhile he wrote to the closest French authority—the consul in Philadelphia—to describe what had happened.[18]

The combined threat of Pierre Michel's nearby troops and the imminent arrival of Louverture sowed fear among the rebels in Le Cap. On March 22 they released Laveaux and Perroud, and Villatte fled. Six days later Louverture marched into Le Cap at the head of a large troop. He found that many townspeople remained wary of Laveaux because of a rumor circulating that two recently arrived ships had brought to Le Cap hundreds of chains that were to be used to reenslave the population. Louverture opened the doors of the administration building to prove that Laveaux was not hiding any chains, and calmed the crowds in the town. Laveaux again took up his post as governor. Louverture had saved the Republic's representative in the colony, and in the process asserted his military and political power in Le Cap.[19]

The Villatte affair has traditionally been interpreted as racial conflict pitting mulattoes against blacks. Laveaux supported such an interpretation and was seconded by Henry Perroud, who wrote indignantly that the men of color to whom France had given so much had turned against the metropole, while the "African chiefs" had "respected the representatives of the Republic." The Africans—"those men who appeared ferocious only so that they could win their liberty"—had in fact saved the governor from the scheming "mulattoes," who were "enemies of the French nation."[20]

While it is tempting to explain the conflict in such terms, and to naturalize the differences between Africans and mulattoes, the reality was more complex. Laveaux listed among Villatte's fellow conspirators several men who were not mulattoes, including several leading black officers and one officer who declared that his "only regret was that he had been born white." The Kongolese Macaya, for example, who had switched sides between Sonthonax and the Spanish auxiliaries in 1793, and who had later been imprisoned by Louverture, put himself under the protection of

Villatte in early 1796. "Every day he organizes dances and assemblies with the Africans of his nation and gives them bad advice," Louverture complained of Macaya at the time. Louverture, meanwhile, had more in common with men like Villatte than with the ex-slave, often African-born, troops he led to the rescue of Laveaux. Indeed his policies toward ex-slaves were in line with those of colored leaders such as Rigaud, who probably had a hand in encouraging the Villatte conspiracy.[21]

Even if it was a simplification of the situation, the accusation that Louverture was an enemy of the colored community was a dangerous one, and he actively sought to dispel it. Those who had tried "by a few quotations from my letters" to convince others that he had "sworn the Destruction of all men of color" were judging him according to their "own hateful and vindictive heart." "It is not color that I am fighting; it is crime," he declared. While he had indeed warned some of his officers to beware of the "men of color" who were "preaching disobedience," he did not confuse the "innocent" with the "guilty." He was not "prejudiced against any particular class" and had men of color whom he admired and respected among his officers. "I cherish all virtuous men," he announced. And he had not hesitated to strike out against "black men" when they were "committing murders."[22]

The question at the heart of the Villatte affair was not racial but political: What role would metropolitan authorities have in Saint-Domingue? Villatte and other free-colored leaders, educated and wealthy, saw themselves as the logical inheritors of colonial power. They were capable of commanding the army, of overseeing the administration, and of rebuilding the plantations. They were frustrated in their ambitions by the actions of Laveaux and Perroud and ultimately turned against them, seeking a bigger political and economic role in the colony. Louverture's intervention, meanwhile, was also an expression of his broader ambitions. His rescue of Laveaux was a strategic move that both ridded him of a political competitor who had undermined his authority, and indebted the governor to him. But his actions were also part of a broader political approach to securing and consolidating emancipation. He considered the link to metropolitan power—particularly to the version of this power embodied in the devotedly egalitarian Laveaux—vital to the survival of emancipation in Saint-Domingue. If he saw a threat to his authority in Villatte, he also saw a threat to the delicate balance of power he believed was necessary to sustain emancipation within the French Republic.[23]

Louverture declared that he would crush all disobedience to the mother country, threatening those who stood in his way with an apocalyptic curse: "let them fall alone into the abyss which they have dug under their Feet; the hand of God, the Avenger, is going to weigh down upon them, for one does not always defy the Supreme Being with impunity." The Bible, he continued, was full of "terrible examples of Divine Justice against Great Criminals."[24]

In the meantime, those whom he had saved embraced Louverture as an avenging angel. A grateful Laveaux declared him the "adjunct to the governor" and described him as "the Spartacus predicted by Raynal, whose destiny was to avenge all the outrages committed against his race." Several years later one visitor in Saint-Domingue would describe how Toussaint Louverture "revered the memory" of Raynal, whom he considered his "precursor." A bust of Raynal, the traveler wrote, was "respectfully conserved" in all the various offices Louverture used throughout the colony. But the task of avenging—and burying—the past turned out to be infinitely more complicated than Raynal had predicted: not an affair of torrents of blood and dancing skeletons, but one of the intricacies of power and politics.[25]

Soon after Villatte's attempted coup was defeated, the new commissioners named by the Directory arrived in Saint-Domingue. In addition to the new French constitution, they carried tens of thousands of guns for the colony's army. Sonthonax's return was celebrated in Le Cap, where the streets were packed with "good citizens" and "lined with flowers." The great emancipator had returned. Curiously, though, some spread the rumor—which had become, and would remain, the standard method for discrediting one's enemies in Saint-Domingue—that he had come to reestablish slavery. The commissioner did everything he could to dispel this impression as he sought to complete what he had begun in 1793, suspending all ongoing litigation involving the sale of slaves, outlawing racial insults, and threatening those who criticized emancipation with deportation. He announced that former slaves in the army were to have the right to proportional representation on military councils. Working with Julien Raimond, he established schools in Le Cap to teach former slaves to read and write. Meanwhile, although he freed many of those who had joined in the uprising against Laveaux, he quickly deported Villatte and his comrades to be put on trial in France.[26]

Welcomed in Le Cap, the commissioners were less warmly received in other parts of the colony. Suspecting Rigaud of a role in encouraging the Villatte conspiracy, and wishing to bring the south more firmly under his command, Sonthonax sent several delegates to the region. Following his orders, they sought to loosen Rigaud's hold on power by turning plantation workers against him. They criticized his plantation regime as tyrannical and publicly destroyed *cachots* (prisons)—which were still used to punish recalcitrant workers on plantations—promising that the commissioners would bring them a truer freedom. In Les Cayes they sought to take control of the administration and the army. Not surprisingly, their actions—coupled with their inept and provocative behavior toward local leaders—incited a hostile reaction. Rigaud and his partisans turned the tables on the delegates, mobilizing plantation workers by spreading the rumor that they had come to restore slavery. Soon an uprising was under way against the delegates, who fled for their lives. Rigaud had preserved his control over the south, and although his actions enraged the commissioners in Le Cap, they could do little to resist him. A second mission in 1797, during which the commissioners sought to use the "African eloquence" of one former slave to gain converts among the workers of the south, made no headway. Rigaud remained loyal to the French Republic and continued fighting the British, but he had secured his autonomy from the rest of the colony.[27]

Although the commissioners had as a political tactic criticized Rigaud's plantation regime, they, too, started to rent plantations to private individuals. Understanding the advantages of this policy—revenue and privately driven development—they stipulated that renters had to pay for repairs, and in so doing ultimately profited the state, which maintained official ownership over the plantations.[28]

Sonthonax imagined that plantation workers might band together to rent their properties—a solution he saw as the "best alternative." In fact, of course, if such groups of plantation workers did seek to rent properties at the public auctions at which they were distributed, they were inevitably outbid by wealthier residents. Wealthy whites and free people of color (notably Julien Raimond) gained control of many plantations, and therefore of the men and women who were required to work there. But the new elites of Saint-Domingue—the military officers, many of them ex-slaves, who had risen to prominence during the war against the British—also took advantage of the new policy. Some ex-slaves, notably Jean-Jacques Dessalines, used their power to amass a bewildering number of plantations. The renting of abandoned plantations therefore incited the "transfer of colonial property" and began a "radical social revolution": it "gave birth to a new property-owning class, and therefore a new managerial class" made up of individuals of African descent. The conflict over plantation labor thus grew more complicated, for it now often involved a struggle between ex-slave workers and ex-slave managers and owners. The seeds of new kinds of social conflict that would haunt postindependence Haiti had been planted.[29]

The new commission also organized elections for new colonial representatives. France's constitution required voters to make an "electoral contribution," a stipulation that excluded most ex-slaves from participation; only 5 to 10 percent of the residents voted. When the electors met in September 1796, the representatives still sitting in Paris—including Jean-Baptiste Belley—were reelected. But a number of new representatives were also chosen. Among them were the two most powerful Frenchmen in the colony: Laveaux and Sonthonax.[30]

In August 1796 Louverture had written to Laveaux, whom he addressed (as he often did) as "my father," that he worried that some "unfortunate event" might befall the Frenchman and his family in the "unhappy land" of Saint-Domingue. He suggested a solution: Laveaux could be elected as a deputy for the colony and return to his "true homeland." Louverture and "all his brothers" would have a "zealous defender" of their cause in Paris, since, among France's many men, Laveaux was the most steadfast "friend of the blacks." Laveaux agreed, and Louverture announced that he would send "trustworthy men" to convince the electors that Laveaux's election would assure the "happiness of the blacks," though he did not specify which methods of pressure they would use. "You will be elected," Louverture announced confidently, and correctly. Laveaux soon left for Paris. Most have interpreted Louverture's support of Laveaux's candidacy as a cynical ploy to rid the colony of a political competitor. Although this may be true, it is worth noting that Laveaux never complained about Louverture's actions and that, once in Paris, he did precisely what he had been asked to do, mounting a spirited—and necessary—defense of emancipation.[31]

Sonthonax's election was more divisive. Just after the elections a new revolt broke out among the plantation workers of the Port-de-Paix region, led once again by Etienne Datty. There were local grievances behind the uprising, notably anger at a recent decision to pay cultivators in paper money when they preferred being paid in commodities, whose value was more dependable. But there are also hints that rebels were responding to the news of Sonthonax's potential departure; some rebels reportedly shouted "Long live Sonthonax!" as they attacked plantations. Datty was executed, and Louverture crushed the remnants of the uprising. But the incident contributed to a feeling among the commissioners that Sonthonax should stay in the colony to use the "talisman of his name and his past actions" to keep order. In fact Raimond declared that if Sonthonax left, he would too. Sonthonax decided to remain at least until March or April of the following year.[32]

During the next months Sonthonax and Louverture came into increasing conflict. The reasons for the tensions were complex. Both men were committed to emancipation, and Louverture seems to have trusted Sonthonax, at least at first. (Indeed, the commissioner took charge of sending Louverture's two sons to study in Paris, placing them on a well-armed ship to make sure that "the sons of one of the greatest defenders of liberty" would not be in danger of "falling back into slavery.") But they had several differences. Sonthonax encouraged Louverture to demobilize some of his troops so that they could return to plantation work, but also requested more troops from France. Louverture probably knew this and was angered by the racism and hypocrisy of this act. Sonthonax, meanwhile, was dismayed by the welcome Louverture gave to returning French planters, many of whom had fled from Sonthonax's previous regime. (Among those Louverture greeted at this time was Bayon de Libertat, the manager who had freed him many decades before.) The two men were also, on another level, competing for the loyalty of the ex-slave population, and for the political power that came from their support. Many cultivators called Sonthonax their "father"; the historian Thomas Madiou, writing in the nineteenth century, remarked on the "enthusiasm" with which many of the old men who had lived through the period spoke of Sonthonax's love for the blacks. He was the only political figure who could compete in popularity with Louverture.[33]

Eventually, in August 1797, Louverture, along with several of his generals—notably Moïse and Henri Christophe—wrote a letter that essentially commanded Sonthonax to leave. There had been good reasons for him to stay, the generals noted, but since "peace, zeal for work, and the reestablishment of culture" had been achieved, he could now go "tell France what you have seen" and defend the cause for which they themselves would be "eternal soldiers." Rightly sensing the best moment to exit the stage, Sonthonax packed up quickly and left a few days later.[34]

His departure did not mark his complete withdrawal from the fray, however. Over the next two years the two men traded accusations. Once in Paris, Sonthonax steadfastly defended emancipation. He was proud, he declared in 1798, to have "contributed" to "the greatest revolution ever experienced on earth: the annihilation of slavery in America"; "I hold it an honor and always will," he later wrote, "that I was the first to dare proclaim the Rights of Man in the new world." But he also vehemently attacked Louverture, claiming that he was a dangerous tyrant bent on concentrating all power in his hands, and portraying him as an enemy of the Republic. "His unenlightened and superstitious mind," Sonthonax declared, "has made him dependent on counterrevolutionary priests who, in Saint-Domingue as in France, are doing all they can to reverse liberty." Louverture was also, he claimed, under the influence of the returning émigrés in their battle against emancipation.[35]

Louverture angrily denied such accusations. He had no problem with the Republican administrators the French government sent to the colony, just with the "strange Republican" Sonthonax. He reminded Laveaux of a conversation they had once had, in which Louverture had argued that the colony should be placed in the hands of "one European chief" who was a "friend of general liberty" and who would be free from the "habits" and "prejudices" of those from the colony. (Sonthonax had made the same point in the middle of 1796, when he wrote to the colonial minister in Paris that to manage the "liberty of the blacks" in such a way as to prevent the population from becoming a "horde of savages" ungoverned by laws, it was necessary for a "European to command in Saint-Domingue"; the point, of course, sounded different coming from him.) He counterattacked with his own accusation against Sonthonax: the commissioner had pushed him to massacre the whites and "make the colony independent of the metropole." The commissioner had therefore become a threat to the "freedom of the blacks."[36]

Both Louverture and Sonthonax knew that most of the embittered and often destitute exiled planters gathered in Jamaica, Philadelphia, and Paris would never accept emancipation. By 1797 they were gathering strength and attacking emancipation with increasing boldness. They were buoyed by a larger wave of reaction in France, which in March of that year swept many conservatives—including several Saint-Domingue planters—into office. By the time Louverture expelled Sonthonax, news of these changes had come to Saint-Domingue. In fact, though neither of them could have known it at the time, a month before Sonthonax's expulsion, parliament had demanded his recall. If Louverture's accusations that Sonthonax advocated independence were true, perhaps Sonthonax saw—prophetically, as it turned out—that with such enemies consolidating their power in France, in the end the only way to preserve the Rights of Man in Saint-Domingue would be for the ex-slaves to proclaim independence. Louverture seems to have used a different, more subtle, tactic. He offered up Sonthonax as a sacrifice to liberty: by handing him over to the planters, he hoped to sate them for a while.[37]

Louverture had ushered his longtime ally Laveaux, as well as Sonthonax, off the stage. The last commissioner in the colony, Julien Raimond, former advocate for the rights of the free coloreds, now deferred to Louverture's authority. The French officer François Kerverseau painted a portrait of Louverture, relaxed and delighted, in the wake of Sonthonax's departure. "I saw the hero of the day," he wrote; "he was radiant. His looks sparkled with joy, his satisfied face announced confidence. His conversation was animated, no longer suspicious or reserved." The black general was now unfettered by any other authority, free at last to shape the liberty of Saint-Domingue on his own terms.[38]

CHAPTER TEN

Enemies of Liberty

W E CONFRONTED DANGERS in order to gain our liberty, and we will be able to confront death in order to keep it," warned Toussaint Louverture in a letter to the French government late in 1797. Slaves had once "accepted their chains" because "they had not experienced a state happier than that of slavery." But those days were over. The people of Saint-Domingue would rather, as Louverture wrote in another letter, be "buried in the ruins of their country" than "suffer the return of slavery."[1]

In writing these words, Louverture was seeking to "conjure away the storm" gathering across the Atlantic. The Saint-Domingue planters in Paris were on the offensive. In May the planter Viénot de Vaublanc, a representative in the newly elected Council of the Five Hundred, gave a strident speech attacking emancipation. Saint-Domingue, he proclaimed, was in a "shocking state of disorder" and under the control of a military government run by "ignorant and gross negroes" who were "incapable of distinguishing" liberty from "unrestrained license." They had "abandoned agriculture"; their "cry" was that the country belonged to them and whites were no longer welcome there. The only solution was to force the ex-slaves to return to the plantations where they had lived "before the revolution." Once there, they should be required to sign multiyear contracts. The excesses of emancipation had to be reigned in, argued Vaublanc, and the population of ex-slaves coerced into serving as laborers for whites once again. Other delegates made similar speeches. In June one proposed that a large military force be sent to reestablish order in the colony, and that the government pay for the return of all exiled planters. As they attacked

France's colonial policy, Vaublanc and his partisans also attacked Louverture, portraying him as a dangerous despot.[2]

Louverture wrote an impassioned response to Vaublanc's speech. If the ex-slaves of Saint-Domingue were ignorant, Louverture argued, it was former slave owners like Vaublanc who were to blame. Furthermore, lack of education did not signify an incapacity for moral and political activity. "Are only civilized people capable of distinguishing between good and evil, of having notions of charity and justice?" The "men of Saint-Domingue" had little education, but they did not deserve to be "classed apart from the rest of mankind" and "confused with animals."[3]

Louverture conceded that there had been "terrible crimes" committed by ex-slaves in Saint-Domingue. But, he insisted, the violence in the colony had been no greater than that in metropolitan France. Indeed, if the blacks of Saint-Domingue were as "ignorant" and "gross" as Vaublanc proclaimed, they should be excused for their actions. Could the same be said of the numerous Frenchmen who, despite "the advantages of education and civilization," had committed horrific crimes during the Revolution? "If, because some blacks have committed cruelties, it can be deduced that all blacks are cruel, then it would be right to accuse of barbarity the European French and all the nations of the world." And if the treason and errors of some in Saint-Domingue justified a return to the old order there, then was not the same true in France? Would not it be justified to claim, on the basis of the violence of the Revolution, that the French were "unworthy of liberty" and "made only for slavery" and that they should be once more put under the rule of kings? How, he further insisted, could Vaublanc gloss over "the outrages committed in cold blood by civilized men like himself" who had allowed "the lure of gold to suppress the cry of their conscience"? "Will the crimes of powerful men always be glorified?" "Less enlightened than citizen Vaublanc," Louverture concluded, "we know, nevertheless, that whatever their color, only one distinction must exist between men, that between good and evil. When blacks, men of color, and whites are under the same laws, they must be equally protected, and they must be equally repressed when they deviate from them."[4]

Instead of frightening the ex-slaves with the threat of a return to slavery, Louverture suggested, white planters should accept and embrace freedom. In so doing, they would assure themselves the "love and attachment" of the ex-slaves. The blacks did not hate the whites, and in fact most of the ex-slaves—including those on the half of the sugar plantations on the north-

ern plain managed by whites—were dutifully working. They were not enemies of order and prosperity. The planters who thirsted for a return to slavery were. Louverture predicted that calls for limits on freedom, which
inevitably raised fears of a return to the old order, would set in motion a
self-fulfilling prophecy, creating the very defiance and rebellion they were
meant to destroy.

Moreover, he warned, any project to reestablish the old order would require a massive army, for the people of Saint-Domingue would have no
choice but to "defend the liberty that the constitution guarantees," even
if it meant fighting France itself. Would not the French take up arms if
their freedom was threatened? What would the white planter Vaublanc do,
Louverture wondered, if he was, "in his turn, reduced to slavery"? "Would
he endure without complaint the insults, the miseries, the tortures, the
whippings? And if he had the good fortune to recover his liberty, would he
listen without shuddering to the howls of those who wished to tear it from
him?" Defending freedom, Louverture suggested, was a universal and inalienable right. And those who fought for it in Saint-Domingue would have
little choice but to win, or to die trying. Louverture reminded the French
government that there were maroons in the Blue Mountains of Jamaica
who had forced the English to grant them "natural rights." He tactfully
avoided invoking events that would have been closer to home for French
readers, assuming they had not yet forgotten the insurrection of 1791. But
he was warning them not to start another war that they would lose.[5]

Julien Raimond similarly struck out against Vaublanc, arguing that his
speech was inflammatory and posed a serious threat to the prosperity of
Saint-Domingue. Raimond supported the policy of allowing exiled planters to return and rebuild their plantations, but he believed it was crucial
to prevent any men wanted to reestablish slavery entering the colony. Indeed he argued that any whites who returned to Saint-Domingue should
have to take an oath never to "pronounce a single word in favor of slavery." Any attempt to restore the old system would, even if it was supported
by the French government, turn Saint-Domingue into a "mountain of
ashes."[6]

Across the Atlantic, Louverture's ally Etienne Laveaux was also following developments in Paris with alarm. He had been unable to take up his
position in parliament, because the conservatives in Paris had annulled the
election in which he had been chosen. As he wrote to Louverture, he had
been dismayed to discover how powerful the enemies of emancipation had

"View of a Temple Erected by the Blacks to Commemorate Their Emancipation."
From Marcus Rainsford, *A Historical Account of the Black Empire of Hayti*
(1805). This monument, probably built under the rule of Louverture, recalled the
emancipation of 1793–94. The tablet listed articles from the 1793 emancipation
decree promulgated by Sonthonax. *Courtesy of the William L. Clements Library,
University of Michigan.*

become. "Men who drink not blood, but the sweat of men," were trying to have the decree of emancipation revoked and to "put the blacks back into slavery." He wrote that "all men who show themselves enemies of general liberty" should be deported from the colony.[7]

In September 1797 there was a political about-face in Paris. A coup d'état annulled the parliamentary elections that had brought Vaublanc and other planters into office. Laveaux soon took up his post, along with several representatives of African descent elected alongside him. Along with other supporters of emancipation in Paris, this group refounded the abolitionist Société des Amis de Noirs and began an energetic campaign to defend emancipation.[8]

In a November speech to the Council of the Five Hundred, Laveaux set out to dispel the "mistaken impressions" the "enemies of liberty"— who were also "enemies of the Republic"—had promulgated about Saint-Domingue and about Louverture himself. Louverture, Laveaux admitted, had indeed fought against France until 1794, but only because he was fighting for liberty. Having rallied to the French side, he had demonstrated his military skills—it was primarily thanks to him that the colony was still in French hands—and his humanity. He had helped destitute white women, Laveaux explained, and these grateful women called the black general their friend and their father. He had been forgiving of whites, even those who had betrayed the Republic, asking of them nothing more than that they take an oath of loyalty to France. "You are French," Louverture had reportedly declared; "I must show you the generosity of a black man who was once a slave." "This is the Republican some call a drinker of blood!" Louverture, along with his officers Moïse and Dessalines, had established order and rebuilt the plantations, and yet, Laveaux mused, "These are the men some would like to see enslaved once again!" Laveaux, like Louverture, insisted that any attempt to reverse emancipation would be disastrous. "The black citizens, at least as passionate as all other Frenchmen in pursuit of their liberty," he declared, were willing to die rather than to "renounce a single article of the Rights of Man." Any who attacked emancipation, he predicted, would "be defeated."[9]

Critics of emancipation had put forth a number of justifications for denying ex-slaves full access to citizenship. Hoping to "diminish the number of citizens among the blacks," as Laveaux put it, they had declared that the majority of them, because they had not been born in the Americas, were "foreigners" who should have to go through naturalization to become

French. Laveaux argued, however, that those who had been "wrenched from their native country and transported to Saint-Domingue" should not be considered foreigners. Because they had been taken across the Atlantic against their will, the colony became a "new place of birth." How could planters—who had "fertilized their sugar plantations" with the work of black men, having stolen them from their wives, children, and homeland, and who had "fattened" their fields with the "corpses of their predecessors"—have the audacity to consider these men foreigners? These were the men who had made the colony grow through their labor. "They have therefore done more for France than all the French who have settled in the islands."[10]

Granting citizenship was not only just; it was also the only way to preserve the colony. In war, the black citizens would be "soldiers, and valiant, because they will be defending their rights and their country." "In peace," they would be "the cultivators of the colony." They were the only ones, Laveaux insisted—echoing, ironically enough, the arguments of proslavery thinkers—who could do the harsh work on the plantations. "In the colonies, there is only one mode of cultivation: to make a lot of sugar, coffee, cotton, and indigo." But the way to keep them working was not to use coercion, but to reward them for their labor. The government should "honor the cultivators" by giving them the rights of citizens, not harass and oppress them. The former masters would indeed be getting off cheaply by rewarding the ex-slaves with citizenship, Laveaux insisted. For those they had oppressed could easily demand much more. Indeed, Laveaux suggested, laying out perhaps for the first time the argument for reparations for slavery, the plantation workers might well say: "Now that the laws have given us back to ourselves, now that, following the example of the French of Europe, we have conquered our liberty, we demand payment for all the time we worked for you, and damages for all the bad treatment we suffered."[11]

Laveaux and his allies succeeded in passing a new law that sanctified the principle of emancipation: "All black individuals," it declared, "born in Africa or in foreign colonies, brought to the French islands, will be free as soon as they set foot on the territory of the Republic." Those who had been "abducted from their homeland" were to enjoy the same rights as those born in France—at least as long as they were working either as cultivators or in a trade, or else enlisted in the army. Furthermore, an exemption from the poll tax was to be granted to all those who had served in the Republican army—though not, as Laveaux had argued it should be, to plantation workers. Thus in Saint-Domingue the many thousands of ex-slaves serving as Republican soldiers were assured the right to vote.[12]

In his November speech Laveaux had predicted that under the rule of Louverture, Saint-Domingue would soon be as "prosperous as it was in 1788," cultivated by "hands forever freed from slavery." To some extent he was right. Louverture would soon bring the imperial war for Saint-Domingue to a close, and in the next years oversee an impressive rebuilding of the economy. But there would not be peace in Saint-Domingue. Soon another war would pit Louverture against Rigaud's power in the south. And when this war ended, another would begin. For if Laveaux had courageously stalled the advance of the enemies of liberty in Paris, he had not stopped them. The 1798 law he crafted, a charter for a multiracial democracy in the New World, would ultimately be swept away by worshipers of the past.[13]

"I found, my dear general and good friend, the colony dismembered, ruined, sacked, occupied by the rebels, the émigrés, the Spanish, and the English," a triumphant Louverture wrote to Laveaux in September 1798. "I am leaving it peaceful, purged of its external enemies, pacified, and advancing toward its restoration." During 1798 Louverture oversaw the withdrawal of the British from Saint-Domingue and the extension of emancipation to the entire colony. It was a major diplomatic and military triumph.[14]

In May 1797 Louverture had written optimistically to Laveaux that Saint-Domingue would soon be "purged of the tyrannical hordes who have infested it for too long." Soon, however, the British drove him out of the Mirabalais region. He counterattacked at Saint-Marc, but as they attempted to take the major fort guarding the town, Louverture's troops found their ladders were too sort to scale the walls, and tried to take the fort by standing on one another's shoulders at the top of the ladders, while "their dead piled up around them." Despite such bravery, the British repelled the attack. The purging of the colony was again delayed, and the war dragged on.[15]

In such engagements black troops faced off against one another, for starting in 1795 the British, who rarely received reinforcements from across the Atlantic, had armed slaves in the regions under their control to buttress their strength. Planters were required to hand over a certain number of male slaves from their plantations, and since they preferred to keep their more experienced workers on plantations, the black units were made up almost entirely of African-born men. One-third of them were from the Kongo. Like the insurgents a few years before, these troops drew on African military traditions of "surprise and ambush" as they fought the Republicans. In addition to pay and food, the slaves were promised freedom in return for their service, an inducement enticing enough that it drew some deserters from the Republican side. By 1798 there were 6,000 locally recruited black soldiers fighting for the British.[16]

The arming of slaves helped shore up the British occupation, but it did so at a cost to the plantation regime, and ultimately did not resolve the basic problem: Saint-Domingue was devouring British money and troops and providing little reward in return. As the fighting continued, occupying troops garrisoned in Port-au-Prince and elsewhere were decimated by disease. A British officer wrote of the horror of soldiers "drowned in their own Blood": "some died raving Mad, others formed Plans for attacking, and others desponding." "Death," he lamented, "presented itself under every form an unlimited Imagination could invent." Furthermore, though many French planters and free-coloreds remained loyal to the British, by 1798 there were increasing complaints, and defections to the Republican side. Many British officials in London and the Caribbean were convinced that the best course would be to evacuate most, if not all, of Saint-Domingue. Although there were some who remained committed to capturing Saint-Domingue, skepticism about the wisdom of continuing the occupation largely permeated the British military command. Among the skeptics was the young General Thomas Maitland, who took over the British army in Saint-Domingue early in March 1798.[17]

When General Maitland arrived, Louverture and Rigaud were in the midst of a "concerted attack" against British positions, and as he watched, the Republicans took a series of important mountain forts built by the British. Slaves in the region under British control escaped to join the armies of Louverture, and, more ominously, some soldiers in the black corps deserted, for the first time, to the Republican side. The prospect of immediate rather than deferred freedom, as well as of serving under black rather than white officers, perhaps drew the deserters. Victor Schoelcher wrote that "at the sight of the tricolor flag," black soldiers serving the British went to the other side, "happy" to be serving under a "general of their race." But these soldiers probably also could see the writing on the wall, and wisely chose to end the war on the winning side. Smelling defeat,

Maitland soon concluded that a withdrawal from most of Saint-Domingue was the only reasonable course of action.[18]

Soon after Maitland came to Saint-Domingue, another newcomer arrived: Gabriel Marie Theodore Joseph d'Hédouville, the new representative of France's Directory regime. He was an officer famous for being the "pacifier" of the Vendée, a French region in which a strong counterrevolutionary movement had been crushed. Although he had left Paris at a time when Laveaux and his allies were in power, he had been chosen for the mission when the planters, including Vaublanc, were still in control of colonial matters. This fact doubtless made Louverture somewhat suspicious of him. Soon after Hédouville arrived in Saint-Domingue, Louverture offered him a bit of pointed advice. "There are men who talk as if they support general liberty," he explained, "but who inside are its sworn enemies." "What I tell you is true," he added. "I know from experience."[19]

Hédouville had been given a difficult mission: to reassert metropolitan control in the colony, wresting it from Louverture and Rigaud. He was make himself their commander, supervising and coordinating their military activities, and take over the colony's administration. He had been given some leeway as to how to approach the two men. Rigaud's rebellion against the commissioners in 1796 concerned officials in France, and the Directory had issued an order for his arrest. But the possibility of reconciliation and an alliance had been left open. Hédouville's attitude toward Louverture, meanwhile, had been shaped by the negative attitudes about him still prevalent in Paris.[20]

Hédouville was in a delicate situation, however, as he had no French troops accompanying him. He disembarked at Santo Domingo, on the Spanish half of the island (which was nominally under the control of a few French administrators stationed there), presumably out of fear of the reception he would receive in Le Cap. During his stay there, the French officer François Kerverseau counseled Hédouville that the only way for him to carry out his mission was to secure the forces he lacked by creating an "intimate link" with Louverture. "With him, you can do everything; without him, nothing." But Hédouville did not follow this advice. In 1798, as so many times before, metropolitan plans were undone in Saint-Domingue. Hédouville's mission, meant to bring peace, prosperity, and metropolitan control to the colony, instead helped trigger a brutal war and paved the way for the final step in Louverture's vertiginous ascent.[21]

General Maitland knew of Hédouville's arrival in the colony, but he also knew that although the agent had the "paper authority," it was Louverture who held the real power. He therefore approached Louverture, rather than Hédouville, as he began to negotiate the British withdrawal. In late April Maitland made an offer to Louverture: in return for a guarantee of "good treatment" for the French planters in the areas under British control, and a promise not to destroy property in the region, he would evacuate peacefully. Louverture dutifully sent the proposals to Hédouville, who authorized his general to negotiate, ordering him to grant amnesty to all "former French" who had not emigrated and had not served in the British army. When Louverture signed a deal with Maitland, however, he stretched the amnesty beyond what Hédouville had ordered, applying it even to those who served in the militia in the areas that had been occupied by the British, as well as all those who had fought with the British but had abandoned them, even if they had done so quite recently.[22]

Louverture's troops occupied Saint-Marc and Arcahaye, then marched triumphantly into the capital of the colony. At the Government House in Port-au-Prince, two British soldiers were still standing guard, having been left behind accidentally in the confusion of retreat, but Louverture's troops convinced the disbelieving men that it was, indeed, time for them to leave. Maitland moved the troops from the Western Province to the two final outposts he had in Saint-Domingue: Jérémie in the south, and the naval fort at Môle in the north. A few French planters struggled aboard ships, carrying what they could, to flee. Others, however, "tore off their Croix de Saint-Louis [a royalist symbol] and made contact with their former slaves in the Republican army." They assumed that personal loyalties had survived the years of turmoil and sought assistance and, perhaps, forgiveness. Louverture, meanwhile, ordered all the cultivators in the areas he had just captured to return to the plantations where they had once been slaves.[23]

Hédouville complimented Louverture on his successes. "The love of liberty and the motherland," the agent noted, had given Louverture qualities that even the best education could not have provided him. In early June, however, when Louverture and Hédouville met for the first time in Le Cap, their meeting was tense, burdened by mutual suspicions. Louverture would later recount that he found the agent surrounded by young officers "without principles" who were enemies of liberty. Wearing counterrevolutionary fashions popular in Paris, they repeated the slogans of Vaublanc, claiming that the "cultivator was unworthy of the freedom he enjoyed." He himself, Louverture wrote, became the butt of their "disdain and derision." Some of these officers joked that with four brave soldiers they could arrest the "monkey with a handkerchief on his head." When one French officer complimented Louverture by telling him it would be an honor to take him to France where he could enjoy the rest he deserved for his service to the nation, Louverture icily replied: "Your ship is not big enough for a man like me."[24]

After meeting with Hédouville, Louverture returned to the west and independently contacted General Maitland to negotiate for the final withdrawal of British troops from Jérémie and the Môle. Hédouville wrote an angry letter to Louverture, warning him that the British were trying to sow divisions among the French, but Louverture ignored the warning. In the coming months he insisted that the British general deal directly with him. When the two men met at the Môle in late August to finalize the transfer of the town, Maitland treated Louverture to a "sumptuous meal" in his tent and presented him with "the splendid silver that had decorated the table" as a gift from the king of England.[25]

Louverture's flouting of metropolitan authority had reached new heights. He was negotiating with Britain independently as the ruler of Saint-Domingue. He had his reasons to be angry with the French government, which had sent a man with no colonial experience, surrounded by a racist entourage, to give him orders. Why, Louverture may have wondered, didn't the Directory regime place its confidence in the hands of those, like him, who had been most responsible for preserving and governing the colony? Why did they send whites to command him, when he had proven his loyalty and competence over the past years? In his writings Louverture expressed hope for reconciliation and for unified Republican support of emancipation. But his actions suggest that he was increasingly wary of the French government and of the fragility of its commitment to freedom. He began to make sure that liberty could be protected, even against France itself.

Hédouville had been given the mission of "reestablishing the prosperity of agriculture in the colony." He was to oversee the return of plantations to their "legitimate" owners (the former planters) and apply a "uniform" policy on plantation labor, one that provided what was "necessary" to the cultivators and "appropriate" to property owners. It was up to Hédouville to decide exactly what "necessary" and "appropriate" meant. And his idea of the capacities and needs of the laborers bore a striking resemblance to the ideas of planters like Vaublanc. The ex-slaves were insensitive to the promise of personal gain; they "never think of tomorrow," he claimed, and were happy if they simply had some cassava and "a few roots" to eat. The best way to counteract the inherent laziness of the workers, he believed (again like Vaublanc), was to force them to sign contracts with their ex-masters, who would carefully supervise them. In July Hédouville ordered all cultivators to sign three-year contracts with those in charge of the plantations to which they were "attached." Louverture would later write that many in Saint-Domingue were surprised to see that the principles of Vaublanc, defeated in Paris, were nevertheless being applied in Saint-Domingue. But initially Louverture seems to have approved of the agent's regulations.[26]

Many plantation laborers, however, saw the new policy as a retraction of their rights. In his 1793 labor regulations, Sonthonax had required cultivators to sign one-year contracts on their plantations, after which they were permitted to move to another plantation if they wished. Rigaud's administration in the south had instituted a similar practice. Louverture had consistently ordered workers to return to their plantations, but he had not issued regulations regarding the length of their terms of contracts. In the areas under his control many former slaves seem to have moved between plantations, seeking better treatment or the company of family and friends, with relative impunity. In the increase in the terms of the contracts, some smelled the scent of slavery. A few laborers claimed they would rather "live in the woods their whole life" than sign three-year contracts, and in some towns the registers in which the contracts were to be signed were ripped up.[27]

The future of plantation laborers was tied to another delicate question: What was to become of Louverture's soldiers now that the war with the British was over? In the regions evacuated by the British, slavery was abolished, but Louverture immediately ordered the newly freed back to "their old plantations," and had his troops gather together "the dispersed cultivators" to make sure they returned to their former homes. But the rank-and-file soldiers who carried out his orders must have done so with some anxiety. For in Louverture's order, the only real alternative to military service available to former slaves was plantation labor. After years of war, many soldiers disdained those who worked on the plantations, whom they called "garden negroes," "poor devils," and, using the old term for recently arrived Africans in the colony, *bossales*. One former slave, a captain named

Patience, had come so far from the plantation that in 1802 he had his former master serving under him as his lieutenant. Indeed many black officers commanded white soldiers, sometimes former masters, throughout the colony. Soldiers who had seen their lives transformed through military service were understandably anxious that they might be demobilized and have to put down their guns and pick up hoes once again.[28]

From the moment of his arrival in the colony, even before the British evacuation had been secured, Hédouville had sought to limit the size and power of Louverture's army. He resented the expenses incurred by the large army, complaining that the "black troops" were given a costly ration of bread when they could easily survive on cassava, bananas, and potatoes gathered in the countryside. (The troops never ate their bread, the agent claimed, selling it instead; but when it was not issued to them they nevertheless "murmured" in complaint.) Hédouville also thought the colony was overpopulated with black officers. Most of these men, he wrote, could barely read and were at the "mercy" of their secretaries, the detritus of the white community. They followed "no law but their will" and exercised an "intolerable despotism." Since their rank was determined by the number of men they commanded, Hédouville claimed, they constantly pulled cultivators from the plantations, sometimes by force; he outlawed such recruitment, unless carried out under his explicit orders, in June 1798. Every "ravine" in the Northern Province possessed an arrogant officer who had been catered to by the "negrophile" policies of the white administrators who had preceded him.[29]

Hédouville's lament was echoed by other writers, such as the French traveler Michel Etienne Descourtilz, who ridiculed the "ignorant" black officers. Some wore so many rings that their fingers were puffed up from lack of circulation; they also wore earrings "like women." He described one named Gingembre-Trop-Fort, who he claimed barely knew French, wore two watches on long chains, and rode his horse with a pillow on top of his saddle. Such portraits were an attempt to counteract, and parody, the dramatic challenge such officers actually represented. As experienced veterans of the war for liberty, some among them would, in a few years, join in trouncing the French army. Many of them had emerged from the "multitude" of Africans who had strengthened the insurgent camps in 1791 and 1792, and were as ready to fight to keep liberty as they had been to win it.[30]

Hédouville's attempts to gain control over the colony's army led him into open conflict with one popular and high-ranking black officer: Moïse. From early on in Louverture's rise to power, Moïse had been beside him, and Louverture had made him his adopted nephew. By 1798 Moïse commanded the garrison at Fort-Liberté (formerly Fort-Dauphin), close to Le Cap. In mid-July Hédouville accused Moïse of gathering cultivators on a plantation, presumably with a seditious intent, though he allowed him to remain at his post. In October, however, using a series of fights in the town as a pretext, Hédouville effectively deposed Moïse, placing a local black official in charge of the town and an officer named Grandet in charge of the troops of Fort-Dauphin. Moïse and his supporters saw this as an attack against the black army, and even against the regime of liberty itself. Indeed, just as the conflict between Hédouville and Moïse was beginning, Moïse complained that Grandet was capturing fugitive blacks who had escaped from slavery on the Spanish side of the island, and was returning them to their masters on the other side of the border. To Moïse and others this policy portended a dangerous retreat from the principle of emancipation.[31]

Moïse left Fort-Dauphin with some of his partisans and began mobilizing laborers on plantations to join him. But he also called on a more daunting supporter. Within days Louverture was on the march. He ordered Dessalines to arrest Hédouville and Christophe to capture the leaders who had replaced Moïse at Fort-Liberté. Soon thousands of troops under Louverture's command, as well as crowds of cultivators, surrounded Le Cap. On October 23 Hédouville, joined by most of the white officers who had come with him, boarded ships in the harbor of Le Cap and sailed back to France. Joining Hédouville in his flight were the commissioner Julien Raimond and several black officers, including Pierre Léveillé, one of the heroes of the Villatte affair, and Jean-Baptiste Belley, who had returned to the colony after serving out his term in Paris. Such men were, like Louverture and unlike Hédouville, deeply committed to defending emancipation and racial equality. But they were disturbed by various aspects of Louverture's increasingly authoritarian exercise of power, his friendly dealings with the British, his generosity to and closeness with returning planters, and his bold dismissal of official French emissaries such as Hédouville. Louverture saw his actions as vital to the preservation and consolidation of liberty. But, increasingly, he was alienating not only metropolitan emissaries but also some who had fought the battle for equality with him.[32]

Before his departure Hédouville had accused Louverture of being "against liberty" and in favor of "independence." "Who must love liberty more," retorted Louverture: a former aristocrat like Hédouville, or the onetime "slave from Bréda"? "Does Hédouville think he scares me?" Louverture wondered. "I've been fighting for a long time, and if I must continue, I can. I have had to deal with three nations, and I defeated all three." The French had already lost 22,000 men in "our country," he noted, and those that it sent in the future would probably suffer the same fate. "I don't want to go to war with France," Louverture proclaimed. "I have preserved this country for her until now, but if she attacks me, I will defend myself." He called up once again the image of the maroons of Jamaica as proof of what blacks could accomplish. "I am black like them, I know how to fight, and, what is more, I have advantages that they did not have, for I can count on support and protection." Louverture was talking not only of the support of French friends of emancipation like Laveaux, but of other allies as well.[33]

Louverture had kept control over the negotiations with the British for a very specific reason. He wanted them to withdraw from Saint-Domingue, but he also wanted their help in rebuilding the colony's economy. Even as he negotiated the withdrawal of the British with Maitland, therefore, he signed a secret treaty with the British general. Louverture promised not to attack or encourage sedition in Jamaica, and in return Maitland agreed to end the British blockade of the island. It was a bold step. France and Britain were still at war, and yet with this agreement—along with a second he signed in 1799 expanding its provisions—he was promising peace between French Saint-Domingue and British Jamaica. And he was agreeing to—indeed encouraging—trade between British merchants and the French Caribbean's major colony. Louverture was making sure that he would have a mechanism to export the coffee and sugar it produced and a source for what it needed to survive. But he was also doing more. He was preparing for the possibility of open conflict with the French government.[34]

Having negotiated an independent agreement between Saint-Domingue and Great Britain, Louverture continued his diplomacy, developing an autonomous foreign policy based on the interests of the colony and not those of France. In June 1798 the U.S. Congress, responding to continuing attacks by privateers against its merchant ships, suspended commercial relations with France. The "Quasi-War" between the two nations would continue for two years, and had an immediate impact on Saint-Domingue: the U.S. merchants who provided the colony an important an outlet for coffee and sugar and a source of provisions and other goods were suddenly outlawed from visiting its ports. Louverture wrote to John Adams complaining that American ships had "abandoned" Saint-Domingue, and expressed hope that commercial relations would be reestablished. He would, he declared, welcome U.S. ships as those of an ally and protect them from attack. Eager to maintain the lucrative trade with Saint-Domingue, American officials quickly found a way to get around the congressional decree that outlawed trade with any region under the control of France. Secretary of State Thomas Pickering argued that if the people of Saint-Domingue no longer acknowledged the power of the French government over them, then there were no obstacles to trading with them. In early 1799 the U.S. Congress passed an act specifically allowing the president to reopen trade with Saint-Domingue. Pickering announced to Louverture that American ships would be allowed back into the ports of the colony if he stopped all French privateering in the area. Soon a new U.S. consul general, Edward Stevens, was on his way to Saint-Domingue to finalize the terms of a trade agreement.[35]

Louverture drafted a public document allowing U.S. merchant ships to come to Saint-Domingue. Stevens asked him to go further, agreeing not to let any French vessels that had been armed outside the colony to enter its ports. Publicly accepting such a provision would have been a provocation to the French government, for it was essentially a declaration of independence: even as armed U.S. and British ships would be entering the ports, French ships arriving from elsewhere would be turned back. But, as Stevens assured Secretary of State Pickering in May 1799, Louverture "privately" agreed to this demand. During the next year, of the nearly 1,800 ships that came in and out of Saint-Domingue for trade, only 15 were French, while most of the rest were British and North American. The trade with the United States was particularly important to Louverture because, unlike the British, whose merchants were primarily supplying provisions, the merchants from the north were a source of guns and ammunition. During the next years merchants came regularly from the United States—one day in July 1801, 32 were counted in Le Cap's port—playing a central role in sustaining Louverture's military might. Early in 1802 General Victor-Emmanuel Leclerc complained that the United States had brought "guns, cannon, and powder" to the colony, convinced that it was the intention of the Americans to encourage the independence not only of Saint-Domingue but of all the Caribbean, so that they could control all the trade in the region.[36]

In fact the U.S. perspective on the revolution in Saint-Domingue was more complex. Working with and supporting Louverture was a delicate matter. He was, after all, the embodiment of a slave revolution that horrified many whites, and the leader of a daunting army of ex-slaves. The commercial opportunities available on the island attracted many merchants, especially from the northern states, but for the south Saint-Domingue was first and foremost a dangerous example for local slaves. Pulling back from Adams' outright support for Louverture after his election in 1800, Thomas Jefferson would ultimately move toward a policy of containment. With his eyes on Louisiana, he was clearly interested in limiting French power in the area, but he was also concerned about limiting the impact of the revolution on North America. In a conversation with a French ambassador in Washington in 1801, Jefferson wondered whether it would be possible to declare the island independent but keep it "under the protection" of France, the United States, and Britain. The three powers, he noted, could work together to "confine this disease to its island." "As long as we don't allow the blacks to possess a ship we can allow them to exist and even maintain very lucrative commercial contacts with them."[37]

Louverture proved his willingness to prevent the export of revolution in 1799, when he betrayed a conspiracy to incite a slave uprising in Jamaica. The plan—a "diabolical attempt to extend the destructive influence of French principles," in Edward Stevens' words—was for the revolt to pave the way for an invasion from Saint-Domingue. The Directory regime supported the idea, though Hédouville was unable to carry it out before he was expelled. In late 1799, however, a man named Sasportas—a Jew involved in contraband trade in the region—entered Jamaica secretly along with another conspirator with the intention of mobilizing slaves there. Louverture let the British know, and the two were soon captured. Sasportas was hung in Kingston, a casualty of Louverture's adroit diplomacy.[38]

The rapprochement with the British and the Americans had its costs for Louverture, however. Although he sought to keep his dealings with these enemy powers secret, news of the 1798 agreement with Maitland circulated widely. In December of that year a London newspaper announced: "With this treaty, the independence of this important island has, in fact, been recognized and guaranteed against any efforts the French might make to recover it." The fact that a "black government has been constituted and organized in the West Indies," the article continued, was a great step forward for the "cause of humanity." Once published in Britain, of course, the news rapidly spread to France, where officials took quite a different view of the matter. Laveaux wrote to Louverture from Paris in September 1799 to warn him that the "villains who abhorred him" in Paris were denouncing him for planning to make the colony independent. He pleaded with Louverture to prove they were wrong by demonstrating his submission to the mother country.[39]

But Louverture was no longer willing to submit to French authorities. After expelling Hédouville, he brought the French agent Roume, who was stationed in Santo Domingo, to Le Cap. Roume was, in principle, serving as the metropolitan representative overseeing Louverture's actions, but in fact the French official was "no more than a dignified prisoner at Le Cap" who possessed only the "semblance of power."[40]

Nevertheless, Louverture never articulated a plan for independence of the kind attributed to him by some British and U.S. observers. In strengthening the autonomy of his regime, Louverture was preparing not to break with France, but to renegotiate its relationship with the colony. Ironically, his regime represented the fulfillment of some of the dreams of autonomy enunciated by the planters of Saint-Marc years before. Like these earlier planter activists, Louverture wanted free trade, control over economic policy within the colony, and political autonomy. Unlike them, he had successfully forced such a regime on the metropolitan officials in the colony. Like the planters, he envisioned a thriving plantation economy. But unlike them, he sought to construct an order without slavery. In a curious reversal of the situation in 1793 and 1794, when the planters sought autonomy to save slavery, Louverture sought it in order to save emancipation.

In 1798 the French naturalist Michel Etienne Descourtilz arrived in Saint-Domingue. He was not alone: many planters were returning to the colony "like bees," hoping to recover their lost fortunes. It was a time of optimism for many whites: the blacks were, because of the "orders of Toussaint Louverture," more "politically submissive" than they had been before— and would be later. Louverture had been actively welcoming white planters back into the colony from the beginning of his service to the Republic, but the victory over the British and the expulsion of Hédouville allowed him to consolidate and expand this policy.[41]

Hédouville had ordered Louverture not to extend the Republic's amnesty to émigrés, but even before the British withdrew he was dismayed to see a "quantity of émigrés flooding into our ports." They clearly trusted, rightly as it turned out, that it was Louverture, and not Hédouville, who would determine their fate in the colony. In Port-au-Prince in mid-August 1798, after a "solemn mass," Louverture declared that, following the teachings of Catholicism, he was willing to pardon those who had sinned by supporting the British occupation. In early September Louverture called on émigrés in the United States to return to Saint-Domingue, where, like the "prodigal son" returning to their father, they would be pardoned. Among those who responded was a wealthy planter named Bernard Borgella, who had been the mayor of Port-au-Prince during the turbulent early years of the Revolution. The returned planter, a longtime proponent of political and economic autonomy from France, would help shape the black general's policies.[42]

As planters returned to Saint-Domingue, they often found themselves in competition with new groups of elites, often ex-slaves, who controlled their properties. Given the economic possibilities opening up during this period, these new managers were not sanguine about handing over plantations to their old owners. The many military officers who were renting abandoned plantations could call on their loyal service to the nation—which contrasted sharply with the treasonous actions of the returning white planters—in laying claim to the land. They were also tightly connected with, and indeed often controlled, the local administrations that were given the responsibility of overseeing the transfer of property back to their original owners. Not surprisingly, then, planters found that it was often difficult to get their former plantations back, despite Louverture's promises. Instead of seeking to resolve the conflicts over land, Louverture pursued a policy that allowed him to sidestep the problem. He gave planters signed papers declaring that their properties were no longer under the control of the state. But when they found themselves powerless to confront and expel those who occupied and controlled their plantations, he did nothing to enforce their claims. One planter, after officially regaining ownership of his plantation, sought to collect rent from the high-ranking officer Laplume, who had been managing the plantation for the previous years. Laplume's response was to claim that the administration had given him a suspension of rent payments for eight to ten months and to refuse to pay, and there was little the planter could do. Another planter complained in

1800 that his property was "in the hands of my former driver," who, along with a free-colored man, were doing everything they could to keep hold of his property and push him out of the colony.[43]

As he traveled in the Artibonite region, the traveler Descourtilz wrote, he saw many devastated plantations whose once-resplendent houses were now denuded and falling apart, seeming to "beg for the return of masters." The men and women who occupied them, however, seemed quite content to be left alone. Descourtilz described a stubborn and brazen refusal on the part of ex-slaves to give up the gains they had been freed. For many planters, the tables were turned in a particularly distressing way, for they found their plantations in the hands of one of their former slaves. As they waited for the local bureaucracy to consider their requests to take back their lands, they were at the mercy of those they had once owned. Descourtilz discovered this firsthand when he traveled to a plantation that had been owned by members of his family. The former slaves who were renting the plantation clearly wanted nothing to do with him; they "pushed their audacious impudence" so far as to refuse to let him and those he was traveling with forage on the property for a few bits of food. "How many times during this unfortunate epoch," he lamented, laying bare his conviction that those who now lived on the plantations were still nothing more than property, "did we, the owners of five leagues of land and 750 blacks, have to serve ourselves!" Some former slaves were even more assertive. In May 1800 one administrator wrote that in certain areas "the cultivators have expelled the white property owners, claiming that the land belonged to them, since they had, as they said, worked it for others for long enough."[44]

Descourtilz was personally involved in one complex struggle for the control of a plantation in the Artibonite. It pitted Descourtilz' uncle, M. Lachicotte, against his "bastard" half-brother, Philippe, both of whom claimed the inheritance of the property of their deceased father. It was a classic family drama—a conflict between a legitimate heir and an illegitimate heir—but it took on a particular cast in postemancipation Saint-Domingue. Philippe was of African descent, and his mother was probably a slave, but he was able to take advantage of the revolutionary context to gain the upper hand on Lachicotte. He became an officer in Louverture's army, outranking and indeed at one point commanding Lachicotte. Their father's property had been declared abandoned by the local administration. Philippe used his connections and salary to rent the plantation, and was so pleased at the reversal of fortune that he announced to Lachicotte: "Your reign is over." In 1798, however, Lachicotte managed to get papers from Louverture ending the state's sequestration of the plantation and declaring him its rightful owner. When he and Descourtilz attempted to take possession of the plantation, however, they found themselves powerless. Expecting a respectful welcome by the plantation residents, they were instead entirely ignored. They were "constrained," Descourtilz wrote in disgust, to go to market to buy their own food and to drive their own mules, which the plantation residents "were not even willing to go get for us in the savanna!" Clearly, whatever fear the former slaves once had for whites seeking to master them had evaporated.[45]

On the plantation, Descourtilz observed, residents had taken over significant stretches of land to cultivate gardens to which they devoted "all their time." Philippe, meanwhile, sought to continue the production of the cotton for which the plantation had once been famous. Descourtilz described Philippe as a horrid tyrant who terrorized the plantation laborers and angered them by flooding their gardens in order to irrigate the cotton fields. They longed, he claimed, for the return of their white masters. The details Descourtilz provided, however, tell a different story. Plantation workers enticed Lachicotte and Descourtilz to the plantation by telling them that they wished to help them regain the plantation, but when they arrived they found that they had been tricked: they were bundled off and presented to local authorities, accused of stirring up trouble on the plantation. Philippe was steadfast in holding on to the plantation, but also quite hospitable to the two interlopers. Though he did not grant them any particular privileges, he did allow them to stay on the plantation and even lent them his carriage for their errands. He seemed to be willing to have them return as residents, just not as masters.[46]

Much had changed in Saint-Domingue since the days of slavery. Whites and blacks, former masters and former slaves, had redefined their relationships and their place in the social order. The landscape was a patchwork shaped by intersecting histories of insurrection, war, and negotiation. A former plantation owner traveling through the colony in 1799 came across some functioning sugar plantations and a few thriving coffee plantations. But he focused on the many ruined properties, where "bushes and trees" had entirely "replaced the houses" and old cane fields were covered with grass and ivy. His biggest shock came when, from the peak of a mountain where once "we stopped in ecstasy to see the plain of Le Cap in all its splendor," he could see only "ruins and bushes" where sugarcane had once covered the land.[47]

On the plains of Le Cap and throughout the colony, a new kind of life was taking root, one based on independence and subsistence, one that for many ex-slaves embodied true freedom. In and around the ruins of old plantations, men and women cultivated small plots of land, growing crops for their families and to sell at the markets. They raised chickens, pigs, and cows, often grazing them in abandoned cane fields. Although they were drawing on traditions developed within slavery, when masters had depended on what slaves produced in garden plots, in the new order they had greater access to land and greater freedom to grow their crops, raise their livestock, and market what they produced. The contrast with slavery was quite clear, and as a result of the better conditions, the number of children seems to have increased among the workers on many plantations. A new culture was being born, one that would shape rural Haiti in the wake of independence. But what for ex-slaves was a new beginning was for many whites, haunted by the specters of the vanished plantations, nothing but loss and darkness. A Polish soldier sent to Saint-Domingue in 1803 captured this sense eloquently. "The air here is most unhealthy," he wrote, "especially since the time of the black revolt twelve years ago." It was as if the uprising that had shaken the colony in 1791 had literally transformed the environment, the very air, making it deadly to Europeans.[48]

CHAPTER ELEVEN

Territory

IN JULY 1798 a carriage bumped its way from Port-au-Prince to Le Cap, carrying the two de facto rulers of Saint-Domingue, Toussaint Louverture and André Rigaud. They were on their way to meet with Hédouville to discuss plans for British withdrawal from the colony. What did the two allies—soon to be bitter enemies—discuss on the journey? Neither left a written account, but oral traditions circulating in the nineteenth century asserted that the two men made a pact during the journey: they would be careful in their dealings with Hédouville and would share with each other any information they gained from him. If they indeed made such an agreement, it soon came undone. Hédouville intentionally treated Rigaud more warmly than he did Louverture, seeking to create jealousy between the two men. Before he was expelled from the colony a few months later, Hédouville planted another "seed of contention" between them. In a letter to Rigaud, Hédouville criticized the "perfidy of General Toussaint Louverture, who is sold to the English, the émigrés, and the Americans." "I absolve you entirely of the authority he was given as general-in-chief," he wrote, and invited Rigaud "to take command of the Department of the South."[1]

Louverture and Rigaud had been allies since 1794, and together they had assured the triumph of the Republic in Saint-Domingue. By 1798, between the two of them, they controlled all the troops and territory of the colony. Louverture was technically Rigaud's superior, but in fact the latter continued to rule over the Southern Province and to command his army independently, as he had since 1793. With the end of the war with the British and the expulsion of Hédouville, however, the relationship between

Louverture and Rigaud rapidly soured. Soon the two were waging a brutal civil war against each other.

The "War of the South," as the conflict is usually called, is often presented as a racial conflict pitting Louverture's black army against Rigaud's free-coloreds. Before the revolution the south was a bastion for wealthy free-coloreds such as the Raimond family, and Rigaud was a member of this social group. Under his regime free-coloreds had filled posts as officers and had gained access to many of the abandoned properties in the south. There were, therefore, consistent tensions between the free-coloreds and the former slaves whose lives they governed and whose labor they often controlled. Although these tensions were driven primarily by the economic differences between the groups, given that so many of the wealthy and powerful in the region were of mixed European and African descent, while those they controlled were not, it was easy for former slaves to see racism at work. In the north, meanwhile, most of Louverture's highest-ranking officers were entirely of African descent, and many had been slaves when they revolted in 1791. The contrast between the two leadership groups makes it tempting to see their conflict as primarily a race war.

In fact, however, there was quite a bit of diversity on both sides. There were many free-coloreds and whites who fought with Louverture's forces during the war, and some of them distinguished themselves for their ferocity against Rigaud's partisans. And there were also ex-slave leaders who, disenchanted with Louverture's regime, and particularly with his close ties to returning white planters, took advantage of the war to strike out against his regime. In the north, several ex-slave officers supported Rigaud during uprisings against Louverture, notably Pierre Michel, who had helped to suppress the Villatte uprising in Le Cap in 1796. In the west the African-born Lamour Desrances, who controlled mountain areas around Port-au-Prince, also sided with Rigaud. The war cannot be explained simply as a conflict between two racial groups.[2]

Louverture did use racial appeals in rallying his followers against Rigaud. Speaking in church in Port-au-Prince in February 1799, Louverture recalled the abandonment of the "Swiss"—the slaves who supported the free-coloreds in 1791—and asked the free-coloreds in the audience: "Why did you sacrifice the Swiss? Because they were *black*." Rigaud, he went on, refused to obey him for the same reason: "because of my color." Once the war began, when some free-coloreds led uprisings in the north in support of Rigaud, Louverture angrily accused the "men of color in general" of conspiring to destroy Saint-Domingue.[3]

Rigaud denied that his resistance to Louverture was motivated by racism. It was, he insisted, simply a response to the vicious treatment he had suffered at Louverture's hands. "I have chiefs, but I have no master," Rigaud wrote, "and never did an irritated and foul-mouthed master treat his slave in a manner as atrocious as I have been treated." Rigaud noted that he had been born, like "General Toussaint," to a mother who was a "négresse." He had a brother who was black whom he had always "obeyed and respected." He had been educated by a black schoolteacher. All these individuals had always given him orders, and he had always followed them. "And is there, in any case," Rigaud continued, "such a difference between Toussaint's color and my own?" "I am too strongly penetrated by the Rights of Man to believe that one color is superior to another," Rigaud declared. It was Louverture, he insisted, who was the real racist.[4]

Louverture also accused Rigaud of rebelling against the French government. But the free-colored general used the letter he had received from Hédouville to claim that it was he who was the legitimate representative of the government, and Louverture the seditious rebel. Both sides also invigorated their polemics with more serious accusations. The U.S. consul Edward Stevens described how Rigaud "studiously propagated" the idea that under Louverture the colony "was to be sold to the British government, and once more brought under the Yoke of Slavery." Louverture, meanwhile, claimed that it was the free-coloreds who were enemies of liberty, and that under Rigaud's command they intended to reestablish slavery as soon as they were able.[5]

Like all enemies, Rigaud and Louverture sought obsessively to highlight their differences. In fact, however, they resembled each other enormously. Both of their regimes were predicated on maintaining former slaves on plantations and on cultivating economic ties with British and U.S. merchants. While free-coloreds made up a larger part of the ruling class in the south, their interests were not substantially different from those of the new class of black property owners that had emerged in the north and west. At base, the conflict between Louverture and Rigaud was not driven by differences in racial identity, or even differences in ideology or practice. It was a conflict over territorial and political power. Louverture was determined to assert his control over the entire colony. But the south had, throughout the history of Saint-Domingue, been a region apart from the rest of the colony, one with a particular culture sustained by its extensive contacts with other Caribbean islands. Building on this foundation of autonomy, Rigaud and his partisans had created a strong and independent regime. They wished, naturally enough, to maintain control, and fought back when Louverture threatened to destroy what they had built.[6]

"My apprehensions of an immediate rupture between the two rival chiefs of this colony have been realized," Edward Stevens wrote in late June 1799. On June 18, 4,000 of Rigaud's troops entered the towns of Petit- and Grand-Goâve, routing the smaller forces under the command of Louverture's officer Laplume. This defeat was a kind of revenge: in 1795 Laplume had brought several thousand troops under Louverture's command rather than submit to the authority of Rigaud. It was also a direct challenge to Louverture, who had insisted on the transfer the towns to his command a few months earlier. Rigaud's bold attack earned him an important ally: the powerful free-colored officer Alexandre Pétion defected to Rigaud's side, swelling the ranks of his army. Composed mostly of "black troops that have served under him since the commencement of the revolution," along with a few "cultivators," his infantry was "well disciplined," and his cavalry, "composed entirely of mulattoes," was "the best in the colony."[7]

Rigaud's partisans were not confined to the south, however. After his victory there were revolts in Le Cap, the Artibonite plain, and, most seriously, in the Môle and the region surrounding Port-de-Paix, where Louverture had faced uprisings consistently during the previous years. The rebels failed to take Port-de-Paix, defended by one of Louverture's loyal officers, but they did surround it. Louverture had enemies everywhere. Indeed, he was the target of two assassination attempts. In the first, his personal physician was killed, and a bullet passed through Louverture's hat. During the second Louverture's carriage was riddled with bullets and his coachman killed. The general escaped "miraculously" only because he was riding behind the carriage.[8]

It was the greatest political challenge Louverture had yet faced. In the north and west he responded with swift brutality. In the months following the uprisings, Louverture's troops executed conspirators without mercy. Descourtilz described Louverture publicly punishing one officer in the town for indiscriminate killings, telling him: "I told you to clear the trees, and you uprooted them." The officer responded by saying: "What do you want? When it rains, everyone outside gets wet." Descourtilz claimed that

Louverture had hypocritically ordered the widespread executions only to publicly disavow them. This may well have been true. But Louverture—who had often been quite merciful to those he defeated—might well have been disturbed by the extent of the revenge. Still, there is little doubt that the officers under his command, notably Christophe and Dessalines, committed numerous atrocities during the campaigns against Rigaud and his partisans.[9]

Having crushed the uprisings in the north, Louverture invaded the south to destroy Rigaud's regime. He had numbers on his side. According to Stevens, Louverture had the support of "most of the Blacks, and all of the Whites of the colony" and was "too powerful" to be defeated." He had 45,000 troops in his army, compared with Rigaud's 15,000. Louverture knew, however, that to win the war he needed to isolate Rigaud. He turned to his new ally, the United States. Writing to John Adams in mid-August, he announced that "in order to satisfy his pride and ambition," Rigaud had started a rebellion "odious" to "all the Governments on earth." He lacked, he explained, one "repressive measure" he needed to end this revolt—a navy. Louverture requested that the United States use its ships to help him "reduce" the "pirates" that were fanning out from Rigaud's ports, attacking both French and foreign ships. Edward Stevens wrote to Washington around the same time, arguing the United States should "cooperate with the British in cutting all supplies of provision and ammunition to Rigaud." To do so would be in the best commercial interests of the United States, for if Louverture should "prove unsuccessful," then "all the arrangements we have made respecting commerce must fall to the ground." Adams was convinced, and soon the U.S. Navy was blockading the southern ports.[10]

Having secured such support and suppressed the uprisings against him in the north and west, Louverture was all but assured of victory. Still, as his army, under the command of Dessalines, marched into the south, the fighting was brutal. The leaders on both sides had demonized their enemies, and the fighting descended into a "delirium" in which neither side showed any mercy. "It never entered anyone's mind to take prisoners." The land, too, suffered; as Rigaud retreated, he commanded his troops to create a "desert of fire," making sure they left behind only trees with their roots in the air. Rigaud lost crucial allies, most devastatingly his longtime comrade Louis-Jacques Bauvais, who, having maintained a tenuous neutrality at the beginning of the conflict, abandoned the colony rather than fight on one side or another. (He died soon after when the ship he was on sank in the Atlantic.) Rigaud also found little support among the cultivators in the Southern Province. Louverture, meanwhile, sought with some success to draw cultivators to his side, sending ex-slave officers, including one named Gilles Bambara, who was probably African-born, to do the recruiting. When Rigaud retreated to Les Cayes, he "rang the tocsins as a signal and call to arms," hoping the cultivators in the surrounding plains would come to his defense. "No one came forward to answer the call." Their refusal to support Rigaud, probably to some extent simply a pragmatic choice, was also a sign of the hostility many felt toward the labor regime to which they had been subjected during the past years. If they hoped for better under Louverture's rule, however, they were to be disappointed.[11]

In June 1800 an emissary from France arrived in Saint-Domingue, carrying a series of proclamations from First Consul Napoleon Bonaparte. One of these confirmed that Louverture was still the "general-in-chief" of the army of Saint-Domingue. Since Rigaud had justified his revolt in part by declaring Louverture's authority illegitimate, this news undermined his position substantially. Sensing that the momentum of the war was on his side, Louverture soon declared a general amnesty for all those who surrendered. In late July, Rigaud fled the colony with his family, and soon afterward Louverture entered Les Cayes. He reiterated his declaration of a general amnesty. Nevertheless, in the wake of the defeat there were reprisals committed against many prisoners. Some have asserted that Louverture ordered these massacres but had his generals do the dirty work so that he could deny knowledge of what was being done in his name. Dessalines's role in this period, in particular, remains controversial. Many see him as the driving force of the brutal reprisals against Rigaud's partisans, though one historian has also noted that he made an effort to preserve the lives of several prisoners. A few years later, some of those who had fought with Rigaud would in fact rally to Dessalines's side as he battled for independence from the French.[12]

Louverture had consolidated his control over all of Saint-Domingue. But his territorial expansion was not over. As he fought against Rigaud, he set his sights beyond the south, looking east. Spanish Santo Domingo had been ceded to France in 1795, but despite the presence of a few French officials the Spanish administration continued to control the colony. Louverture's reasons for wanting to control Santo Domingo were, at least initially, tied to the war against Rigaud. Edward Stevens attributed Louverture's decision to invade to a curious rumor that ships carrying 15,000 troops and the Abbé Grégoire had landed in Guadeloupe and were heading for Santo Domingo. Those who spread this rumor perhaps raised the threat of Grégoire because he was seen as a friend of free-coloreds, and therefore of Rigaud. Although it is doubtful that Louverture trembled at the thought of the arrival of the French priest (who in any case was safely across the Atlantic), he understood the need to prevent Rigaud from receiving any support from the east. To secure his position he needed to control all the ports in the colony. Santo Domingo was an ideal place for hostile new arrivals from Europe to land, as Hédouville had done in 1798, in order to sidestep Louverture's control of Le Cap.[13]

Louverture explained his desire to conquer Santo Domingo, however, in a different way: he claimed that men, women, and children who were "French citizens" were being kidnapped to Santo Domingo and sold as slaves. In April 1800 he announced to the agent Roume that he was determined to end this abuse by sending his troops across the border into the Spanish colony. Convinced that the occupation order had to come from Paris, Roume hesitated to lend his approval to the project, but Louverture simply locked him up. In late December, after defeating Rigaud, he ordered Moïse to lead troops across the border. They were virtually unopposed, and a month later the governor of the Spanish colony capitulated—he and his entourage soon left for Spain—and Louverture's army occupied the capital city, Santo Domingo. Accounts of his army's reign in the colony vary widely. One contemporary presented it in the manner of many imperial apologists, describing how the "principles of French administration" brought "new industry and activity" to the Spanish colony, along with "magnificent" new roads and a new economic prosperity. Others have described a regime in which Louverture's black officers enriched themselves through pillage and seizure of lands.[14]

Before launching his attack, Louverture had assured the governor that, if he surrendered, the property of the residents would be respected. He made no mention of slavery. But a few months earlier, in June 1800, Louverture had discussed the issue with the French officer Pierre Agé, whom he was sending as an envoy to Santo Domingo. "We have often talked," he told Agé, "about the bad way in which general liberty was applied to the French portion of the colony, and how important it is to rule wisely in order to make sure it reigns there without causing problems."

The universal liberty that had been granted to the slaves in the French colony, then, could not be applied: "we must change nothing in the system that currently exists." Like many critics of the 1794 decree in Paris, Louverture seems to have envisioned a process of gradual emancipation as the ideal. Though he did decree slavery abolished in Santo Domingo, it is not clear precisely how or to what extent this was implemented during the occupation.[15]

With the defeat of Rigaud and the conquest of Santo Domingo, Louverture controlled the entire island of Hispaniola. "I have taken flight up high with the eagles," he was heard to say during this period. "I have to be careful as I come back to earth." He needed a rock to set himself down on, he continued: he needed a constitution that would secure his power. Louverture and the colony Saint-Domingue were about to enter the final stage of their history. They would walk part of their journeys together.[16]

"They go from one plantation to another at will, coming and going, paying no attention to cultivation," Louverture complained of the ex-slaves in October 1800. Many "even hide in the cities and towns, and in the mountains, attracted by people who are enemies of order, busying themselves only with stealing and libertinage." The worst of the bunch, he continued, were those who were too young ever to have labored as slaves, and now refused to do plantation work. They were vagabonds, providing a bad example for other cultivators, justifying their behavior by saying that "they were free."[17]

Since 1794 Louverture had consistently enforced limits on the freedom of ex-slaves, arguing that such limits were necessary to consolidate and protect emancipation. It was the responsibility of the "people of Saint-Domingue," as he declared in November 1798, to work to make the colony's economy flourish; the "safety of liberty," he explained in 1801, made the rebuilding of the economy of Saint-Domingue "particularly urgent." In seeking to define the colony's future, he found the past weighing inexorably upon it: Saint-Domingue had developed as a producer of sugar and coffee, and it was difficult to imagine any other role for it in the prevailing Atlantic economy. The colony had long depended on the importation of provisions, and in the late 1790s, with the Franco-British war dragging on, foreign trade was more crucial than ever. To attract foreign merchants, Saint-Domingue had to produce and export its traditional commodities. This was not just an economic necessity; it was also, as Louverture saw it, a matter of political survival. If they were to have a say in their future, the people of Saint-Domingue would need the economic autonomy that could come only from a strong plantation economy. And achieving it would require stifling the aspirations of former slaves who envisioned a future beyond the plantations. But for Louverture this was a price worth paying, as he made abundantly clear in October 1800 by consolidating his labor regulations into one draconian decree.[18]

Louverture militarized plantation labor, applying the ideals of discipline and the methods of punishment used in the armed forces to the colony as a whole. Just as soldiers obeyed their officers, cultivators must obey their superiors. Just as soldiers were court-martialed when they failed in their duties, those who failed in their plantation labor would be punished. Just as soldiers had no freedom of movement and could not leave their units without "the severest punishment," cultivators who left the plantations without permission would be subject to fines or imprisonment. He sought to close off all potential routes of escape from the plantations. He outlawed plantation residents from working as domestics in the towns, and threatened those who employed them as such with fines. He also insisted that military commanders make sure that there were no women in the barracks, unless they were married to soldiers, and specified that no "cultivatrices"—women from the plantations—were to be allowed there under any pretext. The status of the plantation laborer—a status based on a past of enslavement on the very plantations where they were now being ordered to stay—was rendered immutable and permanent. All efforts to escape this past and to create a different future—other than for service in Louverture's army—were criminalized. The plantations were part of the war to preserve liberty, and their residents must accept their roles as soldiers in that war, and the discipline it made necessary.[19]

In February 1801 Louverture issued another decree that further limited the possibilities open to former slaves. In various parts of the colony, the general noted, "one, two, or three cultivators" sometimes joined together to buy a few acres of uncultivated land, and abandoned their plantations to settle there. This practice was common in many postemancipation contexts as former slaves sought to gain what they saw as the ultimate guarantee of independence. Drawing on the traditions of small-scale farming on garden plots that had existed in slavery, they hoped to grow enough food and raise enough livestock to support themselves and sell the excess in local markets. Louverture, however, saw such settlements as a threat to his plan for the plantations. The "agriculture of the colony," he wrote, was "very different from that of other lands" because it required the "reunion of considerable means" in order to be productive. The farming of small plots of land not only did not contribute to this broader productivity; it actually decreased it, by taking "arms" away from the existing plantations. Louverture outlawed the sale of small plots of land under fifty carreaux, or just over three acres. Any sale of larger plots, furthermore, had to be approved by the local administrations under his control, who were to monitor how it was used. The decree made it impossible for relatively poor men and women to acquire land. There were to be only wealthy landowners and landless workers, with nothing in between.[20]

What Louverture was proposing was alarmingly similar in many ways to the old order he was disavowing. There were important differences, of course, most notably the fact that cultivators were to be paid for their work. But the unflinching threat of physical punishment issued by Louverture, finessed by the comparison made to the disciplining of soldiers, meant that ex-slaves were pushed to work as much through fear of violence as through the promise of payment. Not surprisingly, some claimed that it was Louverture's ultimate intention to reestablish slavery. Indeed, days after he issued his decree, Louverture learned that it had been misinterpreted by "badly intentioned people of all colors," particularly by "old planters and property owners," who had gleefully announced to their former slaves: "You say you are free! But you are going to be forced to come back onto my property, and there I will treat you as I did in the past, and you will see that you are not free." Since such statements would inevitably "delay the restoration of Saint-Domingue," Louverture ordered his troops to arrest and punish any individuals who made them. The leader of Saint-Domingue was walking a thin line, seeking to contain simultaneously the aspirations of ex-masters for a return to the old order and the aspirations of the ex-slaves for a fuller freedom.[21]

In 1801 Louverture embodied his control over the colony in a charter for his regime: a constitution. The document built on the foundation of his labor decrees, but it was also a response to dramatic changes taking place across the Atlantic. The French government was now in the hands of Napoleon Bonaparte. Like Louverture, Bonaparte had taken advantage of the revolutionary period to make a vertiginous ascent from the margins of his society—he was born in Corsica, an island recently annexed by France—to its summit. Celebrated as a hero for his brilliant leadership of the armies of the Republic during the 1790s, by the end of the decade he was poised to take power. He organized a coup against the parliament and created a new consular regime, which he dominated. Bonaparte staffed his Colonial Ministry with men who had been devoted defenders of slavery and proponents of colonial autonomy a decade before. Among them was Moreau de St. Méry, who had recently returned to Paris from exile in Philadelphia.[22]

In the early 1790s Moreau and his allies had advocated the formation of "particular laws" for the colonies as a way to prevent the granting of rights to free-coloreds, and the possibility of a reform or elimination of slavery. They had failed to stop the application of the universalist principles of the Revolution in Saint-Domingue; their political ideology had been roundly defeated in 1794. In 1800, however, after years of criticizing emancipation, the planters and their supporters had their revenge. Bonaparte's new constitution decreed that because of the difference in the "nature of things and the climate," the colonies were to be governed by "special laws." Indeed, given differences in "habits, customs, interests," as well as the "diversity" of agriculture and production, there were to be different laws applied to the different colonies of France in the Americas, Asia, and Africa. It was a profound shift away from the colonial policy envisioned by Etienne Laveaux a few years before: the colonies would no longer have representatives in Paris, as they had during the previous years of Revolution. Continental France and her colonies, united under a single legal order for years, were again separated. It was a victory for an old tradition of creole legal thinking embodied in the work of Moreau, although it was a far cry from what many planters had hoped for at the beginning of the revolution: the "special laws" would not be shaped by the residents of the colony, but instead decreed by the metropolitan government.[23]

Bonaparte understood that in the Caribbean the return of the policy of "particular laws" would be seen by many as a looming threat to liberty itself. And so, as they announced their new policy, the consuls also declared to the people of Saint-Domingue that "the sacred principles of the liberty and equality of the blacks will never suffer, among you, any attack or modification." The "brave blacks" should remember that "the French people are the only ones who recognize your right to liberty and equality." In case they forgot, Bonaparte ordered that this statement should be written "in letters of gold" on the flags of all the military units in Saint-Domingue. Louverture, who was confirmed by Bonaparte in his rank of "general-in-chief" of Saint-Domingue, refused to follow this order when he received it several months later. He probably noted that the consul's declaration promised only that liberty and equality would not be touched "among you," that is, in Saint-Domingue; aware of the implications of the idea of "particular laws," he was also probably aware of the opening the new policy allowed for the acceptance of slavery in some parts of the empire. "It is not a circumstantial liberty conceded only to us that we want," he apparently said; "it is the absolute acceptance of the principle that no man, whether born red [i.e., mulatto], black, or white, can be the property of another."[24]

Louverture recognized the opportunity created by these new circumstances and seized on it to propose his own laws for Saint-Domingue. On February 4, 1801—the seventh anniversary of the abolition of slavery by the National Convention—he announced the convocation of a "Constituent Assembly" that would draft a constitution for Saint-Domingue. The time had come to "lay the foundations" for the colony's "prosperity" by creating "laws appropriate for our habits, our traditions, our climate, our industry." He used the language of difference deployed by the French government, but with a different intent. Where it had once served to assert white supremacy in the colony despite the universalist promises of the Revolution, Louverture now used it to justify the creation of a body of law that sanctified and solidified a new regime in which men of African descent were in command. Instead of waiting for Bonaparte to send his own laws, he decided to make his own.[25]

In early March, representatives from each of Saint-Domingue's departments were selected by local assemblies to seats on Louverture's Constituent Assembly. Among those chosen was Julien Raimond, whom Bonaparte had sent back to the colony in late 1799, and whose contribution to Louverture's constitution would be his last political act; in mid-October 1801, he died in Le Cap. Along with Raimond and two other men of color served seven whites, including Bernard Borgella, the returned planter who had become an important adviser to Louverture during the previous year. There were no ex-slaves on the committee—although Moïse had been elected, he refused to take up the post—and most of those on it had once owned slaves. Members of the old elite of Saint-Domingue, those who thanks to their wealth had the luxury of education, were being formed into a new political elite, gathered around the figure of Toussaint Louverture. They were not the only ones giving him advice: Alexander Hamilton sent a letter to Louverture recommending "a lifelong executive and the enrollment of all males in the militia."[26]

An 1822 engraving, part of a series on the history of the Revolution published in Haiti, shows Toussaint Louverture proclaiming his 1801 constitution under God's approving eyes. *Private collection.*

In early May the Assembly completed its constitution, which was signed
by Louverture and promulgated in July 1801. It decreed the colony—com-
prising the entirety of Hispaniola and its coastal islands—a "part of the
French empire" governed by a set of "particular laws." "In this territory,
slaves cannot exist; servitude is permanently abolished," the constitution
declared. "All men within it are born, live, and die free and French." All
residents, "no matter their color," could pursue any employment, and the
only acceptable distinctions would be those based on "virtues and talents."
These initial articles, rephrasings of Bonaparte's constitution, the Declaration of the Rights of Man, and the 1794 abolition of slavery, laid the foun-

dation for an egalitarian society based on the permanent rejection of slavery and racial hierarchy.[27]

The constitution also established a specific religious order for Saint-Domingue. In early January 1800 Louverture had issued a decree outlawing "nocturnal assemblies and dances." Men with "bad intentions," he noted, had been taking "peaceful cultivators" away from their labor by drawing them to such dances, "principally those of Vaudoux." Through these practices, they spread principles that were "absolutely contrary" to those of "friends to their country," and would be subject to physical punishment and imprisonment if they continued their subversive activities. The 1801 constitution built on this earlier decree by declaring that the only "publicly professed" religion was to be Catholicism. The constitution, as Louverture declared, supported "the reign of good habits and the divine religion of Jesus Christ in our climates." Louverture, however, kept direct control over the "extent" of each priest's "spiritual administration." The constitution also declared that those who participated in "civil and religious marriage," which encouraged "purity of habits," would be singled out and protected by the government. Divorce was outlawed. The status and the rights of children were to be defined by laws that aimed at "spreading and maintaining" the "social virtues" and cementing "family ties."[28]

Residents of Saint-Domingue were invited to take part in another kind of family, one not defined by blood. "Every plantation is a factory that requires the union of cultivators and workers; it is the tranquil refuge of an active and loyal family, whose father is necessarily the owner of the soil or his representative." Each "cultivator," the constitution continued, was a "member of this family," and therefore had a right to a part of the plantation's revenues. But since the movement of cultivators from one plantation to another would cause the "ruin of cultivation"—and since the colony was "essentially agricultural" and could not "suffer even the slightest interruption in the work of cultivation"—the regulations set down in Louverture's October 1800 decree were maintained. Cultivators, like children, could not leave the homes of their "fathers," the property owners. Indeed, they were to be joined by new brothers and sisters. "The introduction of cultivators," the constitution proclaimed, was "indispensable for the reestablishment and growth of cultivation." The government would take "appropriate measures" to "encourage" an increase in the number of "arms" in the colony. Louverture was considering working with merchants to bring men and women from Africa as cultivators to work the plantations of Saint-Domingue.[29]

Louverture's constitution represented, as one scholar has argued, the articulation of a "social contract" for Saint-Domingue, one that would have a profound impact on the structuring of postindependence Haitian society. (It is indeed celebrated today as the "precursor" to the nation's first constitution; in 2001 President Jean-Bertrand Aristide dedicated a monument in Port-au-Prince that recalls Louverture's political achievement by reproducing some of the constitution's articles.) It rested on the idea that "all citizens owe their services to the land which feeds them and in which they were born, to the maintenance of liberty and equality, of property, whenever the law calls on them to defend it." As Louverture put it in his speech proclaiming the constitution, the law was the "compass for all citizens," and all should "bend before it." In a sense, the constitution was simply articulating a political classic claim, drawing on the previous policies of Republican France and Republican Saint-Domingue, about the responsibility of citizens to support and sustain their nation. Such claims, which placed the power to define these responsibilities in the hands of a potentially abusive state, always entailed contradictions between liberties and duties. But Saint-Domingue's constitution carried within it particularly powerful contradictions. On the one hand, the project that all the people of Saint-Domingue were called on to support was a project of emancipation, of freedom from racial hierarchy, of liberty for all in a land once dominated by slavery. At the same time, ex-slaves were given very particular responsibilities that were defined by their old status: those who had once worked as slaves were now free, but they were required to work as cultivators. To defend freedom, they had to surrender their freedom to the new state.[30]

This state was literally embodied in one person, Toussaint Louverture, who was declared governor of Saint-Domingue for "the rest of his glorious life." Louverture was even given the right to choose his successor, but the latter's term of office was limited to five years. Although the assembly that had written the constitution was maintained as a consultative body, and municipal administrations and tribunals were established throughout the colony, Governor Louverture would sign and promulgate all laws, control all administrative and military appointments, and oversee enforcement of labor policies and trade. He had the right to censure any publications and to suppress any writings arriving from outside that might bring "disorder" or "corrupt" its residents. Residents were granted few political rights beyond the ability to present petitions to the administration, particularly to the governor, and were warned that "seditious gatherings" would be dispersed, by force if necessary. Louverture's power was based, as it had been since 1794, on the military. In his speech proclaiming the constitution he called on his soldiers to "observe discipline and subordination, activate cultivation, obey your chiefs, and defend and support the Constitution against the internal and external enemies who seek to attack it." The army, according to the constitution, was to be "essentially obedient," could "never deliberate," and was "at the disposition of the Governor."[31]

The French officer Charles Humbert Marie Vincent, who had worked closely with Louverture since 1794, was given the delicate task of carrying the new constitution across the Atlantic to present it to Bonaparte. Vincent warned Louverture that the consul and his Colonial Ministry would probably view it as nothing less than a declaration of independence. "He listened to me attentively," the French officer later wrote, "when I asked him what the French government was to do now, given that according the terms of the constitution they would have no need to name or send representatives to the colony." Louverture explained that he expected the government to send him commissioners to "speak to him." "Why not say," Vincent retorted, "that you wish them to send you chargés d'affaires, ambassadors, as the Americans, the Spanish, and even the British will certainly do?" "You owe all your rights to France," the French officer later scolded Louverture, "and you dare to invade her right to govern her colony!" Louverture was unmoved by the officer's appeals. Vincent, however, turned out to be right. An armada would soon be sailing from France with his regime firmly in its sights. But Louverture also had other enemies closer to home.[32]

"The French in this land are no good, and they are the only ones in our way," General Moïse had explained to his white secretary in the wake of Hédouville's expulsion in 1798. "If it were in my power, I would soon be rid of them," he continued, adding that "you have to finish what you start." "If France sends forces here, what will they do? Nothing." They would ultimately only strengthen the black army of Saint-Domingue. "I hope they send three, four, five thousand men; there would be so many more guns and so much more ammunition for our brothers who are unarmed." "When we began fighting for our liberty," Moïse added, "we had only one rifle, then two, then three, and in the end we had all those of the French who had come here."[33]

Moïse had been one of Louverture's strongest partisans for nearly a decade, since the days when both had served the Spanish, and had become his adopted nephew. By 1801 he was the general of the division of the Northern Province. He also occupied the position of "agricultural inspector" in the region, like Dessalines in the south and west, and was therefore in charge of overseeing and enforcing Louverture's labor regulations. He had the reputation, however, of being "less barbarous" than Dessalines, according to one contemporary; and Louverture criticized him because production levels were lower in the north than elsewhere in the colony. The youthful Moïse responded by declaring that, despite his uncle's orders, he could not "resolve himself" to be the "executioner of my color." "It is always in the name of the interests of the metropole that he scolds me," he explained, "but his interests are those of the whites, and I will love the whites only when they have given me back the eye they took from me in battle." In addition to rejecting the use of violence against cultivators, Moïse was assiduous in his payment of them. He also advocated selling small plots of land to subaltern officers and even to soldiers, going against Louverture's stated aim of preventing the division of plantations. Moïse was further alarmed by the 1801 constitution, particularly by its provision for the importation of Africans as cultivators.[34]

In late October 1801 there was a series of uprisings in the plantation regions of the northern plain. Several hundred whites in the region were killed. Louverture responded swiftly, sending in Dessalines, who suppressed the revolt with brutal efficiency. Christophe, commander of Le Cap, unearthed and crushed a parallel conspiracy in the town. In the wake of the uprising, Louverture summoned Moïse and accused him of being its "soul and leader." "You took up arms because you thought the whites were once again becoming your masters," Louverture apparently told his nephew, adding: "Could I, a former slave, work toward the reestablishment of servitude?" Moïse insisted that he had not organized the revolt, though it seems at the very least he did nothing to stop it and tacitly supported it. Louverture was convinced of his guilt. In late November, Moïse was executed along with another veteran officer, Joseph Flaville.[35]

In the wake of the revolt Louverture issued a proclamation in which he acted as both "preacher" and "dictator." The document is the testament to a kind of delirium, perhaps driven by the horror of what had just happened. Louverture railed against Moïse, complaining that for years he had explained to him how to be a virtuous soldier, disciplined and obedient, and a virtuous man. But instead of listening to the "advice of a father" and to the orders of a "chief devoted to the happiness of the colony," Moïse had let himself be guided "only by his passions." The result: "he has perished miserably!" "This will be the fate of all who imitate him," Louverture warned ominously. "The justice of heaven is slow, but it is infallible, and sooner or later it strikes the wicked and crushes them like thunder."[36]

Louverture did not content himself with fulminating against the departed Moïse. He struck out at seemingly the entire population he was governing. He lashed out against the men "without religion" who had caused disorders in the colony. He blamed such disorders on bad parenting, the "negligence with which fathers and mothers raise their children, shirking religion, obedience, and love of work and instead passing on a disdain for cultivation." Since "bad impressions are difficult to get rid of," the result was the proliferation of "bad citizens, vagabonds, and thieves." The girls became prostitutes, always ready to "follow the urgings of the first conspirator who preaches disorder, assassination, and pillage." Indeed, because the war had killed "many more men than women," the towns were full of women whose "existence is based wholly on libertinage," and who incited others to "banditry." The police and officers of the colony must constantly keep their eyes open and be ready to punish all such "vile" and "dangerous" individuals. Louverture also declared that any married officers or administrators who accepted "concubines" in their houses or who were unmarried but "lived publicly with several women" would be fired.[37]

The plantations were also full of dangerous men and women. "Since the revolution," Louverture claimed, "perverse men" had declared that "liberty was the right to remain idle, to do bad with impunity, to disdain the laws and follow only their whims." Such a "doctrine" was of course accepted happily by "bad subjects, thieves, and assassins." "It is time to strike out against the hardened men who persist in these ideas; all must know that there is no way to live peacefully and respectfully except through work, assiduous work." "As soon as a child can walk," Louverture declared, "he must be put to work on the plantations doing some useful task." "In a well-ordered state," he explained, "idleness is the source of all disorders." Domestics, too, needed stricter surveillance by those they worked for, who should "treat them with justice" but also "force them" to their duty. For since "in the new regime all work deserves a salary, each salary demands work." Louverture's proclamation demanded the strict enforcement of his October 1800 regulations on cultivation. It ratcheted up the threats issued against those officers and administrators—like Moïse—who refused to enforce this decree assiduously. Any officer who tolerated laziness or vagrancy was an "enemy of the government"; any who "tolerated pillage and assassination" was to be executed; any individual who encouraged sedition would also be punished with death.[38]

Louverture ordered the creation of a new system of surveillance. He ordered managers and owners to draw up lists of the laborers on their property to be used for "fixing cultivators on the plantations." "Security cards" listing each individual's name, address, employment, age, and sex were to be issued by local officials. A fee would be charged, and they would be given only to those who had a job and demonstrated "irreproachable conduct." Domestics had to present a "certificate of good conduct" from their employers to get their cards. Those who could not present them on demand would be punished. "Foreigners," especially "metropolitans," that is, European-born Frenchmen, without documents would be deported. "Creoles" would be sent to a plantation. A note at the end of the decree explained that by "creole" the government meant "any individual born in the colony or in Africa." This was a departure from the traditional use of the term, generally used to refer only to American-born and slaves. It was an important step, for it in essence identified the majority in the colony who had come from Africa as natives of Saint-Domingue. It did so, however, not to grant them rights as citizens but to limit those rights.[39]

The November proclamation was a crushing condemnation of the social world of Saint-Domingue, and a charter for a new police state in which the duty of all citizens to work for the state would be strictly enforced. It was a remarkable blend of moralism—indeed, Louverture ordered the decree be read after mass by all the priests in the colony—and bureaucratic innovation. In one way, the draconian regime whose consolidation it articulated turned out to be quite a success: Louverture oversaw a remarkable revival of the shattered plantation economy in Saint-Domingue. By 1801, according to official reports, coffee exports had risen from almost nothing to two-thirds of their level in 1789. Improvements in the sugar industry, where damages were more difficult to repair, were smaller, and included little of the more profitable refined sugar, but by 1802 exports were at one-third those of 1789. These official figures did not include a significant amount of underground and contraband trade, much of it carried out with the support of the regime. Under Louverture's control, the rebuilding of many sectors of Saint-Domingue's plantation economy was well under way.[40]

Louverture would later claim that in early 1802 the colony was "enjoying the greatest tranquility" and that "commerce and cultivation" were flourishing; the island had reached "a degree of splendor that had never been seen before." He had been accused of treating the cultivators as "slaves," but all he was trying to do was to increase the "general happiness of the island" by making the people of Saint-Domingue "taste liberty without license." He had, he added, succeeded, to the point that "you could not see a single idle man in the colony" and the "number of beggars had decreased." "Never have order and tranquility reigned so widely in Saint-Domingue," concurred a French officer in January 1802. And General Charles Victor Emmanuel Leclerc, who arrived in Saint-Domingue soon afterward with decidedly hostile intentions toward Louverture, noted that agriculture in the colony was at a "very high level." In fact he claimed that on the plantations under the command of Louverture's officers, the "blacks" were being worked harder than they ever had been under the whites. He found, furthermore, that he could fulfill the strict orders he had been given to restore order on the plantations and make sure the ex-slaves were working assiduously by using Louverture's regulations, which he deemed were "very good." They were, he noted, so "strong" that he would not have dared propose them himself.[41]

But the strictness of Louverture's November 1801 decree highlighted the strain of the balancing act he had been sustaining for years. Committed to defending liberty at all costs, Louverture had turned himself into a dictator, and the colony he ruled over into a society based on social hierarchy, forced labor, and violent repression. The proclamation was a measure of Louverture's failure to find a middle way by which a true liberty could coexist with the plantation economy. When, a few months later, ships arrived from France to crush Louverture, he would find that among his officers and soldiers, not to mention the cultivators and city-dwellers of Saint-Domingue, there were many who were unwilling to fight to save him. But those French who confused Louverture's regime with slavery were also in for a rude awakening. Despite the many limits he had placed on freedom, the ex-slaves clearly saw the difference between the present and the past. And they were willing to lay down their lives rather than go back.

CHAPTER TWELVE

The Tree of Liberty

OR THIRTY-SEVEN DAYS in late 1801, the winds blew relent-
lessly off the Atlantic into the French port of Brest. Pinned in the
harbor was a fleet of ships packed with some 7,000 troops waiting
to sail. "Never have the western winds blown so persistently," complained
the naval commander, while the general in charge of the troops, Charles
Victor Emmanuel Leclerc, wrote to Napoleon Bonaparte that for days the
wind had not paused for even "one hour" to allow the convoy to set out
to sea.[1]

Leclerc had been by Bonaparte's side for many years. They had fought
together against the British at Toulon in 1793, and then a few years later
in the conquest of Italy, where Leclerc met and married Napoleon's sister,
Pauline. Leclerc had led the troops that dispersed the Parlement during the 1799 coup that made Bonaparte first consul. Now Leclerc was
being sent on a mission of crucial importance: wresting control of Saint-
Domingue from Toussaint Louverture.[2]

In the end the wind let up, and the Leclerc expedition sailed into the
Atlantic. The ships from Brest were joined by convoys from other ports;
once united, the expedition consisted of fifty ships—about half of France's
larger naval vessels—carrying almost 22,000 soldiers, along with approximately 20,000 sailors. Reinforcements followed during the next year; ultimately upward of 80,000 fighting men were sent to Saint-Domingue.[3]

"All of France is coming to Saint-Domingue," Louverture reportedly
exclaimed when he saw part of the armada hovering off the shores of
the colony weeks later. Though he did not yet know it, among its passengers were his two sons, Isaac and Placide, whom he had sent to study
in Paris a few years before. Bonaparte had met with them before their de-

parture, telling them that their father was "a great man." The army he was sending to Saint-Domingue, he assured them, was meant only to strengthen the military forces there. Wishing to see the extent of the education of Louverture's sons, Bonaparte quizzed them on their mathematical skills. Finding them satisfactory, he entrusted them with a letter for their father asking him to submit to the authority of General Leclerc. Within a few months Isaac and Placide would be heading back across the Atlantic, this time as prisoners.[4]

"What are presumably the objects of the French West India expedition?" the British abolitionist James Stephen wondered in early 1802. The question was an important one not only for France but for Britain and its Caribbean colonies. In late 1801 the British government signed the preliminaries of a peace treaty with France that would be finalized as the Treaty of Amiens in March 1802. Although the period of peace between the two empires would be short-lived, it was to have a profound impact in Saint-Domingue, for it made the Leclerc expedition possible.[5]

Emancipation had been decreed in 1793 in large part to secure Saint-Domingue from British occupation, and in the intervening years war had made Louverture and his army necessary allies for the French government. Laveaux and others had celebrated the military services rendered by the ex-slaves in order to mitigate concerns in France about the economic disruption caused by emancipation. With peace, however, military necessity could no longer be used against those clamoring for a reconstruction of the plantation economy. Consistently attacked during the previous years in Paris, Louverture came to be seen in government circles less as a valuable ally than as an obstacle to Bonaparte's new colonial plans. Peace made the Leclerc expedition both politically expedient and militarily possible. The end of the global struggle with the British freed up French forces that had been tied down in Europe. It also rendered the British willing to allow a major military force to cross the Atlantic without hindrance.

In his 1802 letters to Prime Minister Henry Addington, James Stephen examined the potential impact of French policy in Saint-Domingue on Britain's colonies. In doing so he presented a remarkably lucid and prescient account of the real objectives and consequences of Leclerc's mission. Some in Britain, Stephen noted, "speak of St. Domingo as a revolted colony, that, like the United States of America, has renounced its allegiance to the parent state, and is therefore to be reduced by force to its former dependence." Such observers pointed to the treaties Louverture had made with Great Britain and the United States as a tacit declaration of independence. Louverture's diplomacy and his recent constitution certainly demonstrated his bold political autonomy. But, as Stephen seems to have understood, his constitution had also strongly affirmed that Saint-Domingue was a part of France. Though he probably could have done so successfully, Louverture had not in fact declared independence, and he seems to have still believed that the colony would, and should, remain tied to France.[6]

Another theory about the expedition, Stephens noted, was that it was the result of a conflict between "the Constitution lately framed" by Louverture and the "military government" of France's ruler, Bonaparte, and was essentially a "contest of power" between "the Consul of St. Domingo, and the Consul of France." There was much to support this interpretation, even though the conflict was of relatively recent date. After assuming power, Bonaparte resolved to send a military force to Saint-Domingue, and in early 1801 he began organizing an expedition of several thousand soldiers. At the time, however, the aim of the mission was not to attack Louverture. Indeed, in March of that year Bonaparte promoted Louverture to the rank of captain-general of Saint-Domingue, which meant that he would be the "commander-in-chief" over any French officer sent with troops to the colony.[7]

Bonaparte's opinion of Louverture, however, began to shift when news arrived of his takeover of Spanish Santo Domingo. The consul believed that this occupation, while allowed by the 1795 treaty between France and Spain, should have been carried out only under his orders. Bonaparte rescinded his promotion of Louverture and indeed took him off the list of those who were to be maintained as officers in Saint-Domingue. Many of the proplanter advisers whom Bonaparte had placed in the Colonial Ministry encouraged him to eliminate Louverture as a first step to rebuilding the colonial economy. In September 1801 the officer François Kerverseau, who had served in Saint-Domingue, wrote in an official report that the Republic should "examine whether, after having laid down the law for all the monarchs of Europe," it was appropriate for it to "receive laws from a rebel negro in one of its own colonies."[8]

Bonaparte's suspicions of Louverture were cemented when, in October 1801, General Charles Vincent presented him with Saint-Domingue's 1801 constitution. The second consul, Jean-Jacques Régis de Cambacérès, recalled that Bonaparte determined at that point that he must sent a mission to end Louverture's "state of rebellion against the Republic." "The indignation of the first consul was extreme," wrote another contemporary. "The conduct of Toussaint Louverture struck him as an attack on the authority and dignity of the Republic." Bonaparte wrote more diplomatically in the letter he gave to Louverture's sons that the new constitution, which "included many good things," also contained "some that are contrary to the dignity and the sovereignty of the French people, of which Saint-Domingue is only a part." Louverture had suggested to the consul that he send emissaries back to the colony to discuss the terms of the constitution. Bonaparte, however, did not send a "negotiator." Instead, "he sent an army."[9]

In his instructions to General Leclerc, Bonaparte set out a three-stage plan for destroying Louverture's regime. It depended on force, but also on ruse. On his arrival, Leclerc was to rally support in Spanish Santo Domingo, as well as make contact with the "negroes" who were "enemies of Toussaint" in the region of Môle, where Louverture had suffered repeated challenges to his authority. André Rigaud and his comrade Alexandre Pétion, exiled since their defeat by Louverture a few years before, were invited to join the expedition with a similar goal in mind: the French hoped they would help mobilize sectors of the population of free people of color, who they rightly assumed still resented Louverture. (Once in Saint-Domingue, Leclerc realized that Rigaud was a liability and deported him, though Pétion remained in the service of the French for many months.) Even as he sought out counterweights to Louverture's authority in the colony, Leclerc was also to approach the governor, along with those whom Bonaparte singled out as his most dangerous partisans—Moïse (whose death was not yet known in Paris) and Dessalines—and make sure they were "treated well." If they behaved and ceded power to Leclerc, Louverture and his officers would be exiled from the colony but would retain their ranks in the French army. If they resisted, they would be declared "traitors" and pursued until the French had "their heads" and had "disarmed all their partisans." Once their submission or destruction was assured, Leclerc was to carry out the coup de grâce: "On the same day we must, in all points of the colony, arrest all suspicious men who hold positions, of no matter what color, and deport at the same instant all the black generals whatever their habits, their patriotism, and the services they have

Charles Victor Emmanuel Leclerc, 1802. *Courtesy of the Huntington Library.*

rendered." "Do not allow any blacks having held a rank above that of captain to remain on the island," Bonaparte commanded.[10]

"Rid us of these gilded negroes," Bonaparte wrote to Leclerc in July 1802, "and we will have nothing more to wish for." He was "counting on" his brother-in-law to deport "all the black generals" to France by September 1802. "Without this," Bonaparte noted, "we will have done nothing, and an immense and beautiful colony will always remain a volcano, and will inspire no confidence in capitalists, colonists, or commerce." The stakes were enormous, insisted Bonaparte. "Once the blacks have been disarmed and the principal generals sent to France, you will have done more for the commerce and civilization of Europe than we have done in our most brilliant campaigns." A Polish officer setting out for service in Saint-Domingue in 1803 identified the purpose of the mission with more cynicism when he wrote that he was being sent to "fight with the Negroes for their own sugar."[11]

Bonaparte's government presented the expedition to Saint-Domingue as "a crusade of civilized people of the West against the black barbarism that was on the rise in America." In his instructions to Leclerc, Bonaparte noted that "the Spanish, the English, and the Americans also are dismayed by the existence of this black Republic," and encouraged him to impress upon administrators in other Caribbean colonies the "common advantage" to the "Europeans" of "destroying this rebellion of the blacks." The French minister of foreign relations, Charles Maurice de Talleyrand-Périgord, argued in his correspondence with the British that it was "in the interest of civilization in general to destroy the new Algiers that is being organized in the center of America," and that the Leclerc mission deserved the support of all "states that have colonies and commerce." This was in part simply a shrewd diplomatic strategy, since France's ability to send this expedition depended on the acceptance, if not support, of the other major Atlantic powers. But it also reflected a broader sentiment that the new society that had developed in revolutionary Saint-Domingue was a profound threat to the European colonial system as a whole. The British government concurred. Henry Addington, the prime minister, declared that the "interests of the two governments is exactly the same—to destroy Jacobinism, especially that of the blacks." After his arrival in Saint-Domingue Leclerc summed up the sentiment of many in French government circles when he declared, "it is here and at this moment that it will be determined whether Europe will conserve its colonies in the Caribbean."[12]

"The French nation will never place shackles on men it has recognized as free," Bonaparte explained Leclerc's instructions. The "political goal" of the mission in the "French part" of the island was to "disarm the blacks" and to make them "free" cultivators. But this did not mean Bonaparte rejected slavery. In the Spanish part of the island (where Bonaparte wrongly assumed Louverture had abolished slavery), the goal was to disarm the blacks and return them to slavery. And in Martinique, which the British had occupied since 1794 but which was to be returned to France once peace was negotiated, the whites, Bonaparte announced, "need not fear the liberation of the slaves." Such assurances were to be made privately, as a public declaration to this effect might have incited revolt in other colonies. But they make clear that, by late 1801, Bonaparte's regime had decided on a major shift in colonial policy: France would once again accept, and even embrace, the existence of slavery in its empire. The tricolor would no longer signify freedom.[13]

The new policy, as James Stephen noted, would be difficult to enforce. Not far from Martinique was the island of Guadeloupe, where the French had abolished slavery in 1794. Could France really administer one island in which all people were free, and another a short distance away where the majority were enslaved? "To maintain two such opposite systems in islands within sight of each other, would be not more preposterous than impracticable." Were the French simply naive? Stephen thought not. "The true, though unavowed purpose of the French government in this expedition," he concluded, "is to restore the old system of negro slavery in St. Domingo, and in the other colonies wherein it has been subverted."[14]

The promises made by Bonaparte's regime, Stephen suggested, were simply part of this strategy. Knowing that an open announcement of the return of slavery would incite mass insurrection, the governors of France were declaring they respected liberty so that they could position themselves to destroy it. Stephen believed that, at first, this strategy would succeed. "The towns and forts on the coast of St. Domingo will probably be conquered with great facility" and indeed would perhaps offer "no resistance." "Toussaint may submit," he continued, and in any case it would be "an easy game for the Generals of the French army to avail themselves of the discord said already to prevail among the negroes of that Colony, or to scatter the seeds of new dissensions, so as to gain over some of their most powerful leaders, and considerable bodies of their troops." Indeed, "by specious promises of a well regulated freedom," Stephen concluded, "a general submission to the authority of the Republic may be speedily obtained; and thus the whole work may appear to be at once accomplished." The plans laid out in Bonaparte's instructions to Leclerc—which Stephen could not have known about—presented precisely this scenario, with one exception: they assumed that once the submission and deportation of the major officers were accomplished, the war would be over.[15]

Stephen, however, noted that it would only "appear" to be so. "It is when the true design shall be avowed," wrote Stephen, "or begin to unfold itself: when the negroes shall discover, that not to the fasces of the Consul only, but to the whip of the driver, their submission is demanded, when the master shall take possession of his estate, and the bell and the loud report of the driver's whip, announcing the approach of dawn, shall summon again to the field," that the tide would begin to change. The French would learn what the British already had, that there was a "difference between subduing the coast, and ruling the interior, of this extensive Island; between gaining the chiefs, and coercing the new formed people."[16]

Stephen was familiar with Louverture's labor codes and understood that the freedom of the ex-slaves had been extremely limited. Nevertheless, he argued, there was still a fundamental difference between past and present. In the new regime, industry was "considered a duty to be inculcated by persuasion, or enforced by the sanctions of municipal law aided by a military police, and not a mere physical effect to be excited by the application of the lash." Punishment was meted out by agents of the state, and work was not exacted only by the threats of whip-wielding drivers working for their masters. Though Stephen underestimated the troubling continuities between the old and new regimes, he was right to insist that the former slaves in the colonies knew the difference between what they had and what they would be returned to if they were enslaved once again. The "distinctions of political freedom or restraint known in Europe," he noted "shrink to nothing, when compared with the unspeakable difference between the terms 'slave and free,' in the colonies." It would be as impossible to submit the people of Saint-Domingue to slavery as it was "to renew in a philosopher the superstitions of the nursery." There had been not only a "revolution" in their habits, but a dramatic transformation in their "ideas." The French general Pamphile de Lacroix would write in a similar vein that the great failure of Bonaparte and his advisers, most of them former planters, had been failing to see that the blacks were not "as they had left them," and underestimating the profound political consequences of "ten years of revolution" in Saint-Domingue.[17]

"What energies are not likely to be called forth, what desperate struggles to be made, in defending not only private property, but the very capacity of possessing it," Stephen wondered, and "in defending man's title to his own muscles and sinews; in maintaining the common privileges not merely of social, but of rational nature!!" The population of ex-slaves was "a large community of negroes inured by a ten years experience to the habits of freedom," and would embark on a war of resistance whose legitimacy would outshine that of any other war. Drawing on the experience of the

British military occupation in Saint-Domingue, Stephen argued that the black rebels, used to the climate and inured to the diseases of the Caribbean, had an unparalleled "constitutional superiority over their invaders," and would have the clear upper hand in the conflict, which he compared to that between a "seaman and a shark." Once the war had begun, it was clear who would ultimately emerge victorious: not the French, but those they would try to reenslave.[18]

It is difficult to know whether Bonaparte intended to reestablish slavery in Saint-Domingue when he dispatched the Leclerc expedition. He was clearly intent on demolishing Louverture's power and severely restricting the access of the former slaves to political power. Anyone who "discussed the rights of the blacks, who have spilled so much white blood," he wrote in his instructions to Leclerc, was to be "sent to France." Still, he sought a pragmatic approach to the colonies. "The question," he explained in May 1800, was not whether it was a good idea to "abolish slavery," but rather whether it would be reasonable to "abolish liberty" in Saint-Domingue. "My policy is to govern men the way most of them wish to be governed," as this was the best way to "recognize the sovereignty of a people." "It was by making myself Catholic that I ended the war in the Vendée, in making myself a Muslim that I established myself in Egypt," he explained. "If I were governing a Jewish people," he continued, "I would rebuild the temple of Solomon." "And so I will speak of liberty in the free portion of Saint-Domingue [i.e., the French part]; I will confirm slavery in the Ile de France [the Indian Ocean colony where planters had successfully prevented the application of the 1794 emancipation decree], and even in the enslaved portion of Saint-Domingue [i.e., the Spanish portion], and I will reserve the right to soften and limit slavery, where I maintain it, and to reestablish order and introduce discipline, where I maintain liberty." Such a policy, he added, would have advantages that would outweigh its disadvantages. "They may make less sugar than when they were slaves, but they provide us, and serve us as we need them, as soldiers. If we have one less sugar mill, we will have one more citadel occupied by friendly soldiers."[19]

Perhaps even in late 1801 Bonaparte sincerely intended to craft a compromise colonial regime in Saint-Domingue. His public decision to reestablish slavery there did not come until late 1802, after news of Louverture's open resistance to Leclerc had arrived in France. Still, it seems likely that, as Stephen argued, Bonaparte had made his decision about the final goal of his mission before he sent Leclerc across the Atlantic—that the two men had discussed the question of reestablishing slavery in conversations that "left no direct written traces"—and kept it secret only because they knew they had to in order to succeed. The declarations "in favor of the liberty of the blacks of Saint-Domingue," then, were perhaps in the end "nothing but pure diplomacy, trickery, shrewdness, production, technique, and pretense" whose aim was to gain from Louverture through "peaceful means" what the French government "feared having to take from him by force."[20]

Bonaparte did, however, briefly consider another alternative. In mid-November 1801 the British had not yet announced to the French that they would accept the departure of a large expeditionary force to the Caribbean. Bonaparte and his strategists had concluded that in order to be successful his troops must occupy Saint-Domingue before April, because later in the year "the climate of the colonies becomes very dangerous for European troops who are not acclimated to it." If the troops were unable to leave early enough, Bonaparte would have to delay his expedition, and he might well end up having to "recognize Toussaint" and accept the existence of "black Frenchmen" in Saint-Domingue. Although this would mean the loss of income for France—free labor, he was convinced, would be less profitable than slavery, and more black soldiers would mean fewer agricultural workers—it would be to its military advantage. Talleyrand passed on these reflections to the French ambassador in Britain, noting that "Saint-Domingue reconquered by the whites" would "for many years" be a weak power, one that would survive only through "a long peace and support from the mother country." "The government of the blacks recognized in Saint-Domingue and legitimized by France," in contrast, would be a "formidable base for the Republic in the New World." France could collaborate with Louverture, using Saint-Domingue as a military base and deploying its black army against the colonies of its enemies. The Republic could, as it had in the mid-1790s, use emancipation as a potent weapon of imperial war. If a "new power" were "constituted and recognized" in Saint-Domingue, Talleyrand asserted, "the scepter of the New World" would "sooner or later" fall into France's hands. The consequences for Britain would be "incalculable."[21]

James Stephen argued that this possibility was indeed quite dangerous for Britain. France, he argued, could conclude: "Since the negroes will not resume their hoes, let us avail ourselves of their muskets. By means of these African auxiliaries, we shall wound Carthage [i.e., Britain] in its most vulnerable side, clip the wings of her commerce, and enrich ourselves with her spoils!" France would "stand in need of no armies from Europe" to carry out these conquests. In British slave colonies like Jamaica, the "attractions" of emancipation and "the very complexion" of the French troops would "ensure her in every slave Colony she invades, numerous and irresistible allies, ready not only to facilitate, but to perpetuate her conquests."[22]

It is difficult to know how seriously this alternative—certainly articulated in part to threaten the British—was considered by Bonaparte. One contemporary reported that, as Bonaparte's plans unraveled in Saint-Domingue, he angrily declared: "I am for the whites because I am white; I have no other reason, and that one is good." "How is it possible that liberty was given to Africans, to men who had no civilization, who didn't even know what the colony was, what France was? It is perfectly clear that those who wanted the freedom of the blacks wanted the slavery of the whites." But years later Bonaparte would look back with regret on the decisions he had made regarding Saint-Domingue. On his deathbed he explained that he should have "recognized Toussaint" and governed the colony through him, rather than sending his forces against him. But these were the mutterings of a dying man, haunted perhaps by the specters of the tens of thousands of French troops who had gone to their deaths in Saint-Domingue, or else by that of one general who died in a cold and dank prison high in the mountains of France.[23]

In late December 1801 Louverture issued a decree condemning people who, having heard of the imminent peace between France and Britain, had circulated rumors that "France will come with thousands of men to annihilate the colony and liberty." Some claimed that the government planned to gather all the "men of color" and "blacks" in France and make them march at the head of the army that was to come, while others asserted that Louverture's children were being kept as hostages to use as leverage against him. How could these individuals, demanded Louverture, believe that France would, "for no reason," wish to destroy those who had "spilled their blood for the triumph of liberty and the prosperity of the island," who had "conserved" the colony and made it flourish? Such rumors, he insisted, must be baseless. Nevertheless, he warned cryptically: "I am a soldier, I am not afraid of men, I fear only God. If I must die, I will die as an honorable soldier who has nothing to be ashamed of."[24]

Louverture was receiving fragments of information about the Leclerc expedition, and even as he publicly expressed disbelief that France would attack him, he began preparing for war. He increased the size of his army, doing so according to one report by pressing individuals who had recently arrived in the colony—including many creole whites returning from Europe—into service on the pretext that they did not have their required "security cards." With the addition of these new recruits, he had 23,000, and perhaps up to 30,000, regular troops under his command by early 1802. He also had at his disposal local militias numbering 10,000.[25]

Louverture sought to make sure he could depend on his officers in case war broke out. After his execution of Moïse he deported several officers whose loyalties he suspected, replacing them with "military leaders whose devotion and fidelity" to his regime were "indisputable." Among them were Dessalines, who commanded in the west and the south, Maurepas at Port-de-Paix, Christophe at Le Cap, and Sans-Souci at Grande-Rivière on the northern plain. He ordered commanders in coastal towns not to allow any warships, of whatever nation, to enter the ports without his permission. These orders were, he later claimed, simply a way of protecting the colony from "enemies of the Republic." But they certainly put him in a position to respond to such enemies, even if they came from France. Louverture also prepared, however, for the possibility of negotiation, ordering the plantations, squares, government buildings, barracks, and roads to be cleaned up to highlight the good order that was reigning in the colony.[26]

In late January 1802 the ships that had left France weeks before gathered off the eastern coast of Spanish Santo Domingo. Leclerc's plan was to send troops ashore in the island's major port towns—Le Cap, Port-au-Prince (then called Port Républicain), Les Cayes, and Santo Domingo—and then occupy the surrounding territory. He took command of the ships heading for Le Cap, and, hovering off the coast in sight of the town on February 3, sent a message to Christophe. Having made peace with Britain, it announced, the government of France had sent troops to Saint-Domingue to defeat any "rebels" in the colony. He hoped that Christophe would not be among such rebels, but warned him that if he resisted he would be held responsible for the violence that was unleashed.[27]

Accompanying Leclerc's message to Christophe was a letter from Bonaparte to the people of Saint-Domingue, assuring them that the soldiers' sole purpose was to protect them from "enemies of the Republic." Bonaparte had predicted that many would have heard rumors of a more threatening mission, and sought to dispel such fears. "If you are told: these forces are meant to take away your liberty, you must respond: the Republic gave us liberty, and the Republic would not accept that it be taken away from us." Anyone who opposed Leclerc, however, was a "traitor." Reaching for a metaphor he hoped would have a particular local meaning, Bonaparte added that the "rage of the Republic" would "devour" any such traitors "as fire devours your dry sugarcane." In his accompanying proclamation, Leclerc echoed Bonaparte's combined promises of protection and threats of violence. Bonaparte promised to the blacks "the liberty they have fought so hard for," as well as assuring the future prosperity of "commerce and agriculture, without which colonies cannot exist." These promises, Leclerc insisted, would be fulfilled; to doubt that they would be was "a crime."[28]

Before he left France, Leclerc had been encouraged to translate these proclamations into Creole so that they would be understood by the masses in the colony. He did so at some point on the Atlantic crossing, presumably using the expertise of one of the many former residents of Saint-Domingue who accompanied him. Like any process of translation, this one transformed the document in interesting ways. In explaining that peace had come, the creole declaration noted that the "nations that were at war" with France had now "shaken the hand of the Republic." And in encouraging the colony's residents to join in the celebration of peace, it added an interesting phrase: "You are from Saint-Domingue: aren't you French too?" In insisting on the equality of all men, the proclamation added a line that read: "Whites, blacks, are all children of the Republic." Perhaps understanding that, rather than encouraging them to submit, the metaphor of burning cane might serve instead to remind the residents of Saint-Domingue of an all-too-effective tactic of resistance, the translator entirely dropped any such reference, noting simply that those who resisted the mission would be "punished."[29]

These proclamations were delivered to Le Cap from the French fleet and distributed in the town by its black mayor. But they did not convince Christophe or other officers in the area of the wisdom of obeying. Even as Leclerc issued his demands at Le Cap, troops under the command of General Donatien Marie Joseph de Rochambeau disembarking nearby were "assailed by black troops who fired on them, saying that they did not want any whites." The French troops shouted back to the black soldiers that they were "brothers" and "friends" and were "bringing them their liberty." The latter point would have seemed particularly strange to the sol-

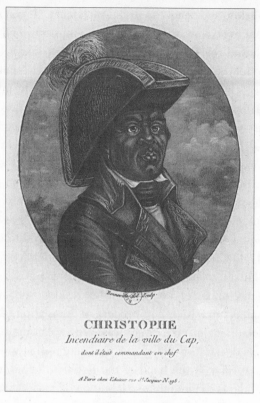

"Christophe, Incendiaire de la ville du Cap."
Courtesy of the Bibliothèque Nationale de France.

diers, many of whom had been part of the revolution of slaves that had brought liberty to Saint-Domingue—and to France—a few years before. The garrison of Fort-Liberté killed sixty of the arriving troops but, surrounded and outnumbered, soon put down their weapons. Rochambeau decided to make an example of the black troops, slaughtering several hundred of them after they had surrendered.[30]

In Le Cap, meanwhile, Christophe dispatched the commander of the town's port, the officer Sangros, to announce that because of Louverture's orders he could not allow the French troops to enter the town. In another missive he backed up his refusal with a threat: "You will enter the town of Le Cap only once it has been reduced to ashes, and even on these ashes I will fight you." Enraged by Christophe's refusal, and convinced it was simply a delaying tactic, Leclerc decided to take the town by force. He would have liked to anchor close in and occupy the town immediately, but Louverture had ordered the beacons that guided ships safely into the harbor removed. The French naval officers demanded that Sangros lead them in, first offering him money, then issuing threats. He refused. The French killed him and dumped his body overboard.[31]

Rather than risk the dangers of a blind entry into the port, Leclerc sent ships to drop off soldiers on either side of Le Cap. They were to encircle the town and capture it from inland. His hope, he wrote to the colonial minister, Denis Decrès, in Paris, had been to force Christophe's troops to abandon Le Cap before they had a chance to "set it on fire and massacre the whites" and also to save as much as he could of the northern plain. As his army marched, cultivators on the plain fled from their plantations. "They had been told the most absurd stories," Leclerc wrote. "They were told it was the Spanish or the English who were coming to conquer the island, and that they would all be killed." He was able to dispel their fears, he claimed, by treating them well. But he failed to prevent the burning of Le Cap. As Leclerc's troops disembarked to the west at Limbé, two French ships fired on the Fort Picolet, which guarded the approach to the town. The gunners in the fort fired back, announcing to the troops in Le Cap that they were under attack. Christophe made good on his threat and ordered his soldiers to set the town alight. For the second time in a decade, it was devoured by flames. It was February 4—eight years to the day since the abolition of slavery had been decreed in Paris. Despite all the protestations made by Leclerc and Bonaparte, many in Saint-Domingue believed that liberty itself was at stake. Several months later one of Louverture's colonels, the African-born Sans-Souci, would describe the officers serving with him as "defenders of liberty." As it turned out, they had good reason. As Leclerc would later admit, a few "negroes" who were arrested soon after the arrival of the expedition were sold as slaves by French officials.[32]

Some contemporaries claimed that Louverture was in fact in Le Cap orchestrating events at the time of Leclerc's arrival. One officer went so far as to claim that the governor had disguised himself as "a Congo negro" in order to be able to set in motion the burning of Le Cap unnoticed. Louverture seems, however, to have been in Santo Domingo at the time the expedition arrived, and to have left for Le Cap only once he was aware of its presence off the coast. On his way to Le Cap, he later recalled, he received news from Christophe about Leclerc's demands, and also met with

Dessalines, who reported that he had seen ships off the western coast of the colony. When he reached the hills at the edge of the northern plain he saw Le Cap burning in the distance. He soon found the roads filled with residents fleeing the city, and Christophe retreating with his army. When Louverture criticized Christophe for having set fire to the town, Christophe protested that the actions of Leclerc and Rochambeau's brutality at Fort Liberté made clear their hostile intentions.[33]

Louverture was soon convinced that war—and its faithful companion in the colony, fire—was the only proper response. He declared that since France had sent forces to "put us back into slavery," there was no choice but to fight back. "They come to take away a freedom they promised to maintain; let us assemble our forces, and all die, if necessary, to make sure our brothers are free!" "The whites of France and of the colony, united together, want to take our freedom from us," he wrote to one of his officers in early February. "Beware of the whites; they will betray you if they can," he added. He ordered cultivators to be recruited to swell the ranks of those who would fight against the French. He wrote to Dessalines, commanding him to send "a few faithful emissaries" into Port-au-Prince—which French troops had occupied thanks to the support of several local officers—to set the town aflame. Louverture explained that, as they waited for the "rainy season that will rid us of our enemies" through disease, their only "resource" was "destruction and fire." It was crucial that "the land bathed in our sweat" not afford any provisions to the invading army. Dessalines should destroy the roads, order that "corpses and horses" be thrown into springs, and "annihilate and burn everything" so that "those who have come to put us back into slavery will always find in front of them the image of the hell they deserve." Dessalines would carry out these orders zealously, and even surpass them, in the coming weeks.[34]

After taking Le Cap, Leclerc sent troops to attack the nearby Port-de-Paix. The commander of the city, Maurepas, after having a conference with Louverture, fought back furiously against the French troops. When Maurepas retreated, he made sure they "conquered only ashes." As they had hoped, the invaders found partisans in the area, which had long harbored rebels against Louverture. But Maurepas continued to fight, retreating to the nearby hills with 2,000 soldiers and several thousand cultivators, and managed to contain the French troops in the town. This effort gave Louverture time to send troops under the command of the Kongolese-born officer Macaya into the region of Acul, near Le Cap, and to organize a line of troops in the mountains bordering the northern plain.[35]

Elsewhere in the colony, however, some of Louverture's officers surrendered to or openly welcomed the arriving French troops. This was the case of his commander in Port-au-Prince, the Frenchman Pierre Agé, as well as of his officer Laplume in the south, who went on to serve the French loyally throughout their campaign. In the occupied Spanish portion of the island, Louverture's brother Paul was in command. Toussaint sent him a letter ordering him to resist the French and to capture Kerverseau, the commander of the convoy sent by Leclerc to take Santo Domingo. He also gave the messengers a false letter ordering Paul to submit, so that if they were captured by the French they could show them this letter and prevent them from knowing Toussaint's true intentions. The emissaries were captured, as Toussaint had feared. His ploy, however, failed. The French executed the men and, searching their bodies, found both letters. They passed them on to Kerverseau, who presented Paul Louverture with the false letter ordering him to submit. He followed what he thought were his brother's orders, putting the entire Spanish colony in the hands of Leclerc's troops.[36]

With conflict raging in many parts of the colony, Leclerc sent Louverture's sons Isaac and Placide to bring their father the letter Bonaparte had written him. "You have a great reputation, and you can preserve it intact," Leclerc wrote in an accompanying letter to Louverture, asking him to submit to his authority. He must "no longer have any worries," he continued, regarding the "liberty" of the citizens of the colony, for it had been won and established too firmly for Bonaparte to imagine "taking it away." But when Leclerc received no immediate response from the governor, he issued a declaration of war.[37]

"They want Saint-Domingue for themselves," Leclerc wrote of the enemy "chiefs," "and if they sometimes speak of France, it is only because they believe they are not strong enough to reject her openly." Leclerc, however, would teach them, and particularly the "rebel" Louverture, about "the strength of the French government." "All the good Frenchmen who live in Saint-Domingue" must recognize the black general as "a monster who preferred the destruction of his country to the surrender of his power." They must also see that for him the word "Liberty," which he spoke so often, was only a means of justifying "the most absolute despotism." Louverture and Christophe were declared outlaws. Those cultivators who had been tricked into following them would be treated like "misled children" and forced back to the plantations. Not to be outdone, Louverture boldly declared Leclerc the outlaw. Within a few days of arriving in the colony, Leclerc had started an all-out war.[38]

As he launched his campaign against Louverture, Leclerc was already aware of several factors that were sapping the strength of his force. Before he had left France, he had already noted a serious lack of decent supplies for the expedition; "the wine is bad, the biscuit no good," he had complained. In Saint-Domingue, on the day he declared war against Louverture, Leclerc wrote in desperation to the colonial minister in Paris to "come quickly to his aid" and to send him "thirty thousand pairs of shoes," for his troops were "barefoot." He had been told in Brest that there were 15,000 pairs of shoes on board, only to find on the other side of the Atlantic that in fact there were only 4,000 "bad pairs." In Saint-Domingue he had difficulty buying appropriate supplies. He complained bitterly about the American merchants, who dominated the commerce of the colony and who he believed were overcharging him—they were "all the most Jewish of Jews," he announced—and about the local merchants who were their agents. There was, finally, an even more serious problem: disease. "I already have 1,200 men in the hospital," he announced, and warned the minister to prepare for a "considerable consumption of men in this land." Just a few days later, pleading for "troops, provisions, and money," he wrote that he had over 2,000 soldiers in the hospital, including 500 wounded. He pleaded for hats to "preserve the soldiers from sunburns that send them to the hospital," as well as medical supplies, noting anxiously that if he did not receive them, "no matter what supernatural efforts I make," he would be unable to "preserve Saint-Domingue for the Republic."[39]

His troops also confronted a new and difficult style of warfare. "This is a war of Arabs," Leclerc complained to Bonaparte. "We have barely passed before the blacks occupy the woods surrounding the road and cut off our communication." His troops suffered at the hands of "rebels" who "hide themselves in the bushes" and in the "impenetrable woods that surround the valleys." When they were repelled, they retreated to safety in the hills. The landscape posed particular problems for the European soldiers. "You have to have seen this land to have an idea of the difficulties you encounter here with each step," Leclerc added. "I haven't seen anything that compares to it in the Alps." Another French officer would recall the irony of the war: "Victors everywhere, we possessed nothing but our rifles. The enemy held nowhere, and yet never ceased to be the master of the country."[40]

Still, French troops advanced steadily in some areas. Thanks to the defection of Laplume and his forces, they rapidly gained control of most of the south. In the north, they attacked Christophe, who commanded a few thousand troops made up of both soldiers and cultivators, and forced him to retreat. French troops occupied Gonaïves on February 23, though not before it had been burned to the ground by its defenders. On the same day Louverture massed more than 3,000 troops along positions overlooking a long valley called the Ravine-à-Couleuvre, a "corridor" that provided an easy passage between key points of the Western Province. In addition to his regular troops, he had the support of several thousand armed cultivators who occupied the hills above the valley. A division commanded by Rochambeau attacked them, and after a furious battle Louverture retreated. The French claimed a great victory, reporting that Louverture lost 800 soldiers and his troops fled in panic. Louverture provided a decidedly different account of the event, noting laconically that after the "affair" that pitted him against Rochambeau he moved to another position, bringing with him a number of prisoners he had taken during the battle. Louverture's maneuver seems to have been meant primarily to cover the retreat of another part of his forces, and to prepare a larger confrontation with the French in the mountains to the south.[41]

Soon afterward Louverture suffered a major blow. Maurepas, who had for a time continued to fight the French forces in the Northern peninsula—aided by a "horrible rain" that slowed down their advance—surrendered. Leclerc had offered to allow Maurepas to keep his rank in the French army, and Maurepas, seeing little hope of success against the French, had accepted. Leclerc wrote optimistically that the "inhabitants of the land" believed Louverture had lost, that his soldiers were "deserting his flags" and cultivators were returning to their plantations. "They all think we are the masters of the colony, and I think so too."[42]

The war was far from over, however. While Louverture was retreating before Rochambeau, another French unit marched on the port town of Saint-Marc, where Dessalines was in command. As they approached, they saw "the flames light up" in front of them. Dessalines had "prepared everything" to make sure the fire spread rapidly once it was set. "Combustibles"—including barrels of power and alcohol—were placed in all the houses, and his soldiers were to set fires everywhere when the order came. Dessalines led by example, setting his splendid, recently completed mansion on fire. By the time the French entered they found the town smoldering and abandoned, with the dead bodies of several hundred residents, mostly white, left to greet them. Dessalines headed toward Port-au-Prince with his troops. Pamphile de Lacroix, the French officer in command there, had recently strengthened his position by securing the loyalty of two local leaders, the onetime maroons Lamour Desrances and Lafortune. Lacroix sent them against a unit of rebel troops approaching the town, who were outflanked and decimated. Dessalines turned back from Port-au-Prince and began a march toward the mountains overlooking the Artibonite plain, where he hoped to join with Louverture's retreating troops.[43]

War brought with it an old question, one that had split the slave insurgents in 1791: What was to be done with the whites? For nearly a decade an uneasy peace had existed in Saint-Domingue between white and black soldiers who served side by side, and between white and black plantation managers and the plantation laborers. Tensions had simmered, and sometimes exploded, as they had in the October 1801 insurrection on the northern plain, but generally whites in the colony were safe under Louverture's regime. With the arrival of the Leclerc expedition, however, many whites soon found themselves hostages of the rebels.

When he retreated from Saint-Marc, Dessalines' troops had taken several hundred whites with them as prisoners. Among them was the French traveler Michel Descourtilz, who had been in the colony since 1798. Writing years later about his "captivity" at the hands of "forty thousand negroes," he described a series of massacres perpetrated by Dessalines. The general, he claimed, had readied his black troops to eliminate white soldiers in the colony who might support a French attack. "Soldiers, these whites from France who are coming; if they are calm, it's good, leave them alone." "But," he warned, "if I find out they have come to trick us, then watch out, soldiers!" When ordered to, his black troops were to arrest their white comrades-in-arms, "herding them like sheep," in order to prevent them from joining the arriving enemy. Dessalines was not indiscriminate in his suspicion of whites, however, making it known that some—notably those who were assimilated enough to eat "callaloo" (a local dish)—might be spared "when needed."[44]

Once the conflict with Leclerc's troops began, whites realized there were "enemies everywhere." "The color white," wrote Descourtilz, was "condemned," and orders had been issued for plantation workers to fire on any whites who were not escorted by black soldiers. The ex-slave officers who held them hostage prodded one another with "stories of cruelties committed by certain white property owners," developing an "ardent desire" to "avenge" the humiliations suffered "in the time of slavery." They also probably—as Descourtilz did not mention—had an eye toward the future, fearing the possibility of the return of those times.[45]

By the time Dessalines had reached the mountains, he had very few white prisoners with him. Questioned by Louverture, he claimed they had been captured by French troops, been killed in combat, or had escaped. Descourtilz wrote that he had witnessed them being slaughtered by the hundreds under Dessalines's direct orders. His account was corroborated by Lacroix, who described finding 800 corpses in the town of Verrettes as he pursued Dessalines's retreating troops, and coming across other piles of bodies along the route they had taken into the mountains. Seeking to spare his troops from the stench of one group of bodies piled up near their camp, and lacking shovels to build a mass grave, he burned them. Instead of removing the odor, this move filled the air with an even more acrid smell, one he was never able to remove from his clothes.[46]

Some black soldiers sought to protect white prisoners. Descourtilz, spared from the initial slaughter because of his ability to "heal people who are sick," had his life saved twice by sympathetic soldiers. One of these, an elderly man named Pompée, held up a revolver to protect Descourtilz and announced that anyone who wished to kill the white doctor would have to kill him first. Those who showed him pity were vindicated: Descourtilz would prove himself useful in taking care of rebel wounded during the dramatic battle that was to come.[47]

In the mountains bordering the Artibonite, at Crête-à-Pierrot, was a small fort that had been built by the British during their occupation of the region. Louverture placed Dessalines in command of a garrison there with orders to resist the French troops marching from Port-au-Prince. He hoped to entice Leclerc into "tangling himself up around the fort by making him think it was a last stand," and then lead some of his troops in a campaign to "bring war to the north." At the time, Louverture did not yet know that General Maurepas had surrendered to Leclerc, and so probably overestimated the possibility of success. Once French forces, led by

Leclerc himself, settled into a siege of the fort at Crête-à-Pierrot, Louverture envisioned an even bolder plan: launching a surprise attack against them. He hoped, he later claimed, to send Leclerc "back to the first consul" and ask that someone else be sent in his place. The battle would not go as Louverture had expected, but neither was it the rapid triumph the French hoped for.[48]

The French hoped that by crushing Louverture's forces they could put an end to the rebellion. One man responsible for plantations in the Artibonite region anticipated that once the army had taken Crête-à-Pierrot from the rebels, "all the cultivators" who had been "swept along" with them would return to their plantations. Some former slaves helped the French troops advance—Lacroix complimented a series of plantation drivers who worked with him for their "intrepidity"—and they reached Crête-à-Pierrot in early March. Arriving by night, they surprised an encampment of sleeping soldiers outside the walls. Awakened, the retreating troops ran toward the fort with the French in hot pursuit, but then suddenly disappeared into the wide trenches that surrounded its walls. The French soldiers found themselves standing out in the open in front of the fort, which "vomited all its fire," mowing most of them down. Another arriving French unit charged the fort and suffered the same fate. The troops inside then tricked their enemy once again, emerging over its walls for an attack, drawing them against them, and then retreating into the trenches around the fort so that their comrades inside could fire murderous volleys into the advancing ranks. Several hundred French soldiers soon lay dead, and many others, including one general, were severely wounded. Understanding the futility of the situation, Lacroix ordered a retreat. The battle, however, continued as the troops retreated, for they were constantly harassed by small attacks and ambushes. As Lacroix wrote, he quickly came to recognize how "war-hardened" the "blacks of Saint-Domingue" had become. The French troops could see, on the plantations near the roads, "cultivators with their families who were observing our movements." Some shot at the soldiers who guarded the flanks of the unit. They fled as soon as detachments of soldiers were sent after them, but when these detachments returned they appeared and started firing again. "It was evident," wrote Lacroix, "that we no longer inspired any moral terror, which is the worst thing that can happen to an army." As a later chronicler wrote: "Everywhere the land harbored enemies—in the woods, behind a rock; liberty gave birth to them."[49]

Imprisoned inside the fort, Descourtilz overheard Dessalines speaking to his troops. His recollection of the speech, published years later, was probably shaped by later events, but it remains one of the few surviving records of the general's words. "Take courage, I tell you, take courage," Dessalines commanded. "The whites from France cannot hold out against us here in Saint-Domingue. They will fight well at first, but soon they will fall sick and die like flies." He warned them not to misunderstand some of the actions he might take along the way to the ultimate defeat of the French. "Listen well! If Dessalines surrenders to them a hundred times, he will betray them a hundred times." They would see that "when the French are reduced to small, small numbers, we will harass them and beat them; we will burn the harvests and then take to the hills. They will be forced to leave." "Then," announced Dessalines, "I will make you independent. There will be no more whites among us." As French reinforcements gathered outside the fort, Dessalines spirited part of his army out by night, leaving those inside under the command of the officer Lamartinière. He intended to mobilize local cultivators in an attempt to attack the French surrounding the fort.[50]

The French, strengthened by the arrival of a unit under the command of Rochambeau, surrounded the fort and began bombarding it with cannon fire. After an artillery barrage, Rochambeau ordered a new frontal assault, only to see his troops shattered as they approached the fort, retreating after the loss of several hundred soldiers. At night, wrote Lacroix, the attacking soldiers heard their enemies singing "patriotic songs" that celebrated "the glory of France." Hearing these songs, some soldiers looked to their officers as if to say: "Could our barbaric enemies be right? Are we no longer soldiers of the Republic?" Had they become, they wondered, "servile instruments" of politics, fighting for an immoral cause? The conflict in Saint-Domingue was, after all, one being fought between "two French armies, two enemy sisters," with veterans of the long revolutionary wars facing off against each other.[51]

Although they held out bravely for three days and three nights, as the siege continued the troops inside the fort became increasingly desperate. Decimated by the cannon fire, on the brink of starvation—before Dessalines left, Descourtilz reported, even he had "contented himself" with two bananas as a meal—and running out of water, they had little hope of holding out for long. Lamartinière decided on a daring attempt to break out of the fort with the 500 soldiers left under his command. In what

Lacroix admitted was a "remarkable feat of arms," he managed to break through the French lines and join with Dessalines's troops. When the French entered the fort, they found Descourtilz among the debris and corpses. He had managed to survive, along with the "white musicians" who had been employed previously by Louverture, and who had been ordered by black officers to play such songs as the revolutionary favorite "Ca Ira!" during the siege. In taking Crête-à-Pierrot, the French had suffered 1,500 soldiers killed and many more wounded, a serious loss for the expeditionary force. Leclerc, embarrassed by the defeat, ordered his officers to misreport the extent of the casualties, as he did in his own reports.[52]

Louverture's army had held out and inflicted heavy losses on their enemy. Most important, it had survived. In the north, the rebel army advanced on the French, taking a number of towns in the mountains. Among their leaders were Henri Christophe, the officers Macaya and Sans-Souci, and Sylla, whose name suggests a Mandingo origin. In late March some of Louverture's troops under the command of Sans-Souci approached Le Cap, reaching the hospital on its outskirts. Meanwhile rebels set fire to so much of the northern plain that "at midnight it was possible" to read in the center of Le Cap "by the light of the flames." In early April Leclerc sent recently arrived French reinforcements into the plain, with some colonial troops as scouts to lead them. The latter, however, defected, and many French troops were killed in ambushes. A hundred were taken prisoner by Sans-Souci and delivered to Louverture. "Toussaint still holds the mountains," Leclerc reported in late April, and he had under his command 4,000 troops and "a very considerable number of armed cultivators." The only way to "end this war" was to conquer and then occupy the mountains of the north and the west, and to hold onto those areas he already controlled. But to do so, he continually reminded the minister in Paris, he would need more troops.[53]

Henri Christophe controlled an important stretch of the northern plain and the nearby mountains, commanding an army of 1,500 soldiers and several hundred armed cultivators. In mid-April, as battles with the French continued in the area, he made contact with Leclerc and indicated he would be willing to negotiate a surrender. The two men met in Le Cap, and after Leclerc assured Christophe that "we had not come here to destroy liberty," Christophe agreed to the same conditions earlier offered to Maurepas: he would preserve his rank and be integrated into the French army.[54]

Why did Christophe, who had started the war against Leclerc by burning Le Cap in February, surrender in April? This remains a puzzle. In March the final peace treaty between Britain and France had been signed, and although the news of this was not officially proclaimed in Saint-Domingue until early May, it was probably already known through unofficial channels. This news may have affected Christophe's decision. He may also have been tired of fighting, and unsure that his loyalty to Louverture would pay off in the end; in a mid-April letter to Christophe, a French officer had invited him to give up the "errant and vagrant" life he was leading as a rebel leader and abandon the cause of the "ambitious" Louverture. According to one recent account, Christophe, having been given assurances by General Leclerc, truly believed that Leclerc could "better guarantee his future and the liberty of his brothers than the former governor, whose star was fading."[55]

It was a major victory for Leclerc, and a turning point in the first stage of the war for Saint-Domingue. Louverture, probably fearing that with peace with the British definitively signed he would be unable to hold out against the French troops for much longer, and understanding that Christophe's defection had severely undermined his military position, soon contacted Leclerc and began negotiating for his own surrender. The two men soon met in Le Cap, where Louverture, surrounded by several hundred members of his honor guard, signed an agreement according to which he was to keep his rank and retire to his plantation at Ennery, while his soldiers would preserve their ranks and be incorporated into the French army. With Louverture came Dessalines, and the two men, along with Christophe, dined with Leclerc and his officer corps in Le Cap to celebrate the event. While Christophe and Dessalines ate the food offered them, Louverture refused everything. He ate only a small piece of cheese, doing so only after having cut large slices off each of its sides, and holding it with his hands rather than using the silverware. He had granted his submission, but not his trust, to the French. He was right to be suspicious, though he miscalculated the kind of poison they were to use against him.[56]

"All the chiefs of the rebels have submitted," Leclerc boasted to Bonaparte in early May. Nevertheless, he explained apologetically, the "moment" had "not yet arrived" to move onto the second stage of Bonaparte's plan: the removal of these officers to France. In fact Leclerc desperately needed these officers, and the troops they brought with them, to maintain his hold on the colony. The troops he had initially brought with him had been severely reduced by battle and disease, and he had not received sufficient reinforcements from across the Atlantic to be able to depend only on French troops. For resistance continued throughout the colony, as many had not followed Louverture, Dessalines, and Christophe into submission. In June Leclerc wrote to Bonaparte that he would try to make the 4,000 troops he expected to arrive soon pass as a force of 6,000. In the meantime, he had no choice but to continue using the colonial troops to fight the insurgents.[57]

Leclerc was aware that the loyalty of the recently surrendered black troops was quite fragile. The colonial minister in Paris had published some of Leclerc's earlier reports in French newspapers, and these publications had made their way back to Saint-Domingue. In order to avoid antagonizing the people in the colony, Leclerc asked the minister to make sure that future publications not include anything that "can destroy the ideas of liberty and equality, which all here have on their lips." Writing to Bonaparte, he requested something more difficult: "I beg you to outlaw the publication of any jokes about blacks in the French newspapers. These undermine my operations here." Leclerc was certainly not committed to antiracism—in the same letter to Bonaparte he complimented General Rochambeau for being an honest man and a good soldier, and added, "he doesn't like blacks"—but he knew that anything that smelled of racism might make it very difficult for him to hold onto Saint-Domingue.[58]

. Leclerc also felt that Louverture's very presence in the colony was a threat. In this belief he was not alone. "Toussaint and the other leaders only appear to have surrendered," wrote one French officer, "and only sought to give their troops an entry into your ranks so that they can surprise you at the first appropriate moment." According to Lacroix, the "spirit" among the cultivators was also still rebellious, and they said that their "submission" was in fact only a cease-fire until the month of August, when many had predicted that the onset of disease would lead to the "annihilation of the entire European army sent to Saint-Domingue." Leclerc would later write that Louverture had surrendered only because Christophe and Dessalines told him that they were no longer willing to fight the French, and in the meantime he was "trying to organize an insurrection among the cultivators in order to make them rise up as a mass."[59]

Among those who were still actively fighting the French were the officers Sans-Souci and Sylla, the latter set up in a camp in an area called

Mapou. It was, wrote one officer at the time, a "rallying point for bad subjects and the last hope of the enemies of France and of all public order." It was also not far from where Louverture was living on his plantation at Ennery, and indeed it seems that Sylla was in regular communication with his old commander. The rebels at Mapou defended their camp skillfully, using the old tactics of the slave insurgents of 1791. They surrounded the approaches with traps: pits covered with branches, and boards studded with nails and covered over with leaves, which as one officer wrote pierced not just "bare feet"—of which there were many among Leclerc's troops—but shoes. The rebels added the "barbarous refinement," in the words of one French officer, of putting "a few rocks or pieces of wood" in front of them, requiring advancing soldiers to leap or jump down into the thin layer of vegetation they took for solid ground.[60]

In late May a French mission sent against Mapou ended in disaster. It was weakened before it began when some of the colonial troops who were to accompany it defected to Sylla's side. The remaining troops tried to attack a position high up on a group of rocks as they were fired on from above, seeking to avoid the rocks rolled down toward them, and falling into the murderous traps that were all around. From the camp women shouted "cries of joy" every time a French soldier fell. Eventually Sylla was dislodged from the Mapou by a force that included colonial troops, though he regrouped elsewhere. Other French columns suffered more; one group of thirty sent to attack a band that had been ambushing French troops were "killed to the last."[61]

Suspecting that Louverture was secretly both in contact with and supportive of the rebel groups led by his former officers, in early June Leclerc decided to rid the island of this "gilded negro." "Toussaint is acting in bad faith," wrote Leclerc to Bonaparte on June 6, "just as I expected." The same day, some of Leclerc's officers, using a clever pretext—that Louverture was needed to work with a local officer to end acts of banditry that had been taking place in the region where he lived—enticed him to a meeting and then overcame the general's light guard and arrested him. "You are now nothing in Saint-Domingue," one of them announced; "give me your sword." "So finished the first of the blacks," writes Lacroix. "For the first time," comments one biographer, "Louverture lost at the dangerous game of deception." His family—including his wife Suzanne, his sons Isaac and Placide, and a niece—were also arrested and sent across the Atlantic with him. As he boarded the ship to exile at Gonaïves, he famously declared: "In overthrowing me, you have cut down in Saint-Domingue only the trunk of the tree of the liberty of the blacks; it will grow back from the roots, because they are deep and numerous."[62]

"Toussaint must not be free," Leclerc wrote to the colonial minister in Paris at the time, and should be "imprisoned in the interior of the Republic. May he never see Saint-Domingue again." "You cannot hold Toussaint far enough from the ocean or put him in a prison that is too strong," Leclerc reiterated a month later. He seemed to fear that the deported man might suddenly reappear. His very presence in the colony, he warned, would once again set it alight. By spiriting Louverture out of the colony, Leclerc felt he had won a great victory. "I have taken away the gathering point of the blacks," he announced to the minister in mid-June. "The blacks have lost their compass," he wrote to Bonaparte the same day; "they are all divided amongst themselves." A few troops rebelled—Leclerc wrote in early July that "after the embarkation of Toussaint some men tried to stir up trouble," and that he had had them "shot or deported"—but for the time it seemed the French were in control.[63]

In July 1802, from Le Cap, Marie-Rose Masson wrote to her former master the marquis de Gallifet, the onetime owner of the richest plantations in the colony. Masson had purchased her freedom from Gallifet's manager, Odeluc, but the transaction was not made official before he was killed in the 1791 insurrection. Masson feared that if the old order returned, she would again be a slave. She pleaded with Gallifet to acknowledge the freedom she had gained before emancipation. "The time of error is finished," she announced, and those with "bad intentions" would no longer be able to "anchor their destructive influence" in Saint-Domingue, for a "protective government" was "working to reestablish order." Soon, she promised Gallifet, "the arms among your property that still exist will, voluntarily or by force, have to return to their useful work." In her bid to preserve her own freedom, Masson used a language similar to that of many French officials, suggesting that the time of freedom had been an aberration, a period of tumult and violence that was best left behind. The same was true of another writer, the representative of Madame de Mauger in Saint-Domingue, who in October 1802 sent news to her of her plantations in the Artibonite region, and of her ever-rebellious former slave, Philipeau. The latter, who after emancipation had continued on as the manager of her indigo plantations, had by 1802 purchased some land in the area where he had once been a slave. He had settled his wife and children there and no longer worked on the plantations. But it would be possible to "remove them," Mauger's representative noted, "when a certain order has been re-established in this country."[64]

Elsewhere in the colony French officers had already begun doing their best to erase what they saw as the perversions of this time of liberty. Soon after the French took Port-au-Prince, Lacroix and another general had found among Louverture's papers a box with a "false bottom." Underneath they found "locks of hair of all colors, rings, golden hearts punctured with arrows, little keys," along with an "infinity of sweet notes," all of which "left no doubt about the success the old Toussaint Louverture had achieved in love!" "He was black, and physically repulsive," wrote Lacroix, "but he had made himself the dispenser of all fortunes, and his power could alter any condition when it wished." Besides shocking the two generals, the discovery frightened them in its implications. For in Bonaparte's instructions to Leclerc he had declared that "white women who have prostituted them-selves to negroes, whatever their rank, will be sent back to France." The archive they had found could have been turned into a list of the guilty. So the two men decided to do a noble thing: before looking too closely at what they had found, they decided to "lose every trace of these shameful memo-ries," and burned much of what could "remind us of our painful discovery," throwing the rest into the ocean.[65]

A few years before, Laveaux had celebrated Louverture in Paris by de-scribing his kindness to white women in the colony, who had called him "father." Now such connections as might have existed between the general and such women were interpreted as a shameful past whose very memory should be destroyed. What did the letters Louverture had collected ac-tually say? What was the meaning of the objects he had received? The French generals made sure there would never be any way to find out, sending the archive's mysteries into the graveyard of fire and water.

CHAPTER THIRTEEN

Those Who Die

I T "APPEARED SUDDENLY, causing sharp pains in the eye sockets, feet, loins and stomach . . . The patient's face became flushed, tears flowed from his glazed eyes." The afflicted found it so difficult to breathe that they were "afraid of suffocation." "A thick, whitish-yellow fluid covered the parched tongue, then the teeth, and soon changed into a black encrustation." The vomit was "yellow from bile," and the "feces and urine red." In the "next phase," the patient could not drink. "Wounds opened up, often with inflamed edges." Then the patient began to heal and feel rejuvenated. This improvement, however, only "signaled the end." The nervous system collapsed, causing "cramps" and nosebleeds, while the pulse "feebled." By then the patient "was already a corpse, putrid and horrible from the blood's decomposition." This, in the words of a French doctor writing in 1806, was what happened to a victim of yellow fever.[1]

Even as they secured victory over Louverture in 1802, French troops increasingly fell prey to another daunting enemy: disease. Watching their troops die around them, bewildered officers counted and reported the dead. Some cast about for an explanation for the virulence of the fever. Descourtilz claimed that he had discovered an old black man who was grinding up the intestines of hastily buried fever victims to make sausages, and in so doing purposely spread the contagion to those who remained healthy. The reality was more banal. Troops arriving in the Caribbean had always been vulnerable to such outbreaks, and many had forewarned Bonaparte of the dangers the scourge might pose to his mission to Saint-Domingue. Aware of the danger, the consul had hoped to avoid the worst by sending his troops early enough in the year to avoid the hot months when the plague was at its worst. He also mistakenly assumed that his troops would accomplish their mission quickly. Instead, the war against Louverture took many months of hard campaigning. By then the season of fever had begun, and the disease showed a rare virulence, spreading rapidly as it fed off the large numbers of unacclimated troops on the island.

As 1802 wore on, the reinforcements that arrived to shore up Leclerc's mission were rapidly reduced by the plague. In mid-1803 two regiments of Polish troops disembarked in the town of Tiburon; ten days later more than half were dead of fever. "They fell down as they walked," a planter noted, "the blood rushing out of their nostrils, mouths, eyes." By late 1802, "an average of one hundred men a day died." The disease killed the entire crew of a Swedish ship harbored in Le Cap, with the single exception of a young cabin boy, and the empty ship was put up for sale.[2]

"If the first consul wants to have an army in Saint-Domingue in the month of October," Leclerc wrote to the colonial minister, Denis Decrès, in June 1802, "he must send one from the ports of France, for the ravages of the sickness here are beyond telling." He had lost 1,200 men during his first month in the colony, 1,800 in the next, and feared that he would lose 2,000 in the coming month. Of the tens of thousands who had arrived a few months before, there were only 10,000 European troops left who could still fight. "Half of the officers in this army are dead" from either battle or disease, he announced weeks later. "Men passed through and disappeared like shadows," Lacroix recalled; "you developed a stoic indifference, and separated yourself from those with whom you lived with less regret than you suffered in Europe when you learned of the light sickness of a friend." In one list of dead officers, Leclerc noted simply of one of them: "I didn't have time to get to know him."[3]

The deadly combination of "yellow fever and an enemy who gave no quarter" steadily undermined Bonaparte's plans for Saint-Domingue. As Leclerc wrote in early June, "the blacks" still fighting against him were "increasingly audacious." In mid-July there were "nighttime meetings" in the northern plain and even in Le Cap itself, animated by conspirators planning "the massacre of the Europeans." With resistance continuing, he found himself in a bind: in order to keep his mission afloat he had to defer, and indeed contradict, its ultimate goal: the destruction of the black army. With his own army becoming smaller and weaker, Leclerc had to depend on officers like Dessalines and Christophe and the colonial troops they commanded to fight the insurgents in the colony. "You order me to send the black generals to Europe," he wrote to Bonaparte in late August, but this was impossible, as he was using them to "stop the revolts" that in some areas had reached "alarming" proportions. His dependence on them was a financial drain—Leclerc complained to Bonaparte that he had to pay the salaries of 3,000 such officers, and 12,000 colonial troops—but it was also a political liability. The more Leclerc depended on the colonial troops, the more he broadcast his weakness. And the loyalty of these troops was, as the general understood, quite fragile. He reported in July that, suspecting a revolt brewing among "some colonial troops," he had shot "several of the leaders." And although he claimed to be the "master" of Dessalines's "spirit," he realized that Dessalines and other black officers were watching for an opportunity to turn against him. He comforted himself with the conclusion that they would not have the courage to do so. They "all hate one another," Leclerc claimed, and "know I will destroy them one by one." They were, furthermore, afraid "to measure themselves against the man who destroyed their chief"—Louverture. "The blacks are not brave," Leclerc concluded, "and this war has scared them."[4]

In fact the black officers serving Leclerc were the main reason his army survived as long as it did. Dessalines was as fearsome an enemy of his former comrades as he had once been of the French. In early August he led a successful attack against the insurgent band led by Macaya and brought back "women and children and prisoners." "I had a few hung, and others shot," Dessalines reported. He hoped that "in ten years" the people of the region would still remember the "lesson." In another letter Dessalines congratulated himself on the "desolation and terror" he had wrought. One French officer noted the "marvels" the black general had performed in capturing hundreds of guns from the insurgents and ridding "the country of more than a hundred incorrigible rascals." Leclerc similarly praised Dessalines as the "butcher of the blacks," noting that he was using him to execute all the most "odious measures" he was enforcing. Another white officer went so far as to call him "a god." As he had been under Louverture, Dessalines held the position of "inspector of agriculture," and punished rebellious plantation workers in the areas under his control swiftly and fiercely. Even if his exemplary justice was part of a broader ploy to trick the French into trusting him so that he could ultimately win the final battle for independence, this was certainly no consolation for those who were his victims during this period.[5]

Finding it impossible to fulfill Bonaparte's orders to dismantle the colonial army, Leclerc sought to carry out another aspect of the first consul's plan: the disarmament of the general population. He initiated the process in the west in June 1802, placing it in Dessalines's able hands, and soon extended the project to the south and eventually the north, collecting hundreds of rifles. According to Descourtilz, Dessalines took advantage of his control of the disarmament process to undermine it, secretly returning to their owners the very weapons he confiscated publicly, and stocking up on ammunition in preparation for the time he rebelled again. The process of taking weapons away, however, confirmed the suspicions many had about the intentions of the French: both Sonthonax and Louverture had warned that the rifle was the guarantor of liberty in Saint-Domingue.[6]

The disarmament process, meant to destroy the population's capacity to defend itself, backfired. It incited uprisings in several parts of the colony, including Port-de-Paix and the island of Tortuga, and helped to propel a series of defections among the colonial troops in the north. Colonel Sans-Souci reemerged as one of the revolt's major leaders. During the month of June he had submitted to the French. In early July, however, Leclerc, suspecting that Sans-Souci was preparing a "new rebellion," ordered his arrest. Before the French could get their hands on him he defected with many of his troops and attacked a French camp. Along with leaders such as Va-Malheureux and Macaya, he soon controlled much of the mountainous territory of the Northern Province, brilliantly repulsing French attacks sent against him. "The insurrection seems to be gaining more and more solidity," wrote one French officer in late July. "The areas that used to be quiet are now in insurrection." The "brigands" were burning plantations, mounting ambushes, and barricading the roads, and when confronted by French forces they "retreat as they burn." Many lower-ranking officers from the colonial army were seen heading with their weapons to areas controlled by rebel leaders.[7]

French officers sought to terrorize the rebels into submission. Giving the order to execute "five negroes" who had been stopped by a patrol with weapons and bayonets, one officer announced: "It is only through terrible examples that we will succeed in disarming the country and give this important colony back its splendor and its prosperity." "I give you permission to hang any rebel or malcontent." He recommended that such examples be made of officers suspected of being sympathetic to the rebels, as well as managers and drivers on the plantations. "They are the ones who are behind the rebellions and who encourage the negroes to revolt," he insisted. The French should show "no mercy today" and should punish crimes, including those committed earlier during the war, with "the rope," "the form of torture that frightens the negroes." Over time the French increasingly practiced such summary justice against black troops, often distinguishing little between soldiers who had remained loyal to them and those who had risen in revolt. Naturally, French brutality ultimately made the decision to change sides easier for those who had remained loyal. Fearing the worst, the French helped bring it about by acting the part of an army bent on destruction.[8]

James Stephen had predicted that once the "true design" of the French mission was unmasked there would be no stopping the resistance against it. The disarmament alarmed many in Saint-Domingue, and news arriving in the colony from across the Atlantic and from other parts of the Caribbean soon confirmed their fears about Leclerc's ultimate mission. In May 1802 Bonaparte signed a decree that publicly declared what had been decided the year before: in colonies such as Martinique that had been returned to France by the Treaty of Amiens, slavery would be "maintained in conformity with the laws and regulations anterior to 1789." The transatlantic slave trade would once again be open to French ships. An explanation attached to the law made clear that the proslavery planters of Paris had succeeded in winning over Bonaparte. "We know how the illusions of liberty and equality were propagated in these far-off countries, where the remarkable difference between men who are civilized and those who are not, and the difference in climates, colors, and habits, and, most important, the security of European families, inevitably require great differences in the civil and political state of people." "Those innovations so ardently desired by zealots"—that is, emancipation—had had "disastrous effects"; "in searching to indiscriminately make all the men of the colonies equal in their rights," they had "only made them all equally miserable." The application of "philanthropy" had "produced in our colonies the effect of the siren's song: with them came miseries of all kinds, despair, and death."[9]

Soon afterward all "black" or "mulatto" soldiers were outlawed from visiting Paris or the French port cities without official permission from the government. (Black sailors, presumably, were expected to remain on board when their ships were in port.) Two months later, more restrictions were put in place: "blacks," "mulattoes," and other "people of color" were not to enter the "continental territory of the Republic" without explicit authorization from officials. All those who entered the territory illegally would be arrested, imprisoned, and deported.[10]

The racial egalitarianism of 1794 had been replaced by a reinvigorated racist regime. The extent to which times had changed was made clear by the fate of the three men who had come from Saint-Domingue bringing news of Sonthonax's emancipation in 1794, and who had been showered with applause in the National Convention as living symbols of the end of the "aristocracy of the skin." In March 1802 the African-born Jean-Baptiste Belley was arrested by Leclerc and deported to France. Belley had long been an enemy of Louverture, and Leclerc's action against him seems to have been motivated by no political consideration other than the fact that he was a black man who had once occupied a high political office in France. Belley spent the next years in prison and died alone and forgotten in France in 1805. His onetime colleague Jean-Baptiste Mills, who was of mixed African and European descent, was arrested and deported to Corsica, where he was joined by hundreds of other deportees from the Caribbean who were condemned to forced labor on the island. The white member of the three-man group, Louis Dufay, who had given the speech celebrating the emancipation Sonthonax had proclaimed in Saint-Domingue, was left free and given permission to return to Saint-Domingue.[11]

Official racism had returned to the French empire with a vengeance. But the fate of those who had been freed in 1794 was left unclear. The May 1802 law on the colonies ended with a vague reference to Guadeloupe and Saint-Domingue, which stated that "a healing system" must be substituted for the "seductive theories" of the revolution. If slavery was not mentioned outright, however, there was less and less doubt about the kind of "healing" Bonaparte's regime intended. His colonial minister, Decrès, wrote: "I want slaves in our colonies. Liberty is a food for which the stomachs of the negroes are not yet prepared. We must seize any occasion to give them back their natural food, except for the seasonings required by justice and humanity."[12]

In Guadeloupe a military expedition sent from France a few months after the Leclerc expedition, led by General Antoine Richepance, had started a war that paralleled the conflict taking place in Saint-Domingue. In May, however, the French defeated the major rebel group, who blew themselves up on a plantation at a site called Matouba rather than surrender. Mass executions and deportations followed, targeting not only the rebels but also officers of African descent who had fought with the French. Richepance received orders from Paris to reestablish slavery but put off the action for fear of inciting new revolt. His secrecy, however, could not hide France's ultimate intentions. Deportees from Guadeloupe imprisoned in ships harbored off the coast of Saint-Domingue escaped and spread news of what had happened on their island. Rumors spread in Saint-Domingue that slavery had been reestablished in Guadeloupe, and were so pervasive that even Leclerc believed them.[13]

The news from Guadeloupe converged with other information flooding into the colony. As news of the reopening of the slave trade arrived, so did letters from France's former slaving companies offering to bring slaves from Africa into Saint-Domingue. "I had asked you, citizen consul," Leclerc lamented to Bonaparte, "not to do anything" that would make the people of Saint-Domingue "fear for their liberty." Now Bonaparte's "plans for the colonies" were "perfectly known." Seeking to hide the truth as long as possible, in late August Leclerc wrote Decrès a letter in a secret numerical code. "Do not consider reestablishing slavery here for some time," he pleaded. He would make it possible for his successor to do so, but given "the innumerable proclamations" he had made "to assure the blacks of their liberty," Leclerc did not want to be in "contradiction with himself."[14]

But it was too late for dissimulation to work as a weapon in Saint-Domingue. Too many now understood that this was a war between slavery and freedom. In October 1802 Leclerc would make this fact unmistakably clear with a proclamation offering liberty to all those individuals freed in the colony by the emancipation decrees of 1793 who joined the French in fighting the insurgents. Planters promised to draw up notary acts assuring freedom to any of their former slaves who volunteered. These declarations made it undeniable that slavery was on the horizon, since otherwise no one in the colony would have any use for the individual freedoms that were being promised.[15]

Already in August Leclerc noted the "true fanaticism" among the rebels, who would rather die than surrender, and lamented that he no longer had any "moral power" in the colony. He had "nothing left but terror" to use against the insurgents, and he deployed this weapon with desperation, hanging sixty insurgents in one day in Le Cap. Still, as he wrote a few days later, the rebels—both men and women—seemed uncowed, and even "laughed at death." Furthermore, as he reminded Decrès, to inflict terror effectively he would need more "money and troops."[16]

Throughout August the French battled against insurgent bands across the colony. The still-loyal troops under Dessalines and Christophe brought them some successes. But insurgent leaders such as Macaya and Sans-Souci fought back, and even when they retreated they were never captured. Each time an insurgent encampment was "destroyed or dispersed" it was "replaced by another, led by the same leaders, striking the same blows against the enemy, nourishing the same hopes." Sans-Souci was particularly successful, using tried-and-true techniques to stave off French advances, fighting a war without clear fronts, in which small groups set up in advance posts would sometimes hold, and sometimes retreat and draw the soldiers into "murderous ambushes." The French lost 400 soldiers in one September attack against Sans-Souci. He managed to hold vast stretches of territory, nearly surrounding Le Cap on one side, while troops under the command of Macaya held the region of Limbé. In the south, too, there were bands made up of defectors from the colonial army, who used artillery effectively against the French, backed up by many plantation laborers. One group, led by officers including Cangé and Gilles Bambara (who were probably African-born), besieged the town of Jacmel and set up ambushes that for a time prevented French reinforcements from breaking through. Such successes were to be expected. Many bands were led by "fighting units of an army of liberation" composed of hardened veterans. Meanwhile there were hundreds of smaller bands who continually harassed the French. Leclerc wrote in late August of "2,000 leaders" he needed to remove from the colony, including plantation managers, who could easily incite their plantation laborers to revolt.[17]

In the middle of August the officer Charles Belair—who in 1793 had signed his name alongside those of Jean-François and Biassou to a plan demanding freedom—launched an audacious plot aimed at drawing colonial troops fighting against the French into the opposition. The powerful Dessalines, however, refused to join, and indeed helped the French crush the uprising and capture and execute Belair. But although Dessalines, Christophe, and Alexandre Pétion—who had played a key role at the siege of Crête-à-Pierrot and had since been serving the French loyally—remained loyal to the French, increasing numbers of soldiers and officers from their units were defecting to join the revolutionaries. Reporting on his September attack against Sans-Souci, Leclerc noted that one column of colonial troops had not returned; he suspected that they had "deserted after having killed their chief." "This is now a war of colors," he noted, adding that the columns made up of "white troops" had suffered heavier casualties "than those composed of blacks," presumably both because of desertions and because some seemingly loyal black troops had fired on their white comrades during the fighting. This was precisely what happened a month later when, during another attack south of Le Cap, two colonial battalions "suddenly turned their fire" against French and Polish units accompanying them, killing many and forcing the rest to retreat.[18]

In early October Leclerc ordered the arrest of a few hundred black soldiers stationed in Jacmel. During the previous weeks these soldiers had demonstrated their loyalty to the French, staying behind as many of their comrades defected to the rebel side, but Leclerc nevertheless suspected them of treason. As they were being transported to Port-au-Prince in the hold of a ship, the prisoners, led by their commanding officer, carried out their final act of war. As Leclerc reported, all but three "strangled themselves," choosing suicide rather than imprisonment by the French. "These are the kind of men we have to fight," Leclerc lamented. In Le Cap, meanwhile, part of another colonial brigade deserted, and the 500 who remained were arrested. Leclerc believed that Dessalines and Maurepas were behind the defections, and issued orders for the arrest of the two officers.[19]

For colonial soldiers throughout the colony, time was running out. They knew they might fall prey at any moment to the increasingly indiscriminate violence exercised by the French against colonial troops whose loyalty they suspected. Even if they survived these reprisals, they might end up dead at the hands of the victorious insurgents. Rumors were spread among the colonial troops that the French troops were preparing to leave the colony. It was time, such rumors suggested, to make a choice between joining the insurgents or dying at their hands.[20]

The way into Le Cap was defended by colonial units loyal to France under the command of Alexandre Pétion and Augustin Clerveaux—both men of color—stationed on the outskirts of Le Cap. On October 13 Pétion and Clerveaux suddenly changed sides, leading their troops to join the rebels under the command of Macaya occupying the plain nearby. They attacked the following night, taking several forts on the edges of Le Cap and forcing the French troops to retreat into the town. The defection of Pétion and Clerveaux was part of a larger coordinated uprising among the colonial troops still allied with Leclerc. Christophe led his troops into the rebel camp, marched on the lightly defended town of Port-de-Paix, and was greeted by a "naked man with epaulettes suspended on his neck" leading a troop who shouted: "Vive le Général Christophe!" The town's commander, Maurepas, had, despite Leclerc's suspicions, in fact remained loyal to the French, but most of his troops had not followed when he retreated from the town. In the Artibonite, meanwhile, Paul Louverture defected to the rebel side with his troops. Dessalines attacked the garrison at Gonaïves, sending the French soldiers into retreat to their ships in the harbor. He wrote to the French officer commanding in nearby Saint-Marc, explaining that the people of Saint-Domingue had come to see clearly the "intentions" of the Leclerc mission, which were "openly manifested" by officers serving under him who "fiercely massacre all the blacks and mulattoes." "I am French, a friend of my country and of liberty," Dessalines continued. "I cannot watch such atrocities with a serene eye." He announced his intention to take Saint-Marc, demanding that the French officers retreat and "return to Europe."[21]

With the battle lines clearly drawn, many soldiers, both white and black, found themselves on the wrong side. In Port-de-Paix, Christophe captured a group of Polish soldiers and took them hostage. He offered Leclerc a deal: he would send the Polish troops to Le Cap in return for the release of his beloved orchestra, which was trapped in the town. When the French general refused, Christophe executed the Poles. In Le Cap, meanwhile, more extensive reprisals were under way. Leclerc ordered the immediate arrest of all the remaining colonial troops in Le Cap and had 1,000 of them loaded on ships in the harbor. Weighted down with sacks of flour tied to their necks, they were all pushed overboard. During the next few days their bodies were washed ashore along the beaches of the town, where "to the disgust and horror of the town's inhabitants" they rotted, untouched, in the equatorial sun. The cycle of revenge continued: insurgents "executed a number of white hostages within view of the city gates."[22]

Orders were sent to officers throughout the colony to arrest and imprison all the black troops still serving with the French. Despite his continuing loyalty, Maurepas was not spared: in early November he and his family were drowned in the harbor of Le Cap on Leclerc's orders. The wife and children of Paul Louverture, who were in Le Cap, suffered the same fate. The French commanders deported whites who were tainted by their affiliation with black generals, including one known as the "black white." In early November one officer fed up with the executions noted that within the past month the French had "drowned" nearly 4,000 colonial troops.

"The Mode of exterminating the Black Army as practised by the French." From
Marcus Rainsford, *A Historical Account of the Black Empire of Hayti* (1805).
Courtesy of the William L. Clements Library, University of Michigan.

"This is how we are fighting our war," he lamented, and concluded: "The
French will never be masters of this country."[23]

Weeks before the major defections began, Leclerc had written to
Decrès advocating a "war of extermination" in the colony. In order to "contain the mountains," he explained, he would have to destroy "a large part"
of the cultivators who lived there. "Accustomed" during the past ten years

"Revenge taken by the Black Army for the Cruelties practised on them by the French." From Marcus Rainsford, *A Historical Account of the Black Empire of Hayti* (1805). *Courtesy of the William L. Clements Library, University of Michigan.*

to "banditry," he wrote, they could never be subjected to work. In early October, when it was clear that he was facing a general insurrection, he put forth an even more forceful and brutal plan. "Here is my opinion on this country," he wrote to Bonaparte. "We must destroy all the blacks of the mountains—men and women—and spare only children under twelve years of age. We must destroy half of those in the plains and must not leave a single colored person in the colony who has worn an epaulette." The only hope, the French commanders had concluded, was to start again in Saint-Domingue with men and women imported from Africa who had never, as one historian writes, known "what it was to have broken the chains and won their freedom in the New World." Otherwise the colony would never be "peaceful," and every year there would be a new "civil war." Leclerc was increasingly desperate. "Since I have been here, I have seen only the spectacle of fires, insurrections, murders, of the dead and the dying," he lamented to Bonaparte. "My soul is withered, and no joyful thought can ever make me forget these hideous scenes."[24]

His body followed his soul speedily. Within a few weeks Leclerc succumbed to the fever that had taken so many of his troops. He was survived by his wife, Pauline, who soon returned to Europe. She would soon marry an Italian nobleman, and one day be immortalized by the sculptor Antonio Canova, to live on in stone, a mute witness to the débacle she had survived in Saint-Domingue.

Late in 1802, crowds in Le Cap lined the streets and covered them with flowers to greet a series of new arrivals in the colony. They were carried into the town in cages: dogs purchased in Cuba, accompanied by trainers who nourished them with blood and had them attack wicker figures—apparently made to resemble "a negro"—stuffed with "animal entrails and blood." Leclerc's replacement, Rochambeau, had ordered this new weapon to help in the floundering campaign against the insurgents. He was following in a venerable tradition: three centuries before, dogs had been introduced on the island by Columbus in order to terrorize the indigenous population. Aiming to "lift white morale," he set up a public demonstration of the dogs' abilities, establishing a "circus" in the courtyard of Le Cap's Government House, the old home of the Jesuits. (Fond of euphemisms for the horrors he was inflicting, Rochambeau referenced the practices of ancient Rome in calling the punishment of being eaten alive by dogs "descending into the arena.") Although some principled individuals refused to attend the event, a huge crowd gathered to watch as a black prisoner—the domestic of a French officer—was placed at the mercy of the dogs. To the dismay of the crowd, the dogs showed little interest in attacking the servant until his master intervened, slicing open the domestic's stomach to draw them into devouring him. Having provided entertainment to whites in Le Cap, the dogs were then let loose on the battlefield. They sometimes proved a liability to their masters, however. Deployed to support one French column sent against the insurgents from Port-au-Prince in March 1803, they contributed to a disastrous defeat. "Ignorant of color prejudice," they attacked those who were fleeing, who "in this circumstance happened to be white." Many of the dogs would end up "eaten by starving French soldiers."[25]

An expert in atrocity, Rochambeau "ordered his victims (both military and civilian) burned alive, drowned in sacks, hung, crucified, asphyxiated by sulphur fumes in ships' holds," and "shot (after digging their shallow graves)." His brutality, like Leclerc's terror, proved counterproductive: it helped expand and cement the alliance that proved crucial for the final victory of the revolutionary army in Saint-Domingue. Just as French killings of colonial troops had united Alexandre Pétion and Jean-Jacques Dessalines—who just a few years before had faced off against each other during the brutal war between Louverture and Rigaud—Rochambeau's actions alienated the most steadfast supporters of the French: portions of the communities of color in the west and south who powerfully resented Louverture and who initially viewed the French as saviors. Witnessing and suffering from the racial violence of Rochambeau, most of these supporters realized that their only hope for survival was to join the revolution. Racist delirium shattered the last fragments of moral authority the French had in Saint-Domingue.[26]

Now calling themselves the "indigenous army," the revolutionaries were by early 1803 jointly led by a solid coalition of ex-slave and colored officers. In March an article published in Port-au-Prince noted that the rebels were still fighting under the French tricolor and that this was a sign that they wished "to remain French" and had no intention of "making the country independent from the metropole." Pétion forwarded the article to Dessalines, who decided it was time to disabuse their enemies of such notions. He and his officers tore the white out of their French tricolor and sewed the blue and the red back together again. In 1793 the tricolor had been a symbol of the unity among whites, people of color, and blacks, all joined in defense of the Republic. The message of the new flag was clear: through their brutality, the French whites had forfeited their right to be included in the new political community being forged in the colony. Black and colored residents were united in opposition to the whites.[27]

The unity of the indigenous army was, however, strained by other divisions. Having defected from the French side, Dessalines and Christophe planned to incorporate the troops that had preceded them in rebellion into their former ranks in the army. This plan did not sit well with Sans-Souci, who—leading preponderantly African-born troops known as the "Congos"—had for months repelled attacks led on behalf of the French by Christophe, and was unwilling to start taking orders from his former enemy. Both Pétion and Dessalines sought to paper over the differences between Christophe and Sans-Souci, and the latter seems to have agreed to submit to the authority of Dessalines. Christophe, however, seeing the leader of the Congos as a threat to his authority, invited him to a meeting and then had him assassinated. The enraged Congos attacked Christophe's troops, sending them into a retreat, and captured Paul Louverture, executing him in revenge. Dessalines then led troops against the remaining Congos, who retreated further into the mountains but continued to harass the insurgent army. The unfinished "war within the war" weakened the insurgent position in the north and continued to haunt postindependence Haiti. After Christophe made himself king of the north of Saint-Domingue, he built a great palace called Sans-Souci, whose name was probably meant in part to erase the memory of his Congo victim.[28]

Despite such internal conflicts, by early 1803 Dessalines had managed to assert his command over most of the insurgents in the colony. He and his officers gradually unified the forces of hundreds of local leaders, continuing to harass the French throughout the colony, and often decimating the troops sent against them. In mid-1803 one unit of Polish soldiers was completely surrounded by insurgents. "Seeing myself surrounded by more than 3,000 negroes," the desperate officer in command of the unit wrote, "I see no prospect of holding out with such a small detachment, and rather than fall into the hands of this savage people fighting for its own freedom, I am taking my own life." Some Polish soldiers made an equally daring choice: they switched sides, joining the rebels. In October 1802 Dessalines had noted that he was joined in his defection by "many European soldiers who are concerned, loyal, and tormented because they are men who, like me, have taken up arms for their own liberty, and they are considered as my friends." He was referring, it seems, to Polish troops with whom he had made connections during his service in the colonial army. The Poles had, years before, enlisted in Bonaparte's army in the hope that the French would support their own bid for national independence. French soldiers often made fun of them, and even spread the rumor that they were cannibals. Many were dismayed by the brutality exercised by the French, and a few, perhaps recognizing in their enemy the same hopes that animated them, concluded that they were fighting an illegitimate war against a just cause. The exact numbers of defections to the rebel side are difficult to know. One Polish officer, however, recalled that Dessalines had "won over 30 fusiliers" from his unit and subsequently turned them into his honor guard.[29]

As their armies grew, the revolutionaries continued to use the "ruse and ingenuity" that had served the insurgents of 1791 so well. One French officer recalled an "African ruse" that was used again and again and "constantly succeeded." "An entirely naked negro appeared in front of one of our posts, a short distance away; he approached, clowning around to amuse the soldiers with his grimaces; then he started making fun of us and provoking us with outrageous gestures." When the French troops, "their patience soon exhausted," fired at him, he dove out of the way. "Irritated," the soldiers approached to fire at him, and soon a group of soldiers enticed into pursuing him ran headlong into an ambush. At one point in 1803, French sentries outside Les Cayes "sighted a magnificent horse, riderless but carrying a saddle and a saber, prancing through the nearby fields." The "gullible" captain offered a reward to any soldier who would capture the horse; four volunteered, but as they sought to approach the horse, they fell into an ambush and were all captured by a group of insurgents.[30]

Although they formed a crucial part of the indigenous army, the veterans of Louverture's war were only one part of the revolution. The war became a mass uprising among the residents of the colony, with plantation laborers fighting in huge numbers. The prospect of defeat was more frightening than the rigors of war. Women fought alongside men. In one battle in the south they made up the first wave of an attack, carrying bundles of brush meant to help the troops behind them cross trenches around a fortification, and were massacred by French musket fire.[31]

According to Descourtilz, Dessalines had convinced the "Congos" who fought with him that it would be a blessing if they were killed by the French, for they would "immediately be transported to Guinea, where they would once again see Papa Toussaint, who was waiting for them to complete his army, which was destined to reconquer Saint-Domingue." This was a return to Africa whose goal was ultimately to take back the colony. Inspired by such promises, wrote Descourtilz, the African fighters marched into battle "with a supernatural intrepidity, singing Guinean songs, as if possessed by the hope that they would soon see their old ac-

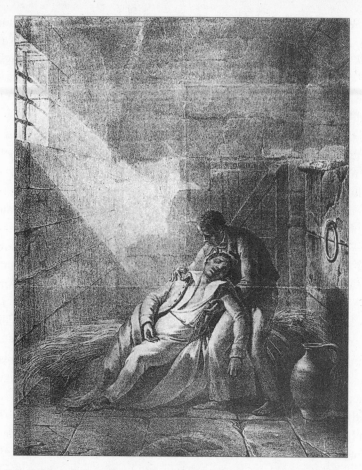

An engraving from the series published in Haiti in 1822.
Louverture is dying in the arms of his domestic servant, who accompanied him to Fort de Joux. *Private collection.*

quaintances." Others responded in a different way, taunting death. A song
probably passed down from the era of the revolution runs: "Grenadiers,
charge! / There is no mother, there is no father. / Grenadiers, charge! /
Those who die, it's their problem!" There was nothing, the song suggested,
other than the battle to be fought—no ancestors, no relatives, no one to go
with the soldier into the grave.[32]

Death was also making its rounds across the Atlantic. On April 8, 1803,
high in the Jura Mountains of France, a doctor was called from a nearby
town to the prison at Fort de Joux to examine a corpse. It was Toussaint

Louverture, who had died the night before. There was "a bit of mucus mixed with blood" in his mouth and on his lips, and an autopsy unveiled the deterioration of the prisoner's hearts and lungs. He had, the doctor declared, died of "apoplexy" and "pneumonia." Louverture was gone at the age of fifty-nine, his body thrown into an unmarked grave near the prison, his soul, if Dessalines was to be believed, on its way to take command of the steadily growing army of the dead waiting for him in Africa.[33]

Two months later, in Saint-Domingue, a judge in Saint-Marc condemned Louverture for having defrauded a group of planters in 1799 by paying them too little for some of their properties in the Artibonite. The planters were invited to take back the properties, while the defendant, having "failed to appear," was condemned to pay the court costs incurred by the planters. It was a gesture in futility on two counts. Louverture, of course, was not going to pay his fine, and there was little hope that the planters would recover their land. In early May the short-lived peace between the French and the British was broken in Europe. It was the coup de grâce for the French troops in Saint-Domingue. Already driven out of much of the colony, they now had no hope of receiving reinforcements from Europe and furthermore had to contend again with the British enemy. Rochambeau withdrew to Le Cap, where his "answer to the blockade of the ports by a British fleet, to the disintegration of his army, to the hospitals glutted with the mutilated and the dying, and to Dessalines' victories, was to throw a ball." During the "last days of Saint-Domingue," with the remaining French forces in Le Cap surrounded by insurgents, the century of French rule ended in a final festival of brutal recrimination and pathetic debauchery.[34]

"Dessalines is coming to the north / Come see what he is bringing," invites a song recalling the general's final march against the French. Passed down and recorded in 1901, the song notes the different weapons he was carrying: "He is bringing a *ouanga nouveau*"—"a new fetish" or "new magic," it announces; "he is bringing muskets, he is bringing bullets . . . He is bringing cannons to chase away the whites." Dessalines's magic triumphed in mid-November 1803. Directing a final attack against French positions outside Le Cap at Vertières on the eighteenth, Dessalines sat on a stone, holding his snuffbox, and watched as his troops took the final, crucial hill, conquering "a country, a nation for his entire race." Finally accepting defeat, Rochambeau negotiated a surrender. The several thousand remaining French troops, along with many white residents of Le Cap, sailed out of the harbor, where they were taken prisoner by waiting British ships. They left behind them upwards of 50,000 dead, the majority of the soldiers and sailors sent to the colony since early 1802. Dessalines marched triumphantly into Le Cap Français, which was soon given a new name: Le Cap Haïtien.[35]

In order to create the new nation of Haiti, Dessalines and his officers invented a new verb. "Le nom français lugubre encore nos contrées," they declared. This sentence translates roughly as "The French name still haunts our lands." But it transformed a French adjective, *lugubre*— "gloomy"—into a verb. The declaration, issued on January 1, 1804, was a furious attack against the brutalities of the French, and a call for the members of the new nation to reject forever the past of empire and slavery.[36]

On December 31, 1803, Dessalines was presented with a draft of the independence declaration. Written by an elderly and educated man of color, "an admirer of the work of Jefferson," the document was modeled on the U.S. Declaration of Independence and "set forth all the rights of the black race, and the just complaints" that the population had against France. Dessalines, however, felt that it lacked the "heat and energy" required for the occasion. A young officer of color named Louis Félix Boisrond-Tonnerre declared: "In order to draw up our act of independence, we need the skin of a white to serve as a parchment, his skull as an inkwell, his blood for ink, and a bayonet for a pen." Dessalines concurred, and put the task of writing a new version of the declaration of independence in Boisrond-Tonnerre's hands. The latter stayed up all night writing the proclamation for the next day's ceremony. The more moderate one it replaced was lost, leaving behind only the trace of its rejection.[37]

"It is not enough to have expelled the barbarians who have bloodied our land for two centuries," the declaration began. "We must, with one last act of national authority, forever assure the empire of liberty in the country that witnessed our birth." The history of French colonialism had left its mark everywhere: "Everything revives memories of the cruelties of this barbarous people: our laws, our habits, our towns, everything still carries the stamp of the French." In declaring independence, the people of Haiti must forever reject their colonizers. "What do we have in common with this people of executioners?" The "difference between our color and theirs," the "ocean" that separated them, all made clear that "they are not our brothers, that they will never be." The people of the colony must "swear to posterity, and the entire universe, to renounce France forever, and to die rather than live under its domination." The nation's "cry" must be "Anathema to the French name! Eternal hatred of France!"[38]

Contemporary sources on the history of the island claimed that its original Taino inhabitants had called the land "Haïti." Versions of this name had been used a few times by residents, notably in a 1788 pamphlet calling for a colonial reform that would include renaming the colony "Aïti." Educated officers such as Boisrond-Tonnerre, who had studied in Paris, were familiar with such historical sources. And the broader population had an "awareness" of the island's former inhabitants who had left remains of their presence scattered throughout the mountains and plains, where they were frequently uncovered by those working the land. Dessalines and his officers decided to baptize the land they had conquered "Haiti."[39]

The choice of this name was not the first use of indigenous symbolism by Dessalines. After going into rebellion in late 1802, Dessalines briefly adopted the term "Army of the Incas" for his troops, who also sometimes called themselves "Sons of the Sun," though these terms eventually gave way to the less poetic term "Indigenous Army." The former slaves who made up the army, and most of the population of the new nation, were of course no more native to the island than were the French colonizers whose expulsion the proclamation of independence demanded. Dessalines's use of symbols derived from indigenous peoples was an attempt to assert a legitimate claim to a land in which a majority of the nation's inhabitants were exiles, having been brought there from Africa against their will. But it also suggested that this claim was based on resistance to, and the ultimate victory over, the brutality of colonialism, something which the enslaved shared with those wiped out by the Spanish centuries before they ever arrived. The choice of the name Haïti, then, infused the declaration of independence with a broader historical significance. Haiti was to be the negation not only of French colonialism, but of the whole history of European empire in the Americas. The new nation was to channel the centuries of suffering of those pushed to the margins by the official activity of colonialism into a new political community meant to guarantee the eternal freedom of its scarred constituency.[40]

The proclamation declared that spirits of the dead who had died at the hands of "those vultures" the French demanded revenge. It was necessary, furthermore, to give "to the nations" a "terrible, but just, example of the vengeance that a people proud of having won back its liberty, and ready to jealously preserve it, must exercise." In the months following the declaration of independence, Dessalines, who like Louverture named himself governor "for life" (though he would soon give himself another title, that of emperor), made good on these threats. In late February he declared that all those who were suspected of participation in the massacres ordered by Leclerc and Rochambeau should be put on trial. He produced a letter written to Bonaparte in late 1802 by a number of residents celebrating Rochambeau's successes and complimenting him for rejecting the "false philosophy" that had been so detrimental to Saint-Domingue, which could be "made fertile" only by Africans held under "strict discipline." It was a thinly veiled call for the return of slavery, Dessalines claimed, and all the signatories were therefore complicit in the terror the French had inflicted during their final year in the colony. Dessalines also feared that whites in the colony were actively conspiring to prepare a new attack aimed at bringing slavery back to the island. He ordered a series of massacres of white inhabitants, although precisely how many perished is difficult to establish.[41]

In the wake of the massacres, Dessalines explained that a "handful of whites" who had "professed" the right "religion"—the rejection of slavery—were under his personal protection. He granted them naturalization papers that welcomed them "among the children of Haiti." In order to receive the papers the whites had to take an oath renouncing France and accepting the laws of their new land. Many of those who were naturalized were white women, presumably widows, who were allowed to retain their property. Their special status was solidified in the constitution proclaimed in 1805. In it Dessalines declared that "no white, no matter what his nation," could come to Haiti as "master or property owner," but he exempted those who had been naturalized. He also singled out two special groups who were not included in the ban: the Poles who had deserted or remained in the colony after the evacuation, and a group of Germans who had been settled in the colony before the revolution. The constitution went on to declare that, in the interest of eliminating all distinctions of "color" in the nation, all Haitians would henceforth be known as "black." Haiti was a black nation, but those who embraced its creed of rejecting France and the slavery it had propagated were welcome to change their official identity and become a part of it, and therefore of the black race.[42]

Such exceptions did not lessen the effect of the killing of whites, which many outside the country pointed to as proof of the barbarity of the new regime. Dessalines defended his actions as the only way to preserve the freedom won at such cost by his army. "These implacable enemies of the rights of man have been punished for their crimes," he declared in an April 1804 proclamation. The ax had been taken to the tree of "slavery and prejudice." The people of Haiti were "mutilated victims" of the "French whites" and had done what was necessary to preserve their freedom. "Yes, we have paid these true cannibals back crime for crime, war for war, outrage for outrage," Dessalines thundered. "I have saved my country. I have avenged America."[43]

Epilogue: Out of the Ashes

IN 1803 WORSHIPERS carrying fruit, meat, fish, milk, and other food gathered around an ancient mapou tree in the Artibonite plain. A call had gone out from the local priests: their "great god, who was fighting for their prosperity and their liberty," had been wounded in the war. He needed food and medicine to help him heal. And so men and women harvested, cooked, and brought what they could to the mapou tree, "happy to be able to do something for their divinity."[1]

Haiti needed to be healed, for it was a nation founded on ashes. Years of insurrection and war had weakened and disrupted the economy. It was being rebuilt when Leclerc's mission had arrived in 1802, but the final, cataclysmic war had brought fire and destruction to most of the cities and plains. There were dead beyond counting—it is estimated that 100,000 or more residents of the colony died during the revolution—and many others were permanently crippled.[2]

The years of conflict left other, more enduring scars: impulses toward democracy would long run up against autocratic and militaristic political traditions, and the social and racial conflicts of the revolutionary years would continue unabated. While some elites rebuilt parts of the colony's plantation economy, producing and profiting from coffee during the nineteenth century, many ex-slaves and their descendants chose what they saw as the true independence of peasant agriculture over the limits of wage labor. In the middle of the century, peasant movements struggled against autocratic governments, seeking to fulfill some of the unachieved promises of the Haitian Revolution, but were ultimately defeated. Burdened by heavy taxes and confronted with the cumulative consequences of environmental degradation, their struggle for a decent life was a difficult one, leaving many in a grinding poverty that impelled migrations to the nation's cities and beyond.[3]

There was little peace in the years after independence. Dessalines's short reign ended with his assassination in 1806, and the young nation again found itself in a civil war pitting the south, under the command of Alexandre Pétion (who hosted a beleaguered Simón Bolívar, encouraging him to abolish slavery in his pursuit of independence in South America), against the north, ruled by Henri Christophe, who crowned himself king. On the slopes of the mountains bordering the northern plain, above his palace at Sans-Souci, Christophe built an impressive fortress. The Citadel, as he called it, was to stand against the continuing threat of a foreign invasion that would bring slavery back to the land.

Such a threat had been evoked before, in April 1804, by Dessalines, who had dared the defeated French to try to return: "Let her come, this power crazy enough to dare attack me!" "At her approach," he promised, "the irritated genie of Haiti" would appear, "emerging from the sea," stirring up the waves, calling up the storms. Its "strong hand" would "shatter and disperse" the ships. It would send "sickness," "hunger," "fire," and "poison" upon its enemies. "But why count on the succor of the climate and the elements?" Dessalines asked. They were not needed; he had under his command "rare souls, nourished on adversity," "sixty thousand men," "war-hardened," ready to fight to avenge their dead brothers. "Let them come, these homicidal troops; I am waiting for them, standing firm, with a steady eye."[4]

The invasions would come, but not precisely as either Dessalines or Christophe expected. They would begin with the simple denial that Haiti existed. Some exiled planters sought to erase what had happened: in 1806 one of them, exiled in Louisiana, noted as part of his property his "Negroes remaining in Saint-Domingue." Many governments reacted similarly. The refusal of diplomatic relations with Haiti pioneered by Jefferson would last until 1862, when Confederate secession made it possible for the abolitionist senator Charles Sumner to lead the way to opening relations with Haiti. The denial of political existence was accompanied by other attacks on sovereignty. In 1825 the Haitian government agreed to pay an indemnity to France in return for diplomatic and economic relations. Exiled planters had been clamoring for such a payment for years: it was meant to repay them for what they had lost in Saint-Domingue, including the money invested in their slaves, and amounted to a fine for revolution. Unable to pay, the Haitian government took loans from French banks, entering a cycle of debt that would last into the twentieth century. When foreign invasion did finally come, it was not by the French, but by the United States, which occupied Haiti in 1915, crushing a resistance movement whose soldiers believed they were fighting a second Haitian Revolution, and departed in 1934, but not before Haiti's constitution was altered to allow whites again to own land there.[5]

Even as Haiti struggled, the ramifications of its revolution reshaped the world around it. The victory of the black troops of Saint-Domingue paved the way for the Louisiana Purchase. Bonaparte's mission to the colony had been the centerpiece of a new colonial policy aimed at reinvigorating the French presence in the Americas—Louisiana was meant to supply food for the reconstructed plantation society of Saint-Domingue—and when it was crushed he had little choice but to give up his ambitions, to the profit of an expanding United States. As a result slavery thrived and expanded in North America during the next decades. In the Caribbean, planters and administrators in Cuba stepped into the vacuum created by the destruction of what had been the most important supplier of the world's sugar. In the nineteenth century sugar plantations sprang up throughout Cuba, sometimes staffed by exiles from Saint-Domingue, and worked by African slaves. The latter were imported into the colony in massive numbers: between 1790 and 1867 nearly as many were introduced to Cuba as had been imported to Saint-Domingue in the entire eighteenth century. The precedent of the Haitian Revolution, however, made some worry about the danger of importing African slaves: one Puerto Rican writer wondered whether they would "come to form a multitude" that might become an "exterminating thunderbolt."[6]

While Haiti represented a nightmare to many slave masters, it was a source of inspiration for slaves throughout the Americas. "Within one month after the 1791 uprising, slaves in Jamaica were singing songs about it," and within a few years masters "from Virginia to Louisiana to Cuba and Brazil were complaining of a new 'insolence' on the part of their slaves, which they often attributed to awareness of the successful black revolution." In Richmond the example of Haiti inspired a slave named Gabriel in 1800 to plan a bold conspiracy that envisioned a collaboration between whites and blacks—perhaps an echo of the alliance that brought down slavery in Saint-Domingue in 1793—in pursuit of emancipation. Years later, in 1861, an anonymous pamphlet was published in Boston, reprinting

Sonthonax's 1793 decrees and arguing that the Union should follow his example by arming and freeing slaves in order to defeat internal rebellion.[7]

Images of the leaders of the Haitian Revolution were an inspiration to people of African descent throughout the Americas. In Rio de Janeiro in 1805, soldiers of African descent wore "medallion portraits of the emperor Dessalines." In Cuba a free black named José Antonio Aponte, who was accused of conspiring to revolt in 1812, had portraits of Henri Christophe, Toussaint Louverture, Jean-François, and Dessalines in his home. Rebels who conspired with Aponte described having been shown these images "in what probably amounted to lessons in the history of the Haitian Revolution." Haiti itself was seen as a source of potential support for rebels. "Word ran through Havana," according to one slave in Cuba, that "generals and captains" from Haiti had come to seek "freedom for all the slaves on the island." Years later Denmark Vesey, who had lived for a short time in Saint-Domingue, would promise "his followers the help of Haitian soldiers once they had taken over the city of Charleston." Though Haiti's rulers never openly supported revolts elsewhere, some did invite any who escaped slavery to take refuge in their land.[8]

Stories of the Haitian Revolution provided "fuel" for "both sides" in public debates on race and slavery. Many writers emphasized the barbarity of the slave insurgents and saw the main result of their emancipation as a descent into laziness and lawlessness, using such arguments, often effectively, to defend slavery where it still existed. But James Stephen used the example of Haiti in arguing for abolition, while another British abolitionist, William Wilberforce, corresponded with Henri Christophe. The example of Haiti reached others as well: as he developed his theory of the master-slave dialectic, the philosopher Hegel seems to have been influenced by reading newspaper accounts about the revolution. As time went on, many were inspired by the story of the Haitian Revolution and of its great leader Toussaint Louverture, who became "the most widely known and sympathetic black hero in the West." Frederick Douglass, who served as the U.S. ambassador to Haiti after diplomatic relations were reestablished, declared in 1893 that when the "black sons of Haiti" had "struck for freedom," they had "struck for the freedom of every black man in the world." Around the same time the French abolitionist Victor Schoelcher, nearing the end of his life, wrote a biography of Louverture, whose example had inspired him as he successfully battled slavery in the remaining French colonies. And as the battle for decolonization in Africa and the Caribbean began, the writer and activist C. L. R. James turned to the example of Haiti to understand both the possibilities and the dangers of revolution.[9]

Through such writings, through conversations, through rumors and nightmares and dreams, those who died for and lived through the Haitian Revolution became part of every society in the Atlantic world. They continue to speak to us, as founders in a long struggle for dignity and freedom that remains incomplete. In the mountains of Haiti, looming over the northern plain, over the ruins of Gallifet's once prosperous plantation, Christophe's Citadel is still standing watch.

NOTES ✳ INDEX

NOTES

PROLOGUE

1. Beaubrun Ardouin, *Etudes sur l'histoire d'Haïti,* 11 vols. (1853–1865; reprint, Port-au-Prince, 1958), 6:9. Little is known about most of the declaration's signers; a series of biographies was published by S. Rouzier, "Les Hommes de l'indépendance," *Moniteur Universelle* 34–66, 1 May–18 August 1924. My thanks to Patrick Tardieu for showing me these articles.

2. Ardouin, *Etudes sur l'histoire d'Haïti;* Thomas Madiou, *Histoire d'Haiti* (1847–48; reprint, Port-au-Prince, 1989).

3. C. L. R. James, *The Black Jacobins: Toussaint Louverture and the San Domingo Revolution* (1938; reprint, New York, 1963); Aimé Césaire, *Toussaint Louverture: La Révolution et le problème colonial* (Paris, 1981), 24.

4. The major recent studies of the Haitian Revolution in English are Carolyn Fick, *The Making of Haiti: The Saint-Domingue Revolution from Below* (Knoxville, 1990); David Geggus, *Slavery, War and Revolution* (Oxford, 1982) and *Haitian Revolutionary Studies* (Bloomington, 2002); and Thomas Ott, *The Haitian Revolution* (Knoxville, 1973). The work that best places the Haitian Revolution within the broader history of the Americas is Robin Blackburn, *The Overthrow of Colonial Slavery, 1776–1848* (London, 1989).

5. M. Dalmas, *Histoire de la Révolution de Saint-Domingue* (Paris, 1814), 1:133.

6. The works that best define the work on "postemancipation" societies in the Americas are Rebecca Scott, *Slave Emancipation in Cuba: The Transition to Free Labor, 1860–1899* (Princeton, 1985); and Thomas Holt, *The Problem of Freedom: Race, Labor, and Politics in Jamaica and Britain* (Baltimore, 1992). See also the introduction and essays in Frederick Cooper, Thomas Holt, and Rebecca Scott, eds., *Beyond Slavery: Explorations in Race, Labor, and Citizenship* (Chapel Hill, 2000).

7. Geggus, *Haitian Revolutionary Studies,* 42; John Thornton, "African Soldiers in the Haitian Revolution," *Journal of Caribbean History* 25, 1 and 2 (1991), 58–80; idem, "I Am the Subject of the King of Kongo: African Political Ideology and the Haitian Revolution" *Journal of World History* 4 (fall 1993): 181–214; Gérard Barthélemy, *Creoles, Bossales: Conflit en Haïti* (Petit-Bourg, Guadeloupe, 2000).

8. For a model approach to the problem of writing historically about race in the Caribbean, see Ada Ferrer, *Insurgent Cuba* (Chapel Hill, 1999).

9. See Michel Rolph Trouillot, *Silencing the Past: Power and the Production of History* (Boston, 1996), chaps. 2 and 3; see also David Barry Gaspar, *Bondsmen and Rebels: A Study of Master-Slave Relations in Antigua* (Baltimore, 1985); and João José Réis, *Slave Rebellion in Brazil: The 1835 Muslim Uprising of Bahia* (Baltimore, 1995).

1. SPECTERS OF SAINT-DOMINGUE

1. Etienne Taillemite, "Moreau de Saint-Méry," introduction to Méderic-Louis-Élie Moreau de St. Méry, *Description topographique, physique, civile, politique et historique de la partie française de l'isle Saint-Domingue,* 3 vols. (1796; reprint, Paris, 1958), 1:xxvii.

2. Malick Walid Ghachem, "Sovereignty and Slavery in the Age of Revolution: Haitian Variations on a Metropolitan Theme" (Ph.D. diss., Stanford University, 2001), chap. 4.

3. Moreau, *Description,* 1:3–4.

4. Ibid., 5–6.

5. Ibid., 6–7; Aimé Césaire, *Toussaint Louverture: La Révolution et le problème colonial* (Paris, 1981), 23.

6. Moreau, *Description,* 1:7.

7. Ibid., 340.

8. Ibid., 340–341.

9. Ibid., 2:543–544, 1055; Louis Sala-Moulins, *Le Code Noir, ou le calvaire de Canaan* (Paris, 1987), 188.

10. Moreau, *Description,* 1:142; 3:1237; 1:185–186; 3:1206; 2:536.

11. Ibid., 3:1253.

12. Peter Hulme, *Colonial Encounters: Europe and the Native Caribbean, 1492–1797* (London, 1986).

13. Richard Turits, *Foundations of Despotism: Peasants, the Trujillo Regime, and Modernity in Dominican History* (Stanford, 2002), 25–26; Noble David Cook, "Disease and the Depopulation of Hispaniola, 1492–1518, *Colonial Latin American Review* 2, 1–2 (1993), 214–220.

14. Bartolomé de Las Casas, *History of the Indies,* trans. and ed. André Collard (New York, 1971), 78, 94.

15. Moreau, *Description,* 1:196, 213–215; Richard L. Cunningham, "The Biological Impacts of 1492," in *The Indigenous People of the Caribbean,* ed. Samuel W. Wilson (Gainesville, 1997), 31–35, 33.

16. Moreau, *Description* 1:212, 244, 141; 3:1381–82; 2:1140–41.

17. Turits, *Foundations of Despotism,* 27–28.

18. Ibid., 29–30; Charles Frostin, *Les Révoltes blanches à Saint-Domingue aux XVIIè et XVIIIè siècles* (Paris, 1975), 40.

19. Pierre Chaunu, *L'Amérique et les Amériques* (Paris, 1964), 113; Kris Lane, *Pillaging the Empire: Piracy in the Americas, 1500–1750* (London, 1998).

20. Philip Boucher, *Cannibal Encounters: Europeans and Island Caribs, 1492–1763* (Baltimore, 1992); Peter Wood, *Black Majority: Negroes in South Carolina from 1670 through the Stono Rebellion* (New York, 1974).

21. Lane, *Pillaging the Empire*, 97; Cunningham, "Biological Impacts of 1492," 33–34.

22. Pierre Pluchon, "Introduction," in Alexandre-Stanislas de Wimpfeen, *Haiti au XVIIIème siècle*, ed. Pluchon (Paris, 1993), 11.

23. Moreau, *Description*, 1:186–187, 210, 229; 3:1177, 1183; Christian Buchet, "L'Expédition de Carthagène des Indes," in *L'Aventure de la Flibuste*, ed. Michel Le Bris (Paris, 2002), 275–288, quotation 279; Pierre Pluchon, ed., *Histoire des Antilles et de la Guyane* (Paris, 1987), 104.

24. Sidney Mintz, *Sweetness and Power: The Place of Sugar in Modern History* (New York, 1985).

25. David Geggus, "Sugar and Coffee Cultivation in Saint Domingue and the Shaping of the Slave Labor Force," in *Cultivation and Culture: Labor and the Shaping of Slave Life in the Americas*, ed. Ira Berlin and Philip Morgan (Charlottesville, 1993), 73–98, esp. 74–75, 84; Mintz, *Sweetness and Power*.

26. Frostin, *Les Révoltes blanches*, 28. For a comparative history of the expansion of American slavery see Robin Blackburn, *The Making of New World Slavery: From the Baroque to the Modern* (London, 1997).

27. Frostin, *Les Révoltes blanches*, 32–33; Carolyn Fick, *The Making of Haiti: The Saint-Domingue Revolution from Below* (Knoxville, 1990), 22; Jean-François Dutrône de la Coutûre, *Précis sur la canne et sur les moyens d'en extraire le sel essentiel, suivi de plusieurs mémoires* (Paris, 1791).

28. Frostin, *Les Révoltes blanches*, 54.

29. Moreau, *Description*, 3:1221; 2:865–867.

30. Françoise Thésée, *Négociants bordelais et colons de Saint-Domingue* (Paris, 1972); Gabriel Debien, *Les Esclaves aux Antilles françaises (XVIIè–XVIIIème siècles)* (Gourbeyre, 1974), 113; Stewart King, *Blue Coat or Powdered Wig: Free People of Color in Pre-Revolutionary Saint Domingue* (Athens, 2001), xvi.

31. John Garrigus, "Redrawing the Colour Line: Gender and the Social Construction of Race in Pre-Revolutionary Haiti," *Journal of Caribbean History* 30, 1 and 2 (1996): 28–50, 33; Geggus, "Sugar and Coffee Cultivation," 73; David Brion Davis, "Impact of the French and Haitian Revolutions," in *The Impact of the Haitian Revolution in the Atlantic World*, ed. David Geggus (Columbia, S.C., 2001), 3–9, 4.

32. Blackburn, *Making of New World Slavery*, 431–449; idem, *The Overthrow*

of Colonial Slavery, 1776–1778 (London, 1989), 167; C. L. R. James, *The Black Jacobins: Toussaint Louverture and the San Domingo Revolution* (1938; reprint, New York, 1963), 47–50; Jean Tarrade, *Le Commerce coloniale de la France à la fin de l'Ancien Régime*, 2 vols. (Paris, 1972), 2:754–755; David Geggus, "Racial Equality, Slavery, and Colonial Secession during the Constituent Assembly," *American Historical Review* 94 (December 1989): 1290–1308, 1291.

33. Moreau, *Description*, 1:296.

34. Ibid., 316, 320.

35. Ibid., 155–156, 320, 345; King, *Blue Coat or Powdered Wig*, 25–26.

36. James E. McClellan II, *Colonialism and Science: Saint Domingue in the Old Regime* (Baltimore, 1992), 3, 85–94; Moreau, *Description*, 1:301; Althéa de Puech Parham, ed., *My Odyssey: Experiences of a Young Refugee from Two Revolutions, by a Creole of Saint Domingue* (Baton Rouge, 1959), 20.

37. King, *Blue Coat or Powdered Wig*, 23; McClellan, *Colonialism and Science*, 94–97; Moreau, *Description*, 1:312.

38. McClellan, *Colonialism and Science*, 83; Thomas Ott, *The Haitian Revolution, 1789–1804* (Knoxville, 1974), 6; Moreau, *Description*, 1:119; Parham, *My Odyssey*, 21; Gabriel Debien, Jean Fouchard, and Marie Antoinette Menier, "Toussaint Louverture avant 1789: Légendes et réalités," *Conjonction* 134 (June–July 1977): 65–80.

39. McLellan, *Colonialism and Science*, 24–25, 80.

40. King, *Blue Coat or Powdered Wig*, 34–36; Wimpffen, *Haiti aux XVIIIè siècle*, 174–175.

41. Moreau, *Description*, 2:717–723; McClellan, *Colonialism and Science*, 72.

42. Moreau, *Description*, 3:1165–67.

43. Ibid., 3:1240–41; John Garrigus, "Blue and Brown: Contraband Indigo and the Rise of a Free Colored Planter Class in French Saint-Domingue," *The Americas* 50 (October 1993): 233–263, 238; Frostin, *Les Révoltes blanches*, 59.

44. King, *Blue Coat or Powdered Wig*, 16.

45. Moreau, *Description*, 1:330.

46. Frostin, *Les Révoltes blanches*, 172, 182–183, 189–191, 205.

47. McLellan, *Colonialism and Science*, 38; Frostin, *Les Révoltes blanches*, chap. 7. Following French usage, I use "metropole" to refer to continental France, since Saint-Domingue was considered by many to be part of France—first a province, then a department—although it was a colony.

48. Frostin, *Les Révoltes blanches*, 28; McLellan, *Colonialism and Science*, 3, 75–76; Moreau, *Description*, 1:185; 2:627, 619.

49. Sala-Moulins, *Le Code Noir;* Jean-Philippe Garran-Coulon, *Rapport sur les troubles de Saint-Domingue* (Paris, 1798–99), 4:26.

50. Debien, *Esclaves aux Antilles françaises*, 485–486; Ghachem, "Sovereignty and Slavery," 157–164.

51. Debien, *Esclaves aux Antilles françaises*, 486–487; idem, *Les Colons de Saint-Domingue et la Révolution: Essai sur le Club Massiac (août 1789–août 1792)* (Paris, 1951), 53–57; Ghachem, "Sovereignty and Slavery," chap. 2; Frostin, *Les Révoltes blanches*, 371; Blackburn, *Overthrow of Colonial Slavery*, 166, 175.

52. Blackburn, *Making of New World Slavery*, 279–283; Tarrade, *Le Commerce coloniale*.

53. Frostin, *Les Révoltes blanches*, 43; Tarrade, *Le Commerce coloniale*, 1:101–112; David Geggus, *Slavery, War and Revolution: The British Occupation of Saint-Domingue, 1793–1798* (Oxford, 1982), 40.

54. Frostin, *Les Révoltes blanches*, 152–157; Chaela Pastore, "Merchant Voyages: Michel Marsaudon and the Exchange of Colonialism in Saint-Domingue, 1788–1794" (Ph.D. diss., University of California at Berkeley, 2001), 224.

55. Frostin, *Les Révoltes blanches*, 274; Tarrade, *Le Commerce coloniale*, 538–547 and chaps. 9–14 generally; Ghachem, "Sovereignty and Slavery," chap. 3.

56. Bryan Edwards, *The History, Civil and Commercial, of the British Colonies in the West Indies* (London, 1801); 1:11; Moreau, *Description*, 1:37, 43; Michel Etienne Descourtilz, *Voyages d'un naturaliste, et ses observations*, 3 vols. (Paris, 1809), 2:52, 57–58.

57. Andrew O'Shaughnessy, *An Empire Divided: The American Revolution and the British Caribbean* (Philadelphia, 2000); Sylvia Frey, *Water from the Rock: Black Resistance in a Revolution Age* (Princeton, 1997).

58. Debien, *Esclaves aux Antilles françaises*, 91; Frostin, *Les Révoltes blanches*, 71, 319–320; Descourtilz, *Voyages d'un naturaliste*, 3:380.

2. FERMENTATION

1. Gabriel Debien, "Sur les plantations Mauger à l'Artibonite (Saint-Domingue 1763–1803)" in *Enquêtes et documents: Nantes, Afrique, Amérique* (Nantes, 1981), 219–314, 219–220, 288–290; idem, *Les Esclaves aux Antilles françaises (XVIIème–XVIIIème siècles)* (Gourbeyre, 1974), 108.

2. Debien, "Sur les plantations," 290–291.

3. Pierre Pluchon, "Introduction," in Alexandre-Stanislas de Wimpffen, *Haiti aux XVIIIème siècle*, ed. Pluchon (Paris, 1993), 11; Debien, *Esclaves aux Antilles françaises*, 105–117, 159.

4. Debien, *Esclaves aux Antilles françaises*, 119–133.

5. Ibid., 147; Carolyn Fick, *The Making of Haiti: The Saint-Domingue Revolution from Below* (Knoxville, 1990), 30.

6. Debien, "Sur les plantations," 292–295.

7. Ibid., 295–298.

8. Debien, *Esclaves aux Antilles françaises*, 69–71.

9. *DuBois Slave Trade Database* (Cambridge, 1999); Paul Lovejoy, *Transforma-

tions in Slavery: A History of Slavery in Africa, 2d ed. (Cambridge, 2000), 47–48; Philip Curtin, *The Atlantic Slave Trade: A Census* (Madison, 1969), 268; Pluchon, "Introduction," 28.

10. Debien, *Esclaves aux Antilles françaises*, 345, 347; Arlette Gauthier, *Les Soeurs de solitude: La condition féminine dans l'esclavage aux Antilles du XVIIème au XIXème siècle* (Paris, 1985), 36; Thomas Ott, *The Haitian Revolution, 1789–1804* (Knoxville, 1974), 17.

11. Lovejoy, *Transformations in Slavery*, 55–57; Patrick Villiers, *Traite des noirs et navires négriers au XVIIIè siècle* (Grenoble, 1982), 64–65.

12. *DuBois Slave Trade Database;* Lovejoy, *Transformations in Slavery*, 49–55.

13. David Geggus, "Sugar and Coffee Cultivation in Saint Domingue and the Shaping of the Slave Labor Force," in *Cultivation and Culture: Labor and the Shaping of Slave Life in the Americas*, ed. Ira Berlin and Philip Morgan (Charlottesville, 1993), 80, 83–84, 88; Louis Méderic Moreau de St. Méry, *Description topographique, physique, civile, politique et historique de la partie française de l'isle Saint-Domingue*, 3 vols. (1796; reprint, Paris, 1958), 1: 47–54.

14. Debien, *Esclaves aux Antilles françaises*, 60–66, 74, and chap. 2 generally; Howard Justin Sosis, "The Colonial Environment and Religion in Haiti: An Introduction to the Black Slave Cults of the Eighteenth Century" (Ph.D. diss., Columbia University, 1971), 139–142 and chap. 8 generally; Geggus, "Sugar and Coffee," 73–98, 79–81; Odette Menesson-Rigaud Papers, box 1, folder 7/8, no. 42, Bibliothèque Haïtienne des Pères du Saint-Esprit, Port-au-Prince.

15. Debien, *Esclaves aux Antilles françaises*, 60; Geggus, "Sugar and Coffee," 81.

16. Moreau, *Description*, 1:44, 55, 59; Gérard Barthélemy, *Créoles-Bossales: Conflit en Haïti* (Cayenne, 2000).

17. Moreau, *Description*, 3:1316; 1:56; Michel Etienne Descourtilz, *Voyages d'un naturaliste, et ses observations*, 3 vols. (Paris, 1809), 3:163, 176.

18. Moreau, *Description*, 1:57.

19. Ibid., 46, 54–55; Michel DeGraff, "Relexification: A Reevaluation," *Anthropological Linguistics*, 44:4 (Winter 2002): 321–414.

20. Fick, *Making of Haiti*, chap. 2; Donald Cosentino, ed., *The Sacred Arts of Haitian Vodou* (Los Angeles, 1995); Joan Dayan, *Haiti, History, and the Gods* (Berkeley, 1995); Karen McCarthy Brown, *Mama Lola: A Vodou Priestess in Brooklyn* (Berkeley, 1992).

21. Moreau, *Description*, 1:64–68; Fick, *Making of Haiti*, 39–44.

22. Jean-François Dutrône de la Coutûre, *Précis sur la Canne et sur les moyens d'en extraire le sel essentiel, suivi de plusières Mémoires* (Paris, 1791), 334; Debien, *Esclaves aux Antilles françaises*, 135–136, 139, 153.

23. Dûtrone de la Coutûre, *Précis*, 101–106; Debien, *Esclaves aux Antilles françaises*, 97, 316.

24. Debien, *Esclaves aux Antilles françaises*, 90–91, 96, 98.

25. Ibid., 142–144; Geggus, "Sugar and Coffee," 76–77; Gros, *Isle de Saint-Domingue: Précis historique* (Paris, 1793), 21.

26. Barbara Bush, "Hard Labor: Women, Childbirth and Resistance in British Caribbean Slave Societies," in *More than Chattel: Black Women and Slavery in the Americas,* ed. David Gaspar and Darlene Clark Hine (Bloomington, 1996), 193–217; Gauthier, *Soeurs de solitude,* chap. 4, esp. 107–120; David Geggus, "Les Esclaves de la plaine du Nord à la veille de la Révolution française," *Revue de la Société Haïtienne d'Histoire et de Géographie* 142 (1984): 15–44, 34; Moreau, *Description,* 3:1272; Descourtilz, *Voyages d'un naturaliste,* 3:117–120.

27. See Gauthier, *Soeurs de solitude,* 168–172.

28. Debien, *Esclaves aux Antilles françaises,* chap. 11.

29. Ibid., 183, 193–95; Moreau, *Description,* 3:1239.

30. Moreau, *Description* 1:435–436, 2:679–680; 1:162–163; Sidney Mintz, *Caribbean Transformations* (New York, 1979).

31. Debien, *Esclaves aux Antilles françaises,* 156, 243–244; Moreau, *Description,* 1:338; Sue Peabody, "'A Dangerous Zeal': Catholic Missions to Slaves in the French Antilles, 1635–1800," *French Historical Studies* 25, 1 (2002): 53–90, 82.

32. Debien, *Esclaves aux Antilles françaises,* 156, 243–244; Moreau, *Description,* 1:63–64, 243; 3:1038.

33. Louis Sala-Molins, *Le Code Noir, ou le calvaire de Canaan* (Paris, 1987), 122–124; Debien, *Esclaves aux Antilles françaises,* 156.

34. James Stephens, *The Crisis of the Sugar Colonies; or, an Enquiry into the Objects and Probable Effects of the French Expedition to the West Indies* (1802; reprint, New York, 1969), 72; Pierre de Vassière, *Saint-Domingue: La société et la vie créoles sous l'ancien régime, 1629–1789* (Paris, 1909), 189–190; Fick, *Making of Haïti,* 37.

35. De Vassière, *Saint-Domingue,* 190–194; C. L. R. James, *The Black Jacobins: Toussaint Louverture and the San Domingo Revolution* (1938; reprint, New York, 1963), 12–13.

36. Pierre Pluchon, *Vaudou, sorciers, empoissoneurs de Saint-Domingue à Haïti* (Paris, 1987), 170–172; Moreau, *Description,* 1:630–631.

37. Moreau, *Description,* 1:631; David Geggus, "Marronage, Voodoo, and Saint-Domingue," in *Proceedings of the Fifteenth Meeting of the French Colonial Historical Society,* ed. Patricia Galloway and Philip Boucher (Lanham, Md., 1992), 22–35, 29; Peabody, "'A Dangerous Zeal,'" 79.

38. Fick, *Making of Haïti,* 59–63; Moreau, *Description,* 1:630–631.

39. Debien, *Esclaves aux Antilles françaises,* 422–424, 441, 446–452, 460; Gauthier, *Soeurs de solitude,* 227–238; Jean Fouchard, *Les Marrons de la liberté* (Paris, 1972); Yvan Debbasch, "Le Marronage: Essai sur la désertion de l'esclave antillais," *L'Année Sociologique,* 1961, 1–112.

40. Debien, *Esclaves aux Antilles françaises,* 156, 452.

41. Ibid., 432, 457–458.

42. Sala-Moulins, *Code Noir,* 166; Debien, *Esclaves aux Antilles françaises,* 432–433, 453, 465.

43. Moreau, *Description,* 1:163, 183.

44. Gauthier, *Soeurs de solitude,* 231, 243; Pluchon, *Vaudou,* 179.

45. Fouchard, *Les Marrons;* Fick, *Making of Haiti,* chap. 2; Geggus, "Marronage, Voodoo, and Saint-Domingue."

46. Robin Blackburn, *The Overthrow of Colonial Slavery* (London, 1989), 208, emphasizes this point, as does Fick, *Making of Haiti.*

47. Debien, *Esclaves aux Antilles françaises,* 402; Pluchon, *Vaudou.*

48. Pluchon, *Vaudou,* 176.

49. Malick Walid Ghachem, "Sovereignty and Slavery in the Age of Revolution: Haitian Variations on a Metropolitan Theme" (Ph.D. diss., Stanford University, 2001), 259–278; de Vassière, *Saint-Domingue,* 186–188; Fick, *Making of Haiti,* 37–38.

50. Fick, *Making of Haiti,* 62; Pluchon, *Vaudou,* 80; *Songs, Choruses, &c in King Caesar; or, the Negro Slaves* (London, 1801).

51. Louis Sebastien Mercier, *L'An deux mille cent quarante: Rêve s'il en fût jamais* (1770; reprint Paris, 1977), 127.

52. Guillaume Thomas Raynal, *Histoire philosophique et politique des établissements et du commerce des Européens dans les Deux Indes* (Geneva, 1780), 3:204–205.

53. Mercier, *L'An,* 1:184; Marcel Dorigny, "Le Mouvement abolitionniste français face à l'insurrection de Saint-Domingue ou la fin du mythe de l'abolition graduelle," in *L'Insurrection des esclaves de Saint-Domingue (22–23 août 1791),* ed. Laennec Hurbon (Paris, 2000), 97–113.

54. Mercier, *L'An,* 3:8; see also generally Michèle Duchet, *Anthropologie et histoire au siècle des lumières* (Paris, 1971); and Edward Seeber, *Anti-Slavery Opinion in France during the Second Half of the Eighteenth Century* (Baltimore, 1937).

55. Jean-Philippe Garran-Coulon, *Rapport sur les troubles de Saint-Domingue* (Paris, 1798–99), 4:18; Abbé Grégoire, *Mémoire en faveur des gens de couleur ou sang-mêlés de St.-Domingue, & des autres Isles françoises d'Amérique, adresse à l'Assemblée Nationale* (Paris, 1789), 33, 36.

3 · INHERITANCE

1. Julien Raimond, *Observations sur l'origine et le progrès du préjugé des colons blancs contre les hommes de couleur* (Paris, 1791), 26–28.

2. John Garrigus, "The Free Colored Elite of Saint-Domingue: The Case of Julien Raimond, 1744–1801," manuscript, 5; idem, "Blue and Brown: Contraband

Indigo and the Rise of a Free Colored Planter Class in French Saint-Domingue," *The Americas* 50 (October 1993): 259–260. See also Mercer Cook, *Five French Negro Authors* (Washington, D.C., 1943), 3–37.

3. Louis Sala-Molins, *Le Code Noir, ou le calvaire de Canaan* (Paris, 1987), 196–199; Yvan Debbasch, *Couleur et liberté: Le jeu du critère ethnique dans un ordre juridique esclavagiste* (Paris, 1967), 1:30–33.

4. Léo Elisabeth, "The French Antilles," in David Cohen and Jack Greene, eds., *Neither Slave nor Free: The Freedmen of African Descent in the Slave Societies of the New World* (Baltimore, 1972), 134–171, 162; Stewart King, *Blue Coat or Powdered Wig: Free People of Color in Pre-Revolutionary Saint Domingue* (Athens, Ga., 2001), 166–168; Garrigus, "Blue and Brown," 248; Malick Walid Ghachem, "Sovereignty and Slavery in the Age of Revolution: Haitian Variations on a Metropolitan Theme" (Ph.D. diss., Stanford University, 2001), chap. 1.

5. Raimond, *Observations*, 2–3; King, *Blue Coat or Powdered Wig*, 130.

6. Raimond, *Observations*, 3, 5; Garrigus, "Free Colored Elite," 3–6.

7. Intendant Montholon to Conseil de Marine, 20 February 1723, reprinted in Charles Frostin, *Les Révoltes blanches à Saint-Domingue aux XVIIè et XVIIIè siècles* (Paris, 1975), 392; Raimond, *Observations*, 4–6.

8. Raimond, *Observations*, 6-7, 9; Garrigus, "Free Colored Elite," 5–6; Debbasch, *Couleur et liberté*, 1:73–74.

9. King, *Blue Coat or Powdered Wig*, 45, 124, 145, and chaps. 6 and 7 generally; John Garrigus, "Redrawing the Colour Line: Gender and the Social Construction of Race in Pre-Revolutionary Haiti," *Journal of Caribbean History* 30, 1 and 2 (1996): 28–50.

10. Garrigus, "Redrawing the Colour Line," 42; King, *Blue Coat or Powdered Wig*, 84.

11. John Garrigus, "Catalyst or Catastrophe? Saint-Domingue's Free Men of Color and the Battle of Savannah, 1779–1782," *Revista Interamericana* 22 (spring 1992): 109–124, 109; M.L.E. Moreau de St. Méry, *Description topographique, physique, civile, politique et historique de la partie française de l'isle Saint-Domingue*, 3 vols. (1796; reprint, Paris, 1958), 1:186–187; 229–230.

12. Garrigus, "Catalyst or Catastrophe?" 109–110, 115–119; Moreau, *Description*, 1:229; King, *Blue Coat or Powdered Wig*, 65–66.

13. Garrigus, "Catalyst or Catastrophe?" 113–115; King, *Blue Coat or Powdered Wig*, 61–63, 71; Moreau, *Description*, 1:181; Charles Frostin, *Les Révoltes blanches*, 301–303, 310–313.

14. Garrigus, "Catalyst or Catastrophe?" 117; Gabriel Debien, *Les Esclaves des Antilles françaises (XVIIè–XVIIIème siècles)* (Gourbeyre, 1974), 487; see also generally King, *Blue Coat or Powdered Wig*, chaps. 4, 11.

15. Garrigus, "Catalyst or Catastrophe?" 111–113; King, *Blue Coat or Powdered Wig*, 58, 236–237.

16. Frostin, *Les Révoltes blanches*, 382; Abbé Grégoire, *Mémoire en faveur des gens de couleur ou sang-mêlés de St.-Domingue, & des autres Isles françoises d'Amérique, adresse à l'Assemblée Nationale* (Paris, 1789), 17, 29; idem, *Lettre aux philanthropes, sur les malheurs, les droits et les réclamations des gens de couleur de Saint-Domingue, et des autres îles françoises de l'Amérique* (Paris, 1790), 14.

17. Ghachem, "Sovereignty and Slavery," 82; Debbasch, *Couleur et liberté*, 54–55.

18. Garrigus, "Redrawing the Colour Line," esp. 47; and idem, "Sons of the Same Father: Gender, Race, and Citizenship in French Saint-Domingue, 1760–1789," in *Society, Politics, and Culture in Eighteenth-Century France*, ed. Jack Censer (College Station, 1997).

19. Delafosse de Rouville, *Essai sur la situation de Saint-Domingue en 1791, précédé d'un éloge historique du Chevalier Mauduit-Duplessis* (1817; reprint, Port-au-Prince, 1983), 76–77; Alexandre Stanislas de Wimpffen, *Haiti au XVIIIè siècle*, ed. Pierre Pluchon (Paris, 1993); Moreau, *Description*, 1:103–104. See also Garrigus, "Redrawing the Colour Line," 35–37, whose translations I have used; and Arlette Gauthier, *Les Soeurs de solitude: La condition féminine dans l'esclavage aux Antilles du XVIIè au XIXè siècle* (Paris, 1985), 160–161.

20. Michel Etienne Descourtilz, *Voyages d'un naturaliste, et ses observations*, 3 vols. (Paris, 1809), 2:51–52.

21. Moreau, *Description*, 1:107; Raimond, *Observations*, 12; King, *Blue Coat or Powdered Wig*, 187, 193; Susan Socolow, "Economic Roles of Free Women of Color in Cap Français," in *More than Chattel: Black Women and Slavery in the Americas*, ed. David Gaspar and Darlene Clark Hine (Bloomington, 1996).

22. Frostin, *Les Révoltes blanches*, 317; Garrigus, "Blue and Brown," 259.

23. Moreau, *Description*, 1:96–100; Roger Norman Buckley, ed., *The Haitian Journal of Lieutenant Howard, York Hussars, 1796–1798* (Knoxville, 1985), 110; *Moniteur Général de Saint-Domingue*, 16 December 1791, 130.

24. Grégoire, *Mémoire*, 22, 44; Julien Raimond, *Réponse aux Considérations de M. Moreau, dit Saint-Méry* (Paris, 1791), quoted in Cook, *Five French Negro Authors*, 17.

25. M. L. E. Moreau de St. Méry, *Discours sur l'utilité du musée établi à Paris prononcé dans la scéance publique du 1er Décembre 1784* (Parma, 1805), 4–5; Marquis de Condorcet, *Réflexions sur l'esclavage des Nègres*, 2d ed. (Paris, 1788); Jacques Thibau, *Le Temps de Saint-Domingue: L'esclavage et la Révolution française* (Paris, 1989), 102–106.

26. Edward Seeber, *Anti-Slavery Opinion in France during the Second Half of the Eighteenth Century* (Baltimore, 1937); Sue Peabody, *"There Are No Slaves in France": The Political Culture of Race and Slavery in the Ancien Régime* (Oxford, 1996).

27. Robin Blackburn, *The Overthrow of Colonial Slavery* (London, 1989), 169–

172; Marcel Dorigny and Bernard Gainot, *La Société des Amis des Noirs, 1788–1799: Contribution à l'histoire de l'abolition de l'esclavage* (Paris, 1998).

28. Thibau, *Le Temps de Saint-Domingue,* 100.

29. Blackburn, *Overthrow of Colonial Slavery,* 172; Thibau, *Le Temps de Saint-Domingue,* 103; Aimé Césaire, *Toussaint Louverture: La Révolution et le problème colonial* (Paris, 1981), 171; David Geggus, "Racial Equality, Slavery, and Colonial Secession during the Constituent Assembly," *American Historical Review* 94 (December 1989): 1292–93.

30. Gabriel Debien, *Les Colons de Saint-Domingue et la Révolution: Essai sur le Club Massiac (août 1789–août 1792)* (Paris, 1953), 63–65; Césaire, *Toussaint Louverture,* 39; Mitchell Bennett Garrett, *The French Colonial Question, 1789–1791* (Ann Arbor, 1916), 7–10; Debien, *Colons,* 64–65, 153.

31. Debien, *Colons de Saint-Domingue,* 68–73; Garrett, *Colonial Question,* 12.

32. Blackburn, *Overthrow of Colonial Slavery,* 173–174; Debien, *Colons de Saint-Domingue,* 73–75; Ghachem, "Sovereignty and Slavery," 325–330.

33. Blackburn, *Overthrow of Colonial Slavery,* 174; Geggus, "Racial Equality," 1294; Olympe de Gouges, *L'Esclavage des noirs, ou l'heureux naufrage* (1792; reprint, Paris, 1989), 15.

34. Debien, *Colons de Saint-Domingue,* 63, 83, 91–96, 120, 130, 138–139, and chap. 4 generally; Blackburn, *Overthrow of Colonial Slavery,* 176.

35. *Lettres des députés de Saint-Domingue à leurs comettants en date du 12 août 1789* (Paris, 1790); Garrett, *Colonial Question,* 18–19; Debien, *Colons de Saint-Domingue,* 77.

36. Debien, *Colons de Saint-Domingue,* 97, 158–159; Garrett, *Colonial Question,* 23; Chaela Pastore, "Merchant Voyages: Michel Marsaudon and the Exchange of Colonialism in Saint-Domingue, 1788–1794" (Ph.D. diss., University of California at Berkeley, 2001), 59.

37. Antoine Dalmas, *Histoire de la Révolution de Saint-Domingue* (Paris, 1814), 1:23; Félix Carteau, *Soirées bermudiennes, ou entretiens sur les événements qui ont opéré la ruine de la partie française de l'isle Saint-Domingue* (Bordeaux, 1802).

38. Garrett, *Colonial Question,* 37–39, 58–59; Debien, *Colons de Saint-Domingue,* 214–215; Blackburn, Overthrow *of Colonial Slavery,* 183.

39. Garrett, *Colonial Question,* 60–61; Blackburn, *Overthrow of Colonial Slavery,* 167–168.

40. Ghachem, "Sovereignty and Slavery," 247–250; Moreau de St. Méry, *Considérations presentées aux vrais amis du repos et du bonheur de France, à l'occasion des nouveaux mouvements de quelques soi-disant amis-des-noirs* (Paris, 1791), 19–20.

41. Dalmas, *Histoire,* 1:34. On Martinique see David Geggus, "The Slaves and Free Coloreds of Martinique during the Age of the French and Haitian Revolu-

tions: Three Moments of Resistance," in *The Lesser Antilles in the Age of European Expansion*, ed. Robert Paquette and Stanley Engerman (Gainesville, 1996), 280–301.

42. Debien, *Colons de Saint-Domingue*, 178–179; Debbasch, *Couleur et liberté*, 172; Bryan Edwards, *The History, Civil and Commercial, of the British Colonies in the West Indies* (London, 1801), 3:23–24; Césaire, *Toussaint Louverture*, 67–68.

43. Garrett, *Colonial Question*, 25–26; Debien, *Colons de Saint-Domingue*, 163–164.

44. Debien, *Colons de Saint-Domingue*, 156–163; Geggus, "Racial Equality," 1298–1300; Jean-Philippe Garran-Coulon, *Rapport sur les troubles de Saint-Domingue* (Paris, 1798–99), 4:20. See also Marcel Dorigny, "Grégoire et le combat contre l'esclavage pendant la Révolution: Précis historique," in *Grégoire et la cause des noirs (1789–1831)*, ed. Yves Benot and Marcel Dorigny (Paris, 2000), 51–68.

45. Debien, *Colons de Saint-Domingue*, 98, 102, 163, 168; idem, *Etudes antillaises (XVIIIè siècle)* (Paris, 1956), 154.

46. Geggus, "Racial Equality," 1300; Ghachem, "Sovereignty and Slavery"; Victor Schoelcher, *Vie de Toussaint Louverture* (1889; reprint, Paris, 1982), 14; Debien, *Colons de Saint-Domingue*, 180–181; Louis Médéric Moreau de St. Méry, *Opinion de M. Moreau de St. Méry, député de la Martinique, sur la motion de M. de Curt* (Paris, 1789).

47. Moreau, *Considérations*, 36–38, 44.

48. Grégoire, *Mémoire*, 28–29, 32, 44; Debien, *Colons de Saint-Domingue*, 171, 176, 179, 184.

49. Daniel Piquet, *L'Emancipation des noirs dans la Révolution française* (Paris, 2002), 79; Moreau, *Considérations*, 48.

50. Debien, *Colons de Saint-Domingue*, 188–193; Garrett, *Colonial Question*, 43–51; Blackburn, *Overthrow of Colonial Slavery*, 178–179.

51. Debien, *Colons de Saint-Domingue*, 193–195; Garrett, *Colonial Question*, 51–56.

52. Debien, *Colons de Saint-Domingue*, 195–196.

53. Garrett, *Colonial Question*, 60–61; Edwards, *History*, 3:33: Pamphile de Lacroix, *La Révolution de Haiti* (1819; reprint, Paris, 1995), 58–60.

54. Lacroix, *Révolution de Haiti*, 57–65, quotation p. 58; Garrett, *Colonial Question*, 61–65; Debien, *Etudes antillaises*, 154.

55. Garrett, *Colonial Question*, 65–76; Debien, *Colons de Saint-Domingue*, 228–234; Grégoire, *Lettre aux philanthropes*.

56. Grégoire, *Lettre aux philanthropes*, 3, 14; Debien, *Colons de Saint-Domingue*, 196, 222; Lacroix, *Revolution de Haiti*, 68; Thomas Ott, *The Haitian Revolution, 1789–1804* (Knoxville, 1974), 36.

57. Lacroix, *Révolution de Haiti*, 69–70; Carolyn Fick, *The Making of Haiti: The Saint-Domingue Revolution from Below* (Knoxville, 1990), 82–84.

58. Lacroix, *Révolution de Haiti*, 71–73; Edwards, *History*, 3:52.

59. Debien, *Colons de Saint-Domingue*, 286–287; Geggus, "Racial Equality," 1296.

60. Piquet, *Emancipation des noirs*, chap. 2.

61. Ibid., 94; Geggus, "Racial Equality," 1303; Ott, *Haitian Revolution*, 39.

62. Madame Rouvray to Madame de Lostanges, 30 July 1791 and 12 July 1791, in *Une correspondence familiale au temps des troubles de Saint-Domingue*, ed. M. E. McIntosh and B. C. Weber (Paris, 1959), 15, 22–24; David Geggus, *Slavery, War, and Revolution: The British Occupation of Saint-Domingue, 1793–1798* (Oxford, 1982), 270, 274.

4. FIRE IN THE CANE

1. James E. McClellan II, *Colonialism and Science: Saint Domingue in the Old Regime* (Baltimore, 1992), 168–171; M.L.E. Moreau de St. Méry, *Description topographique, physique, civile, politique et historique de la partie française de l'isle de Saint-Domingue*, 3 vols. (1796; reprint, Paris, 1958), 1:278, 286–290; Simon Schama, *Citizens: A Chronicle of the French Revolution* (New York, 1989), 123.

2. Millot to Gallifet, August 1791, 107 AP 128, folder 1, Archives Nationales (hereafter AN); Mossut to Gallifet, September 19, 1791, 107 AP 128, folder 3, AN.

3. David Geggus, "Les Esclaves de la plaine du Nord à la veille de la Révolution française," *Revue de la Société Haïtienne d'Histoire et de Géographie* 142 (1984): 15–44, 25; Moreau, *Description*, 1:278.

4. Geggus, "Esclaves de la plaine," 24–36; Moreau, *Description*, 1:288.

5. Carolyn Fick, *The Making of Haiti: The Saint-Domingue Revolution from Below* (Knoxville, 1990), 98–99; Antoine Dalmas, *Histoire de la Révolution de Saint-Domingue* (Paris, 1814), 1:120.

6. Dalmas, *Histoire*, 1:121; Bryan Edwards, *The History, Civil and Commercial, of the British Colonies in the West Indies* (London, 1801), 3:72; Fick, *Making of Haiti*, 96.

7. Pamphile de Lacroix, *La Révolution de Haiti* (1819; reprint, Paris, 1995), 87–88.

8. Mossut to Gallifet, September 19, 1791, 107 AP 128, folder 3, AN.

9. Fick, *Making of Haiti*, 100; Dalmas, *Histoire*, 1:123.

10. "Le Début de la révolte de Saint Domingue dans la Plaine du Cap, vécu par Louis de Calbiac," *Généalogie et Histoire de la Caraïbe* 48 (April 1993): 774–784, 774; Edwards, *History*, 3:76–78; *Philadelphia General Advertiser*, October 10, 1791; Thomas Ott, *The Haitian Revolution, 1789–1804* (Knoxville, 1974), 49; Dalmas, *Histoire*, 1:132; Althéa de Puech Parham, ed., *My Odyssey: Experiences of a Young Refugee from Two Revolutions, by a Creole of Saint Domingue* (Baton Rouge, 1959), 29.

11. *Philadelphia General Advertiser*, October 10, 1791.

12. Mossut to Gallifet, September 19, 1791, 107 AP 128, folder 3, AN; Fick, *Making of Haiti,* 105.

13. Fick, *Making of Haiti,* 92; David Geggus, *Haitian Revolutionary Studies* (Bloomington, 2002), 84–85.

14. Gabriel Debien, *Les Esclaves aux Antilles françaises (XVIIème–XVIIIème siècles)* (Gourbeyre, 1974), 124.

15. Fick, *Making of Haiti,* 91.

16. Ibid., 91–92; Geggus, *Haitian Revolutionary Studies,* 87–88.

17. *A Particular Account of the Commencement and Progress of the Insurrection of the Negroes of St. Domingo* (London, 1792), 4–5; Fick, *Making of Haiti,* 98–99, 103.

18. Fick, *Making of Haiti,* 93–94 and app. B; Geggus, *Haitian Revolutionary Studies,* 86–87. See Robin Law, "La Cérémonie du Bois-Caïman et le 'pacte de sang' dahoméen," in *L'Insurrection des esclaves de Saint-Domingue (22–23 août 1791),* ed. Laennec Hurbon (Paris, 2000), 131–147.

19. Dalmas, *Histoire,* 1:117–118; Geggus, *Haitian Revolutionary Studies,* 82.

20. Hérard Dumesle, *Voyage dans le nord d'Hayti, ou, Révélation des lieux et des monuments historiques* (Les Cayes, 1824), 85–90. There has been great controversy surrounding the sources relating to the Bois-Caïman ceremony; the most detailed discussions are Geggus, *Haitian Revolutionary Studies,* 81–92; Fick, *Making of Haiti,* app. B; and Léon-François Hoffman's controversial intervention, "Un Mythe national: La cérémonie du Bois-Caïman," in *La République haïtienne: Etat des lieux et perspectives,* ed. Gérard Barthélemy and Christian Girault (Paris, 1993), 434–448.

21. John Thornton, "African Soldiers in the Haitian Revolution," *Journal of Caribbean History* 25, 1 and 2 (1991): 58–80; Lacroix, *Révolution de Haiti,* 87; Fick, *Making of Haiti,* 139; *Philadelphia General Advertiser,* October 11, 1791; Gros, *Isle de Saint-Domingue: Précis historique* (Paris, 1793), 14.

22. Maya Deren, *Divine Horsemen: The Living Gods of Haiti* (New York, 1953), 62; Joan Dayan, *Haiti, History, and the Gods* (Berkeley, 1995), chap. 1; Laurent Dubois, "The Citizen's Trance: The Haitian Revolution and the Motor of History," in *Magic and Modernity,* ed. Birgit Meyers and Peter Pels (Stanford, forthcoming).

23. Parham, *My Odyssey,* 33–34; Fick, *Making of Haiti,* 111.

24. *Philadelphia General Advertiser,* October 11, 1791; Mossut to Gallifet, 19 September 1791, 107 AP 128, folder 3, AN; Madame de Rouvray to de Lostanges, September 4, 1791, in *Une Correspondance familiale au temps des troubles de Saint-Domingue,* ed. M. E. McIntosh and B. C. Weber (Paris, 1959), 27; *Philadelphia General Advertiser,* October 10 and 11, 1791.

25. *Moniteur Général de la Partie Française de Saint-Domingue* (hereafter *Moniteur Générale*), November 15, 1791, 1; Dalmas, *Histoire,* 1:159.

26. Gros, *Isle de Saint-Domingue,* 13; Marquis de Rouvray to de Lostanges,

December 6–7, 1791, in McIntosh and Weber, *Correspondence familiale*, 40; Proclamation of Etienne Polverel and Légér Félicité Sonthonax, May 5, 1793, in Gabriel Debien, "Documents—aux origines de l'abolition de l'esclavage," *Revue d'Histoire des Colonies* 36 (1er trimestre, 1949): 24–55, 35; *Moniteur Générale*, February 27, 1793, 410.

27. J. Ph. Garran de Coulon, *Rapport sur les troubles de Saint-Domingue, fait au nom de la Commission des Colonies, des Comités du Salut Public, de Législation et de Marine, réunis*, 4 vols. (Paris, 1798), 2:194; 209, 4:58.

28. *Philadelphia General Advertiser*, November 11, 1791.

29. Ibid., October 10 and 11, 1791; "Début de la révolte," 776.

30. Fick, *Making of Haiti*, 92, 113, 127–128; Gros, *Isle de Saint-Domingue*, 13–14, 26; *Philadelphia General Advertiser*, October 11, 1791; Garran de Coulon, *Rapport sur les troubles*, 2:193.

31. Jean-François and Biassou to Commissioners, December 12, 1791, DXXV 1, folder 4, no. 8, AN; Garran de Coulon, *Rapport sur les troubles*, 2:209–210.

32. *Moniteur Général*, December 19, 1791, 143; Biassou to Commissioners, December 23, 1791, DXXV 1, folder 4, no. 20, AN; *Moniteur Général*, February 28, 1793, 419; Robert Louis Stein, *Légér Félicité Sonthonax: The Lost Sentinel of the Republic* (London, 1985), 98.

33. Gros, *Isle de Saint-Domingue*, 13, 19; Geggus, *Haitian Revolutionary Studies*, 173–174; Jane Landers, "Rebellion and Royalism in Spanish Florida," in *A Turbulent Time: The French Revolution and the Greater Caribbean*, ed. David Barry Gaspar and David Geggus (Bloomington, 1997), 156–171, 162.

34. Fick, *Making of Haiti*, 128, 151; *Philadelphia General Advertiser*, October 10 and November 12, 1791.

35. Garran de Coulon, *Rapport sur les troubles*, 2:209; Stein, *Légér Félicité Sonthonax*, 98; John Thornton, "I Am the Subject of the King of Kongo: African Political Ideology and the Haitian Revolution" *Journal of World History* 4 (fall 1993): 181–214, 186.

36. John Thornton, "African Soldiers in the Haitian Revolution," *Journal of Caribbean History* 25, 1 and 2 (1991): 58–80; Lacroix, *Révolution de Haiti*, 87; *Philadelphia General Advertiser*, October 10, 1791; *Moniteur Général*, March 18, 1793, 487; Jean-François and Biassou to Commissioners, December 12, 1791, DXXV 1, folder 4, no. 8, AN.

37. *Philadelphia General Advertiser*, November 12, 1791; Fick, *Making of Haiti*, 111–112; Michel Etienne Descourtilz, *Voyages d'un naturaliste, et ses observations*, 3 vols. (Paris, 1809), 3:206.

38. Fick, *Making of Haiti*, 110; Lacroix, *Révolution de Haiti*, 88; Thomas Madiou, *Histoire d'Haiti* (1847–48; reprint, Port-au-Prince, 1989), 1:97; *Philadelphia General Advertiser*, October 11, 1791.

39. *Particular Account*, 7; Camille Desmoulins, *J. P. Brissot démasqué* (Paris,

1792), 40; quoted in Eléni Varkis, "Préface," in Olympe de Gouges, *L'Esclavage des noirs, ou l'heureux naufrage* (1792; reprint, Paris, 1989), 25.

40. Edwards, *History*, 3:67, 79.

41. Ibid., 80–81; *Particular Account*, 10; Fick, *Making of Haiti*, 95–96, 108–109, 113.

42. *Particular Account*, 11.

43. Fick, *Making of Haiti*, 97, 106–107.

44. *Philadelphia General Advertiser*, November 9, 1791.

45. Marie Rose Masson to Gallifet, 8 Thermidor An 10 (July 27, 1802), 107 AP 127, folder 1, AN.

5 . NEW WORLD

1. Madame de Rouvray to Madame de Lostanges, September 4 and 15, 1791, in *Une Correspondence familiale au temps des troubles de Saint-Domingue*, ed. M. E. McIntosh and B. C. Weber (Paris, 1959), 27, 33.

2. *Philadelphia General Advertiser*, November 11, 1791; Carolyn Fick, *The Making of Haiti: The Saint-Domingue Revolution from Below* (Knoxville, 1990), 105.

3. *Philadelphia General Advertiser*, November 9, 12, and 14, 1791.

4. Pamphile de Lacroix, *La Révolution de Haiti* (1819; reprint, Paris, 1995), 95; *Philadelphia General Advertiser*, November 14, 1791; Althéa de Puech Parham, ed., *My Odyssey: Experiences of a Young Refugee from Two Revolutions, by a Creole of Saint Domingue* (Baton Rouge, 1959), 30.

5. Bryan Edwards, *The History, Civil and Commercial, of the British Colonies in the West Indies* (London, 1801), 3:82; Lacroix, *Révolution de Haiti*, 95; *Philadelphia General Advertiser*, October 10 and November 14, 1791; Thomas Ott, *The Haitian Revolution, 1789–1804* (Knoxville, 1974), 49; de Rouvray to de Lostanges, September 15, 1791, in McIntosh and Weber, *Correspondence familiale*, 34.

6. *Moniteur Général*, November 19, 1791, 17; ibid., December 7, 1791, 92.

7. Edwards, *History*, 3:v–vii, ix–x; David Geggus, *Slavery, War and Revolution: The British Occupation of Saint-Domingue, 1793–1798* (Oxford, 1982), 53 and n. 51, and chap. 3 generally.

8. Lacroix, *Révolution de Haiti*, 90.

9. Ibid., 105–106.

10. Edwards, *History*, 3:7; *Philadelphia General Advertiser*, November 14, 1791; Lacroix, *Révolution de Haiti*, 105.

11. Fick, *Making of Haiti*, 119–120.

12. David Geggus, *Haitian Revolutionary Studies* (Bloomington, 2002), 99–102; Fick, *Making of Haiti*, 120; H. Pauléus Sannon, *Histoire de Toussaint Louverture* (Port-au-Prince, 1938), 1:88–89.

13. Concordat, September 11, 1791, printed in Edwards, *History,* 3:228–235; Fick, *Making of Haiti,* 121.

14. Fick, *Making of Haiti,* 122–125; Concordat, September 11, 1791; *Concordat, ou Traité de paix entre les Citoyens Blancs et les Citoyens de Couleur des quatorze paroisses de la Province de l'Ouest de la partie Française de Saint-Domingue* (Paris, October 19, 1791).

15. Geggus, *Haitian Revolutionary Studies,* 103–115; Jean-Philippe Garran-Coulon, *Rapport sur les troubles de Saint-Domingue* (Paris, 1798–99), 3:65–68; Fick, *Making of Haiti,* 124–125.

16. Fick, *Making of Haiti,* 125–126; Sannon, *Histoire de Toussaint Louverture,* 106–107; Commissioners of Saint-Marc to Governor-General, December 2, 1791, DXXV 1, folder 3, no. 10, AN.

17. Commissioners of Saint-Marc to Governor-General, December 2, 1791; Sannon, *Histoire de Toussaint Louverture,* 107–108; Fick, *Making of Haiti,* 133–134.

18. Gros, *Isle de Saint-Domingue: Précis historique* (Paris, 1793), 6.

19. Ibid., 6–7.

20. Ibid., 8–9; "Adresse à l'assemblée générale . . . par MM. les citoyens de couleur, de la Grand Rivière," DXXV 1, folder 4, no. 4, AN.

21. Gros, *Isle de Saint-Domingue,* 9, 12.

22. Ibid., 11, 13, 17, 21; Biassou to Commissioners, December 23, 1791, DXXV 1, folder 4, no. 20, AN; Fick, *Making of Haiti,* 75.

23. Fick, *Making of Haiti,* 103; Antoine Dalmas, *Histoire de la Révolution de Saint-Domingue* (Paris, 1814), 1:219; Thomas Madiou, *Histoire d'Haiti* (1847–48; reprint, Port-au-Prince, 1989), 1:97; *Moniteur Général,* December 22, 1791, 154; Gros, *Isle de Saint-Domingue,* 14.

24. *Moniteur Général,* November 22, 1791, 31–32.

25. Ibid., November 22, 1791, 29–31; ibid., December 9, 1791, 101–102.

26. Ibid., December 9, 1791, 101–102; ibid., December 17, 1791, 134–136; Deputy of Le Cap to the Civil Commissioners, December 15, 1791, DXXV 1, folder 4, no. 9, AN.

27. *Moniteur Général,* December 17, 1791, 134–136; ibid., December 19, 1791, 142–143; "Adresse à l'assemblée générale . . . par MM. les citoyens de couleur, de la Grand Rivière," DXXV 1, folder 4, no. 4, AN; Fick, *Making of Haiti,* 115.

28. *Moniteur Général,* December 16, 1791, 132; ibid., December 23, 1791, 158; Lacroix, *Révolution de Haiti,* 115–118, and quotation from editor's note on 118; Commissioner Roume to Minister of the Colonies, April 12, 1792, DXXV 1, folder 4, no. 1, AN; the debate on the name of the assembly was printed in the *Moniteur Général* starting with December 9, 1791.

29. Jean-François and Biassou to Commissioners, December 12 and 15, 1791; "Note des Commissaires," December 16, 1791; Jean-François and Biassou to

Commissioners, December 17, 1791, all DXXV 1, folder 4, nos. 8, 42–44, AN; Lacroix, *Révolution de Haiti*, 118–119; *Moniteur Générale*, December 23, 1791, 157.

30. Jean-François and Biassou to Commissioners, December 21, 1791, DXXV 1, folder 4, no. 19, AN.

31. Gros, *Isle de Saint-Domingue*, 21, 27.

32. Fick, *Making of Haiti*, 117; Lacroix, *Révolution de Haiti*, 123.

33. Florence Gauthier, "Comment la nouvelle de l'insurrection des esclaves de Saint-Domingue fut-elle reçue en France (1791–1793)?" in *L'Insurrection des esclaves de Saint-Domingue*, ed. Laënnec Hurbon (Paris, 2000), 15–27, 21–22; Thomas Clarkson, *The True State of the Case Respecting the Insurrection at St. Domingo* (Ipswich, 1792), 8; *L'Ami du Peuple*, December 12, 1791, in Jacques De Cock and Charlotte Goëtz, *Jean-Paul Marat: Oeuvres Politiques, 1789–1793* (Brussels, 1993), 3788.

34. Olympe de Gouges, preface to *Black Slavery, or the Happy Shipwreck* (Paris, 1792), trans. Maryann De Julio, in *Translating Slavery: Gender and Race in French Women's Writing, 1783–1823*, ed. Doris Y. Kadish and Françoise Massardier-Kenney (Kent, Ohio, 1994), 87–117, 88; Gauthier, "Comment la nouvelle"; Marcel Dorigny and Bernard Gainot, *La Société des Amis des Noirs, 1788–1799* (Paris, 1998).

35. Ott, *Haitian Revolution*, 65; Robin Blackburn, *The Overthrow of Colonial Slavery, 1776–1778* (London, 1989), 206.

36. "Loi relative aux colonies et aux moyens d'y apaiser les troubles, donnée à Paris, le 4 Avril 1792", AD VII 20A, AN; Blackburn, *Overthrow of Colonial Slavery*, 193–204.

6. DEFIANCE

1. Gabriel Debien, "Sur les plantations Mauger à l'Artibonite (Saint-Domingue 1763–1803)," in *Enquêtes et Documents: Nantes, Afrique, Amérique* (Nantes, 1981), 298–299.

2. Ibid., 282–283.

3. Ibid., 284–285.

4. Ibid., 286–287.

5. Ibid., 300–301.

6. Ibid., 301–302.

7. Carolyn Fick, *The Making of Haiti: The Saint-Domingue Revolution from Below* (Knoxville, 1990), 137–138.

8. Ibid., 131–133.

9. Ibid., 132, 141.

10. Pamphile de Lacroix, *La Révolution de Haiti* (1819; reprint, Paris, 1995),

127–128; Jean-Philippe Garran-Coulon, *Rapport sur les troubles de Saint-Domingue* (Paris, 1798–99), 3:75–76.

11. David Geggus, "The Arming of Slaves in the Haitian Revolution," in *The Arming of Slaves*, ed. Philip Morgan and Christopher Brown (New Haven, forthcoming), 15–17; Lacroix, *Révolution de Haiti*, 129–130; Fick, *Making of Haiti*, 139–140; Thomas Madiou, *Histoire d'Haiti* (1847–48; reprint, Port-au-Prince, 1989), 1:131–132.

12. Madiou, *Histoire d'Haiti*, 1:133; Geggus, "Arming of Slaves," 17–18.

13. Lacroix, *Révolution de Haiti*, 135–139; Madiou, *Histoire d'Haiti*, 1:140–143; Fick, *Making of Haiti*, 139.

14. Chaela Pastore, "Merchant Voyages: Michel Marsaudon and the Exchange of Colonialism in Saint-Domingue, 1788–1794" (Ph.D. diss., University of California at Berkeley, 2001), 134; Madiou, *Histoire d'Haiti*, 1:211; Lacroix, *Révolution de Haiti*, 131–138; Fick, *Making of Haiti*, 140.

15. Lacroix, *Révolution de Haiti*, 138; Garran-Coulon, *Rapport*, 3:101; Fick, *Making of Haiti*, 140.

16. Fick, *Making of Haiti*, 141–142.

17. Ibid., 143–144.

18. Ibid., 144–145; Madiou, *Histoire d'Haiti*, 1:149; Lacroix, *Révolution de Haiti*, 143–146.

19. Fick, *Making of Haiti*, 145–146.

20. Ibid., 146–151; Pastore, "Merchant Voyages," 176.

21. Fick, *Making of Haiti*, 148–150; Bernard Foubert, "Les Volontaires nationaux de l'Aube et de la Seine-Inférieure à Saint-Domingue (octobre 1792–janvier 1793)," *Bulletin de la Société d'Histoire de la Guadeloupe* 51 (1er trimestre 1982): 3–54, 17–18, 29, 41; Pastore, "Merchant Voyages," 167.

22. Nathalie Picquionne, "Lettre de Jean-François, Biassou et Belair, Juillet 1792," *Annales Historiques de la Révolution Française* 311 (January–March 1998): 132–139, 133–135; Fick, *Making of Haiti*, 161.

23. Fick, *Making of Haiti*, 145, 154–156; Pastore, "Merchant Voyages," 154; Garran-Coulon, *Rapport*, 3:141–144.

24. Robert Louis Stein, *Légèr Félicité Sonthonax: The Lost Sentinel of the Republic* (London, 1985), 82; Fick, *Making of Haiti*, 315

25. Stein, *Légèr Félicité Sonthonax*, 22–25, 42–43; Jacques de Cauna, "Polverel et Sonthonax: Deux voies pour l'abolition de l'esclavage," *Revue Française d'Histoire d'Outre-mer* 84 (1997): 47–53, 48–49; Marcel Dorigny, "Sonthonax et Brissot: Le cheminement d'une filiation politique assumée," ibid., 29–40.

26. Dorigny, "Sonthonax et Brissot," 35–36; Stein, *Légèr Félicité Sonthonax*, 22–23.

27. Stein, *Légèr Félicité Sonthonax*, 23–25; Garran-Coulon, *Rapport*, 3:128–129; Madiou, *Histoire d'Haiti*, 1:151; Dorigny, "Sonthonax et Brissot," 31.

28. Stein, *Légèr Félicité Sonthonax*, 42–45.

29. Garran-Coulon, *Rapport*, 3:133–134.

30. Stein, *Légèr Félicité Sonthonax*, 46–48; Dorigny, "Sonthonax et Brissot," 31–32.

31. Fick, *Making of Haiti*, 157.

32. Pastore, "Merchant Voyage," 164–165; Garran-Coulon, *Rapport*, 3:118–124; Fick, *Making of Haiti*, 157.

33. Stein, *Légèr Félicité Sonthonax*, 51–52.

34. Ibid., 56; Madiou, *Histoire d'Haiti*, 1:153; *Moniteur Générale*, February 9, 1793, 337.

35. Stein, *Légèr Félicité Sonthonax*, 54–55, 58.

36. Ibid., 59–60; Garran-Coulon, *Rapport*, 3:227–242.

37. Madiou, *Histoire d'Haiti*, 1:159; Pamphile de Lacroix, *Révolution de Haiti*, 153; Stein, *Légèr Félicité Sonthonax*, 61.

38. Garran-Coulon, *Rapport*, 3:246–247; Madiou, *Histoire d'Haiti*, 1:163–164.

39. *Moniteur Général*, February 4, 1793, 319; February 5, 1793, 323; February 7, 1793, 331; February 12, 1793, 349–350; February 26, 1793, 406.

40. Fick, *Making of Haiti*, 155–156; Madiou, *Histoire d'Haiti*, 1:166.

41. David Geggus, *Haitian Revolutionary Studies* (Bloomington, 2002), 137–145; Foubert, "Les Volontaires," 33–35; *Moniteur Général*, February 28, 1793, 419.

42. Madiou, *Histoire d'Haiti*, 1:215; *Moniteur Général*, February 9, 1793, 339–340; ibid., March 5, 1793, 434–435; ibid., February 28, 1793, 419; Julius Scott, "The Common Wind: Currents of Afro-American Communication in the Era of the Haitian Revolution" (Ph.D. diss., Duke University, 1986).

43. Garran-Coulon, *Rapport*, 3:394; *Moniteur Général*, February 9, 1793, 339–340; ibid., March 8, 1793, 446–447; ibid., March 5, 1793, 434–435.

44. *Moniteur Générale*, February 24, 1793, 399; ibid., February 21, 1793, 388; ibid., February 8, 1793, 336; ibid., February 12, 1793, 352.

45. Ibid., February 19, 1793, 380; ibid., February 25, 1793, 403; ibid., February 8, 1793, 336.

46. Thomas Madiou, *Histoire d'Haiti*, 1:263; *Moniteur Générale*, February 5, 1793, 322.

47. *Moniteur Général*, March 22, 1793, 504; *DuBois Slave-Trade Database* (Cambridge, 2000).

7. LIBERTY'S LAND

1. David Geggus, *Haitian Revolutionary Studies* (Bloomington, 2002), 175; idem, *Slavery, War and Revolution: The British Occupation of Saint-Domingue, 1793–1798* (Oxford, 1982), 103, 338.

2. David Geggus, "The Arming of Slaves in the Haitian Revolution," in *The Arming of Slaves,* ed. Philip Morgan and Christopher Brown (New Haven, forthcoming), 23–25; idem, *Haitian Revolutionary Studies,* 179–180.

3. Geggus, *Slavery, War and Revolution,* 58–64.

4. Ibid., 103; Jean-Philippe Garran-Coulon, *Rapport sur les troubles de Saint-Domingue,* 4 vols. (Paris, 1798–99), 4:24, 30–31; Robert Louis Stein, *Légér Félicité Sonthonax: The Lost Sentinel of the Republic* (London, 1985), 69, 78.

5. Stein, *Légér Félicité Sonthonax,* 83, 64.

6. Proclamation of Etienne Polverel and Légér Félicité Sonthonax, May 5, 1793, in Gabriel Debien, "Aux origines de l'abolition de l'esclavage," *Revue d'Histoire des Colonies* 36 (1er trimestre, 1949): 24–55, 35–43; Garran-Coulon, *Rapport,* 4:31–33, 55–56.

7. Stein, *Légér Félicité Sonthonax,* 69–72; Garran-Coulon, *Rapport,* 3:400–409; 4:26, 35–36. For some of Boissière's writings, see *Moniteur Général,* February 3, 1793, 315; ibid., February 7, 1793, 330.

8. Stein, *Légér Félicité Sonthonax,* 70–73.

9. Ibid., 70–73; Pierre Pluchon, *Toussaint Louverture* (Paris, 1989), 81; Garran-Coulon, *Rapport,* 3:366–370, 395–399; "Précis des faits relatifs à la malheureuse colonie de Saint-Domingue," DXXV 14, folder 127, no. 6, AN.

10. Stein, *Légér Félicité Sonthonax,* 74–75; Garran-Coulon, *Rapport,* 3:437–446; Thomas Madiou, *Histoire d'Haiti* (1847–48; reprint, Port-au-Prince, 1989), 1:178–179; Pamphile de Lacroix, *La Révolution de Haiti* (1819; reprint, Paris, 1995), 162.

11. Garran-Coulon, *Rapport,* 3:446–447, 474; Stein, *Légér Félicité Sonthonax,* 75; Carolyn Fick, *The Making of Haiti: The Saint-Domingue Revolution from Below* (Knoxville, 1990), 158–159; Pailleux to the Colonial Commission, 30 Frimaire An 3 (December 20, 1794), DXXV 125, folder 991, no. 1, AN.

12. Stein, *Légér Félicité Sonthonax,* 75; Fick, *Making of Haiti,* 159.

13. Pailleux to the Colonial Commission, 30 Frimaire An 3 (December 20, 1794); Garran-Coulon, *Rapport,* 4:41–42.

14. Lacroix, *Révolution de Haiti,* 164–165; Paillieux to the Colonial Commission, 30 Frimaire An 3 (December 20, 1794); Stein, *Légér Félicité Sonthonax,* 76.

15. Stein, *Légér Félicité Sonthonax,* 76; Fick, *Making of Haiti,* 159; Geggus, *Haitian Revolutionary Studies,* 126.

16. Garran-Coulon, *Rapport,* 4:6, 43; Geggus, *Haitian Revolutionary Studies,* 267.

17. Stein, *Légér Félicité Sonthonax,* 98; Lacroix, *Révolution de Haiti,* 166–67; John Thornton, "I Am the Subject of the King of Kongo: African Political Ideology and the Haitian Revolution," *Journal of World History* 4 (fall 1993): 181–183.

18. Garran-Coulon, *Rapport,* 4:11–14, 48–51; Fick, *Making of Haiti,* 161; Stein, *Légér Félicité Sonthonax,* 76; Madiou, *Histoire d'Haiti,* 1:185.

19. Fick, *Making of Haiti,* 163–164.

20. Lacroix, *Révolution de Haiti,* 169.

21. Proclamation of Etienne Polverel, August 27, 1793, in Debien, "Aux origines," 43–55, quotations on 43–45.

22. Ibid., 45–46, 48.

23. Ibid., 49, 52.

24. Geggus, *Haitian Revolutionary Studies,* 126; Garran-Coulon, *Rapport,* 4:53–57.

25. Florence Gauthier, "Le Rôle de la députation de Saint-Domingue dans l'abolition de l'esclavage," in *Les Abolitions de l'Esclavage de L. F. Sonthanax à V. Schoelcher, 1793, 1794, 1848,* ed. Marcel Dorigny (Paris, 1995), 200–211, 203; Lacroix, *Révolution de Haiti,* 170; Proclamation of Sonthonax, August 29, 1793, in Gabriel Debien, "Aux origines de l'abolition de l'esclavage," *Revue d'Histoire des Colonies* 36 (3ème et 4ème trimestres 1949): 348–356.

26. Bramante Lazzary, August 30, 1793, D XXV 23, 231, no. 98, AN.

27. Etienne Polverel, "Proclamation relative à la liberté générale différée," Port-au-Prince, September 4, 1793; "Proclamation aux Africains et descendants d'Africains," September 10, 1793; "Proclamation relative à l'émancipation des esclaves appartenant à l'Etat dans la province de l'Ouest," September 21, 1793; "Proclamation relative à l'émancipation des esclaves appartenant à l'Etat dans la province du Sud," Les Cayes, October 7, 1793; "Proclamation relative à la liberté générale," October 31, 1793; reprinted in Debien, "Aux origines," 356–387.

28. Proclamation of Sonthonax, August 29, 1793, in Debien, "Aux origines," 348–356; Beaubrun Ardouin, *Etudes sur l'histoire d'Haïti,* 11 vols. (1853–1865; reprint, Port-au-Prince, 1958), 3:101.

29. Etienne Polverel, "Proclamation relative à la liberté générale," October 31, 1793, in Debien, "Aux origines," 372–387.

30. Geggus, *Slavery, War and Revolution,* 65–66, 107–108.

31. Ibid., 125, 395–399; Lacroix, *Révolution de Haiti,* 173–177.

32. Geggus, *Slavery, War and Revolution,* 66, 109; Madiou, *Histoire d'Haiti,* 1:205–211; Geggus, *Slavery,* 109.

33. Madiou, *Histoire d'Haiti,* 1:234–236; Geggus, *Haitian Revolutionary Studies,* 78, 124.

34. Madiou, *Histoire d'Haiti,* 1:232–233; Lacroix, *Révolution de Haiti,* 186–188; "Notes divers d'Isaac sur la vie de Toussaint-Louverture," in Antoine Métral, *Histoire de l'expédition des Français à Saint-Domingue* (1825; reprint, Paris, 1985), 333.

35. Gauthier, "Le Rôle de la députation," 200–211, 204; "Procès verbal de l'Assemblée électorale des deputés du nord de St. Domingue," September 23, 1793, C[181], 84, AN.

36. *Lettre écrite à New York par les députés de Saint-Domingue, à leurs commetans, imprimée par ordre de la Convention Nationale* (Paris, 1794), 3–9.

37. M. J. Mavidal and M. E. Laurent, eds., *Archives parlementaires de 1787 à 1860, première série (1787–1799)* (Paris, 1962), 84:276–285.

38. Madiou, *Histoire d'Haiti*, 1:226–228.

8. THE OPENING

1. Gabriel Debien, Jean Fouchard, and Marie Antoinette Menier, "Toussaint Louverture avant 1789: Légendes et réalités," *Conjonction* 134 (June–July 1977): 68, 73–74; Stewart King, "Toussaint L'Ouverture before 1791: Free Planter and Slave-Holder," *Journal of Haitian Studies* 3 and 4 (1997–98): 68; David Geggus, *Haitian Revolutionary Studies* (Bloomington, 2002), 230.

2. Debien, Fouchard, and Menier, "Toussaint Louverture," 67; C. L. R. James, *The Black Jacobins: Toussaint Louverture and the San Domingo Revolution* (1938; reprint, New York, 1963), 25; "Notes divers d'Isaac sur la vie de Toussaint-Louverture," in Antoine Métral, *Histoire de l'expédition des Français à Saint-Domingue* (1825; reprint, Paris, 1985), 325–326; Geggus, *Haitian Revolutionary Studies*, 16.

3. "Notes divers d'Isaac," 331; "Extrait de l'esquisse historique légendaire et descriptive de la Ville de Pontarlier et du Fort de Joux par Edouard Girou," N.A. 6894, 22–26, Bibliothéque Nationale (hereafter BN); Geggus, *Haitian Revolutionary Studies*, 127.

4. Pamphile de Lacroix, *La Révolution de Haiti* (1819; reprint, Paris, 1995), 244, 354; Geggus, *Haitian Revolutionary Studies*, 16, 19; James, *Black Jacobins*, 418.

5. Lacroix, *Révolution de Haiti*, 245, 355.

6. Madison Smartt Bell, *Master of the Crossroads* (New York, 2000); in Haitian Vodou the crossroads are the symbolic site where the *lwa* (gods) intersect with the living.

7. Victor Schoelcher, *Vie de Toussaint Louverture* (1889; reprint, Paris, 1982), 94–95; James, *Black Jacobins*, 125; Geggus, *Haitian Revolutionary Studies*, 127.

8. Bramante Lazzary to Toussaint Louverture, D XXV 23, 231, no. 96, AN.

9. Geggus, *Haitian Revolutionary Studies*, 125; James, *Black Jacobins*, 124–125.

10. Toussaint Louverture to General Laveaux, May 18, 1794, in Gérard Laurent, *Toussaint Louverture à travers sa correspondence, 1794–1798* (Madrid, 1953), 103–107; Laurent's work reprints the correspondence between Louverture and Laveaux, along with some other documents, in Manuscrits Occidentaux, 12101–03, BN. The sleight-of-hand was the work of T. Gragnon-Lacoste, in *Toussaint Louverture* (Paris, 1877); see Geggus, *Haitian Revolutionary Studies*, 126; Schoelcher, *Vie de Toussaint Louverture*, 98–100; James, *Black Jacobins*, 125–126.

11. Geggus, *Haitian Revolutionary Studies*, 128; idem, *Slavery, War and Revolution: The British Occupation of Saint-Domingue, 1793–1798* (Oxford, 1982), 108.

12. Geggus, *Haitian Revolutionary Studies*, 133.

13. Laplace, "député des émigrés Français," to "son excellence," April 4, 1794, 12102, 55, BN; Pierre Pluchon, *Toussaint Louverture* (Paris, 1989), 101–102; Schoelcher, *Vie de Toussaint Louverture*, 97; Geggus, *Haitian Revolutionary Studies*, 121.

14. Geggus, *Haitian Revolutionary Studies*, 122–123, 135–136.

15. Ibid., 123–124; Jean-Philippe Garran-Coulon, *Rapport sur les troubles de Saint-Domingue* (Paris, 1798–99), 4:298–300; Louverture to Laveaux, May 18, 1794, in Laurent, *Louverture*, 103–107; Pluchon, *Toussaint Louverture*, 99–100; Carolyn Fick, *The Making of Haiti: The Saint-Domingue Revolution from Below* (Knoxville, 1990), 184.

16. Geggus, *Slavery, War and Revolution*, 114, 118; Louverture to Laveaux, July 7, 1794, in Laurent, *Louverture*, 118–120.

17. Beaucorps to Rodrigue, July 9, 1794, 12102, 92–94, BN; Geggus, *Slavery, War and Revolution*, 119; idem, *Haitian Revolutionary Studies*, 176, 180.

18. Robert Louis Stein, *Légér Félicité Sonthonax: The Lost Sentinel of the Republic* (London, 1985), 104.

19. Proclamation by Laveaux to the Inhabitants of Saint-Marc, September 12, 1794, in Laurent, *Louverture*, 130–133; Geggus, *Slavery, War and Revolution*, 121, 126–128.

20. Louverture to Laveaux, July 7, 1794, in Laurent, *Louverture*, 118–120; Geggus, *Slavery, War and Revolution*, 128.

21. Louverture to Laveaux, October 4, 1794, in Laurent, *Louverture*, 133–136.

22. Geggus, *Slavery, War and Revolution*, 122, 128–129, 150–154; Thomas Madiou, *Histoire d'Haiti* (1847–48; reprint, Port-au-Prince, 1989), 1:266–268.

23. Louverture to Laveaux, October 21, 1794, and January 7, 1795, in Laurent, *Louverture*, 137–138 and 145–147; Schoelcher, *Vie de Toussaint Louverture*, 108, 113–117.

24. Pluchon, *Toussaint Louverture*, 134–135.

25. The letter is attached to Louverture to Laveaux, June 18, 1795, and reprinted in Laurent, *Louverture*, 181–183.

26. Louverture to Laveaux, October 5, October 28, and November 8, 1795, in Laurent, *Louverture*, 237–239, 249, 253–255; Jean-François to Laveaux, December 28, 1794, 12102, 162, BN.

27. Geggus, *Slavery, War and Revolution*, 182; idem, *Haitian Revolutionary Studies*, 179–203; Jane Landers, "Rebellion and Royalism in Spanish Florida," in *A Turbulent Time: The French Revolution and the Greater Caribbean*, ed. David Barry Gaspar and David Geggus (Bloomington, 1997), 156–171.

28. Louverture to Laveaux, August 31 and September 14, 1795, 12103, 128 and 218, BN; in Laurent, *Louverture,* 222–232; Schoelcher, *Vie de Toussaint Louverture,* 142–144; Geggus, *Slavery, War and Revolution,* 165.

29. Louverture to Laveaux, September 30 and December 7, 1795, 12103, 237 and 368, BN; in Laurent, *Louverture,* 233–236, 271–272; Schoelcher, *Vie de Toussaint Louverture,* 121–122; Lacroix, *Révolution de Haiti,* 214.

30. Fick, *Making of Haiti,* 168–169; Etienne Polverel, "Réglement sur les proportions du travail et de la récompense," February 7, 1794, in Gabriel Debien, "Aux origines de l'abolition de l'esclavage," *Revue d'Histoire des Colonies* 36 (3ème and 4ème trimestres 1949): 391–402.

31. Fick, *Making of Haiti,* 170; Judith Kafka, "Action, Reaction, and Interaction: Slave Women and Resistance in the South of Saint-Domingue, 1793–94," *Slavery and Abolition* 18 (August 1997): 48–49, 54.

32. Fick, *Making of Haiti,* 171; Kafka, "Action, Reaction, and Interaction," 60.

33. Fick, *Making of Haiti,* 172–173.

34. Louverture to Laveaux, July 19, 1794, 12102, 95, BN; in Laurent, *Louverture,* 121–124.

35. Schoelcher, *Vie de Toussaint Louverture,* 109.

36. Ibid., 127–129; Proclamation of Louverture, March 22, 1795; Louverture to Laveaux, June 17, June 26, and September 14, 1795, 12103, 95, 117, and 218, BN; in Laurent, *Louverture,* 171–173, 183–188, 228–232.

37. Louverture to Laveaux, September 14, 1795, 12103, 218, BN; in Laurent, *Louverture,* 228–232; Schoelcher, *Vie de Toussaint Louverture,* 145–146; Geggus, *Haitian Revolutionary Studies,* 23.

38. Louverture to Laveaux, August 6 and September 14, 1795, 12103, 193 and 218, BN; in Laurent, *Louverture,* 213–219, 228–232; Pluchon, *Toussaint Louverture,* 421.

39. Louverture to Laveaux, January 31 and June 17, 1795, 12103, 16 and 95, BN; in Laurent, *Louverture,* 157–161 and 183–186; Schoelcher, *Vie de Toussaint Louverture,* 129. There has been surprisingly little research into the details of how Louverture's work policies were applied, and resisted, on the plantations.

40. Procés-verbal de Toussaint Louverture, 1 Ventôse An 4 (February 20, 1796), in Laurent, *Louverture,* 314–315, 316.

41. Ibid., 317–318.

42. Louverture, "Proclamation," April 25, 1796, ibid., 380–385.

43. Procés-verbal of Louverture, February 20, 1796, and Louverture to Laveaux, May 11, 1796, 12104, 230, BN; in Laurent, *Louverture,* 385–387.

44. Lacroix, *Révolution de Haiti,* 201; Marquis de Condorcet, *Réflexions sur l'esclavage des Nègres,* 2d ed. (Paris, 1788).

45. Odette Menesson-Rigaud Papers, box 1, folder 7/8, no. 74, Bibliothéque Haitïenne des Pères du Saint-Esprit, Port-au-Prince.

1. Jean-Baptiste Belley, *Le Bout d'oreille des colons où le système de l'Hotel de Massiac, mis au jour par Gouli* (Paris, 1795).

2. Darcy Grimaldo Grigsby, *Extremities: Painting Empire in Revolutionary France* (New Haven, 2002), 52.

3. Belley, *Le Bout d'oreille*.

4. Ibid.; Grigsby, *Extremities*, 53.

5. Speech of Defermont and Decree of the National Convention, July 23, 1795, in Gérard Laurent, *Toussaint Louverture à travers sa correspondence, 1794–1798* (Madrid, 1953), 244–247.

6. *Débats entre les accusateurs et les accusés dans l'affaire des colonies* (Paris, 1795).

7. Florence Gauthier, "La Convention thermidorienne et le problème coloniale, Septembre 1794–Septembre 1795," in *Le Tournant de l'an III: Réaction et terreur blanche dans la France révolutionnaire*, ed. Michel Vovelle (Paris, 1997), 109–119, 113–115; Victor Schoelcher, *Vie de Toussaint Louverture* (1889; reprint, Paris, 1982), 177.

8. Schoelcher, *Vie de Toussaint Louverture*, 119.

9. Carolyn Fick, *The Making of Haiti: The Saint-Domingue Revolution from Below* (Knoxville, 1990), 186–188; Beaubrun Ardouin, *Etudes sur l'histoire d'Haïti*, 11 vols. (1853–1865; reprint, Port-au-Prince, 1958), 3:81.

10. Fick, *Making of Haiti*, 185–187.

11. David Geggus, *Slavery, War and Revolution: The British Occupation in Saint-Domingue, 1793–1798* (Oxford, 1982), 183–184.

12. Louverture to Laveaux, February 12, 1796, in Schoelcher, *Vie de Toussaint Louverture*, 136–137.

13. Ibid., 138–139; Fick, *Making of Haiti*, 188.

14. Geggus, *Slavery, War and Revolution*, 180; Louverture to Laveaux, April 26 and June 18, 1795, in Laurent, *Louverture*, 175–177, 179–181.

15. Louverture to Laveaux, July 2, 1795, Jan. 19, 1796, ibid., 189–192, 293–295.

16. Pierre Pluchon, *Toussaint Louverture* (Paris, 1989), 121; Ardouin, *Etudes sur l'histoire d'Haïti*, 3:28; Laurent, *Louverture*, 173–174.

17. Laurent, *Louverture*, 349–354; Thomas Madiou, *Histoire d'Haiti* (1847–48; reprint, Port-au-Prince, 1989), 1:303–304.

18. Pluchon, *Toussaint Louverture*, 118–119; Schoelcher, *Vie de Toussaint Louverture*, 159; Laurent, *Louverture*, 355–357.

19. Laurent, *Louverture*, 358; Pluchon, *Toussaint Louverture*, 128; Madiou, *Histoire d'Haiti*, 1:305–306.

20. Henry Perroud, *Précis des derniers troubles qui ont eu lieu dans la partie du Nord de Saint-Domingue* (Le Cap, 1796), 2–4.

21. Ardouin, *Etudes sur l'histoire d'Haïti,* 3:28–29; Louverture to Laveaux, February 22, 1796, 12104, 86, BN, in Laurent, *Louverture,* 333–335; Geggus, *Slavery, War and Revolution,* 180; Pluchon, *Toussaint Louverture,* 140.

22. Proclamation of Toussaint Louverture, March 1796, in *Toussaint Louverture,* ed. George Tyson Jr. (Englewood Cliffs, N.J., 1973), 31–34.

23. Geggus, *Slavery, War and Revolution,* 181.

24. Proclamation of Toussaint Louverture, March 1796, in Tyson, *Louverture,* 31–34.

25. Ardouin, *Etudes sur l'histoire d'Haïti,* 3:32; Pamphile de Lacroix, *La Révolution de Haiti* (1819; reprint, Paris, 1995), 193; Schoelcher, *Vie de Toussaint Louverture,* 172; Michel Etienne Descourtilz, *Voyages d'un naturaliste, et ses observations* (Paris, 1809), 3:246.

26. Robert Louis Stein, *Légèr Félicité Sonthonax: The Lost Sentinel of the Republic* (London, 1985), 132–134; Madiou, *Histoire d'Haïti,* 1:318.

27. Fick, *Making of Haiti,* 192–196; Gaetan Mentor, *Histoire d'un crime politique: Le Général Etienne Victor Mentor* (Port-au-Prince, 1999), 36.

28. Stein, *Légèr Félicité Sonthonax,* 148.

29. Ibid.; Pluchon, *Toussaint Louverture,* 153–155.

30. Stein, *Légèr Félicité Sonthonax,* 160–161. The official report of the electoral assembly is in N.A.F. 6847, 44–53, BN.

31. Schoelcher, *Vie de Toussaint Louverture,* 181–182; Stein, *Légèr Félicité Sonthonax,* 161.

32. Stein, *Légèr Félicité Sonthonax,* 163, 166–167; Ardouin, *Etudes sur l'histoire d'Haïti,* 3:49–50.

33. Ardouin, *Etudes sur l'histoire d'Haïti,* 3:50; Sonthonax to Louverture, June 12, 1796, FR 8986, 12–13, BN; in Laurent, *Louverture,* 467–468; Pluchon, *Toussaint Louverture,* 175–177, 194; Schoelcher, *Vie de Toussaint Louverture,* 191; Stein, *Légèr Félicité Sonthonax,* 128; Madiou, *Histoire d'Haïti,* 1:335, 341–342.

34. Stein, *Légèr Félicité Sonthonax,* 168.

35. Ibid., 178–181; Ardouin, *Etudes sur l'histoire d'Haïti,* 3:77–79.

36. Louverture to Laveaux, May 22 and June 5, 1798, 12104, 380 and 384, BN; in Laurent, *Louverture,* 439–450; Pluchon, *Toussaint Louverture,* 163.

37. Louverture to Laveaux, May 22 and June 5, 1798, in Laurent, *Louverture,* 439–450; C. L. R. James, *The Black Jacobins: Toussaint Louverture and the San Domingo Revolution* (1939; reprint, New York, 1963), 188–190; Fick, *Making of Haiti,* 196–196; Stein, *Légèr Félicité Sonthonax,* 169–170; Pluchon, *Toussaint Louverture,* 180, 186–187; Ardouin, *Etudes sur l'histoire d'Haïti,* 3:75–76.

38. Ardouin, *Etudes sur l'histoire d'Haïti,* 3:82–83; Pluchon, *Toussaint Louverture,* 188–189.

1. Aimé Césaire, *Toussaint Louverture: La Révolution française et le problème colonial* (1961; reprint, Paris, 1981), 252–253; Gérard Laurent, *Toussaint Louverture à travers sa correspondence, 1794–1798* (Madrid, 1953), 436; Pierre Pluchon, *Toussaint Louverture* (Paris, 1989), 231.

2. Césaire, *Toussaint Louverture*, 253; "Refutation de quelques assertions d'un discours prononcé . . . par Vienot Vaublanc," October 29, 1797, in *La Révolution française et l'abolition de l'esclavage* (Paris, 1968), vol. 11; an English translation of part of the document is in George Tyson Jr., ed., *Toussaint Louverture* (Englewood Cliffs, N.J., 1973), 36–43; Césaire, *Toussaint Louverture*, 248–249, 253; Beaubrun Ardouin, *Etudes sur l'histoire d'Haïti*, 11 vols. (1853–1865; reprint, Port-au-Prince, 1958), 3:83; Robert Louis Stein, *Légér Félicité Sonthonax: The Lost Sentinel of the Republic* (London, 1985), 178–179.

3. Toussaint Louverture, Letter to the Directory, October 27, 1797, in Tyson, *Louverture*, 36–43.

4. Ibid.

5. Ibid.; Pluchon, *Toussaint Louverture*, 197–198.

6. Pluchon, *Toussaint Louverture*, 196–197.

7. Bernard Gainot, "La Constitutionnalisation de la liberté générale sous le Directoire," in *Les Abolitions de l'esclavage*, ed. Marcel Dorigny (Paris, 1995), 213–229; idem, "Le Général Laveaux, gouverneur de Saint-Domingue, député Jacobin," in *Esclavage, colonisation, libération nationales de 1789 à nos jours* (Paris, 1990), 169–183, 178–179; Victor Schoelcher, *Vie de Toussaint Louverture* (1889; reprint, Paris, 1982), 184.

8. Gainot, "La Constitutionnalisation," 213–229; Marcel Dorigny and Bernard Gainot, *La Société des Amis des Noirs, 1788–1799: Contribution à l'histoire de l'abolition de l'esclavage* (Paris, 1998).

9. Etienne Laveaux, *Discours prononcé par Laveaux, député de Saint-Domingue* (Paris, 1797), 1, 6–8.

10. Ibid., *Discours*, 3.

11. Etienne Laveaux, *Opinion de Laveaux, sur les colonies* (Paris, 1798), 7–9.

12. "Loi concernant l'organisation constititionale des colonies," 12 Nivôse An 6 (January 1, 1798), AD VII 20 A, AN; Gainot, "La Constitutionnalisation," 222–223.

13. Laveaux, *Discours*, 12.

14. Louverture to Laveaux, September 24, 1798, 12104, 401, BN; in Laurent, *Louverture*, 451–454.

15. David Geggus, *Slavery, War and Revolution: The British Occupation in Saint-Domingue, 1793–1798* (Oxford, 1982), 224, 318; Schoelcher, *Vie de Toussaint Louverture*, 218; Michael Duffy, *Soldiers, Sugar and Seapower: The British Expe-*

ditions to the West Indies and the War against Revolution France (Oxford, 1987), 302.

16. Geggus, *Slavery, War and Revolution*, 315–318.

17. Roger Norman Buckley, ed., *The Haitian Journal of Lieutenant Howard, York Hussars, 1796–1798* (Knoxville, 1985), 49–50; Duffy, *Soldiers, Sugar and Seapower*, 303–304.

18. Geggus, *Slavery, War and Revolution*, 375–376; Schoelcher, *Vie de Toussaint Louverture*, 218.

19. Pluchon, *Toussaint Louverture*, 209, 213.

20. Ibid., 210; Ardouin, *Etudes sur l'histoire d'Haïti*, 3:85.

21. Ardouin, *Etudes sur l'histoire d'Haïti*, 3:87; Pluchon, *Toussaint Louverture*, 212.

22. Duffy, *Soldiers, Sugar and Seapower*, 306; Ardouin, *Etudes sur l'histoire d'Haïti*, 3:87–88; Pluchon, *Toussaint Louverture*, 215–216.

23. Geggus, *Slavery, War and Revolution*, 376; Duffy, *Soldiers, Sugar and Seapower*, 305–307; Ardouin, *Etudes sur l'histoire d'Haïti*, 3:89.

24. Pluchon, *Toussaint Louverture*, 216–217; Ardouin, *Etudes sur l'histoire d'Haïti*, 3:90, 94; Pamphile de Lacroix, *La Révolution de Haiti* (1819; reprint, Paris, 1995), 210.

25. Geggus, *Slavery, War and Revolution*, 380–381; Lacroix, *Révolution de Haiti*, 212; Pluchon, *Toussaint Louverture*, 218–220.

26. Pluchon, *Toussaint Louverture*, 210, 224, 226; Schoelcher, *Vie de Toussaint Louverture*, 236; Ardouin, *Etudes sur l'histoire d'Haïti*, 3:101–102.

27. Ardouin, *Etudes sur l'histoire d'Haïti*, 3:101, 106. There has been remarkably little examination by historians of the details of how Louverture's labor regulations were implemented on the plantations.

28. Louverture to Laveaux, September 24, 1798, in Laurent, *Louverture*, 451–454; Lacroix, *Révolution de Haiti*, 214–215, 222, 302; Michel Etienne Descourtilz, *Voyages d'un naturaliste, et ses observations*, 3 vols. (Paris, 1809), 3:277.

29. Pluchon, *Toussaint Louverture*, 223–225.

30. Descourtilz, *Voyages d'un naturaliste*, 3:247–248.

31. Pluchon, *Toussaint Louverture*, 237–238; Ardouin, *Etudes sur l'histoire d'Haïti*, 3:104–105; Carolyn Fick, *The Making of Haiti: The Saint-Domingue Revolution from Below* (Knoxville, 1990), 199.

32. Ardouin, *Etudes sur l'histoire d'Haïti*, 3:92.

33. Pluchon, *Toussaint Louverture*, 241–243.

34. Duffy, *Soldiers, Sugar and Seapower*, 309–310; Schoelcher, *Vie de Toussaint Louverture*, 230; Geggus, *Slavery, War and Revolution*, 381.

35. "Letters of Toussaint Louverture and of Edward Stevens, 1798–1800," *American Historical Review* 16 (October 1910): 64–67; Pluchon, *Toussaint Louverture*, 297–298.

36. Stevens to Pickering, May 3, 1799, in "Letters of Louverture and Stevens," 67–72; Thomas Ott, *The Haitian Revolution, 1789–1804* (Knoxville, 1973), 132; Leclerc to Minister, February 1802, in *Lettres du Général Leclerc,* ed. Paul Roussier (Paris, 1937), 79–82; Pluchon, *Toussaint Louverture,* 307, 417.

37. Marcel Bonaparte August and Claude Bonaparte Auguste, *La Participation étrangère à l'expédition française de Saint-Domingue* (Quebec, 1980), 33–34; Tim Matthewson, "Jefferson and Haiti," *Journal of Southern History* 61 (May 1995): 209–247; Douglas R. Egerton, "The Empire of Liberty Reconsidered," in *The Revolution of 1800: Democracy, Race, and the New Republic,* ed. James Horn, Jan Ellen Lewis, and Peter S. Onuf (Charlottesville, 2002), 309–330.

38. Stevens to Pickering, September 30, 1799, and January 16, 1800, in "Letters of Louverture and Stevens," 82–85, 88–92; Pluchon, *Toussaint Louverture,* 303–304.

39. Stevens to Pickering, June 23, 1799, in "Letters of Louverture and Stevens," 74–76; Pluchon, *Toussaint Louverture,* 258–259, 320.

40. Stevens to Pickering, June 24, 1799, in "Letters of Louverture and Stevens," 76–81; Pluchon, *Toussaint Louverture,* 256–264, 284–290.

41. Descourtilz, *Voyages d'un naturaliste,* 2:211, 240; Geggus, *Slavery, War and Revolution,* 381.

42. Ardouin, *Etudes sur l'histoire d'Haïti,* 3:99, 102.

43. David Geggus, *Haitian Revolutionary Studies* (Bloomington, 2002), 23; Pluchon, *Toussaint Louverture,* 403, 425.

44. Descourtilz, *Voyages d'un naturaliste,* 2:91–92; 3:265–266; Pluchon, *Toussaint Louverture,* 427.

45. Descourtilz, *Voyages d'un naturaliste,* 2:91–92, 125–135.

46. Ibid., 94–97.

47. Pluchon, *Toussaint Louverture,* 418–420.

48. Gabriel Debien, "Sur les plantations Mauger à l'Artibonite (Saint-Domingue 1763–1803)" in *Enquêtes et Documents: Nantes, Afrique, Amérique* (Nantes, 1981), 219–314, 314; Jan Pachonski and Reuel K. Wilson, *Poland's Caribbean Tragedy: A Study of Polish Legions in the Haitian War of Independence, 1802–1803* (Boulder, 1986), 123.

11. TERRITORY

1. Beaubrun Ardouin, *Etudes sur l'histoire d'Haïti,* 11 vols. (1853–1865; reprint, Port-au-Prince, 1958), 3:93–94; Victor Schoelcher, *Vie de Toussaint Louverture* (1889; reprint, Paris, 1982), 245; Pierre Pluchon, *Toussaint Louverture* (Paris, 1989), 256.

2. Ardouin, *Etudes sur l'histoire d'Haïti,* 4:24–27.

3. Pluchon, *Toussaint Louverture,* 266–268; Ardouin, *Etudes sur l'histoire d'Haïti,* 4:7.

4. *Réponse du Général de Brigade André Rigaud, à l'écrit calomnieux du*

Général Toussaint Louverture (Cayes, 1799), 6; Ardouin, *Etudes sur l'histoire d'Haïti*, 4:13.

5. Pamphile de Lacroix, *La Révolution de Haiti* (1819; reprint, Paris, 1995), 228; Stevens to Pickering, June 24, 1799, in "Letters of Toussaint Louverture and of Edward Stevens, 1798–1800," *American Historical Review* 16 (October 1910): 64–101, 76–81; Ardouin, *Etudes sur l'histoire d'Haïti*, 4:31.

6. Ardouin, *Etudes sur l'histoire d'Haïti*, 4:18, 25, 27.

7. Stevens to Pickering, June 24, 1799, in "Letters of Louverture and Stevens," 76–81; Pluchon, *Toussaint Louverture*, 265.

8. Stevens to Pickering, June 24, 1799, in "Letters of Louverture and Stevens," 76–81; Ardouin, *Etudes sur l'histoire d'Haïti*, 4:24, 26; Schoelcher, *Vie de Toussaint Louverture*, 252.

9. Ardouin, *Etudes sur l'histoire d'Haïti*, 4:25; Michel Etienne Descourtilz, *Voyages d'un naturaliste, et ses observations* (Paris, 1809), 3:261–262.

10. Louverture to Adams, August 14, 1799, and Stevens to Pickering, June 24, 1799, in "Letters of Louverture and Stevens," 76–82; Pluchon, *Toussaint Louverture*, 270.

11. Lacroix, *Révolution de Haiti*, 228, 232, 237; Ardouin, *Etudes sur l'histoire d'Haïti*, 4:26–30, 39; Carolyn Fick, *The Making of Haiti: The Saint-Domingue Revolution from Below* (Knoxville, 1990), 202–203; Schoelcher, *Vie de Toussaint Louverture*, 253–255.

12. Schoelcher, *Vie de Toussaint Louverture*, 263–268; Fick, *Making of Haiti*, 205; Ardouin, *Etudes sur l'histoire d'Haïti*, 4:52. No recent historian has yet provided a study of the war between Rigaud and Louverture, or sought to evaluate the competing claims regarding the atrocities committed.

13. Ardouin, *Etudes sur l'histoire d'Haïti*, 4:37; Stevens to Pickering, April 24, 1800, in "Letters of Louverture and Stevens," 97–98.

14. Ardouin, *Etudes sur l'histoire d'Haïti*, 4:36; Schoelcher, *Vie de Toussaint Louverture*, 279; Lacroix, *Révolution de Haiti*, 258; Pluchon, *Toussaint Louverture*, 292–293. Remarkably little has been written about Louverture's occupation of Santo Domingo.

15. Ardouin, *Etudes sur l'histoire d'Haïti*, 4:38; Lacroix, *Révolution de Haiti*, 253.

16. Lacroix, *Révolution de Haiti*, 259.

17. Ardouin, *Etudes sur l'histoire d'Haïti*, 4:54.

18. Ibid., 53–55.

19. The decree is printed in ibid. and in Claude Moïse, *Le Projet nationale de Toussaint Louverture et la Constitution de 1801* (Port-au-Prince, 2001), 91–97; an English translation is in George Tyson Jr., ed., *Toussaint Louverture* (Englewood Cliffs, N.J., 1973), 51–56.

20. Ardouin, *Etudes sur l'histoire d'Haïti*, 4:68–69; Fick, *Making of Haiti*, 207.

21. Ardouin, *Etudes sur l'histoire d'Haïti*, 4:55–56.

22. Paul Roussier, ed., *Lettres du Général Leclerc* (Paris, 1937), 25; Yves Benot, *La Démence coloniale sous Napoléon* (Paris, 1991).

23. Schoelcher, *Vie de Toussaint Louverture*, 262–263.

24. Ibid., 263–264.

25. Ardouin, *Etudes sur l'histoire d'Haïti*, 4:67–68; Moïse, *Projet nationale*, 20.

26. Ardouin, *Etudes sur l'histoire d'Haïti*, 4:75; Moïse, *Projet nationale*, 21; Carlo Avierl Celius, "Le Contrat social haïtien," *Pouvoirs dans la Caraïbe* 10 (1998): 27–70, 52; Claude Bonaparte Auguste and Marcel Bonaparte Auguste, *L'Expédition Leclerc, 1801–1803* (Port-au-Prince, 1985), 15. On Hamilton's letter, which Louverture may never have received, see Thomas Ott, *The Haitian Revolution, 1789–1804* (Knoxville, 1973), 119; and Doulgas R. Egerton, "The Empire of Liberty Reconsidered," in *The Revolution of 1800: Democracy, Race, and the New Republic*, ed. James Horn, Jan Ellen Lewis, and Peter S. Onuf (Charlottesville, 2002), 309–330, esp. 331.

27. Constitution of 1801, reprinted in Moïse, *Projet nationale*, 72–85, quotation 72.

28. Ardouin, *Etudes sur l'histoire d'Haïti*, 4:34; Moïse, *Projet nationale*, 73, 87.

29. Moïse, *Projet nationale*, 74.

30. Celius, "Contrat social haïtien," esp. 29; Moïse, *Projet nationale*, 84–85, 88. I explore the parallel contradictions of the contemporary regime in Guadeloupe in "'The Price of Liberty': Victor Hugues and the Administration of Freedom in Guadeloupe," *William and Mary Quarterly* 3d. ser., 56 (April 1999): 363–392.

31. Moïse, *Projet nationale*, 76–79, 83–84, 88.

32. Lacroix, *Révolution de Haiti*, 261–262.

33. Pluchon, *Toussaint Louverture*, 253–254.

34. Lacroix, *Révolution de Haiti*, 274–276; Thomas Madiou, *Histoire d'Haiti*, (1847–48; reprint, Port-au-Prince, 1989), 2:144–145.

35. Moïse, *Projet nationale*, 102; Madiou, *Histoire d'Haiti*, 3:145–152; Pluchon, *Toussaint Louverture*, 433–438; Fick, *Making of Haiti*, 208–210.

36. Schoelcher, *Vie de Toussaint Louverture*, 305; the proclamation, from November 25, 1801, is printed in Moïse, *Projet nationale*, 98–109; Ardouin, *Etudes sur l'histoire d'Haïti*, 3:91–94.

37. Moïse, *Projet nationale*, 100–102.

38. Ibid., 101–105.

39. Ibid., 104–108; Auguste and Auguste, *Expédition Leclerc*, 81, 88.

40. Mats Lundahl, "Toussaint Louverture and the War Economy of Saint Domingue, 1796–1802," *Slavery and Abolition* 6 (September 1985): 122–138; David Geggus, *Haitian Revolutionary Studies* (Bloomington, 2002), 23; Pluchon, *Toussaint Louverture*, 405–41.

41. Toussaint Louverture, *Mémoires du Général Toussaint Louverture* (Paris,

1853), 29, 59–60; Auguste and Auguste, *Expédition Leclerc*, 82; Leclerc to Minister, May 6 and February 9, 1802, in Roussier, *Lettres du Général Leclerc*, 134–138, 79–82.

12. THE TREE OF LIBERTY

1. Claude Bonaparte Auguste and Marcel Bonaparte Auguste, *L'Expédition Leclerc, 1801–1803* (Port-au-Prince, 1985), 58; Leclerc to Bonaparte, December 8 and 11, 1801, in Paul Roussier, ed., *Lettres du Général Leclerc* (Paris, 1937), 55–59.

2. Henri Mezière, *Le General Leclerc, 1772–1802, et l'expédition de Saint-Domingue* (Paris, 1990).

3. Auguste and Auguste, *Expédition Leclerc*, 28–30, 40.

4. Leclerc to Bonaparte, December 11, 1801, in Roussier, *Lettres du Général Leclerc*, 58–59; Pamphile de Lacroix, *La Révolution de Haiti* (1819; reprint, Paris, 1995), 283; "Mémoires d'Isaac Louverture," in Antoine Métral, *Histoire de l'expédition des Français à Saint-Domingue* (1825; reprint, Paris, 1985), 229–230.

5. James Stephens, *The Crisis of the Sugar Colonies; or, an Enquiry into the Objects and Probable Effects of the French Expedition to the West Indies* (1802; reprint, New York, 1969), 5.

6. Ibid., 6.

7. Pierre Pluchon, *Toussaint Louverture* (Paris, 1989), 456.

8. Pluchon, *Toussaint Louverture*, 456–457; Auguste and Auguste, *Expédition Leclerc*, 27; Yves Benot, *La Démence coloniale sous Napoléon* (Paris, 1991), 46–56.

9. Beaubrun Ardouin, *Etudes sur l'histoire d'Haïti*, 11 vols. (1853–1865; reprint, Port-au-Prince, 1958), 4:97–98; Jean-Jacques Régis de Cambacérès, *Mémoires inédits* (Paris, 1999), 1:587–588; Bonaparte to Louverture, November 18, 1801, in Roussier, *Lettres du Général Leclerc*, 307–309; Pluchon, *Toussaint Louverture*, 398.

10. "Notes pour servir aux instructions à donner au Capitaine Général Leclerc," in Roussier, *Lettres du Général Leclerc*, 263–274; Auguste and Auguste, *Expédition Leclerc*, 171–172.

11. Bonaparte to Leclerc, July 1, 1802, in Roussier, *Lettres du Général Leclerc*, 305–306; Jan Pachonski and Reuel K. Wilson, *Poland's Caribbean Tragedy: A Study of Polish Legions in the Haitian War of Independence, 1802–1803* (Boulder, 1986), 140.

12. Marcel Bonaparte Auguste and Claude Bonaparte Auguste, *La Participation étrangère à l'expédition française de Saint-Domingue* (Quebec, 1980), 21, 47–53; Benot, *Démence coloniale sous Napoléon*, 59–62; "Notes pour servir aux instructions," 269; Leclerc to Minister, February 27, 1802, in Roussier, *Lettres du Général Leclerc*, 102–111.

13. "Notes pour servir aux instructions," 269, 272; Germain Saint-Ruf, *L'Epopée Delgrès: La Guadeloupe sous la Révolution française (1789–1802)* (Paris, 1977), 88.

14. Stephens, *Crisis of the Sugar Colonies*, 7, 36.

15. Ibid., 44–45.

16. Ibid., 45–46.

17. Ibid., 24, 46, 75–76; Lacroix, *Révolution de Haiti*, 282.

18. Stephens, *Crisis of the Sugar Colonies*, 47–48, 55–56, 69.

19. Pluchon, *Toussaint Louverture*, 449–450.

20. "Notes pour servir aux instructions," 274; Benot, *Démence coloniale sous Napoléon*, 58; Auguste and Auguste, *Expédition Leclerc*, 18.

21. Auguste and Auguste, *Participation étrangère*, 11, 57–58; Benot, *Démence coloniale sous Napoléon*, 62.

22. Stephens, *Crisis of the Sugar Colonies*, 89, 91.

23. Benot, *Démence coloniale sous Napoléon*, 89; Pluchon, *Toussaint Louverture*, 451–452.

24. Louverture, Address, December 20, 1801, in Lacroix, *Révolution de Haiti*, 437–439.

25. Auguste and Auguste, *Expédition Leclerc*, 14–15, 79, 82–85.

26. Ibid., 15, 87; Toussaint Louverture, *Mémoires du Général Toussaint Louverture* (Paris, 1853), 30.

27. Auguste and Auguste, *Expédition Leclerc*, 91; Leclerc to Christophe, February 3, 1802, in Roussier, *Lettres du Général Leclerc*, 61.

28. Leclerc to Christophe, February 3, 1802; Proclamation of Leclerc, February 3, 1802; Proclamation of the Consuls, November 8, 1801, all in Roussier, *Lettres du Général Leclerc*, 62–63.

29. Creole translation of Proclamation of the Consuls, ibid., 64–65.

30. Auguste and Auguste, *Expédition Leclerc*, 93–94; Leclerc to Minister, February 9, 1802, in Roussier, *Lettres du Général Leclerc*, 66–74.

31. Auguste and Auguste, *Expédition Leclerc*, 95–96.

32. Ibid., 99, 148; Leclerc to Minister, February 9 and August 14, 1802, in Roussier, *Lettres du Général Leclerc*, 66–74, 212–213.

33. Auguste and Auguste, *Expédition Leclerc*, 98; Louverture, *Mémoires*, 30–37.

34. Michel Etienne Descourtilz, *Voyages d'un naturaliste, et ses observations,* 3 vols. (Paris: Dufart, 1809), 3:284; Lacroix, *Révolution de Haiti*, 319–321.

35. Lacroix, *Révolution de Haiti*, 315; Leclerc to Minister, February 27, 1802, in Roussier, *Lettres du Général Leclerc*, 102–111; Auguste and Auguste, *Expédition Leclerc*, 101.

36. Louverture, *Mémoires*, 41–42; Auguste and Auguste, *Expédition Leclerc*, 102–113.

37. Leclerc to Louverture, February 12, 1802, in Roussier, *Lettres du Général Leclerc*, 85–87.

38. Leclerc to Minister, February 15, 1802; Proclamation, February 17, 1802, ibid., 91–92, 98–100; Louverture, *Mémoires*, 53.

39. Leclerc to First Consul, December 11, 1801, Leclerc to Minister, February 15, 17, 19, and 27, and March 4, 1802, in Roussier, *Lettres du Général Leclerc*, 58–59, 87–91, 95–96, 101–111, 113–114.

40. Leclerc to First Consul, February 19, 1802; Leclerc to Minister, February 27, 1802, ibid., 101–111; Pluchon, *Toussaint Louverture*, 487–488.

41. Auguste and Auguste, *Expédition Leclerc*, 132–135; Leclerc to Minister, February 27, 1802, in Roussier, *Lettres du Général Leclerc*, 101–111.

42. Leclerc to Minister, February 27, 1802, ibid., 101–111; Lacroix, *Révolution de Haiti*, 317–319.

43. Lacroix, *Révolution de Haiti*, 322–324, 326.

44. Descourtilz, *Voyages d'un naturaliste*, 3:279–281.

45. Ibid., 294, 305.

46. Louverture, *Mémoires*, 58; Lacroix, *Révolution de Haiti*, 328, 332.

47. Descourtilz, *Voyages d'un naturaliste*, 3:310–311, 325.

48. Auguste and Auguste, *Expédition Leclerc*, 138; Louverture, *Mémoires*, 52–57.

49. Gabriel Debien, "Sur les plantations Mauger à l'Artibonite (Saint-Domingue 1763–1803)," in *Enquêtes et Documents: Nantes, Afrique, Amérique* (Nantes, 1981), 219–314, 308; Lacroix, *Révolution de Haiti*, 330–332; Métral, *Histoire*, 83.

50. Descourtilz, *Voyages d'un naturaliste*, 3:359; Carolyn Fick, *The Making of Haiti: The Saint-Domingue Revolution from Below* (Knoxville, 1990), 211–212; Auguste and Auguste, *Expédition Leclerc*, 140–141.

51. Lacroix, *Révolution de Haiti*, 330–333.

52. Descourtilz, *Voyages d'un naturaliste*, 3:358, 361–373; Lacroix, *Révolution de Haiti*, 335–336; Auguste and Auguste, *Expédition Leclerc*, 140–141.

53. Auguste and Auguste, *Expédition Leclerc*, 144, 147–149, 158; Leclerc to Minister, April 21, 1802, in Roussier, *Lettres du Général Leclerc*, 130–132.

54. Leclerc to Minister, May 6, 1802, in Roussier, *Lettres du Général Leclerc*, 140–142.

55. Ibid.; Auguste and Auguste, *Expédition Leclerc*, 152–153.

56. Leclerc to Minister, May 6, 1802, in Roussier, *Lettres du Général Leclerc*, 140–142; Pluchon, *Toussaint Louverture*, 495–496.

57. Leclerc to Bonaparte, May 7 and June 6, 1802, in Roussier, *Lettres du Général Leclerc*, 145–148, 161–164.

58. Leclerc to Minister, May 6, 1802; Leclerc to Bonaparte, May 7, 1801, ibid., 140–142, 145–148.

59. Auguste and Auguste, *Expédition Leclerc*, 161; Lacroix, *Révolution de Haiti*, 351–352; Leclerc to Minister, June 11, 1802, in Roussier, *Lettres du Général Leclerc*, 168–170.

60. Auguste and Auguste, *Expédition Leclerc*, 162–165.

61. Ibid., 160, 163–167.

62. Leclerc to Bonaparte, June 6, 1802, in Roussier, *Lettres du Général Leclerc*, 161–164; Auguste and Auguste, *Expédition Leclerc*, 173–176; Pluchon, *Toussaint Louverture*, 497–498; Lacroix, *Révolution de Haiti*, 354.

63. Leclerc to Minister, June 11 and July 6, 1802; Leclerc to Bonaparte, June 11, 1802, all in Roussier, *Lettres du Général Leclerc*, 168–173, 182–183.

64. Marie-Rose Masson to Gallifet, 8 Thermidor An 10 (July 27, 1802), 107 AP 128, AN; Debien, "Sur les plantations," 306, 311.

65. Lacroix, *Révolution de Haiti*, 304–305.

13. THOSE WHO DIE

1. Jan Pachonski and Reuel K. Wilson, *Poland's Caribbean Tragedy: A Study of Polish Legions in the Haitian War of Independence, 1802–1803* (Boulder, 1986), 54–55.

2. Michel Etienne Descourtilz, *Voyages d'un naturaliste, et ses observations* (Paris, 1809), 3:377–378; Pachonski and Wilson, *Poland's Caribbean Tragedy*, 57, 84, 170.

3. Leclerc to Minister, June 6, 11, and 24, 1802; Leclerc to Bonaparte, June 6, 1802, all in Paul Roussier, ed., *Lettres du Général Leclerc* (Paris, 1937), 154–157, 161–167, 176–177; Pamphile de Lacroix, *La Révolution de Haiti* (1819; reprint, Paris, 1995), 351.

4. Leclerc to Minister, June 6, July 6 and 12, August 25, 1802; Leclerc to Bonaparte, June 11, 1802, all in Roussier, *Lettres du Général Leclerc*, 155–157, 171–173, 182–183, 192–193, 216–218.

5. Leclerc to Bonaparte, June 6 and September 16, 1802; Leclerc to Minister, August 25, 1802, ibid., 161–165, 216–218, 228–237; Claude Bonaparte Auguste and Marcel Bonaparte Auguste, *L'Expédition Leclerc, 1801–1803* (Port-au-Prince, 1985), 206–208.

6. Descourtilz, *Voyages d'un naturaliste*, 3:381; Auguste and Auguste, *Expédition Leclerc*, 186–188.

7. Auguste and Auguste, *Expédition Leclerc*, 189–192; Michel Rolph Trouillot, *Silencing the Past: Power and the Production of History* (Boston, 1995), 41–42; Leclerc to Minister, July 23, 1802, in Roussier, *Lettres du Général Leclerc*, 196.

8. Auguste and Auguste, *Expédition Leclerc*, 196.

9. "Loi rélative à la traite des noirs et au régime des colonies," 30 Floréal An X (May 20, 1802), ADVII 21A, no. 54, AN.

10. "Arrêté portant défense aux noirs, mulâtres ou autres gens de couleur, à entrer sur le territoire continental de la République," 13 Messidor An X (July 2, 1802), ADVII 21A, no. 55, AN.

11. Auguste and Auguste, *Expédition Leclerc*, 172, 179.

12. "Loi rélative à la traite des noirs et au régime des colonies," 30 Floréal An X (May 20, 1802), AN ADVII 21A, no. 54, AN; Denis Decrès, "Rapport," Section Outre-Mer, Aix-en-Province, C7A 55, 248–252, AN.

13. On the events in Guadeloupe in 1802 see Laurent Dubois, "The Promise of Revolution: Saint-Domingue and the Struggle for Autonomy in Guadeloupe, 1797–1802," in *The Impact of the Haitian Revolution in the Atlantic World*, ed. David Geggus (Columbia, S.C., 2001), 122–134; and the essays and documents in Jacques Adélaïde-Mérlande, René Bélénus, and Frédéric Régent, *La Rébellion de la Guadeloupe, 1801–1802* (Basse-Terre, Guadeloupe, 2002).

14. Leclerc to Minister, August 6, 9, and 25, 1802; Leclerc to Bonaparte, August 6, 1802, all in Roussier, *Lettres du Général Leclerc*, 199–206, 219; Beaubrun Ardouin, *Etudes sur l'histoire d'Haïti*, 11 vols. (1853–1865; reprint, Port-au-Prince, 1958), 5:67.

15. Ardouin, *Etudes sur l'histoire d'Haïti*, 5:67.

16. Leclerc to Bonaparte, August 6, 1802; Leclerc to Minister, August 9, 1802, in Roussier, *Lettres du Général Leclerc*, 201–206.

17. Auguste and Auguste, *Expédition Leclerc*, 220–223, 233–234; Carolyn Fick, *The Making of Haiti: The Saint-Domingue Revolution from Below* (Knoxville, 1990), 216–227; Leclerc to Minister, August 25, 1802, in Roussier, *Lettres du Général Leclerc*, 216–218; Trouillot, *Silencing the Past*, 42.

18. Auguste and Auguste, *Expédition Leclerc*, 211–220; Leclerc to Bonaparte, September 16, 1802, in Roussier, *Lettres du Général Leclerc*, 228–237; Pachonski and Wilson, *Poland's Caribbean Tragedy*, 90.

19. Leclerc to Bonaparte, October 7, 1802, in Roussier, *Lettres du Général Leclerc*, 253–259.

20. Auguste and Auguste, *Expédition Leclerc*, 237.

21. Ibid., 238–245; Pachonski and Wilson, *Poland's Caribbean Tragedy*, 96–98; Fick, *Making of Haiti*, 227–228.

22. Pachonski and Wilson, *Poland's Caribbean Tragedy*, 99.

23. Auguste and Auguste, *Expédition Leclerc*, 247–249, 314.

24. Leclerc to Minister, September 17, 1802; Leclerc to Bonaparte, October 7, 1802, in Roussier, *Lettres du Général Leclerc*, 237–239, 253–260; Fick, *Making of Haiti*, 222; Auguste and Auguste, *Expédition Leclerc*, 227.

25. Pachonski and Wilson, *Poland's Caribbean Tragedy*, 113–114, 337; Auguste and Auguste, *Expédition Leclerc*, 272; Ardouin, *Etudes sur l'histoire d'Haïti*, 5:84–86; Joan Dayan, *Haiti, History, and the Gods* (Berkeley, 1996), 155.

26. Pachonski and Wilson, *Poland's Caribbean Tragedy*, 113, 157–158; Auguste and Auguste, *Expédition Leclerc*, 171–172.

27. Ardouin, *Etudes sur l'histoire d'Haïti*, 5:83–84.

28. Trouillot, *Silencing the Past*, 43–44, 65; Auguste and Auguste, *Expédition Leclerc*, 276, Fick, *Making of Haiti*, 231–233; Ardouin, *Etudes sur l'histoire d'Haïti*, 5:80–81. On the conflict between "Congos" and "creoles" see more generally Gérard Barthélemy, *Créoles-Bossales: Conflit en Haïti* (Petit-Bourg, Guadeloupe, 2000).

29. Pachonski and Wilson, *Poland's Caribbean Tragedy*, 103, 130–131, 192, 335.

30. Fick, *Making of Haiti*, 110; Pierre Pluchon, *Toussaint Louverture* (Paris, 1989), 489; Pachonski and Wilson, *Poland's Caribbean Tragedy*, 183.

31. Pachonski and Wilson, *Poland's Caribbean Tragedy*, 179.

32. Descourtilz, *Voyages d'un naturaliste*, 3:384; the song was sung to me by Erol Josué.

33. "Autopsie cadaverique," 18 Germinal An 11 (April 8, 1803), in *Pour que la Mémoire: Toussaint Louverture, Precurseur de l'indépendance d'Haïti* (Port-au-Prince, 2001), 21.

34. "Extrait des minutes du greffe de Saint-Marc," 22 Prairial An 11 (June 11, 1803), Papiers Descheaux, Fouchard Library, Port-au-Prince, Haiti; Dayan, *Haiti, History, and the Gods*, 160.

35. Dayan, *Haiti, History, and the Gods*, 39–40; Ardouin, *Etudes sur l'histoire d'Haïti*, 5:98; Auguste and Auguste, *Expédition Leclerc*, 316.

36. Ardouin, *Etudes sur l'histoire d'Haïti*, 6:8.

37. Ibid., 7; David Geggus, *Haitian Revolutionary Studies* (Bloomington, 2002), 208.

38. Ardouin, *Etudes sur l'histoire d'Haïti*, 6:8.

39. Geggus, *Haitian Revolutionary Studies*, 208, 215–217.

40. Ibid., 214; Ardouin, *Etudes sur l'histoire d'Haïti*, 6:17.

41. Ardouin, *Etudes sur l'histoire d'Haïti*, 5:74–75, 6:8–9; Gérard M. Laurent, *Six Etudes sur J. J. Dessalines* (Port-au-Prince, 1950), 93–114.

42. Ardouin, *Etudes sur l'histoire d'Haïti*, 6:15–17, 33–34.

43. Ibid., 16–17.

EPILOGUE

1. Michel Etienne Descourtilz, *Voyages d'un naturaliste, et ses observations*, 3 vols. (Paris, 1809), 3:209–210.

2. Claude Bonaparte Auguste and Marcel Bonaparte Auguste, *L'Expédition Leclerc, 1801–1803* (Port-au-Prince, 1985), 316.

3. Mimi Sheller, *Democracy after Slavery: Black Publics and Peasant Radical-*

ism in Haiti and Jamaica (Gainesville, 2000), part 2; Michel Rolph Trouillot, *State against Nation: Origins and Legacy of Duvalierism* (New York, 1990), part 1; David Nicholls, *From Dessalines to Duvalier: Race, Color, and National Independence in Haiti* (New Brunswick, N.J., 1979).

4. Beaubrun Ardouin, *Etudes sur l'histoire d'Haïti*, 11 vols. (1853–1865; reprint, Port-au-Prince, 1958), 6:17.

5. Paul Lachance, "Repercussions of the Haitian Revolution in Louisiana," in *The Impact of the Haitian Revolution in the Atlantic World*, ed. David Geggus (Columbia, 2001), 209–230, 223; Hans Schmidt, *The United States Occupation of Haiti, 1915–1934*, 2d ed. (New Brunswick, N.J., 1995).

6. Lachance, "Repercussions in Louisiana," 209–211; Christopher Schmidt-Nowara, *Empire and Antislavery: Spain, Cuba and Puerto Rico, 1833–1874* (Pittsburgh, 1999), 4, 41.

7. David Geggus, "Preface," in Geggus, *Impact of the Haitian Revolution*, x; James Sidbury, *Ploughshares into Swords: Race, Rebellion, and Identity in Gabriel's Virginia, 1730–1810* (Cambridge, 1998), 39–48; Douglas Egerton, *Gabriel's Rebellion* (Chapel Hill, 1993); Julius Scott, "The Common Wind: Currents of Afro-American Communication in the Era of the Haitian Revolution" (Ph.D. diss., Duke University, 1986); *The Lesson of Santo Domingo: How to Make the War Short and the Peace Righteous* (Boston, 1861).

8. Geggus, "Preface," x, xii; Matt Childs, "'A Black French General Arrived to Conquer the Island': Images of the Haitian Revolution in Cuba's 1812 Aponte Rebellion," in Geggus, *Impact of the Haitian Revolution*, 135–156, 137, 144.

9. David Brion Davis, "Impact of the French and Haitian Revolutions"; Seymour Drescher, "The Limits of Example"; and Robin Blackburn, "The Force of Example," in Geggus, *Impact of the Haitian Revolution*, 3–20; Susan Buck-Morss, "Hegel and Haiti," *Critical Inquiry* 26 (summer 2000): 821–865.

INDEX

Jean-François: as insurgent leader, 106, 109, 123–129, 141, 148, 287, 305; service with Spanish, 152, 159–160, 166, 177, 180, 182

Jeannot, 79, 112, 115, 123

Jefferson, Thomas, 225, 298, 303

Jérémie, 27, 166, 218, 219

Jesuits, 12, 22, 49, 292

Jumecourt, Hanus de, 119, 137, 145

Jura, 296

Kerverseau, François, 208, 217, 253, 267

Kina, Jean, 148–149, 182

Kongo, 40, 41, 42, 43, 49, 51, 54, 83, 168, 198; political ideologies from, 108–109, 160; military tactics from, 109

Labor regulations: under Polverel and Sonthonax, 162, 164–165, 185–186, 220; under Louverture, 184, 187–189, 214, 220, 233, 239–240, 244–245, 247, 248, 258; under Rigaud, 220, 232, 233

Lacroix, Pamphile de, 172, 184, 258, 270, 271, 272, 273–274, 276, 277, 279, 281

Lafortune, 270

Lamartinière, 273

Land, for ex-slaves, 162, 164–165, 185, 192, 193, 197, 228, 239–240, 247

Laplume, 199, 227, 234, 267, 269

La Rochelle, 20, 82

Las Casas, Bartolomé de la, 14–15

Laveaux, Etienne: and integration of army units, 146–147; as military commander, 147–148, 168, 180–181, 197, 199; and Louverture, 177, 179–180, 183, 187, 188, 205, 207–208, 223, 279; and Villatte affair, 200–203; as representative, 205, 211, 213–215, 217, 241

Lazzary, Bramante, 163, 176

Le Cap, 9, 11, 28–29, 48–49, 51, 78, 86, 88, 222, 226; description of, 22–24; conflict in, 80, 145, 155–159, 177, 200–203, 247; and 1791 insurrection, 96–97, 110, 113, 124; demands for abolition in, 162–163; and Leclerc expe-

dition, 262–265, 274, 281, 288, 289; and Rochambeau, 292–293, 297

Leclerc, Charles Victor Emmanuel, 250, 251–252, 254–256, 259, 262–269, 274–278, 280–284, 286–292, 300

Le Jeune, Nicholas, 56

Léogane, 182

Léopardins, 86–87

Les Cayes, 15, 27, 135, 139–140, 160, 204, 236, 262, 295

Léveillé, Pierre, 200, 222

Libertat, Bayon de, 171, 206

Liberty taxes, 55, 74–75

Limbé, 30, 51, 94, 97, 99, 124, 179, 265, 287

London, 166, 216

Louis XVI, 73, 106, 125, 145, 152

Louisiana, 225, 303

Louisiana Purchase, 304

Louverture: François Dominique Toussaint, 2, 4, 6, 26, 119, 305; and 1791 insurrection, 125, 128, 176–177; service with Spanish, 166, 176–180; background of, 171–176; name of, 172; administration of emancipation by, 173–175, 184–193, 238–240; Catholicism of, 173, 175, 176, 199, 203, 227, 261; joins French, 178–180; as military commander, 181–184, 196–199; and occupation of Santo Domingo, 183; and white planters, 187, 188–189, 226–227; reconstruction of plantation economy by, 188–189, 238, 249–250; plantations of, 189; uprisings against, 190–191, 234; and Villatte affair, 199–203; and elections, 205–208; criticisms of, 207, 210; defense of emancipation by, 209–211, 240–241, 283; and white women, 213, 279; and withdrawal of British, 215, 216–217, 218–219; suspicions on French, 218–219; diplomacy of, 223–226, 246; and United States, 223–225, 235; and independence, 224–226, 252–253; autonomy of, 226; conflict with André Rigaud, 231–236; assassination attempts against, 234;

Odeluc, 91, 92, 94, 95, 113–114, 278

Ogé, Vincent, 26, 80, 82, 87–88, 120, 125, 134–135

Ollivier, Vincent, 65–66

Ouanaminthe, 129, 147

Perroud, Henry, 200, 201

Petion, Alexandre, 234, 254, 287, 288, 293, 294, 303

Petite-Rivière, 187

Petit-Goâve, 234

Petits blancs, 35, 77–78, 136, 145

Philadelphia, 8, 10, 159, 169, 201, 207, 241

Philipeau, 36–39, 132, 169, 278–279

Pickering, Thomas, 224

Pierrot, 158, 159, 160, 162, 200

Pinchinat, Pierre, 119, 121, 137, 146–147, 167

Piracy, 16, 17, 32

Pitt, William, 117

Plaisance, 179, 187

Plantations: functioning of, 18–19, 20, 36–39, 45–48; numbers of, 19; protests on, 53; prisons on, 53; destruction of, 96, 113, 229–230; return of ex-slaves to, 127–128, 184; and transfer of land to ex-slaves, 161–162, 185; post-emancipation management of, 162, 184–189, 214, 220, 232, 233; renting of, 204–205, 227; attempts of returning planters to recover, 226–229

Platons, 139–140, 148, 160

Poison, 51–52, 55–56, 58

Polish troops, 256, 281, 288, 289; defections of, 294–295, 300

Polverel, Etienne: background of, 142–143; as commissioner, 143–148, 172, 179; and abolition of slavery, 154–165, 168, 179; trial of, 180, 196; administration of emancipation by, 184–187, 197; death of, 196

Population, 19, 20, 27, 28, 30

Port-au-Prince, 12, 23, 26, 49, 54, 64, 155, 232; political conflicts in, 86, 119–122, 136–137; and British occupation, 167–168, 179, 181–182, 198, 218; and Leclerc expedition, 262, 266,

270, 279; and war of independence, 293

Port-de-Paix, 168, 184, 289; uprisings in, 190, 191, 234, 262, 283

Port-Salut, 139

Priests, and 1791 uprising, 103, 108; and Louverture, 207, 244, 249

Prostitution, 248, 279

Puerto Rico, 304

Quasi-War, 223–224

Racial categories, 5–6, 70–71, 151; and free people of color, 61–62; and revolutionary conflicts, 201–202, 232–233; in post-independence Haiti, 300

Racial equality: in elections, 120; and British occupation, 166–167; celebration of, 169, 210, 215; elimination of, 284–285

Raimond, Julien, 28, 60–64, 67, 70, 103, 135, 143; family history of, 61, 63, 71; activism of, 76, 80, 82, 83, 89; as commissioner, 196, 203, 208, 222; renting of plantations by, 204; defense of emancipation, 211; and 1801 Constitution, 242; death of, 242

Ravine-à-Couleuvre, 269

Raynal, Abbé Guillaume Thomas François, 57–58, 59, 103, 172, 203

Reestablishment of slavery: in Guadeloupe, 4, 285–286; rumors of, 189–191, 201, 203, 204, 240, 286; threat of, 211, 233, 257–258, 265; decisions about, 259–260, 284–286

Refugees, 8, 115, 153, 159, 168–169, 177–178; and Louverture, 188–189, 218, 219, 226–229, 242; and attacks on emancipation, 207–208, 209, 211, 241

Regiment du Cap, 146–147

Religion, 11–12, 43–45, 49, 51, 244, 302; and 1791 uprising, 55, 99–103. *See also* Catholicism; Priests; Vodou

Reparations, for slavery, 214

Representation, for colonies, 74–75, 77, 168–170, 194

Richepance, Antoine, 285–286

Richmond, 304